High Performance with MongoDB

Best practices for performance tuning, scaling, and architecture

Asya Kamsky, Ger Hartnett, Alex Bevilacqua

High Performance with MongoDB

Copyright © 2025 Packt Publishing

Portfolio Director: Sunith Shetty
Relationship Lead: Sathya Mohan
Project Managers: Aniket Shetty & Sathya Mohan
Content Engineer: Siddhant Jain
Technical Editor: Aniket Shetty
Copy Editor: Safis Editing
Indexer: Hemangini Bari
Proofreader: Siddhant Jain
Production Designer: Deepak Chavan

First published: September 2025

Production reference: 1051225

Published by Packt Publishing Ltd.
Grosvenor House
11 St Paul's Square
Birmingham
B3 1RB, UK.

ISBN 978-1-83702-263-2
www.packtpub.com

To Ben and Mark for their unwavering support

— Asya

To Luci, Clíodhna, Hannah, and Jane. Thank you for all of your support.

— Ger

Thanks to all my amazing friends and colleagues at MongoDB for helping me get the word out about how awesome MongoDB can be.

— Alex

Acknowledgements

We'd like to thank everyone who developed, documented, managed, and supported the MongoDB products over the years. In particular, we'd like to thank colleagues who made suggestions or put together internal content that contributed to this book, including Cesar Albuquerque de Godoy, Pierre Depretz, Dave Walker, Steve Wotring, Chris Harris, and Xiaochen Wu.

Contributors

About the authors

Asya Kamsky is a Principal KnowItAll at MongoDB, where she has worked since 2012. Before discovering MongoDB, she spent nearly two decades coaxing relational databases into doing what they were never designed to do at a series of startups, most of which no one remembers. Asya has an extensive background in software development, databases, and telling people what they're doing wrong.

Ger Hartnett is a Lead Engineer on MongoDB's product performance team, where he loves working on fascinating optimization and scaling challenges. Before MongoDB, he founded a startup that built a project communication platform (that had scaling issues). Prior to that, he architected and tuned embedded software at Intel, where he co-authored a book. Even before that, he developed systems at companies including Tellabs, Digital, and Motorola.

Alex Bevilacqua is the Lead Product Manager at MongoDB for Developer Experience. Prior to joining MongoDB in 2018, he worked as a software engineer and systems architect, implementing solutions in a number of languages, technologies, and frameworks. Aside from his passion for programming that consumes more than just his working hours, Alex can typically be found at an arena with one of his kids, both of whom play rep hockey.

About the reviewers

Keith Smith is a systems and storage expert with decades of experience in operating systems and data infrastructure. Based in the U.S., he has contributed to innovations at companies like Sun Microsystems, NetApp, and MongoDB. Keith started his career designing real-time UNIX systems and went on to build extensible operating systems at Harvard, where he earned his PhD. His work has spanned object-based storage, metadata catalogs, and file system architectures. Since 2020, he has led storage engine development at MongoDB. Keith is passionate about scalable systems and continues to push the boundaries of data storage technology.

John Page is a full-stack engineer who joined MongoDB in 2013. Since then, he has held senior technical roles focused on customer success across all phases of the development lifecycle. Before MongoDB, he spent 18 years building document database systems for law enforcement and the U.S. military. Trained as a geologist, John can find silicon in the wild, build a computer from raw components, and write everything from operating systems and databases to front ends and documentation.

James Kovacs is a director of engineering in Database Experience at MongoDB. He focuses on client libraries, object-document mappers, framework integrations, and AI/ML. He has over 25 years of professional software engineering experience, having worked in a wide variety of companies and industries over that time. When not in front of a keyboard, you can find him playing board games/TTRPGs, cooking tasty vegan meals in the kitchen, or at the dojo teaching karate.

Stephanie Eristoff is a software engineer on the Storage Execution team at MongoDB, which she joined in 2024. She brings experience in performance testing of time-series collections and indexes and has also contributed to the Performance and Query Execution teams. Outside of work, Stephanie enjoys baking, running, and biking.

Katya Kamenieva is a product manager at MongoDB, where she has been driving improvements to the aggregation framework, change streams, and other features since 2019. Her work focuses on enhancing how users interact with data in MongoDB. Outside of work, she's a mom to two young daughters and finds mindfulness through quiet moments, a good cup of coffee, yoga, and watercolor painting.

Jawwad Asghar is a software engineer at MongoDB, where he has been a key member of the performance team since 2022. He helps drive changes to the database by optimizing its performance for diverse and demanding customer use cases. Prior to joining MongoDB, he spent 10 years as a control software engineer in the locomotive industry. When not behind his desk, he enjoys biking around New York City, camping, and going hiking upstate.

Alice Doherty is a software engineer at MongoDB, having joined the Product Performance team in 2023. She offers valuable experience in root-causing unique performance problems, both for customers and for internal engineering teams, as well as driving performance improvements in MongoDB's products. Outside of work, Alice enjoys staying active, cooking, and any adventures in the outdoors.

Linda Qin is a staff technical services engineer at MongoDB. She joined MongoDB in 2013 and has worked in the technical support team since then. Linda specializes in issue diagnosis and performance tuning, with deep expertise in sharding. She is also involved in developing tools to streamline diagnostics and improve efficiency. Outside of work, Linda enjoys cooking and bushwalking.

Matt Panton is a product manager at MongoDB. Since joining in 2022, Matt has focused on delivering improvements to key distributed systems features such as sharding and replication. His work is centered on making MongoDB scalable and resilient. Outside of work, Matt enjoys playing soccer, running, and cooking.

Sebastien Mendez (but call him Seb) is a lead engineer on MongoDB's Query Execution team. Back in the day, he was active in the demoscene as "rakiz," hacking Z80 assembly demos, creating diskmags on his Amstrad CPC 6128, and organizing coding parties. After exploring several industries, Seb discovered a passion for data processing—building a persistence layer, a query engine, and a highly configurable streaming data pipeline. Today, he specializes in MongoDB's change streams, helping shape their roadmap around observability, performance, and new features. Outside of work, Seb enjoys video gaming, reading sci-fi and fantasy, tinkering with Arduinos, and growing his pop culture T-shirt collection.

Kevin Arhelger is a staff engineer on the Technical Services team at MongoDB, where he focuses on improving performance for customers across diverse environments. He has been professionally administering Linux systems since 2006 and has specialized in software and database performance since 2008. With deep expertise in server administration, cloud automation, and full-stack performance tuning, Kevin brings a holistic approach to solving complex technical challenges.

Manuel Fontan is a senior technologist on the Curriculum team at MongoDB. Previously, he was a senior technical services engineer in the Core team at MongoDB. In between, Manuel worked as a database reliability engineer at Slack for a little over two years and then for Cognite until he rejoined MongoDB. With over 15 years of experience in software development and distributed systems, he is naturally curious and holds a Telecommunications Engineering MSc from Vigo University (Spain) and a Free and Open Source Software MSc from Rey Juan Carlos University (Spain).

Parker Faucher is a self-taught software engineer with over six years of experience in technical education. He has authored more than 100 educational videos for MongoDB, establishing himself as a knowledgeable resource in database technologies. Currently, Parker focuses on AI and search technologies, exploring innovative solutions in these rapidly evolving fields. When not advancing his technical expertise, Parker enjoys spending quality time with his family and maintains an avid interest in collecting comic books.

Sarah Evans is a curriculum engineer at MongoDB, where she specializes in making complex technical concepts accessible for all learners. With over ten years of experience in software engineering, education, and developing curriculum for technical bootcamps, she's all about making learning MongoDB less intimidating and more exciting. When she's not helping developers level up their database skills, Sarah can be found having spontaneous dance parties with her family, exploring the great outdoors with her dog, or tending to her garden.

Dave Walker has been directly supporting MongoDB users in public cloud environments for 15 years. He served as Director of Solutions at mLab, which was acquired by MongoDB in 2018. As a Staff Engineer on the Technical Services team, Dave's focus is helping Atlas users make well-informed decisions to achieve ongoing and long-term success through workload optimization and performance tuning. When not working with Atlas users, Dave skis the mountains of Colorado and plays acoustic stringed instruments with his wife and two daughters.

Table of Contents

Chapter 9: Transactions   175

Chapter 11: Managing Connections and Network Performance   225

Chapter 15: Debugging Performance Issues   325

Preface

In today's data-driven world, performance is not just a feature; it's a necessity. As data volumes grow exponentially and user expectations for speed and reliability increase, the ability to build and maintain high-performance database systems has become crucial for competitive applications. MongoDB is a popular, powerful database built for modern application needs. It stores data in documents that align naturally with the data structures used in programming languages. Its distributed architecture provides built-in scalability, high availability, and performance for mission-critical workloads. By understanding MongoDB's architecture, operational patterns, and optimization techniques, you can fully harness its performance potential to build fast, scalable, and resilient applications with ease.

This book offers a practical guide to understanding and improving MongoDB performance. It covers how to identify the most common performance issues, analyze query and system behavior using built-in tools, and apply proven techniques for optimization. Topics range from schema design and indexing strategies to tuning storage settings and managing system resources. Whether you're running a single replica set or operating a large sharded cluster, the book aims to help you make informed decisions that improve stability and efficiency in real-world deployments.

How this book will help you

This book delves into both fundamental concepts and advanced optimization techniques, providing you with the knowledge and practical tools to design, build, and operate high-performance MongoDB deployments at any scale.

Whether you're troubleshooting a slow query, designing schemas for a new application, or scaling a large cluster to handle growing workloads, this book serves as your trusted resource. The goal of this book is to demystify MongoDB performance optimization and equip you with strategies that work in real-world environments.

The chapters are designed to be modular, allowing you to focus on specific areas of interest, whether it's fine-tuning indexes, resolving slow queries, or configuring system resources. However, those new to performance tuning may benefit from reading linearly to build a solid conceptual foundation. While some topics naturally build on earlier chapters, most sections are designed to be understandable on their own. This makes the book flexible as both a continuous read and a reference guide for solving specific performance issues as they arise. Throughout the book, you'll find practical examples, diagnostic techniques, and code snippets that you can adapt to your environment for hands-on learning.

Who this book is for

This book is written for developers, system architects, DevOps engineers, and database administrators who are serious about MongoDB performance optimization. Whether you're building data-intensive applications, responsible for scaling and managing MongoDB in production, designing distributed systems for future growth, or integrating MongoDB into CI/CD pipelines, you'll find practical guidance tailored to your needs. An understanding of MongoDB basics is assumed, and while experience with schema design or database operations is helpful, each chapter builds progressively to support learners at all levels.

What this book covers

Chapter 1, Systems and MongoDB Architecture, introduces core systems thinking concepts and shows how they apply to MongoDB's architecture, performance tuning, and identifying bottlenecks.

Chapter 2, Schema Design for Performance, covers how document modeling choices directly affect read and write efficiency, one of the most critical aspects of MongoDB performance.

Chapter 3, Indexes, dives deep into indexing strategies, the primary tool for optimizing query performance.

Chapter 4, Aggregations, shows you how to use the aggregation framework to perform complex data analysis efficiently.

Chapter 5, Replication, discusses MongoDB's replication mechanism and how to leverage it effectively for high availability.

Chapter 6, Sharding, explains horizontal scaling techniques to distribute data and workloads across multiple servers.

Chapter 7, Storage Engines, focuses on the WiredTiger, MongoDB storage engine and explains its configuration options and performance characteristics.

Chapter 8, Change Streams, shows how to build reactive systems with real-time data change notifications.

Chapter 9, Transactions, covers multi-document ACID transactions, their use cases, and their performance implications.

Chapter 10, Client Libraries, examines how to configure and use MongoDB drivers for optimal application performance.

Chapter 11, Managing Connections and Network Performance, details connection pooling strategies and network optimization techniques.

Chapter 12, Advanced Query and Indexing Concepts, explores advanced indexing topics and **MongoDB Query Language** (**MQL**) best practices.

Chapter 13, Operating System and System Resources, provides guidance on configuring your operating system and hardware for MongoDB workloads.

Chapter 14, Monitoring and Observability, provides a comprehensive guide to monitoring your MongoDB deployment and establishing proactive performance management.

Chapter 15, Debugging Performance Issues, equips you with methodologies to identify, diagnose, and resolve performance bottlenecks in production.

To get the most out of this book

You will require the following software:

Software covered in the book	Operating system requirements
MongoDB version 8.0	Windows, macOS, or Linux
MongoDB Shell	Windows, macOS, or Linux

After reading this book, we encourage you to check out some of the other resources available at https://www.mongodb.com/developer and https://learn.mongodb.com/.

Download the example code files

The code bundle for the book is hosted on GitHub at `https://github.com/PacktPublishing/High-Performance-with-MongoDB/`.

We also have other code bundles from our rich catalog of books and videos available at `https://github.com/PacktPublishing`. Check them out!

Download the color images

We also provide a PDF file that has color images of the screenshots/diagrams used in this book. You can download it here: `https://packt.link/gbp/9781837022632`.

Conventions used

There are a number of text conventions used throughout this book.

`CodeInText`: Indicates code words in text, database table names, folder names, filenames, file extensions, pathnames, dummy URLs, user input, and X (Twitter) handles. For example: "`$project` and `$addFields` serve different purposes and have different performance implications."

A block of code is set as follows:

```
# A simple document representing a user
user = {
    "name": "Jane Doe",
    "age": 30,
    "email": "janedoe@example.com",
    "address": {
        "street": "123 Main St",
        "city": "Anytown",
        "state": "CA",
        "zip": "12345"
    },
    "interests": ["hiking", "photography", "travel"]
}
```

Any command-line input or output is written as follows:

```
db.adminCommand({ serverStatus: 1 })
```

Bold: Indicates a new term, an important word, or words that you see on the screen. For instance, words in menus or dialog boxes appear in the text like this. For example: "In Grafana, navigate to the **Import** screen (click the + icon, then select **Import**)"

Warnings or important notes appear like this.

Tips and tricks appear like this.

Get in touch

Feedback from our readers is always welcome.

General feedback: If you have questions about any aspect of this book or have any general feedback, please email us at customercare@packt.com and mention the book's title in the subject of your message.

Errata: Although we have taken every care to ensure the accuracy of our content, mistakes do happen. If you have found a mistake in this book, we would be grateful if you reported this to us. Please visit http://www.packt.com/submit-errata, click **Submit Errata**, and fill in the form.

Piracy: If you come across any illegal copies of our works in any form on the internet, we would be grateful if you would provide us with the location address or website name. Please contact us at copyright@packt.com with a link to the material.

If you are interested in becoming an author: If there is a topic that you have expertise in and you are interested in either writing or contributing to a book, please visit http://authors.packt.com/.

Share your thoughts

Once you've read *High Performance with MongoDB*, we'd love to hear your thoughts! Scan the QR code below to go straight to the Amazon review page for this book and share your feedback.

https://packt.link/r/1837022631

Your review is important to us and the tech community and will help us make sure we're delivering excellent quality content.

Free Benefits with Your Book

This book comes with free benefits to support your learning. Activate them now for instant access (see the "*How to Unlock*" section for instructions).

Here's a quick overview of what you can instantly unlock with your purchase:

PDF and ePub Copies

Next-Gen Web-Based Reader

Free PDF and ePub versions

Next-Gen Reader

Access a DRM-free PDF copy of this book to read anywhere, on any device.

Use a DRM-free ePub version with your favorite e-reader.

Multi-device progress sync: Pick up where you left off, on any device.

Highlighting and notetaking: Capture ideas and turn reading into lasting knowledge.

Bookmarking: Save and revisit key sections whenever you need them.

Dark mode: Reduce eye strain by switching to dark or sepia themes.

How to Unlock

UNLOCK NOW

Scan the QR code (or go to packtpub.com/unlock). Search for this book by name, confirm the edition, and then follow the steps on the page.

Note: Keep your invoice handy. Purchases made directly from Packt don't require one.

1

Systems and MongoDB Architecture

Every database deployment operates within a larger system that includes networks, applications, hardware, and users. To scale or optimize MongoDB effectively, we must approach it with the mindset of a system designer, rather than thinking only as database engineers. This chapter introduces that shift in thinking. It will help you see how small changes in one area can lead to significant and sometimes unexpected effects across an entire system. Solving performance problems is not just about tuning technical settings; it also requires a deep understanding of how systems behave.

We will begin by looking at systems more broadly, starting with examples from nature and the real world. You will be introduced to key concepts such as delays, feedback loops, and bottlenecks. These ideas will help explain why systems sometimes behave in counterintuitive or surprising ways when we attempt to change them. As the chapter progresses, we will gradually narrow our focus. We will move from general systems to software systems, then to data services, and finally, to MongoDB. Along the way, we will provide a high-level overview of common bottlenecks and examine two specific examples in more detail. We will also introduce a step-by-step process that you can use to diagnose and resolve performance and scalability issues.

Every system contains a limiting factor, or bottleneck. When a system has multiple inputs and components, the true limiting factor is not always obvious. Improving other parts of the system will not increase overall performance unless the bottleneck itself is addressed. In my experience, many people spend time optimizing the wrong part of the system because they make incorrect assumptions about where the bottleneck lies. A structured approach, based on measurement and experimentation, makes it easier to identify and address the real issue.

This chapter will cover the following topics:

- Examining the fundamental characteristics of systems
- Exploring a typical software system and identifying potential performance bottlenecks
- Introducing MongoDB architecture and its foundations
- Understanding the connection between core MongoDB components and their role in application performance
- Discussing strategies for managing complexity in modern data platforms
- Reviewing performance monitoring tools and observability techniques
- Finding bottlenecks and the iterative process for tuning

What are systems?

A system is an interconnected set of elements organized in a way that fulfills a purpose. Donella Meadows defines systems as follows:

> *A set of things—people, cells, molecules, or whatever—interconnected in such a way that they produce their own pattern of behavior over time. The system may be buffeted, constricted, triggered, or driven by outside forces. But the system's response to these forces is characteristic of itself, and that response is seldom simple in the real world. [1]*

We see systems at many scales. Our solar system is a system of planets. Earth has weather and climate systems, as well as political and social systems such as countries and cities. A city contains institutional systems such as universities, which, in turn, have academic systems such as faculties, professors, and students. The engineering faculty has a lab system with multiple computers connected through a network system of bridges and routers. Each computer is a system of hardware and software components, including processors, memory, and applications.

A store in the city is a system that manages products such as computers, with processes for inventory replenishment from suppliers and factories. Beyond the city, a forest is an ecological system containing trees, each a system of roots, branches, and leaves. A wild boar in the forest has biological systems, including skeletal, nervous, circulatory, and digestive systems. Even a single cell within the boar's ear is a system, with its own internal subsystems such as mitochondria, a nucleus, and ribosomes.

The common thread unifying all these different systems is that their elements interact with each other within the system and with other systems around them.

A system's performance is often not determined by the strongest or fastest element, but by the weakest link. This is sometimes referred to as the **bottleneck** or the **limiting factor**. This is the element within a system that significantly restricts the system's overall performance or growth. Bottlenecks can change over time. If you fix a bottleneck, another element will then become the bottleneck. Remember, everything that is true for general systems is true for software systems, as well. In later sections, we'll look at typical software bottlenecks and some of the tactics you can use to fix them.

Characteristics of systems

In this section, we'll look at the potential pitfalls we can encounter when changing systems. We'll see how buffers and delays can make it hard to understand a system's behavior, and how changes can lead to unexpected outcomes.

Changing systems is a risky business

The elements of a system can interact in non-linear ways. For example, a school is a system with elements such as students, classrooms, playgrounds, and basketball hoops. The behavior of the system doesn't always emerge in a predictable way, as discussed here:

- **Small changes can have big effects (butterfly effect)**: An insignificant action can lead to massive, unpredictable consequences. For example, a student starts running in the playground. Another student starts running after the first one. Soon, more and more students see the fun and join in. Suddenly, half the playground is playing tag.

- **Feedback loops (chain reaction)**: This is a direct, step-by-step process where one event leads to another. In the cafeteria, a student tells a joke. If it's funny, a few others laugh. Their laughter makes others in the cafeteria curious, and soon, everyone is laughing, even those who didn't hear the joke. The laughter spreads in a way that builds on itself. This is called a **positive feedback loop**.

- **More than the sum of its parts (synergy)**: A system can produce results that are greater than just adding up its components. During band practice, a single drum beat sounds simple. A single trombone note is cool. But when a whole band plays together, the music sounds much better than just adding up individual sounds.

- **Unexpected outcomes (emergence)**: Systems can create results that aren't obvious from the individual parts. For instance, during art class, a student mixes red and yellow paint to get orange, which surprises them.

Non-linear interactions mean small actions can trigger big changes, feedback loops can amplify their effects, elements can work together unexpectedly, and new outcomes can emerge. In general, humans struggle to comprehend non-linear interactions between different elements of the system and tend to see behavior as a series of discrete events, making it easy to miss the underlying patterns.

We can build models of systems and see how they behave. Of course, the real world is always going to be more complex than any model we can build. A model of a system has inputs, stocks, variables, and feedback loops. An example of a store/inventory system is shown in *Figure 1.1*.

We'll use this example to explain the concepts of stocks, variables, and feedback loops. Reading from the top left in an anticlockwise direction, the system has an inflow of deliveries and an outflow of sales. The products in the store are in stock, called the inventory.

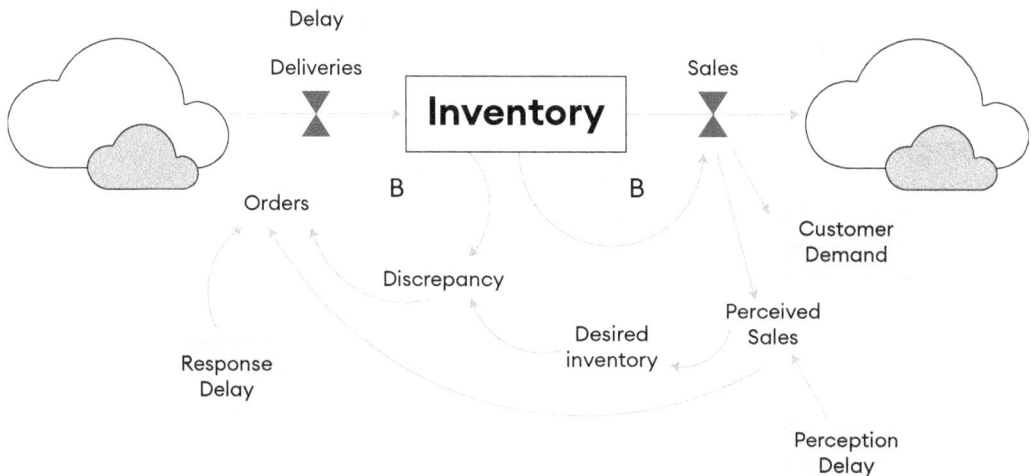

Figure 1.1: An example system model showing store inventory management

The delivery delay and customer demand are inputs regulating the flow of products. **B** signifies a balancing feedback loop. Customer demand causes the products to flow out of the system as sales, reducing inventory. The manager doesn't want to keep checking the stock every day, so there's a perception delay variable. After the delay, the manager compares perceived sales with the desired inventory. The manager doesn't want to overreact to a change in customer demand, so they have a response delay variable limiting the size of an order to the supplier, who then delivers more product after a delay.

This model only uses balancing feedback loops. The other kind of feedback loop is a reinforcing loop, which typically increases the size of stocks. For example, in a bank savings account, the more money you have in the account, the more you earn in interest, which, in turn, increases the amount of money in the account.

A system with no delays is simple

Let's say the manager wants to keep 10 days of demand in inventory, and the demand is 200 items per day. This means the desired inventory is 2,000. On day 10, demand increases by 10%. Customers are now buying 220 items per day. The manager increases the size of the order, and more inventory is delivered on the same day. The desired inventory goes up to 2,200.

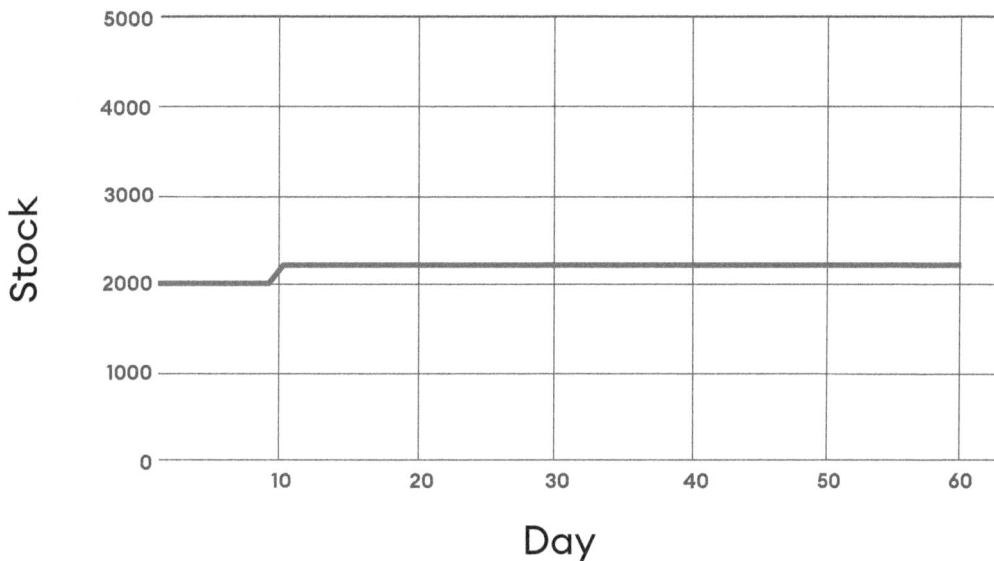

Figure 1.2: Behavior over time in a simple system with no delays

When there are no delays in the system, adjustments can be made instantly to changes in demand, making the system's behavior straightforward and predictable.

A system with delays can behave in unexpected ways

In complex systems, there are often delays between taking an action and seeing its effect, as described by Donella Meadows:

> *Because of feedback delays within complex systems, by the time a problem becomes apparent it may be unnecessarily difficult to solve. [1]*

For example, if inventory orders take several days to arrive, a sudden increase in demand might not be addressed quickly enough. This lag can cause overcorrections or shortages, creating instability. Understanding and managing these delays is crucial to maintaining smooth system performance.

Now, let's add some delays:

- **Perception delay**: Before changing the order, the manager averages sales over a 5-day period
- **Response delay**: The manager makes up 40% of the inventory shortfall when changing the order
- **Delivery delay**: The factory takes 5 days to deliver the order

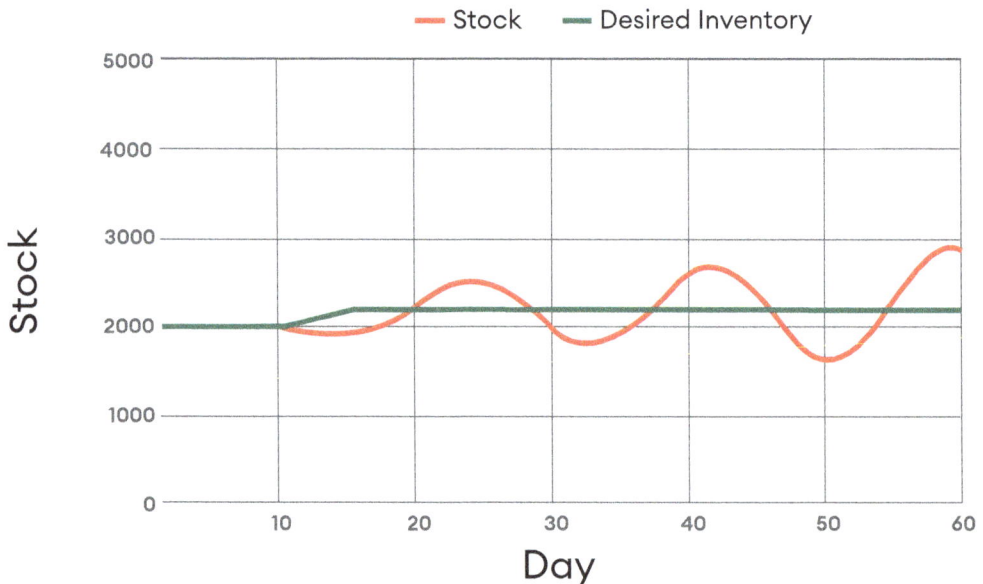

Figure 1.3: Inventory levels oscillate after demand rises due to delayed order adjustments

As you can see in *Figure 1.3*, after day 10, when demand increases by 10% first, we see the stock levels start to drop. Then, after 5 days, the manager adjusts the order to make up 40% of the shortfall. The increased deliveries start to arrive, and on day 20, the stock equals the desired inventory. However, the increased deliveries continue, and by day 25, the store is overstocked. The manager reduces the order. The cycle continues, and the inventory oscillates between under- and over-stocked.

Trying to fix oscillations

Here are three options you could try to fix this unwanted behavior:

- Faster perception (reduce delay)
- Faster response (increase order)
- Slower response (decrease order)

Close your eyes for a minute and decide which of these options you'd try first. We'll examine the outcome of each option.

First, we'll reduce the perception delay from five days to two, as shown in *Figure 1.4*.

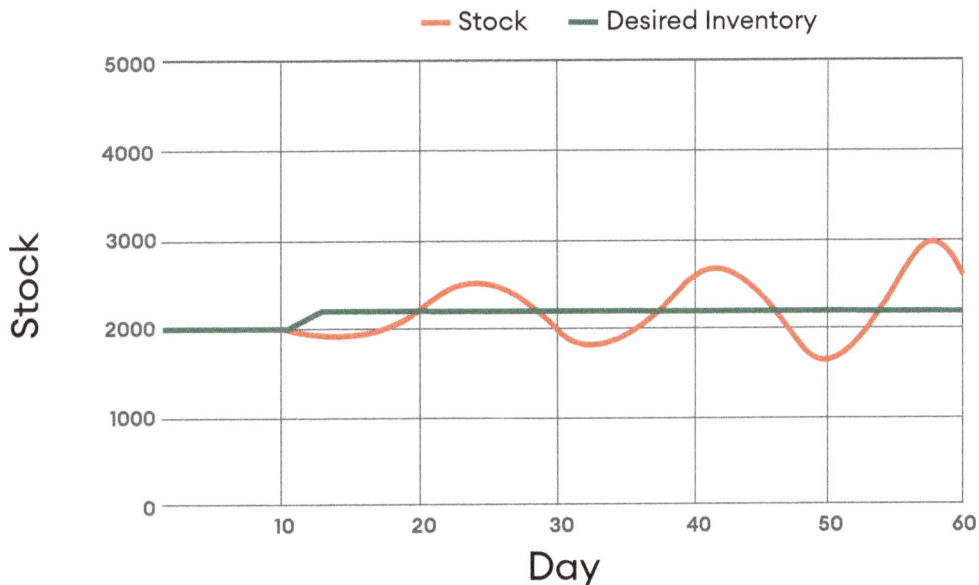

Figure 1.4: Reducing perception delay from five days to two days for faster response

So, the manager reacts sooner, and the desired inventory goes up to 2,200 faster, but if anything, the oscillations start a little sooner, and they are slightly higher. The peak inventory just before the 60-day mark is now 2,994 items. It was 2,981 before changing the perception delay.

Next, we'll try responding faster by changing the order to make up 60% of the shortfall, which was originally 40%. As you can see in *Figure 1.5*, the behavior gets even worse. The oscillations get much bigger, and the peak inventory goes even higher to 3,800 and falls to 1,400 some days.

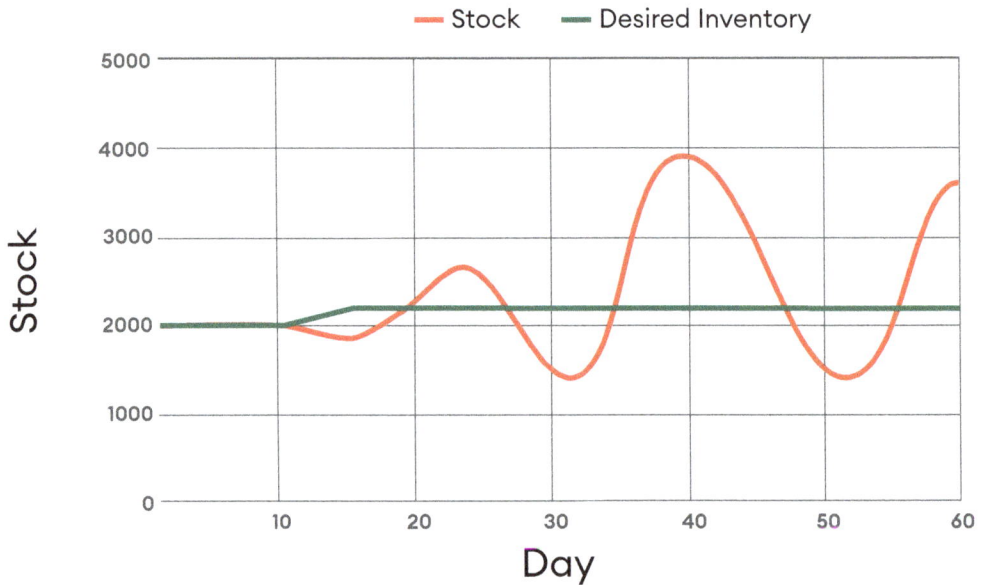

Figure 1.5: Reducing response delay – inventory swings grow larger

Finally, we'll try a slower response, reducing the response delay (the change in the order) to 25% instead of 60%, as we saw in the previous example.

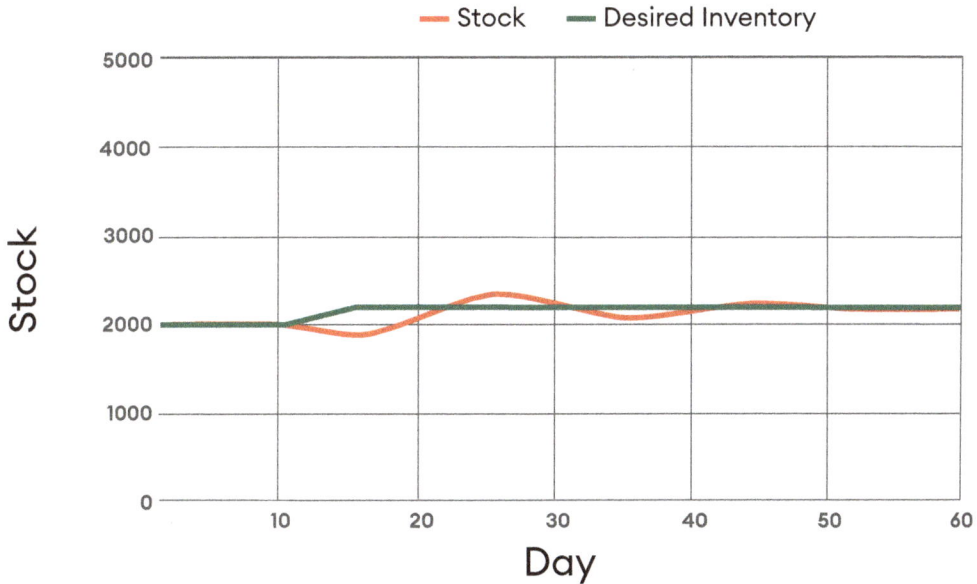

Figure 1.6: Slower order changes reduce inventory oscillations

As shown in *Figure 1.6*, the behavior of the system is much better now. The inventory still oscillates, but it starts to settle close to the desired inventory around 20 days after the change in demand.

Systems surprise us

Systems can react in counterintuitive ways. In this relatively simple system, the store manager was reacting too quickly. Our natural inclination was toward faster perceptions and responses, but they made the system behave even worse. It was only when we tried something that seemed counterintuitive (slower responses) that the behavior of the system improved. This is also true of software systems, and we'll see some practical examples later in this chapter. Changing some variables can have a big impact on the overall behavior, but others might have little to no effect. In these examples, we saw that a perception delay had little effect, but a response delay did.

Real systems are always more complex than models and can have hidden variables or feedback loops. This system was relatively simple. A more complex system can have multiple stocks and more feedback loops. Systems are inherently oscillatory. System behavior is revealed as a series of events over time. Our human minds are not good at understanding non-linear growth and interactions between elements. We make assumptions about what the current bottleneck is and try to improve elements of the system that will not increase performance unless the limiting factor is improved.

A typical software system

Now, let's apply what we've discussed about systems in general to a software system. We'll begin by looking at a typical software system at a high level, as shown in *Figure 1.7*, and describe some of the potential bottlenecks.

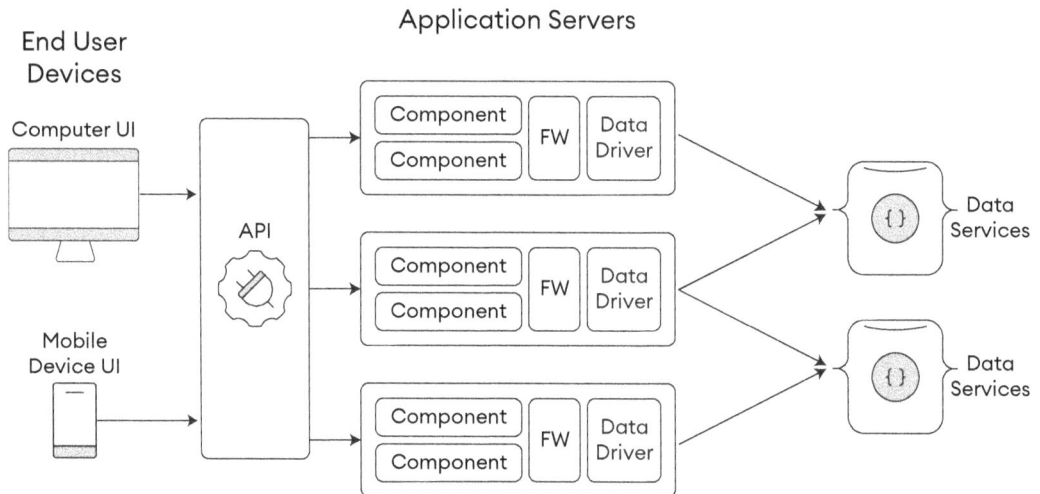

Figure 1.7: High-level view of a software system showing a client-to-database request flow

Looking from left to right, we see two clients. These could be a desktop computer and a mobile device. These clients connect via the internet to an **application programming interface** (**API**) gateway, which sends requests and receives notifications. The API gateway connects to multiple application servers. These modify, route, and forward client requests to one or more software components running on those application servers. Each application server can have multiple software components using one or more **frameworks** (**FW**) such as Spring or Rails. These typically contain data service abstractions or object modeling components that use a database-specific driver (sometimes called a client library) that talks to the data services.

Any of these components (the computers they run on or the networks connecting them) could be a bottleneck to the performance or scalability of the overall application.

Here are two examples of performance bottlenecks in a software system:

- **An API gateway bottleneck**: As the system gains popularity and more users connect to the API gateway, the API reaches a point where it is handling so many connections and requests that the CPU is fully utilized. This could be identified by looking at the idle CPU available on the computer running the API gateway. This could be solved by vertically scaling the computer or the cloud instance running the API gateway.

- **A framework bottleneck:** The application software may send seemingly simple requests to the framework, but under the hood these requests can trigger expensive database operations, such as a full collection or table scan on the database. This inefficient querying uses CPU and storage bandwidth on the database while also sending more data than necessary back to the application servers. As a result, unnecessary network bandwidth is used, and additional CPU resources are required on the application server to process the data.

This latter bottleneck could be identified in a number of ways:

- Profiling the application could find that the requests to the framework are taking a surprising amount of time.
- During development, an end-to-end trace can be used to track a user request from a client through the application code, framework, and data services abstraction to see what kind of query is run on the data services and the subsequent **input/output** (I/O) operations.
- This could identify read or write amplifications, where a small client request results in a disproportionately large database operation. For example, a client query for one data point of 32 bytes could make its way through the full system and result in a table scan on the database that pulls 32 GB of data through I/O and caches for no reason. This could be remedied by configuring the framework to be more efficient.

We will provide specific examples of these kinds of bottlenecks and solutions throughout the book, culminating in a number of specific case studies in *Chapter 15, Debugging Performance Issues*.

Identifying potential bottlenecks is only the first step in optimizing a software system. To remove these bottlenecks, we need a structured approach applying performance engineering principles.

Performance engineering principles span a range from algorithmic theory to Little's law. By applying these principles, developers can minimize bottlenecks, improve scalability, and maximize resource efficiency. In the next subsections, we'll explore some of these principles and see how they guide the design of high-performing systems, which you can keep in mind as you read this book.

Algorithmic efficiency (complexity)

The choice of algorithm and data structure is typically where most computer science courses first introduce performance. An algorithm that scales linearly or logarithmically with input size will perform better than one that scales exponentially. No amount of micro-optimization will compensate for an inherently slow algorithm. In modern systems, this might mean using built-in libraries (often optimized in C or assembly) or leveraging parallel algorithms.

Avoid premature optimization

As the saying goes, *"Make it work, then make it fast."* In other words, focus on building a correct and reliable system before worrying about performance.

This idea is echoed by computer scientist Donald Knuth, who famously warned that *"premature optimization is the root of all evil."* Developers often guess wrong about what's slowing their systems down; profiling tools regularly uncover performance bottlenecks in unexpected places. Modern processors can also execute compiled code in ways that defy human intuition.

By resisting the urge to optimize too early, you keep your code clean and maintainable. You also ensure that your performance efforts are grounded in real data, not assumptions.

Amdahl's law (limit of parallel speedup)

Amdahl's law explains why certain workloads don't speed up proportionally with more cores. If a fraction S of a program must run sequentially, for example, to protect a shared data structure, then even with infinite processors, the speedup is limited to $1/S$. For example, if 10% of a task is serial, the best overall speedup you can get approaches 10x (assuming the other 90% runs on many processors). When using multicore processors and distributed computing, one must identify and reduce the serial portions of the workload.

Locality and caching

Programs typically access a relatively small portion of data or code repeatedly in a short period of time. Caches can be used to speed up access to frequently used data. Systems use caches at various levels: in-memory caches for database results, and CPU caches to avoid recomputation or slow accesses by storing results of expensive operations and reusing them. However, caching introduces complexity, such as stale data and memory overhead. This is why it's mentioned in the following joke:

> *There are 2 hard problems in computer science: cache invalidation, naming things, and off-by-1 errors.*
>
> *Leon Bambrick*

Ironically, there's now a counterpoint to that joke:

> *There's 2 hard problems in computer science: we only have one joke and it's not funny.*
>
> Phillip Scott Bowden

The use of caching (e.g., in I/O operations) is crucial to get good performance out of slow devices, but it's also applicable at other layers of distributed systems.

Little's law (throughput versus latency)

Performance is multi-dimensional. Sometimes the goal is to handle a high volume of operations (throughput), while other times, the priority is to minimize the delay between the start and completion of a single operation (latency). In many cases, both are equally important.

You can increase concurrency to improve throughput (e.g., using multithreading, asynchronous I/O, or non-blocking event loops). However, these techniques might introduce queuing delays that affect latency. Having too many concurrent operations can push a system into an inefficient state. It's important to first identify your performance target and then optimize accordingly. For high throughput, maximize resource utilization (CPU, network, and disk) with concurrency. For low latency, minimize waiting and depth of processing. Balancing these is an art, guided by analysis and benchmarks.

In summary, performance engineering should be data-driven, using profilers and monitors to identify bottlenecks. It should be informed by both classic insights (such as algorithmic complexity and Amdahl's law) and modern techniques (such as parallel computing, vectorization, and distributed load balancing). Focus optimization efforts where they yield the most benefit, and always verify the impact with measurements.

Understanding MongoDB architecture

Now that you understand systems in general, it's time we start looking at MongoDB systems in particular. Before we do that, let's take a look at MongoDB architecture at a high level. We'll dive deeper into each of these components throughout the book.

First, it's important to understand the foundations of MongoDB. MongoDB was created to bridge the gap between traditional relational databases and simple key-value stores. The central idea was to bring together the best aspects of both worlds (flexibility, speed, and an easy-to-understand data model), while offering features such as powerful querying, indexing, and complex aggregations. In addition, from the early days, MongoDB had native libraries for many languages, built-in replication, horizontal scaling via sharding, and an intuitive document data model.

Key-value stores are often praised for their speed and simplicity. MongoDB, however, goes beyond that simple approach by letting you store and query entire documents (objects) with rich relationships and structure. Relational databases, on the other hand, organize data into tables with predefined columns and relationships and enforce strict schemas.

In the next section, we'll take a closer look at the MongoDB document model and how it differs from a relational database.

The document model: MongoDB's foundation

In a relational database, data is typically normalized into separate tables to support a wide range of use cases. This can require complex joins for application-specific views. In contrast, MongoDB encourages you to model data as application-specific documents, optimized for how your application accesses and uses it. This flexibility allows for representing complex relationships and hierarchical data within a single document.

JavaScript Object Notation (JSON) is a lightweight, human-readable data format used to store and exchange data between applications. MongoDB's document model stores data in JSON-like structures called **Binary JSON (BSON)** documents.

Here's an example of a document:

```
# A simple document representing a user
user = {
    "name": "Jane Doe",
    "age": 30,
    "email": "janedoe@example.com",
    "address": {
        "street": "123 Main St",
        "city": "Anytown",
        "state": "CA",
        "zip": "12345"
    },
    "interests": ["hiking", "photography", "travel"]
}
```

This contains a number of properties about a user. In a relational database, the user's interests would be stored in a separate table, which would have to be queried separately or joined with every time you needed the user's interests alongside the other user information. From a performance perspective, in MongoDB, the array of interests is stored with the user information, so all user information can be read from storage in one access and received by an application in one query. In addition, interests can be indexed so that it's simple and fast to query for all users interested in hiking, for example.

Have you ever tried to model hierarchical data in a relational database? If you have, you know it often feels like trying to fit a square peg into a round hole. In MongoDB, nested structures are a natural fit, with no complex joins or entity-relationship diagrams required.

Key architectural components of MongoDB

The MongoDB server uses a single mongod process that can run anywhere. You can deploy the mongod process on many classes of computers, including laptops, self-managed servers within data centers within your business, cloud instances managed by your business, and cloud instances managed by MongoDB Atlas.

Many of the concepts we'll discuss apply to this server process; however, it's also a building block of the MongoDB distributed system. A basic deployment in production would usually at a minimum be a **replica set** with three computers, each running a mongod process. One of them would be the primary, and the other two would be secondaries. All members of a replica set have the same copy of the data. You will learn more about this in *Chapter 5, Replication*, but the most important thing to know is that replication provides high availability for your application by monitoring the health of all members and electing a new primary automatically should there be a failure of the old primary.

When you horizontally scale MongoDB, you would treat your replica set as the first **shard** and then add as many additional shards as you need. Each shard is a replica set. Each shard holds a subset of the data, and a smart **router** process directs operations to the correct shard, eliminating the need for your application to know how the data is distributed. You'll learn more about this in *Chapter 6, Sharding*.

Atlas is an integrated suite of cloud database and data services to accelerate and simplify how you build with data. Atlas extends MongoDB's flexibility and ease of use to enable you to build full-text search, real-time analytics, and event-driven features.

MongoDB client libraries (or drivers) allow your application code to communicate with the database using a native library and APIs that look like any other API in the language you're using. You construct a request in your preferred programming language, and the driver converts it to messages MongoDB understands.

MongoDB provides official drivers for most of the popular programming languages, including Python, Java, C#, and Node.js, among others. You can find the full list in the MongoDB documentation at https://www.mongodb.com/docs/drivers/.

Here's a simple example of how to connect to MongoDB and insert a document using PyMongo, the official MongoDB driver for Python:

```python
from pymongo import MongoClient

# Connect to MongoDB
client = MongoClient('mongodb://localhost:27017/');
db = client['store_database'];
collection = db['products'];

# Define a product document with nested information
product = {
    "name": "Ergonomic Keyboard",
    "price": 129.99,
    "category": "Computer Accessories",
    "details": {
        "weight": 1.2,
        "dimensions": "18 x 6 x 1 inches"
    },
};

# Insert the document
collection.insert_one(product);
```

What you don't see in the preceding code is all the heavy lifting the client library is doing: managing connections, communicating the MongoDB wire protocol to the server, handling network timeouts, implementing retry logic, and transforming Python dictionaries to BSON and back.

The following code queries the products collection for affordable products (less than $100):

```python
# Find affordable products
affordable_products = collection.find({'price': {'$lt': 100}});
for product in affordable_products:
    print(f"Found affordable product: {product['name']}");
```

When MongoDB returns a document, it arrives as a native data structure in your language, which is a Python dictionary in this case. No awkward conversion is needed. This natural mapping between your application code and database representation is a significant advantage for developer productivity.

The data services system

Let's zoom in now to the data services part of the overall software system that we looked at earlier in *Figure 1.7*.

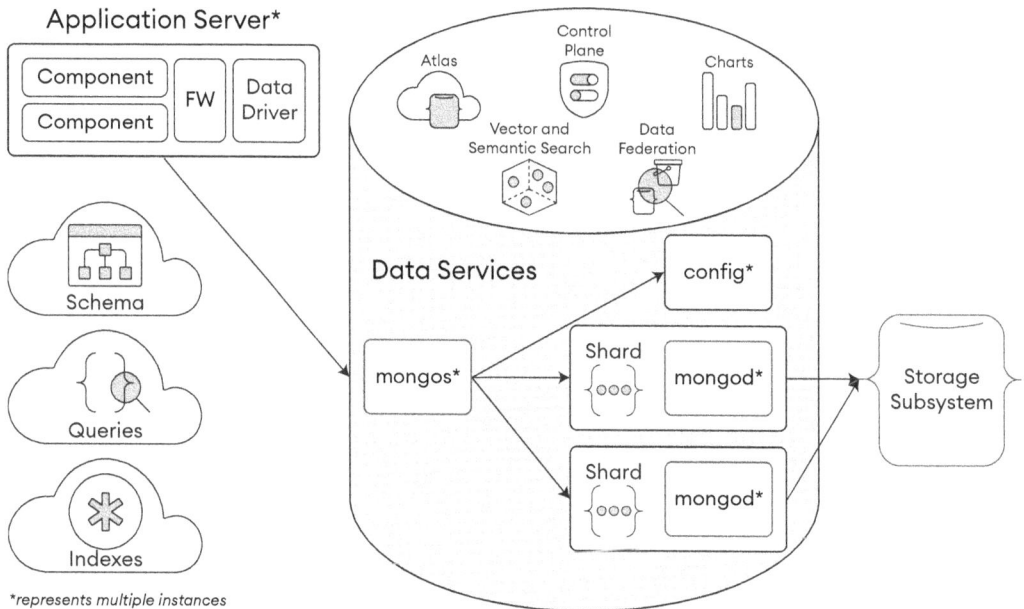

Figure 1.8: MongoDB architecture showing the connections between core database components

Looking from left to right in *Figure 1.8*, we see that the application servers are communicating with the data services through a driver or client library. In this case, we are showing a sharded cluster. For simpler deployments, the application server could connect to a single replica set without the mongos and config server. Conceptual elements such as the schema, queries, and indexes are shared between the application server and the data services layer. Some performance and scalability issues can be caused by these conceptual elements, and changing them might be the source of some improvements.

In this case, we are looking at a diagram of an Atlas deployment that includes elements such as the Atlas UI (which includes monitoring and backup), the Atlas control plane, charts, and features such as Vector and Semantic Search, and Data Federation.

The rest of the components are considered the **core** database, and they are as follows:

- mongod: A single server process. Atlas can deploy multiple mongod processes in replica sets (for high availability) and shards (for horizontal scaling).

- mongos: A router process for a sharded cluster. It routes queries to one or more shards and combines results from multiple shards into responses.

- config: A special, internal database that stores the metadata for a sharded cluster. The metadata reflects the state and organization of all data within the sharded cluster. mongos uses this metadata to route read and write operations to the correct shards. It also maintains a cache of this data.

Finally, in *Figure 1.8*, the mongod processes will save and retrieve the data via the storage subsystem. This could be a disk in a self-managed MongoDB system or cloud storage, such as the following:

- **Elastic Block Storage (EBS)** in AWS and Alibaba Cloud
- **Managed Disks** in Azure
- **Persistent Disks (PD)** in GCP
- Locally attached ephemeral SSDs

When using Atlas, we present the overall data services system as a black box with a small number of settings you need to consider. Atlas takes care of the details for you. The settings from an Atlas perspective are as follows:

- The number of shards and replica set members.

- The instance size, which determines the number of **virtual central processing units (vCPUs)**, the amount of memory, and network performance.

- The storage configuration, which includes the size and throughput of the device. Throughput is usually defined as **input/output operations per second (IOPS)**.

If you are self-managing MongoDB on your own cloud or physical servers, you have visibility of many of the component settings inside the server and software that the mongod process is running on. This is a double-edged sword. You have more settings you can tune to improve performance. However, you also have more elements to manage and potential bottlenecks to explore.

Now, if we zoom in to the mongod, we find that it is itself a system with multiple elements. The following diagram (*Figure 1.9*) shows the main elements inside the MongoDB server (mongod):

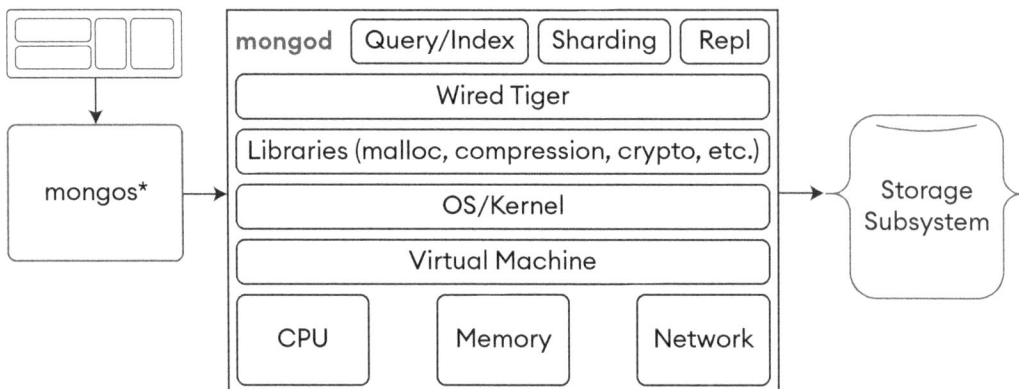

Figure 1.9: Elements inside the MongoDB server

Query engine

MongoDB's query engine takes your query, determines the most efficient way to find the data you need, and returns the results. It uses indexes to optimize query execution and passes requests to the storage engine to execute operations.

An index is like the index at the back of a book. Instead of reading every page of a book to find a topic, you can use the index to directly find out which pages contain the topic. Similarly, in a database, an index helps the query engine locate data more efficiently.

MongoDB allows you to do a lot more than a key-value store. MongoDB's query and indexing capabilities rival (and, in some ways, surpass) traditional relational databases:

- You can query on any field, not just the primary key
- You can perform complex logical operations
- You can query inside nested documents and arrays
- You can aggregate and analyze data
- You can create indexes on any combination of fields, including arrays and subdocuments
- You can add multiple indexes to a collection of documents

Indexes make queries more efficient. As with many aspects of performance, there are costs to indexes, too. When creating/inserting new documents, every index will necessitate an additional write operation to storage. Similarly, when updating an indexed field of a document, an extra write will be needed to update the index.

You can get the query system to provide **explain plans**, which provide details about how a query ran. This can provide valuable information for finding potential bottlenecks and generating ideas for improvements.

 We'll go into a lot more detail about indexes and queries in *Chapters 3, Indexes,* and *Chapter 12, Advanced Query and Indexing Concepts.*

Storage engine/WiredTiger

Each mongod process needs to store the data on disk. The storage engine is MongoDB's filing system; it's the component responsible for managing how data is stored, retrieved, and maintained on disk. Since MongoDB 3.2, WiredTiger has been the default storage engine.

The storage engine takes care of persisting data and indexes on disk, fetching the data from disk, as well as handling the compression and encryption of the data on disk. It also handles the journal known as the **write-ahead log** in many databases. The storage engine also contains an in-memory cache of the most recently accessed documents. You can change the size of the WiredTiger cache using the `wiredTigerCacheSizeGB` setting. The remaining memory will be used by the operating system's filesystem (page) cache. You'll learn more about storage engines in *Chapter 7, Storage Engines.*

Libraries

When developing MongoDB, we used many other building blocks and libraries. These also have settings that can be changed to improve performance.

Starting with MongoDB Server 8.0, a newer version of the memory allocator (TCMalloc) supports per-CPU caches, instead of per-thread caches. This can reduce memory fragmentation and make your database more resilient to high-stress workloads. A number of system configuration settings may need to be modified to use per-CPU caches. You'll find more details on system settings in *Chapter 13, Operating System and System Resources.* If you really know what you are doing, you can change controls such as the logical page size, but this could necessitate changing the settings in the MongoDB source code and rebuilding the server. Again, Atlas provides defaults and implements best practices.

Compression algorithms are more accessible. You can specify the storage compression algorithm to be used either when creating a collection or via configuration options when starting the server. By default, Atlas uses an algorithm called **Snappy**. When running self-managed MongoDB, you have four compressor options:

- None
- **Snappy**: Fastest, lowest CPU consumption; doesn't compress data as much
- **Zstd**: A middle ground between Snappy and Zlib
- **Zlib**: Slowest, highest CPU consumption; compresses data better

You can also use network compression between the driver and the MongoDB server. In this case, you can select the compression algorithm via the driver in your application code, whether the server is on Atlas or not.

MongoDB uses OpenSSL to handle TLS/SSL encryption for the following:

- Client-server connections (e.g., mongod $\rightleftarrows$ MongoDB Shell)
- Replication and sharded cluster communication
- MongoDB drivers connecting to the database

Different versions of OpenSSL have different performance characteristics and scalability on higher-tier instances/servers.

Other system components that mongod uses

MongoDB runs within an operating system, which, in turn, is managed by a kernel. In operating systems such as Linux, parameters such as `vm.dirty_ratio` and `vm.dirty_writeback_centisecs` tune the kernel's mechanisms for managing virtual memory. They change how data is handled before being written from memory to disk.

MongoDB can run inside **virtual machines (VMs)**. However, you need to make sure it's configured correctly from the VM perspective. For example, over-allocating vCPUs can lead to CPU contention among VMs running on the same host, which can degrade performance. You can learn more about concepts such as ballooning and how to configure MongoDB for VMs in the MongoDB server production notes at `https://www.mongodb.com/docs/manual/administration/production-notes/`.

MongoDB runs on many types of CPUs in networked systems with different amounts of memory. These typically depend on the cloud instance size or computer server on which you deploy MongoDB. In general, larger instances or servers will have more CPUs, memory, and higher network bandwidth.

As we saw earlier, with Atlas, you can select different types and configurations of cloud storage. You typically have the same options when running your own cloud instances or self-managed storage. In addition, you can choose different filesystems and settings, such as readahead. When a program reads a file, Linux anticipates future reads and loads additional data into memory. This reduces the number of disk access operations, making sequential reads faster. This will be discussed in more detail in *Chapter 13, Operating System and System Resources*.

Managing complexity in modern data platforms

Let's zoom back out from a single mongod process to look at the data services layer again. To your application, the data services element is one component, but in reality, it can be a complex distributed system in its own right with multiple individual servers.

MongoDB's approach is to provide a data services API that simplifies this complexity using three key principles: a flexible data model, built-in redundancy and resilience, and horizontal scaling.

Flexible data model with rigorous capabilities

The document model allows you to represent relationships naturally while still supporting rigorous data governance when needed. One MongoDB user explained it perfectly: "*We can push updates to our application without having to coordinate complex database migrations. The schema evolves with our code, not against it.*" You can learn more about this flexible data model in *Chapter 2, Schema Design for Performance*.

Built-in redundancy and resilience

Rather than treating high availability as an add-on feature, MongoDB bakes resilience into its core architecture through replication:

- **Automatic failover**: If the primary node fails, an election determines a new primary within seconds
- **Self-healing**: When failed nodes recover, they automatically catch up and rejoin the replica set

Again, Atlas provides defaults, implements best practices, and simplifies the number of settings you need to consider. When self-managing MongoDB, you can dig deeper into replication settings. For example, if running MongoDB on your own servers, you can change server parameters to tune how replication data is batched. Larger batches reduce network traffic and the number of IOPS required on secondaries, but can add latency for writes. You can also configure **flow control**, which can prevent replication lag by slowing down writes if secondaries are falling behind. You can learn more about replication in *Chapter 5, Replication*.

Horizontal scaling with intelligent distribution

MongoDB's sharding capability distributes data across multiple replica sets while keeping related data together:

- **Automatic balancing**: MongoDB continuously rebalances data across shards as your data grows

- **Query routing**: The MongoDB router (mongos) intelligently directs operations to the appropriate shards

- **Zone sharding**: You can align data distribution with your infrastructure (keeping European customer data in European servers, for example)

MongoDB Atlas simplifies sharding by automating key processes, enabling best practices, and providing built-in features to ensure optimal performance. You can read more about this in *Chapter 6, Sharding*.

Performance tools

You can use performance monitoring tools to help find potential bottlenecks or limiting factors. These could be in any of the components or elements we mentioned earlier. More details will be provided in *Chapter 14, Monitoring and Observability*.

The mongod and mongos processes write log files with performance information. They also support the serverStatus command, which returns information about the running process. The query engine can "explain" how a query will run and supports a profiler feature. Command-line tools, such as mongostat and mongotop, are provided to monitor a running mongod process.

To monitor utilization of all kinds of system resources, you can use operating system commands, MongoDB Atlas monitoring, and other GUI tools that are designed specifically for monitoring multiple servers.

For system resources specifically, Linux commands such as top, vmstat, iostat, and netstat can be used to monitor CPU, memory, storage, and network at a point in time on a single server. Tools such as dstat and sar can be used to combine data from simpler tools and view it over a period of time.

MongoDB Atlas monitoring provides historical and real-time system resource data, which is integrated with database-specific metrics. It has tools such as **Real-Time Performance Panel (RTPP)**, Performance Advisor, Namespace Insights, and Query Profiler. You can also set alerts for specific performance events.

For self-managed deployments, you can use graphical tools such as Netdata, Prometheus + Grafana, Zabbix, Munin, or Observium. You can use observability frameworks such as OpenTelemetry. Finally, you can use commercial **application performance monitoring (APM)** tools such as AppDynamics, Datadog, Dynatrace, LogicMonitor, New Relic, SolarWinds, and Splunk Observability.

Finding bottlenecks

As mentioned at the start of this chapter, every system has a limiting factor or bottleneck. With multiple inputs to a system, it's not always clear what the limiting factor is. We need to find the element or component that is the current bottleneck. To do this, we need to use the tools mentioned previously to analyze the performance of all of the potential bottlenecks we mentioned so far.

In summary, the following table lists the potential bottlenecks you might encounter when tuning a typical software application. The first column shows the potential bottlenecks you could encounter on both Atlas and self-managed systems. The second column shows the additional bottlenecks you are responsible for with self-managed deployments. As you can see, using Atlas significantly reduces the number of bottlenecks you need to consider.

Atlas and self-managed (private cloud)	Self-managed (private cloud)
UI/application code	Network
Framework	Replication
Driver	Storage engine
Network	Libraries (allocator, compression, and encryption)
Schema/model	OS/kernel
Queries	Virtual machine
Indexes	Memory (extra details)
Sharding	CPU (extra details)
Cloud storage	Storage (extra details)
CPU	—
Memory	—

Table 1.1: Atlas vs. self-managed (private cloud)

For the remainder of this section, we'll look in more detail at two example bottlenecks.

We'll look at a storage bottleneck first, including the measurements and indicators that will help us identify it. In this example, we have a workload that's mostly reading data:

- 95% of the database operations in the steady state are reads of documents using the _id field (primary key)
- The documents are being retrieved in random order, meaning the _id values are being accessed in a different order from when they were inserted
- The dataset is 10x larger than the memory on the database server, so most of the read operations cannot be satisfied by a cache read and they need to access the storage device.]
- The storage device is specified to provide 4,000 IOPS

We see the system is running 5,500 database operations per second using mongostat or Atlas monitoring. We try to increase performance by scaling up the instance type. The database performance stays at 5,500 operations per second. After running this experiment, we know the bottleneck is not the CPU or memory size of the systems running the MongoDB server. We scale the instance size down again.

Next, we look at measurements of I/O:

- If running self-managed instances, you can look at the number of IOPS using the iostat command on Linux
- If running in Atlas, you can observe the number of IOPS being used on the **Max Disk IOPS** metric when you look at monitoring

To try and improve performance, we now increase the number of storage IOPS from 4,000 to 8,000. Database performance doubles to 11,000 operations per second. We see this situation quite frequently with customers. They assume they need to use a more powerful database instance when, in reality, they really need more IOPS from the storage subsystem.

In the second example, we'll focus on a subset of *Figure 1.8*. Here, we have an application server interacting with a data services layer:

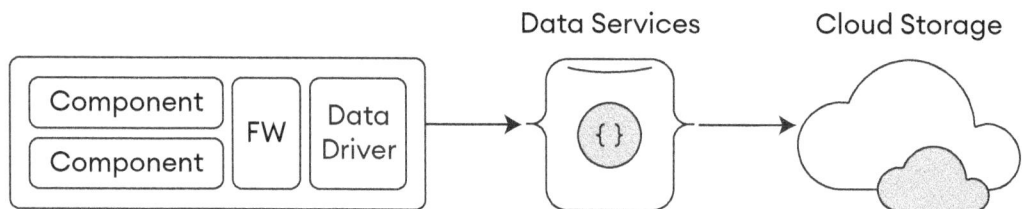

Figure 1.10: Application server connects to storage through data services

Initially, we assume the bottleneck is somewhere in the data services layer or below, but when we look at CPU and I/O utilization, we see idle CPU time, and the storage IOPS and bandwidth are not being reached. So, we assume the limiting factor is further upstream. Through measurements on the application server, we see it has no idle CPU time, so it is the bottleneck. It is not generating enough requests to fully load the data services or cloud storage layers.

As a general model of a service in a system, requests come in and are executed by a number of threads within the service. Some threads can interact via shared resources; for example, in a MongoDB server, a query being run by one thread could use space in the storage engine cache, slowing other threads.

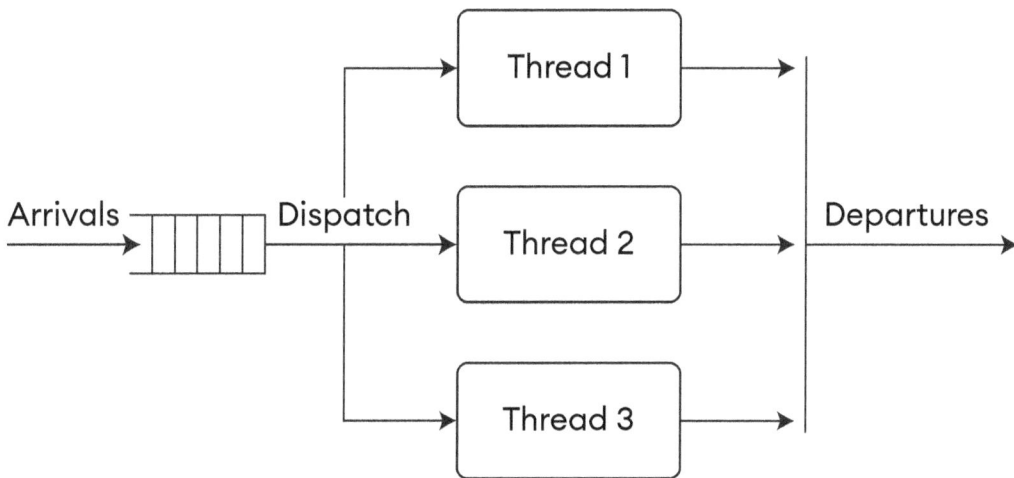

Figure 1.11: Service threads handle requests

In this example, the application server is not sending enough requests that can be dispatched to be run in multiple threads within the data services layer. The general performance of a system with this kind of model is as follows:

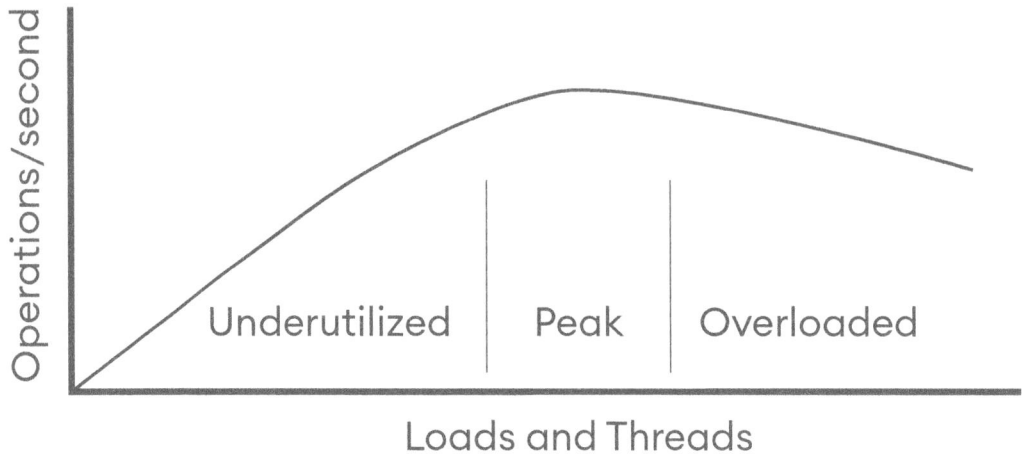

Figure 1.12: Performance improves as load and threads grow until the system is overloaded

As the load and number of active threads increase, the performance in IOPS also increases until the system reaches a point where the threads start to contend for shared resources. Beyond this point, further increasing the load and number of threads can cause performance to decline. Most systems have this characteristic. Peak performance tends to be a factor of the following:

- The amount of work being performed for each request
- The ratio of threads to CPU cores
- The contention for shared resources

The best way to understand this load/performance graph for your application or workload is to run stress/load experiments before you put your product into production.

To resolve this issue, we add a second application server; overall performance improves, but doesn't reach our performance goal.

We re-analyze the load of the components and now see that the CPU on the server running the mongod process is fully utilized. Performance goes from the *Underutilized* part of the graph to the *Overloaded* part. We now see that the MongoDB server is the bottleneck.

Now that we have doubled the load from the application servers, we can reduce it in a finer-grained way by reducing the number of concurrent operations or threads running in the server. You could manage this from your application servers, but another way to do so is to lower the maxPoolSize limit in your database driver or framework/**object-relational mapper (ORM)**. This will reduce the maximum number of connections to the database, which will reduce the maximum number of threads that can be active from your application server at a time. It brings the mongod performance back to the *Peak* part of the graph in *Figure 1.12*. With these two changes, we have now reached our performance goal.

This is another example of what seems like a counterintuitive change. Reducing something can improve performance.

An incremental process for optimization

In general, you can follow a seven-step process with a five-step loop. When we've seen people struggle with performance tuning and scaling, it is because they start in the middle, skip steps, or don't know where they are in the process:

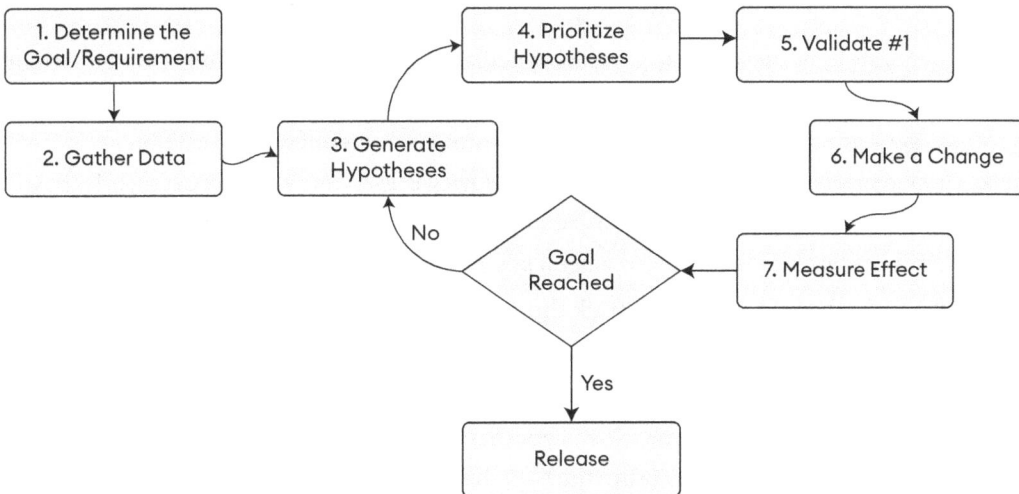

Figure 1.13: An incremental process for optimization and tuning

Let's go through these steps in detail:

1. **Determine the goal/requirement:** There's always room for improvement somewhere in a complex system. Without an agreed goal at the start of the process, performance tuning can become a never-ending task. The goal can become a moving target as the market or requirements change. Get agreement for what the performance requirements will be from project sponsors and stakeholders before starting the project. A performance requirement should be **SMART**, which stands for **specific, measurable, achievable, relevant, and time-bound**. *Make it as fast as possible* is not very specific, achievable, or time-bound. *1M queries per second on a 1GHz 4-core CPU, with 3k IOPS* is not achievable. The requirement should also be relevant to your end user.

This is also a good time to think about the limits of scalability of the system. Presuming data can't increase unbounded forever, how will data expire or be archived over time? What are the performance targets when data is being archived?

2. **Gather data:** Start by gathering data. The working set is the size of the frequently used data and indexes. Does the working set fit in memory? We'll see examples of this calculation later in the book. In general, be aware of the costs of a particular operation. For example, if your application has an administrator feature that runs an occasional query over a large dataset, it's likely that the data won't be in any of the many caches. Worst case, the database will have to retrieve each document from a different disk location, resulting in I/O operations. Your system will have some limit on I/O bandwidth, and this is shared among all the queries running at the same time.

3. **Generate hypotheses:** Next, generate hypotheses, or possible explanations for the current bottleneck. Typically, there will be more than one possible hypothesis. It's a good idea to get a group of people together to brainstorm. Each person will have different levels of experience in different parts of the system. However, everyone will have pet theories based on their experience. Sometimes discussions can get bogged down in one area. At first, focus on quantity; try to get people to suggest possible hypotheses without judgment or analysis.

4. **Prioritize hypotheses:** Then, walk through each hypothesis and try to prioritize them. Note any evidence or data that might support a hypothesis. Again, it's important to time-box the discussion and not spend too much time on any one hypothesis.

5. **Validate #1:** Now that we have a #1 hypothesis or a prime suspect, we need to identify a test that could prove or disprove the hypothesis. For example, if we think a specific part of the system could be CPU-bound, try increasing the size of the server it's running on.

6. **Make a change:** Next, make a change that should improve the situation and prove the hypothesis. For example, you could increase the number of IOPS or reduce or increase the number of threads in your application. Ideally, you should make one change at a time.

7. **Measure effect:** Finally, measure the change in performance. Hopefully, it's an improvement. If the overall performance requirement is met, you can release and celebrate. If not, you'll need to undo the changes that didn't work, then iterate and look at the next hypothesis and bottleneck.

Optimization is not a one-time task. It is a structured, iterative process. By following the steps in order and avoiding the temptation to skip ahead, you can prevent common pitfalls and achieve measurable improvements in system performance.

Summary

This chapter started by describing the characteristics of systems in general and how they can behave in surprising ways when you change them. We then looked at software systems and performance principles in general before looking at data services and MongoDB at a high level. We listed some of the potential bottlenecks or limiting factors before looking at two specific examples, and described a process that can be used when tuning a system for performance.

We also explored MongoDB's architecture, which is designed with performance in mind. Its document model bridges the gap between rigid relational databases and simple key-value stores, providing flexibility without sacrificing power. We looked at components such as the storage engine, the query optimizer, and the replication mechanism.

By consolidating what would traditionally require multiple specialized systems, MongoDB helps organizations reduce operational complexity while still meeting their diverse data needs. The approach isn't about sacrificing power for simplicity; it's about making powerful capabilities more accessible through thoughtful design.

In the next chapter, we'll dive deeper into MongoDB's architecture by exploring how it approaches schema design and how you can design for optimal performance.

References

1.   Meadows, Donella H. *Thinking in Systems: A Primer*. Chelsea Green Publishing, 2008.

Get This Book's PDF Version and Exclusive Extras

UNLOCK NOW

Scan the QR code (or go to `packtpub.com/unlock`). Search for this book by name, confirm the edition, and then follow the steps on the page.

Note: Keep your invoice handy. Purchases made directly from Packt don't require an invoice.

2

Schema Design for Performance

MongoDB was created to bridge the gap between fast, horizontally scalable key-value stores and traditional relational databases. To achieve the best performance, you need to understand MongoDB's strengths and design your application to take advantage of them. Whether you're handling large volumes of reads, writes, or both, the goal is to balance readability, maintainability, and speed. MongoDB's flexible schema design offers unique opportunities, but it requires thoughtful planning to avoid common pitfalls.

In this chapter, we'll cover fundamental principles of designing MongoDB schemas for high performance. We'll start by covering the key principles of schema design in MongoDB and clearing up some common misunderstandings. Then, we'll look at how MongoDB's document model makes it easier to build flexible and efficient schemas. After that, we'll review common mistakes and anti-patterns that can hurt performance or make your data harder to manage. Finally, we'll share practical schema design patterns to help you optimize reads and writes. To bring it all together, we'll apply these ideas to a sample app so you can see how they work in practice.

This chapter will cover the following topics:

- Core principles of schema design
- Strengths of MongoDB's schema model
- Using schema validation for data integrity
- Schema design patterns organized by benefits

Understanding the core principles of schema design

Schema design in MongoDB is driven by how your application accesses and modifies data; there's no single *correct* structure that applies to every use case. This is a shift from the relational model, where normalization is the default starting point and denormalization is a performance tuning step. In MongoDB, you begin by understanding your workload and then design your schema to match.

In this section, we'll cover key principles such as data collocation, read and write trade-offs, document sizing, and common pitfalls. These guidelines will help you build data models that are both efficient and aligned with your application's behavior.

There is no single right way

Here's the most important thing about schema design that you may not realize: *there is no single correct way to structure your documents*. Yes, you read that right! Each use case demands a unique balance between read and write efficiency. The key is to think about your application's workload first; *data that's frequently retrieved together should be stored together to avoid costly lookups*.

This is fundamentally different from how you may have learned to manage data in relational databases. In that model, data normalization is the expected approach from the start. Only when performance cannot keep up with a fully normalized data model will you begin selectively denormalizing some of the data based on how it's used. With MongoDB, we start with the question, *How will this data be used?* and create a data model that best fits our access patterns.

Think of urban planning. Some towns isolate residential, commercial, and industrial zones into distinct areas. But in a well-designed city, areas are not organized strictly by type, but instead, as neighborhoods where daily necessities are within easy reach for their inhabitants. Similarly, MongoDB gives you the flexibility to organize your data based on how your application actually uses it, not by arbitrary categorization.

Data collocation

Once you've identified the entities your application will work with, the main decision is whether to embed related data or store it separately and reference it. You'll repeatedly ask yourself whether an object is an independent entity that should be stored in its own collection or whether it is an attribute of another object and should be stored as part of that object. Similarly, for each attribute of an object, you'll need to consider whether to embed it directly or store it separately.

This is where the principle of *data that's used together should be stored together* comes in. It might sound simple at first glance, but it's powerful when you understand its implications. Here's how it plays out in practice:

- **Embed data that is always retrieved together**: This reduces the number of round trips to the database and keeps reads efficient. For example, embedding order line items within an order document makes sense if they are usually accessed together.

- **Separate infrequently accessed data**: Keep large but rarely used fields out of the main document. This helps prevent overhead if most queries don't need them. Storing large attributes that are only occasionally needed in a document increases disk I/O and wastes RAM. For example, storing a full-size image of a user in the primary user document isn't efficient if only a small thumbnail is displayed on most user pages.

The worst mistake would probably be to treat MongoDB like a relational database, normalizing data across multiple collections and then joining it back together for every query. On the other hand, over embedding can also be suboptimal if it bloats your documents to an extreme extent. You will end up needing significantly more cache, **input/output operations per second** (**IOPS**), and network bandwidth than if you structured the data more in line with your application needs.

Read and write trade-offs

When designing your schema, you may face conflicting requirements between optimizing for reads versus writes. This is not unique to MongoDB, but the document model gives you more options for resolving these conflicts. Here are a few common factors to consider when balancing read and write performance in your schema design:

- **Indexing**: Indexes speed up reads but add overhead to writes and use other resources. Adding multiple indexes to a collection can dramatically improve query performance but will add cost to write operations. It is a classic trade-off, but one worth making if the indexes are correctly designed for your application.

- **Strict service level agreements (SLAs)**: Prioritize operations with the strictest latency requirements. Sometimes you optimize for writes and other times for reads, rarely both equally. For instance, an order processing system may prioritize fast writes, while a reporting system may optimize for read efficiency.

- **Reducing I/O**: Work to minimize the amount of data reads and writes. Every data block you access has a cost. If you can eliminate unnecessary reads or writes, all operations become cheaper and faster.

These considerations also influence whether to model data using large or small documents, which affects how efficiently your application can read, write, and update data.

Small versus large documents

Understanding how MongoDB stores documents on disk is crucial for optimizing performance. MongoDB's WiredTiger storage engine, which is covered in more detail in *Chapter 7, Storage Engines*, uses a page-oriented architecture, where documents are stored on pages that are loaded into memory as needed.

Here is why this matters:

- **Minimum page size**: WiredTiger has a minimum uncompressed page size of 32 KB. Documents smaller than this threshold (under 32 KB uncompressed) share a page with other documents, allowing multiple small documents to be retrieved in a single page read.

- **Related document fragmentation**: If related data is split across multiple documents, your application ends up making multiple queries to retrieve the complete dataset. Additionally, these documents may reside on different pages, requiring more I/O operations to retrieve all related data.

- **Write amplification**: When large documents are updated, even with small changes, the entire document must still need to be written to disk during checkpoints. The larger the document, the more likely it is to cause larger than necessary writes.

Understanding this leads us to our next important principle: *high read velocity workloads benefit from embedded document patterns*. This is because related data is stored in one place, on one page. On the other hand, for high write velocity workloads, where you're frequently updating small portions of data, multiple document patterns may be more efficient.

Common myths

Let's bust some common misunderstandings about MongoDB schema design:

- **Denormalization**: Denormalizing data does not always mean *more storage* or *data duplication*. In some cases, embedding related data in one place lowers overall space usage and reduces the number of required indexes. For example, embedding line items within an order document eliminates the need for order ID indexes in both the orders and line items collections, and can help reduce the total data size. Embedding frequently accessed domain data that rarely or never changes will also reduce additional lookups and improve overall performance.

- **Dynamic schema**: MongoDB offers flexibility, but you don't have to use it. You can enforce a strict schema through your application layer or through MongoDB's own schema validation capabilities, or even both. Flexible schema is an option, not a requirement.

- **Intentional design**: If you didn't consciously design your data structure, it's not really a schema. Someone passing you JSON that you store directly in the database is not schema design; it's just storing payload. True schema design reflects the specific needs and requirements of your application.

- **Indexing is not automatic**: It is not a common myth, but it's out there. Each collection automatically creates a unique index on the required `_id` field, which is the primary key for each record, and if you don't supply it with the document when inserting it, it will be generated automatically. But an important part of schema design is figuring out which secondary attributes you'll be querying by and making sure you create all indexes that are necessary to efficiently support those queries. You'll learn more about indexes in *Chapter 3, Indexes*.

Remember when relational database practitioners would debate *whether every table needed a surrogate key or a natural key?* Now, we have more interesting discussions about *whether to embed or reference related data*, conversations that directly impact application performance!

Key strengths of the MongoDB schema design

Compared to relational databases, MongoDB's document model enables patterns that simplify data access, reduce query complexity, improve performance for read-heavy and write-heavy workloads, and adapt more readily to evolving application requirements. Instead of enforcing a rigid structure, MongoDB allows developers to model data in ways that reflect real-world use cases and access patterns. This flexibility is at the heart of MongoDB's approach to schema design, enabling developers to build applications optimized for speed and scalability. In this section, we'll cover the key strengths of MongoDB's schema design, including handling one-to-many relationships, embedding weak entities, supporting dynamic attributes, leveraging caching and snapshots, optimizing for common use cases, and accommodating seamless schema evolution.

One-to-many relationships

One-to-many relationships in MongoDB are treated as first-class citizens, with arrays, objects, and arrays of objects enjoying full querying, updating, and indexing capabilities. This capability is baked into the foundation of MongoDB's document model, rather than added as an afterthought.

This makes MongoDB perfect for storing structured, repeating data such as comments in a blog post, tags for a product, or variations in merchandise. For example, in a blogging platform, a blog post document can contain its comments in an array, allowing the application to retrieve the post and its comments in a single query. By storing related data together, MongoDB eliminates the need for costly joins, reduces query complexity, and minimizes disk I/O operations, improving overall performance.

Embedding weak entities

Weak entities (items that rely on a parent entity for context) are ideal candidates for embedding in MongoDB. For example, order line items in an e-commerce platform are inherently dependent on their parent order. Embedding these line items within the order document ensures all related data is stored together, without the need for separate lookups or joins. An order without its line items serves little value, and keeping them together allows developers to query and update order data efficiently. This approach improves performance by reducing I/O operations and query complexity, making data retrieval faster and simplifying application logic at the same time.

Dynamic attributes

Relational databases often struggle with modeling entities where field names or the number of attributes are not known ahead of time. These challenges typically involve costly schema migrations to add new columns or require storing the attributes in cumbersome, inefficiency-prone formats. MongoDB, however, embraces dynamic data modeling natively. For instance, a product catalog can include variable attributes such as `"color"` for clothing items or `"engine size"` for vehicles, without requiring rigid definitions or structural changes. Documents can easily store attribute names as keys with corresponding values or use arrays of key-value pairs, both of which support efficient indexing and querying. This eliminates operational overhead and ensures faster queries, even as data evolves.

Caches and snapshots

In traditional databases, data normalization discourages redundancy, but MongoDB allows selective duplication to optimize frequent access patterns. For example, storing a customer's shipping address directly within each order document ensures quick retrieval of this information without querying a separate collection. Similarly, storing a handful of a user's most recent actions, such as posts or reviews, within their parent document reduces repeated queries and speeds access to frequently requested data. This use of data duplication acts as an effective cache or point-in-time snapshot, reducing I/O overhead and ensuring faster queries for applications subject to high user traffic.

Optimization for common use cases

Some of the examples mentioned previously allow you to optimize your system for operations that happen thousands of times a minute, such as users looking at their orders or their friends' posts, and allow you to worry less about operations that may happen once in a blue moon, if at all (how often does a user change their name, and does that operation really need to be instantaneous?). This optimization allows developers to focus on key workflows, such as retrieving user posts or order details, while deprioritizing rare operations, such as users changing their account information. MongoDB's schema flexibility allows developers to focus on optimizing these frequent operations, reducing unnecessary processing overhead and ensuring smooth, fast performance for everyday transactions.

Schema evolution

Have you ever tried to add a column to a large table in a relational database in production? With MongoDB's dynamic schema, you can start using new fields immediately while either lazily updating old documents or not at all, depending on your requirements. Applications should gracefully handle new fields or shapes in documents. This can ensure backward compatibility and smooth transitions during schema updates. Good data access layers in MongoDB applications understand schemas can evolve over time without requiring a full data conversion.

MongoDB's schema design strengths provide flexibility and efficiency for modern applications, empowering developers to build tailored data models that maximize real-world performance. Whether handling one-to-many relationships, embedding weak entities, supporting dynamic attributes, leveraging caching and snapshots, optimizing for high-frequency operations, or accommodating schema evolution, MongoDB enables developers to create high-performance applications that adapt to changing needs. By simplifying queries, reducing latency, and streamlining data access patterns, MongoDB delivers the power and versatility required for scalable, modern workloads. Its document model is not just a convenience; it's a cornerstone of performance optimization for real-world applications.

Schema validation

While much of schema design focuses on how data is structured and accessed, one often overlooked but critical aspect is schema validation. Just because MongoDB is flexible doesn't mean you should allow just any data structure to be stored. Schema validation is an important tool for maintaining data integrity and is almost completely free in terms of performance impact. The performance cost of validating documents as they're inserted or updated is negligible compared to the total cost of the write, and it offers several practical benefits:

- **Catch errors early**: Validation prevents incorrect or malformed data from entering your database

- **Enforce business rules**: You can define requirements such as minimum values or valid patterns directly in your data model

- **Document your schema**: Validation rules serve as living documentation for your data model

- **Smooth evolution**: You can easily adapt validation rules as your schema evolves

While MongoDB offers great flexibility, schema validation ensures that flexibility doesn't come at the cost of data integrity. By defining clear rules for your data model, you not only prevent errors and enforce business logic but also lay the groundwork for maintainable, evolving schemas. Let's now look at common schema design mistakes, many of which can be avoided with thoughtful validation and a solid understanding of your data's structure and usage patterns.

Common schema design mistakes

MongoDB's flexible document model offers powerful advantages when used thoughtfully. The same features that enable high performance and developer agility can lead to inefficiencies or bottlenecks if applied incorrectly. Common schema design mistakes can undermine performance, increase complexity, or negate the benefits of MongoDB's model. Understanding these pitfalls will help you make more informed design choices and avoid costly rewrites down the line.

Overnormalizing

This often happens when developers with a relational database background apply the same normalization principles to MongoDB. Here are some signs that you might be overnormalizing:

- Your code makes frequent $lookup operations (MongoDB's version of JOIN)

- You have multiple collections representing entities that are usually accessed together

- Read queries require piecing together data from multiple collections

- You need multi-document transactions to update related fields stored in separate documents that could be stored together and updated atomically without transactions

If you have the same number of collections in MongoDB as you would in a relational database, there's a good chance that you've overnormalized your schema.

Cost of overnormalization

I was reviewing an application where developers had created a separate collection for user preferences, another for user profiles, another for user settings... You get the idea. Every user page load required seven different queries! We consolidated the frequently accessed fields into a single user document, and page load times dropped from 600 ms to under 100 ms.

Overembedding

This is the opposite problem: when developers get excited about MongoDB's document model and try to put too much into a single document. Here are some signs you might be overembedding:

- Document size keeps growing without bounds
- You have very large documents
- You're storing data you rarely access within documents you frequently access
- You have arrays that grow indefinitely (such as comments on popular posts)
- Writing queries to return just specific parts of the document becomes complicated
- Updates to deeply embedded fields require complex update operators
- Creating effective indexes for deeply nested fields becomes challenging

If your documents are approaching the 16 MB document size limit, that's a strong indication that you must reconsider your schema design.

Other common anti-patterns

In addition to overnormalizing and overembedding, there are several schema design patterns that often cause problems, or what we call **anti-patterns**. Recognizing and avoiding these pitfalls can help you build more efficient, maintainable, and scalable applications:

- **Requiring transactions for everything**: Designing schemas that always need multi-document transactions negates the benefits of the document model. With proper embedding, most operations can be atomic without transactions.
- **Poor indexing strategy**: Not knowing how to index properly for your query patterns leads to full collection scans and poor performance.
- **Complex updates to embedded data**: If you can't easily update deeply nested fields, your schema may be too complex or over-embedded.

- **Inefficient querying**: If you can't easily query for just the relevant parts of your documents, reconsider your schema design.

- **Treating MongoDB like a relational database**: Spreading related data across collections and joining it back with $lookup for every query negates the benefits of the document model. Excessive use of $lookup slows down queries and can be avoided with strategic embedding or denormalization.

- **Unbounded array growth**: Embedding arrays that could grow indefinitely (such as comments on a viral post) can lead to document size issues and poor performance.

- **Ignoring write patterns**: Optimizing only for reads when your application is write-heavy can lead to contention and performance bottlenecks.

- **Over-indexing**: Creating indexes on every field *just in case* adds overhead to writes and doesn't necessarily improve query performance.

- **Storing large binary data in documents**: While MongoDB can store binary data, very large files (>16 MB) should either use GridFS or be stored externally, with references in your documents.

Now that you're familiar with common pitfalls in schema design, let's focus on patterns that optimize the efficiency of reads, writes, querying, storage, and more.

Schema design patterns by benefit

Now that we've covered the fundamentals, let's explore a set of practical schema design patterns, each organized by the specific benefits they offer, such as improving read performance, write efficiency, or query flexibility. These patterns aren't just theoretical; they're grounded in real-world use cases and common challenges.

Throughout this section, we'll use examples from a social media application called **Socialite** to illustrate schema design patterns. Socialite consists of three main data stores:

- **Content store**: Holds posts, media, and comments
- **User graph**: Manages users and relationships between users (followers, following)
- **Timeline cache**: Optimized for fast display of relevant content when a user logs in

This separation allows Socialite to optimize each store for its specific access patterns. As we explore different schema design patterns, we'll refer back to these components to demonstrate some practical applications. But next, let's discuss some MongoDB-specific schema strengths.

Patterns for read performance optimization

In this section, we'll look at schema design patterns that are beneficial for optimizing read performance. These include the embedding pattern, which allows frequently accessed related data to be stored together; the extended reference pattern, which balances embedding and referencing for flexibility and performance; and the subset pattern, which helps retrieve only the most relevant parts of a document without loading unnecessary data.

Embedding pattern

In MongoDB, the embedding pattern involves including related data within the same document instead of normalizing it and referencing it from another collection. In the following example, this pattern is used in a sample document from the `users` collection to store hierarchical and related information:

```
{
  _id: ObjectId("5f4e5b6d3c1e2a1b3c4d5e6f"),
  username: "jane_smith",
  name: "Jane Smith",
  email: "jane.smith@example.com",
  profile: {
    bio: "Travel enthusiast and photographer",
    location: "San Francisco, CA",
    birthdate: ISODate("1988-04-12T00:00:00Z"),
    avatar: "https://socialite.com/images/avatars/jane_smith.jpg"
  },
  preferences: {
    theme: "dark",
    emailNotifications: true,
    privacySettings: {
      profileVisibility: "friends",
      activityStatus: "everyone"
    }
  }
}
```

Let's go over this document to understand how the embedding pattern has been applied here:

- **Profile data as sub-document**: The profile field is embedded as a sub-document, containing details such as bio, location, birthdate, and avatar. Instead of storing this information in a separate collection and referencing it, all user profile-related data resides together as one cohesive unit. This keeps the data localized for quick access and retrieval.

- **Preferences data as sub-document**: Similarly, the preferences field includes the user-specific settings, such as theme, emailNotifications, and nested privacySettings. By embedding these preferences directly into the main document, it avoids the complexity of separate collections and joins, making it easier to query and update user settings in one operation.

- **Nested privacy settings**: privacySettings, which is a sub-document within preferences, demonstrates a deeper embedding as it stores profileVisibility and activityStatus. This shows MongoDB's flexibility to create multi-level embeddings while retaining a logical structure.

By using the embedding pattern for the profile and preferences sub-documents, the design achieves data denormalization, reduces the need for costly joins, and ensures data locality for optimized performance in reads and writes. This pattern works well in scenarios where related data is frequently accessed together, eliminating the need for multiple queries.

Extended reference pattern

The extended reference pattern is used in MongoDB when we need to reference another document in a related collection while also including some of its key fields for convenience and performance when querying. This approach helps avoid unnecessary lookups, especially when frequently accessed fields are readily available.

The following example is a document from the posts collection that contains a reference to the author and author-related data:

```
{
  _id: ObjectId("5f4e5b6d3c1e2a1b3c4d6f4h"),
  content: "Just visited the Golden Gate Bridge! #travels #sanfrancisco",
  postDate: ISODate("2023-04-07T09:15:30Z"),
  media: ["https://socialite.com/images/posts/golden_gate.jpg"],
  likes: 42,
  comments: 7,
  author: {
```

```
    _id: ObjectId("5f4e5b6d3c1e2a1b3c4d5e6f"),   // Reference to complete
user
    username: "jane_smith",                       // Duplicated for display
    name: "Jane Smith",                           // Duplicated for display
    avatar: "https://socialite.com/images/avatars/jane_smith.jpg" //
Duplicated for display
  }
}
```

In this example, the posts document utilizes the extended reference pattern by including an author sub-document:

- **Embedded reference:** The author sub-document contains an _id field, which is a reference to the complete Author/User document stored elsewhere in a users collection. This allows linking the post back to its author.

- **Duplicated key fields for display:** Instead of just storing the _id value of the user, additional author-related details such as username, name, and avatar are included directly within the posts document. These fields are copied from the referenced users document to enhance performance and allow displaying author details without needing to perform additional queries or a lookup operation.

- **Optimized read operations:** By embedding username, name, and avatar, the posts document ensures that common queries, such as showing posts content along with the author's basic information, can be handled seamlessly without additional database calls. This reduces latency and improves efficiency for applications that frequently display posts and their authors.

Using the extended reference pattern here strikes a balance between normalization and denormalization. While _id provides a definitive link to the original Author/User document for updates or deeper data retrieval, the duplicated fields, such as username and avatar, ensure fast rendering of posts with essential author information. This pattern is particularly useful in read-heavy applications such as social media platforms.

Subset pattern

The subset pattern is used in MongoDB to store frequently accessed data separately from infrequently accessed data, optimizing reads for common queries while keeping more detailed or less frequently needed information available in a related document.

The following is an example of data from a single media post that is stored in two separate documents:

```
// Document 1: Frequently accessed media post data
{
  _id: ObjectId("5f4e5b6d3c1e2a1b3c4d6f5i"),
  postType: "video",
  title: "My Trip to Yosemite",
  authorId: ObjectId("5f4e5b6d3c1e2a1b3c4d5e6f"),
  thumbnailUrl: "https://socialite.com/thumbnails/yosemite-trip.jpg",
  duration: "3:42",
  viewCount: 1287,
  likeCount: 328,
  commentCount: 57
}


// Document 2: Infrequently accessed media post data
{
  _id: ObjectId("5f4e5b6d3c1e2a1b3c4d6f6j"),
  postId: ObjectId("5f4e5b6d3c1e2a1b3c4d6f5i"),
  highResVideo: "https://socialite.com/videos/yosemite-trip-hd.mp4",
  rawMetadata: {
    codec: "H.264",
    resolution: "1920x1080",
    fps: 60,
    bitrate: "12Mbps"
  },
  processingHistory: [
    { timestamp: ISODate("2023-04-05T14:20:00Z"), action: "uploaded" },
    { timestamp: ISODate("2023-04-05T14:25:12Z"), action: "processed" },
    { timestamp: ISODate("2023-04-05T14:30:45Z"), action: "published" }
  ]
}
```

Let's go over this example to understand how the subset pattern has been applied here. The subset pattern is designed to split a dataset into two separate documents (one storing frequently accessed data and another holding infrequently accessed data) to optimize performance for common queries while still retaining access to detailed information when necessary.

The first document (Document 1) contains the highly queried fields about the media post, including the following:

- postType: The type of media (e.g., "video")
- title: The name of the media post
- Engagement metrics, such as viewCount, likeCount, and commentCount
- authorId: A reference to the author's profile
- Lightweight media information, such as thumbnailUrl and duration

This document is designed for use cases such as rendering a feed of posts, showing trending content, or loading summaries of media posts. By keeping this document small and focused on frequently accessed fields, queries against it are fast and lightweight.

The second document (Document 2) stores detailed data that is rarely needed in everyday queries, such as the following:

- The full video URL, stored in highResVideo for streaming or downloading the original video file.
- rawMetadata, containing technical details about the media, such as its codec, resolution, FPS, and bitrate, which are relevant for backend processing but not user-facing queries.
- A processingHistory array that logs the workflow of the media file, including timestamps for actions such as uploading, processing, and publishing.
- A reference to the first document with postId, which establishes a relationship between the two. This enables applications to fetch the detailed document only when necessary, such as when preparing the video for streaming or accessing historical processing data.

This document is larger and more detailed. It is stored separately to ensure that common queries (e.g., listing posts in a feed) are not burdened with loading unnecessary technical or historical information.

Using the subset pattern allows you to split data into two separate documents: one with frequently accessed fields, and the second document, stored separately, holds large and infrequently accessed information. This approach balances efficiency for frequent queries with the ability to retrieve detailed data when needed, making it an ideal solution in scenarios where different parts of the dataset have significantly different access patterns.

Patterns for write performance optimization

In this section, we'll look at schema design patterns that are beneficial for optimizing write performance. These include the document versioning pattern, which allows you to manage changes to frequently updated documents efficiently by storing previous versions within the same document or a separate collection; the bucketing pattern, which groups multiple related records into a single document to reduce the number of writes and improve the efficiency of write-heavy workloads; and the key prefixing pattern, which engineers the value of the _id field to avoid the creation of secondary indexes.

Document versioning pattern

Instead of updating existing documents and storing what changed, create new versions and maintain a pointer to the current version. This is particularly useful when there's a requirement to always keep the full history of changes to an entity.

The following is an example of feature rollout configuration in the Socialite app that shows two documents containing two different versions:

```
// Current version (in main collection)
{
  _id: "feature_story_sharing",
  name: "Story Sharing Feature",
  isEnabled: true,
  userPercentage: 75,
  configuration: {
    maxDurationSeconds: 30,
    allowedFilters: ["sepia", "noir", "vintage"],
    maxFileSize: 15728640
  },
  version: 3,
  lastUpdated: ISODate("2023-04-12T16:30:00Z")
}
```

```
// History collection (previous versions)
{
  _id: ObjectId("5f4e5b6d3c1e2a1b3c4d7f2o"),
  featureId: "feature_story_sharing",
  name: "Story Sharing Feature",
  isEnabled: true,
  userPercentage: 50,   // Was 50%, now 75%
  configuration: {
    maxDurationSeconds: 30,
    allowedFilters: ["sepia", "noir"],   // "vintage" filter added later
    maxFileSize: 15728640
  },
  version: 2,
  updatedAt: ISODate("2023-04-10T09:15:00Z")
}
```

Let's go over this example to understand how the document versioning pattern has been applied here. The document versioning pattern is used to track changes to a document over time by storing the current version in a `main` collection and previous versions of the document in a separate `history` collection:

- **Current version document (the `main` collection)**: The first document represents the active configuration of the feature, storing the following:

    - The current state of the feature (`isEnabled: true`, `userPercentage: 75`)
    - The latest configuration settings (`allowedFilters` now includes `"vintage"`)
    - The current version number (`version: 3`) and the timestamp (`lastUpdated`), indicating when it was last modified

    This document is stored in the `main` collection, which focuses on the current version, serving applications that need to access or modify the latest feature configuration. This optimizes for fast reads and updates as it represents the most up-to-date data.

- **Previous versions document (the `history` collection)**: The second document provides a snapshot of an earlier version of the feature configuration, including the following:

    - Historical settings, such as `userPercentage: 50` and `allowedFilters`, before the `"vintage"` filter was added

- The version: 2 field clearly shows this is an earlier version of the feature
- The updatedAt timestamp documents when this version was replaced by a newer one

This document is stored in a separate history collection dedicated to maintaining versions of documents. Storing older versions separately ensures that the main collection remains lightweight while still enabling access to historical data for use cases such as audits, debugging, or comparative analysis.

The document versioning pattern avoids the need for a second write to record "what changed" by separating the current version of a feature configuration from its historical versions. This pattern is best suited for applications that require maintaining an audit trail, tracking changes over time, or supporting rollbacks, such as configuration management systems, content publishing platforms, or any system needing historical data without compromising performance for active workflows.

Bucketing pattern

For time-series or high-volume data, you can use the bucketing pattern to group related data points into "buckets" to reduce the number of documents, when using a special time-series collection is not possible for some reason.

The following is an example of a timeline cache in the Socialite app that tracks a user's daily activity:

```
// With bucketing (optimized for fast timeline displays)
{
  _id: ObjectId("5f4e5b6d3c1e2a1b3c4d5f2f"),
  userId: ObjectId("5f4e5b6d3c1e2a1b3c4d5e6f"),
  date: ISODate("2023-04-10T00:00:00Z"),
  activities: [

      {
    type: "post",
    postId: ObjectId("5f4e5b6d3c1e2a1b3c4d6f4h"),
    timestamp: ISODate("2023-04-10T10:00:00Z"),
    content: "Just posted a new photo!",
    mediaUrl: "https://socialite.com/images/photo123.jpg",
    likes: 42
  },
```

```
    {
      type: "follow",
      timestamp: ISODate("2023-04-10T10:15:12Z"),
      targetUser: {
        id: ObjectId("5f4e5b6d3c1e2a1b3c4d6f7j"),
        username: "travel_adventures"
      }
    },
    {
      type: "like",
      timestamp: ISODate("2023-04-10T10:25:30Z"),
      postId: ObjectId("5f4e5b6d3c1e2a1b3c4d6f8k"),
      postAuthor: "mountain_explorer",
      postSnippet: "Summit day at Mt. Rainier..."
    }

    // ... more activities within this day
  ],
  activityCount: 27
}
```

Let's go over this example to understand how the bucketing pattern has been applied here:

- **Grouping activities**: Instead of storing each user activity (such as posts, likes, and follows) as individual documents, all activities for the user on a specific date (`date: ISODate("2023-04-10T00:00:00Z")`) are grouped into a single document under the `activities` array. Each entry in the array represents an activity, making it easy to track related actions within that timeframe.

- **Metadata for aggregation**: The document includes an `activityCount` field, providing an aggregated summary of the number of activities stored within the bucket for quick reference.

In this example, the bucketing pattern is applied by grouping a user's daily activities into a single document, rather than creating individual documents for each activity. This pattern dramatically reduces write operations and makes displaying a user's timeline extremely fast, as one query can retrieve a full day's worth of activity. The bucketing pattern is well suited for use cases involving time-based or logically grouped data, such as activity logs, event tracking, IoT sensor readings, or time-series data, where natural clustering of records exists and querying grouped records is common.

Key prefixing pattern

The key prefixing pattern involves adding meaningful prefixes or identifiers to a field (usually the _id field) to group related data, enable efficient querying, and reduce the need for secondary indexes. The key prefixing pattern is best for workloads with many small, related documents that need to be efficiently retrieved together without using additional indexes.

The following example from the Socialite app includes documents that contain data about user notifications:

```
{
  _id: "user_5f4e5b6d3c1e2a1b3c4d5e6f",   // Main user document
  username: "jane_smith",
  email: "jane.smith@example.com"
  // ... other user fields
}


{
  _id: "user_5f4e5b6d3c1e2a1b3c4d5e6f_notif_001",   // Notification with
prefix
  type: "like",
  message: "Alex liked your post",
  timestamp: ISODate("2023-04-10T10:30:00Z"),
  read: false
}


{
  _id: "user_5f4e5b6d3c1e2a1b3c4d5e6f_notif_002",   // Another notification
  type: "comment",
  message: "Sarah commented on your post",
  timestamp: ISODate("2023-04-10T11:15:00Z"),
  read: false
}
```

Let's go over this example to understand how the key prefixing pattern has been applied. Here, the pattern is used to structure the _id field to associate notifications with a specific user by prefixing _id with the user identifier:

- **Main document prefix**: The primary user document has an _id value (user_5f4e5b6d3c1e2a1b3c4d5e6f) where the prefix user_ clearly identifies it as a user record. This structured _id value helps organize documents logically and simplifies queries targeting specific types of records.

- **Related notifications**: Notifications related to the user use the same prefix (user_5f4e5b6d3c1e2a1b3c4d5e6f) followed by an additional suffix (_notif_001, _notif_002). This ensures all notifications are directly associated with the user and can be queried efficiently using _id.

With the default index on the _id field, you can efficiently retrieve all notifications for a user using a range query. Additionally, if the prefix part after user_ is an object ID, notifications are naturally sorted by time as well.

Patterns for query and analytics optimization

In this section, we'll look at schema design patterns that are beneficial for query and analytics optimization. These include the computed pattern, which precomputes and stores derived or aggregated data to reduce the cost of on-the-fly calculations during query execution; the schema versioning pattern, which tracks changes in document structures over time to ensure compatibility across versions and facilitate analytics on evolving datasets; and the polymorphic pattern, which allows storing different types of related data in a unified collection by leveraging flexible schemas, enabling efficient querying and analytics without the need for multiple collections.

Computed pattern

With the computed pattern, you precalculate and store aggregation results to avoid expensive computation during read operations. This includes incrementing counters when operations happen, so that the totals always reflect current metrics.

The following is a sample document from the Socialite database that contains post analytics:

```
{
  _id: ObjectId("5f4e5b6d3c1e2a1b3c4d6f7k"),
  content: "Check out my new photography portfolio!",
  postDate: ISODate("2023-04-10T14:30:00Z"),
```

```
  // Pre-computed metrics
  engagementMetrics: {
    totalViews: 1432,
    uniqueViewers: 1053,
    likeCount: 287,
    commentCount: 43,
    shareCount: 18,
    avgTimeViewed: 12.5,   // in seconds
    conversionRate: 0.086  // % of viewers who took action
  },

  // Demographics of engagers (pre-computed)
  audienceBreakdown: {
    genderDistribution: {
      male: 0.48,
      female: 0.51,
      other: 0.01
    },
    ageGroups: {
      "18-24": 0.32,
      "25-34": 0.45,
      "35-44": 0.15,
      "45+": 0.08
    }
  }
}
```

Let's go over this example to understand how the computed pattern has been applied. Here, the pattern is used to store precomputed engagement metrics and audience demographic breakdowns alongside the main post content:

- **Engagement metrics**: The document includes a precomputed engagementMetrics field containing aggregated data such as totalViews, uniqueViewers, likeCount, commentCount, shareCount, avgTimeViewed, and conversionRate. Instead of calculating these metrics dynamically for every query, they are stored directly in the document for instant retrieval.

- **Audience demographics**: The audienceBreakdown field provides precomputed data about viewers' gender distribution and age group percentages. This eliminates the need to perform analytics calculations or run expensive aggregation pipelines at query time.

By precomputing this data and embedding it into the document, queries related to engagement statistics and audience demographics can be executed quickly, without requiring access to raw event logs or other related datasets.

This pattern eliminates the need for complex aggregation queries during read operations. Note that this increases the cost of what would normally be just a read or a write by adding an additional write; to avoid this cost, you can queue the additional write to be performed as an async write rather than making it required during the original operation.

Schema versioning pattern

When applying the schema versioning pattern, you include a version field to track schema changes over time, allowing for smooth transitions during schema evolution.

The following example includes two sample user documents from the Socialite database:

```
// New document with schema version 3
{
  _id: ObjectId("5f4e5b6d3c1e2a1b3c4d5e6f"),
  schemaVersion: 3,
  username: "jane_smith",
  name: {  // In schema v3, we split name into first/last
    first: "Jane",
    last: "Smith"
  },
  email: "jane.smith@example.com",
  // ... other fields
}

// Older document with schema version 2
{
  _id: ObjectId("5f4e5b6d3c1e2a1b3c4d5e7a"),
  schemaVersion: 2,
  username: "john_doe",
  fullName: "John Doe",  // In schema v2, we used a single name field
  email: "john.doe@example.com",
  // ... other fields
}
```

Let's go over this example to understand how the schema versioning pattern has been applied here:

- **Version identification:** The schemaVersion field explicitly indicates which version each document conforms to, enabling application-level logic to handle variations in the schema during queries, updates, or reads.

- **Schema evolution:** In the example, the two documents are associated with different schema versions. For version 3, the name is stored in two fields (first and last), while in version 2, the name is stored as a single fullName field.

This pattern allows your application to handle documents with different schema versions gracefully. It may not be necessary to use a schemaVersion field unless it's needed for schema validation or parts of the application cannot make due with just using the absence of a field as an indication of the schema version.

Polymorphic pattern

The polymorphic pattern stores similar but not identical entities in the same collection for flexible querying.

The following example includes documents from the Socialite database that contain activity feed data, including post, following, and group join activity:

```
// Post activity
{
  _id: ObjectId("5f4e5b6d3c1e2a1b3c4d5e6f"),
  activityType: "post",
  userId: ObjectId("5f4e5b6d3c1e2a1b3c4d5e7a"),
  timestamp: ISODate("2023-04-10T15:30:00Z"),
  content: "Just posted a new photo!",
  mediaUrl: "https://socialite.com/images/photo123.jpg"
}

// Follow activity
{
  _id: ObjectId("5f4e5b6d3c1e2a1b3c4d5e7b"),
  activityType: "follow",
  userId: ObjectId("5f4e5b6d3c1e2a1b3c4d5e7a"),
  timestamp: ISODate("2023-04-10T16:45:00Z"),
  targetUserId: ObjectId("5f4e5b6d3c1e2a1b3c4d5e8c"),
  targetUsername: "alex_wong"
}
```

```
// Group join activity
{
  _id: ObjectId("5f4e5b6d3c1e2a1b3c4d5e8d"),
  activityType: "group_join",
  userId: ObjectId("5f4e5b6d3c1e2a1b3c4d5e7a"),
  timestamp: ISODate("2023-04-10T17:15:00Z"),
  groupId: ObjectId("5f4e5b6d3c1e2a1b3c4d5e9e"),
  groupName: "Photography Enthusiasts"
}
```

Let's go over this example to understand how the polymorphic pattern has been applied here:

- **Shared collection**: All activities are stored in the same collection. Each document represents a distinct activity type but shares common fields such as _id, activityType, userId, timestamp, and additional fields specific to the activity.
- **Type-specific fields**: The activityType field specifies the type of activity (post, follow, or group_join). Based on this value, type-specific fields are included in each document. For example, a post activity includes content and mediaUrl.

Now, instead of maintaining separate collections for each type of activity, queries can target the single collection using activityType as a filter.

This pattern allows for efficient querying across different types of activities while maintaining type-specific fields.

Archive pattern for storage optimization

In this section, we'll look at the archive patterns which is beneficial for storage optimization. This pattern helps reduce active storage costs by moving infrequently accessed or historical data to a separate collection or database optimized for long-term storage.

To apply the archive pattern, you move old or infrequently accessed data to separate collections to improve the performance of the main collection.

The following example includes message documents from two collections: one for active messages that are recent and frequently accessed, and another for long-term storage of old message documents:

```
// Active messages collection
{
  _id: ObjectId("5f4e5b6d3c1e2a1b3c4d7f5q"),
  conversationId: ObjectId("5f4e5b6d3c1e2a1b3c4d7f6r"),
  sender: ObjectId("5f4e5b6d3c1e2a1b3c4d5e7a"),
  recipient: ObjectId("5f4e5b6d3c1e2a1b3c4d5e6f"),
  content: "Are we still meeting tomorrow?",
  timestamp: ISODate("2023-04-10T14:30:00Z"),
  read: true
}

// Archived messages collection (older than 90 days)
{
  _id: ObjectId("5f4e5b6d3c1e2a1b3c4d7f7s"),
  conversationId: ObjectId("5f4e5b6d3c1e2a1b3c4d7f6r"),
  sender: ObjectId("5f4e5b6d3c1e2a1b3c4d5e7a"),
  recipient: ObjectId("5f4e5b6d3c1e2a1b3c4d5e6f"),
  content: "Hey, how's it going?",
  timestamp: ISODate("2023-01-05T10:15:00Z"),
  read: true,
  archivedAt: ISODate("2023-04-05T00:00:00Z")
}
```

Let's go over this example to understand how the archive pattern has been applied here:

- **Active messages collection:** The first document is part of the active collection, which stores recent data that is frequently accessed or updated, such as messages exchanged between users. This document represents a message sent on 2023-04-10 and remains in the active collection because it is considered part of ongoing interactions.

- **Archived messages collection:** The second document is part of an archived messages collection, which stores older messages that are no longer part of active interactions. This document represents a message sent on 2023-01-05, which was archived on 2023-04-05 after exceeding a 90-day threshold. The archivedAt field captures the timestamp when this message was moved to the archive.

By separating data into active and archived collections, this pattern keeps your active collections lean while preserving historical data. You can archive data into another collection in the same cluster, another cluster, or the Atlas online archive.

Real-world application: The Socialite app

In real-world applications, achieving optimal performance often requires more than simply adopting a single schema design pattern; it involves combining multiple patterns. MongoDB's flexibility allows developers to do just that! This section explores how combining schema design patterns can enhance performance, illustrated through practical examples of scenarios from the Socialite app.

Scenario 1: User profile and activity feed

In the following scenario, the Socialite app needs to efficiently display a user's profile alongside their recent activity feed. The traditional approach would be to store user data, posts, comments, likes, and follows in separate collections, and then perform complex joins across these collections every time a profile page is viewed. This method can be slow and resource-intensive, especially as the volume of data grows. However, with MongoDB, we can optimize this process by using a combination of schema design patterns: the computed pattern and the subset pattern.

The following example demonstrates this approach. It shows a single document from the users collection:

```
// User document
{
  _id: ObjectId("5f3d7eb8c242d20df83d3a8c"),
  username: "jane_smith",
  name: "Jane Smith",
  bio: "Photographer and travel enthusiast",
  profileImage: "https://socialite.com/images/profiles/jane_smith.jpg",
  followerCount: 1245,  // Computed pattern
  followingCount: 362,  // Computed pattern

  // Subset pattern - most recent activities
  recentActivities: [
    {
      type: "post",
      timestamp: ISODate("2023-04-07T10:22:15Z"),
      content: "Just posted photos from my Japan trip!",
      imageUrl: "https://socialite.com/images/posts/japan123.jpg",
      likeCount: 48
    },
```

```
  {
    type: "like",
    timestamp: ISODate("2023-04-07T09:15:30Z"),
    targetPost: {
      id: ObjectId("5f3d7eb8c242d20df83d3a94"),
      author: "travel_adventures",
      snippet: "My day at Mount Fuji..."
    }
  }
  // 3-5 more recent activities
  ]
}
```

Let's go over this example to understand how the computed and subset patterns have been applied here:

- **Computed pattern**:
  - Fields such as followerCount and followingCount are calculated ahead of time and stored directly in the user document
  - It reduces the need for on-the-fly aggregation or queries to count followers/ following during profile views

- **Subset pattern**:
  - It embeds an array of recentActivities directly in the user document
  - It includes only the most recent posts, likes, or actions, optimized for quick access during profile page loads
  - More comprehensive activity history is deferred to a separate collection for less frequent queries

This design optimizes profile page loads by including recent activities directly in the user document. Complete activity history is stored in a separate collection that's only queried when a user views more activities.

Scenario 2: Chat system

In the following scenario, the Socialite app needs to implement a messaging system that handles both real-time chat and access to a user's message history efficiently. We might be tempted to store all messages in a single collection and query it repeatedly for both real-time updates and historical data, but this can result in performance bottlenecks as the volume of messages grows over time. However, with MongoDB, we can optimize this by combining the subset, bucketing, and archive patterns.

The following example demonstrates this approach and includes two documents, the first from an active messages collection and the second from an archived messages collection:

```
// Active messages collection - current conversation state (for fast
access)
{
  _id: ObjectId("5f4e5b6d3c1e2a1b3c4d7f6r"),
  participants: [
    ObjectId("5f3d7eb8c242d20df83d3a8c"),   // jane_smith
    ObjectId("5f4e5b6d3c1e2a1b3c4d5e7a")    // john_doe
  ],
  lastMessage: {
    sender: ObjectId("5f4e5b6d3c1e2a1b3c4d5e7a"),
    content: "See you tomorrow!",
    timestamp: ISODate("2023-04-12T18:45:22Z")
  },
  unreadCount: {
    "5f3d7eb8c242d20df83d3a8c": 0,
    "5f4e5b6d3c1e2a1b3c4d5e7a": 1
  },

  // Recent messages (subset pattern)
  recentMessages: [
    {
      sender: ObjectId("5f4e5b6d3c1e2a1b3c4d5e7a"),
      content: "See you tomorrow!",
      timestamp: ISODate("2023-04-12T18:45:22Z"),
      read: false
    },
    {
      sender: ObjectId("5f3d7eb8c242d20df83d3a8c"),
      content: "Yes, 3 PM works for me.",
      timestamp: ISODate("2023-04-12T18:44:15Z"),
      read: true
    }
```

```
      // 10-15 most recent messages
  ]
}


// Archived messages collection - for older messages, using bucketing
pattern
{
  _id: ObjectId("5f4e5b6d3c1e2a1b3c4d8f1t"),
  conversationId: ObjectId("5f4e5b6d3c1e2a1b3c4d7f6r"),
  date: ISODate("2023-04-11T00:00:00Z"),   // One bucket per day
  messages: [
    {
      sender: ObjectId("5f3d7eb8c242d20df83d3a8c"),
      content: "How about meeting tomorrow?",
      timestamp: ISODate("2023-04-11T15:30:12Z"),
      read: true
    }
    // More messages from this day
  ]
}
```

Let's go over this example to understand how the subset, archive, and bucketing patterns have been applied here:

- **Subset pattern:**
  - The recentMessages field in the first document from the active messages collection stores the most recent 10–15 messages directly within the document
  - It enables quick access to the latest messages without the need for a separate query to a larger data store

- **Archive pattern:**
  - The second document uses the archive pattern to store older messages. The conversationId field links the bucket to a specific conversation, ensuring logical grouping by conversationId. The date field represents the day covered by the bucket, allowing for chronological organization of messages.

- This pattern ensures efficient storage and retrieval of older, less frequently accessed messages and reduces overhead when querying or analyzing historical conversations, as queries can target specific buckets based on `date` and `conversationId`.

- **Bucketing pattern:**

  - Older messages are grouped into daily buckets in the `messages` array in a separate collection with one document per conversation per day

  - It organizes historical messages efficiently to reduce the overhead of querying massive datasets and improves scalability for long-running conversations.

This approach allows fast access to recent messages while maintaining scalability by organizing and querying archives of historical messages efficiently.

Summary

By aligning your schema with the actual patterns of data usage (how you read, write, or update documents), you can minimize I/O and resource contention. MongoDB's flexible structure can help, but only if used thoughtfully, with the right combination of embedding, referencing, and indexing.

There are many important takeaways here. It's critical to understand your workload and to consider both read and write patterns before designing your schema. Make sure you think in documents, not tables. Embrace the document model's flexibility rather than forcing relational patterns. Remember to design for common operations and optimize operations with the strictest performance requirements. Test with realistic data volumes: what works with 100 documents might fail with 10 million. Finally, always be intentional: deliberate schema design will always outperform arbitrary storage of data.

Schema design in MongoDB is as much an art as it is a science. By understanding your application's workload and balancing read and write efficiency, you can create schemas that are both performant and maintainable.

MongoDB bridges the gap between fast, horizontally scalable key-value stores and feature-rich relational databases. To fully leverage its power, design your schema to take advantage of the document model's strengths: embedding related data, avoiding unnecessary lookups, and optimizing for your specific access patterns. In the next chapter, we'll build upon these schema design principles to explore indexing strategies that further enhance your application's performance.

Get This Book's PDF Version and Exclusive Extras

UNLOCK NOW

Scan the QR code (or go to packtpub.com/unlock). Search for this book by name, confirm the edition, and then follow the steps on the page.

Note: Keep your invoice handy. Purchases made directly from Packt don't require an invoice.

3

Indexes

What's the most common database operation? It's a query, or a read of a single document or several documents. We insert documents once, we update them sometimes, and we read them a lot. So, it's important to ensure that those reads are as fast as they can possibly be.

In this chapter, you'll learn how to use indexes to improve the performance of your queries. You'll start by understanding what indexes are and how MongoDB uses them. Then, you'll explore query plans and how to interpret them to identify slow or inefficient operations. You'll also practice creating and using indexes to speed up queries and see how MongoDB chooses which index to use. By the end of this chapter, you'll be able to make informed decisions about when and how to use indexes to optimize performance.

This chapter will cover the following topics:

- Indexes and the types of indexes MongoDB supports
- Cardinality, selectivity, and how they affect indexes
- Best practices for optimizing compound indexes
- Why partial indexes and covered index queries are important for performance

Introduction to indexes

Let's begin by looking at a basic example. Say you have a collection of orders, and you want to find the order with the ID value of 295:

```
db.orders.find({ orderId: 295 })
```

Without an index, MongoDB has to examine every document in the collection to check whether it has an `orderId` field, and then see whether its value is 295. For a collection with millions of documents, this can be painfully slow. It results in a time complexity of $O(n)$, meaning the time it takes grows linearly with the number of documents.

This is analogous to packing everything into boxes for a move. If you don't take the time to organize, group, and label the boxes, then finding a specific item later means looking through everything. This isn't very efficient, but it does save you time when packing. Database indexes work the same way. You have to decide whether it's more important to spend time organizing and labeling items when packing (writing) or whether you can afford to take extra time when searching for an item (reading). In most cases, the smart move is to spend a bit of time up front so that finding things is easier later.

What is an index?

In the database world, an index is a data structure that allows you to find records quickly without scanning the full collection. MongoDB uses a type of data structure called a **B-tree** for most of its indexes.

A B-tree is a self-balancing tree data structure that maintains data in sorted order and allows various operations in logarithmic time, which is $O(log\ n)$. This means that as your data grows, the time to find a document increases much more slowly compared to a collection scan, which scales linearly with the size of your data, or $O(n)$ time.

Let's take a peek under the hood. If we create an index on our orderId field, the simplified B-tree might look something like *Figure 3.1*:

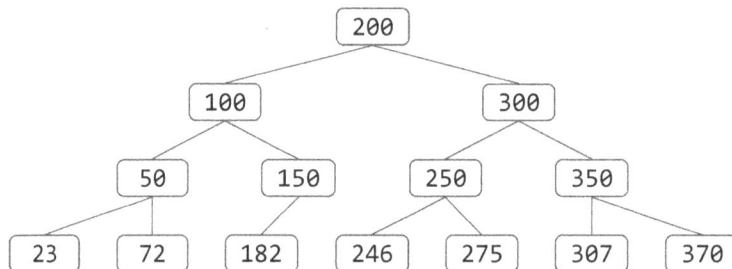

Figure 3.1: Simplified view of B-tree on the orderId field

When searching for the order ID 295, MongoDB would follow these steps:

1. Start at the root node, [200].

2. Compare 295 to 200. Since 295 > 200, go right.

3. Arrive at node [300].

4. Compare 295 to 300. Since 295 < 300, go left.

5. Arrive at node [250].

6. Compare 295 to 250. Since 295 > 250, go right.

7. Continue right until 295 is found or determine that it doesn't exist.

This process takes $O(log\ n)$ time, which is dramatically faster than the $O(n)$ time required for a collection scan.

The leaf nodes store the indexed values as well as pointers (`recordID`) to the documents containing those values. So, when we reach the leaf node containing a value of 295, we find the associated `recordID`, which is a pointer or reference to the actual document location. If multiple documents share the same value, the leaf node contains multiple record IDs. A B-tree usually has more than two branches from each node, and like a typical B+-tree, MongoDB B-trees only have data in leaf nodes; the inner nodes are for navigation only.

Interestingly, the specific data structure used isn't as important as the fact that the indexed values are stored in a **sorted** data structure that can be efficiently searched and traversed in order. If you think of an index as a sorted list or a binary search tree, you're not far off. The important thing is that you can easily access data and find it in sorted order, and because it's sorted, it's relatively quick ($O(log\ n)$ time) to jump to a particular value or range of values.

Resource efficiency and trade-offs

Indexes aren't just about speeding up queries; they're also key to using your system's resources efficiently. When you do a full collection scan, you're forcing MongoDB to load the entire collection into memory (specifically, the WiredTiger cache). Not only does this take longer, but it also consumes a limited resource (cache memory) and can cause a lot of disk I/O due to constant churn.

Alternatively, when you use an index, MongoDB only needs to load the relevant parts of the index (typically smaller than a collection) and then fetch the specific document(s) that match the query criteria. This saves precious memory and IOPS that can be used for other operations, making your entire database more efficient.

Beyond faster lookups, indexes also support requirements to return results in a specific order. If the documents are read in order from the index, you can avoid expensive in-memory sort operations. In a nutshell, indexes speed up queries, minimize disk I/O, lower RAM requirements, and reduce overall CPU load.

But indexes aren't free; there's a trade-off. Every index you add requires that it be atomically updated whenever an indexed value is changed, a new document is written, or an existing document is deleted. This slows down write operations. Maintaining indexes in memory uses more RAM, and writing to both indexes and documents increases disk usage.

The performance impact on write latency for each index can range from 5–70%, depending on the number of fields, the overall size and type of index, and on your workload based on tests performed by the MongoDB performance team. There isn't a formula, and the only reliable way to know how much your write latency is impacted is to benchmark your actual data and workload. That's why you should be strategic about which indexes you create, avoid maintaining redundant indexes, and don't just index everything.

Resource usage

We mentioned indexes requiring disk space and RAM, but how much RAM do they use? You can see the size of your index using $collStats, but the size of the index doesn't necessarily mean that all of it must fit in RAM. Not all indexes are created equal when it comes to resource usage. There is a myth that all your indexes must fit in RAM to achieve the best performance, but that would only be true if you were always accessing the full index. This may not be necessary in a well-designed application.

Imagine your application processes orders with sequentially increasing IDs. New orders always have higher IDs than existing ones. In your B-tree index, all new writes occur on the *right side* of the tree, as shown in *Figure 3.2*.

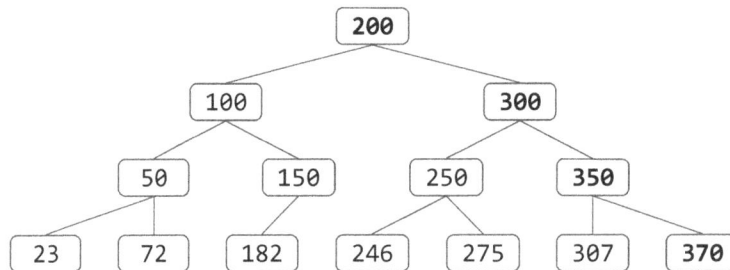

Figure 3.2: B-tree with all recent activity on the right side

New orders are always inserted to the right side of the index (highest values), and the majority of updates happen to recent orders, not to mention the fact that older orders are seldom read as well. This creates what we call a **right-balanced** index. The part of the index with older orders is seldom accessed and, therefore, won't be loaded into RAM and can stay "cold" on disk. Only the accessed part of the index (the active part containing recent data) needs to be in memory.

Fields that can create a right-balanced index include anything that's naturally increasing, for instance:

- Auto-incrementing IDs such as order IDs

- Timestamps and/or dates
- MongoDB's automatically generated object IDs (because they include a timestamp component as the first four bytes)

In contrast, when you index a random value, access patterns will span the entire B-tree, eventually requiring the entire index to be loaded into memory, making it much less efficient. Types of random values that can force the entire index to stay in RAM include the following:

- UUID
- Most string values (names, usernames, etc.)
- Any hashed value

So, while index size matters, how you access that index matters even more. Designing your data access patterns thoughtfully can significantly reduce memory usage and boost performance.

Common misconceptions about indexes in MongoDB

There are a few common myths about MongoDB (and NoSQL in general). One is that MongoDB is so fast that it doesn't need indexes. This might only hold true if your dataset is so tiny that everything fits into RAM and every query is fast, even though it's doing a full collection scan. This would never be the case for a real production system. Another myth is that every field is automatically indexed. In MongoDB, only the primary key (the _id field) is automatically indexed. To achieve acceptable performance in production environments, you need to analyze your query patterns and create the right secondary indexes accordingly.

Types of indexes in MongoDB

MongoDB offers multiple types of indexes to optimize different query patterns. The majority of them use B-trees, but not all of them. This chapter will focus on the ones that do use B-trees as their underlying structure.

> **Field versus attribute in index types**
>
> The *type* of index can refer to either what fields you are indexing or what attributes you assign to the index. The former specifies the fields that will be stored in the B-tree; the latter is more about attributes of the index as a whole.

Let's take a look at some of the more common index types.

Single-field indexes

A single-field index in MongoDB is an index created on a single field of a collection. This is how you create a basic index on a single field:

```
db.collection.createIndex({ fieldName: 1 })
```

In the *What is an index?* section, we already saw an example using {orderId:1}, which speeds up queries for specific order IDs, as well as sorts or range queries by order ID.

A single-field index that exists in every regular collection is the _id index, which enforces uniqueness, though it doesn't explicitly display the unique attribute when you run a command to list the indexes:

```
// Command to show all indexes on collection
db.collection.getIndexes()
// output showing _id index only
[ { "v" : 2, "key" : { "_id" : 1 }, "name" : "_id_" } ]
```

This is how you can see the indexes that exist for a particular collection. Most indexes you create in real life will not be single-field indexes; however, each regular collection will have at least one index by default: a unique index on the _id field, which is the primary key.

Compound indexes

Compound indexes are created on multiple fields. Here is an example that creates an index on three fields:

```
db.collection.createIndex({ status: 1, country: 1, zipString: 1 })
```

Compound indexes store multiple field values from each document, so each entry has multiple values concatenated together. The B-tree stores the data sorted by the combined values. Let's look at an example indexing by status, country, and zip:

Values for status, country, and zip in your collection	The order in which these values are stored in the index
"processing","US","10007"	"done","FR",""
"done","US","95401"	"done","US","14850"
"done","FR",""	"done","US","90210"
"done","US","90210"	"done","US","95401"
"done","US","14850"	"processing","US","10007"

Table 3.1: How index ordering affects document retrieval

First, the records are sorted by status, then by country, and finally, by zip. You can probably see that the order of fields when you create a compound index is very important. It allows you to use the compound index for querying on just the first field or any prefix fields of it. More on that shortly.

Multikey indexes

A multikey index isn't technically a separate type of index that you create explicitly; you still create an index on one or more fields. But if any one of those fields contains an array, MongoDB creates an index entry for *each element* in the array and tags the index as being a multikey index. Here's a simple example:

```
// If documents have: { tags: ["electronics", "sale", "new"] }
db.collection.createIndex({ tags: 1 })
// Creates index entries for "electronics", "sale", and "new"
// all of which point to the same recordID
```

Single-field, compound, and other indexes can all be tagged as multikey if any indexed field contains an array. We'll revisit the implications of this throughout the rest of this chapter and again in *Chapter 12, Advanced Query and Indexing Concepts*.

Sparse indexes

If you specify that the index should be sparse, then only documents that have the fields being indexed will be inserted into the B-tree. This is in contrast to regular (non-sparse) indexes, which will index every document in the collection, even ones that don't have the fields being indexed.

Here's how you create a sparse index in MongoDB:

```
// sparse is an attribute of index being created
db.collection.createIndex({a:1}, {sparse:true})
```

The preceding creates an index on the a field, which only contains documents where the a field is present.

Because of **MongoDB Query Language** (**MQL**) null semantics, non-sparse indexed documents in which a field is missing are indexed the same as documents in which the field exists with a value of null. In a sparse index, a null entry means the field is present and set to null. We'll explore this further in *Chapter 12, Advanced Query and Indexing Concepts*.

Wildcard indexes

Wildcard indexes allow you to specify an index without knowing the names of the fields in advance. This is not uncommon with a dynamic schema:

```
// Index fields inside attr subdocument
db.collection.createIndex({ "attr.$**": 1 })
// Sample document
// { ...,
//   attr: {
//       genre: "Mystery",
//       author: "John Smith",
//       pages: NumberInt(298),
//       ...
//   }
// }
// query using the index
db.collection.find({"attr.pages":{$gt:500}})
```

This allows you to query using an index on any of the attributes stored under attr without having to create a separate index for each one of them. Wildcard indexes are sparse by default.

Partial indexes

Sometimes, you may want to only index and query a subset of your documents. Partial indexes will only index documents that match a specified filter. This command creates an index on two fields, but only indexes documents where status is equal to "processing":

```
db.orders.createIndex(
   { country: 1, dateOrdered: 1 },
   { partialFilterExpression: { status: "processing" } }
)
```

A query with {status:"processing"} among other query predicates will be able to use this partial index.

Using partial indexes can significantly reduce index size and save on resources. This is particularly useful when your queries target only a small portion of the collection. For instance, if you frequently query only active documents, which make up a small subset of your data, an index with a partial filter of {active:true} will be both compact and efficient. When a document is updated to {active:false}, it is automatically removed from the index.

This isn't an exhaustive list of all index types and attributes; you can read more about them in the MongoDB Server documentation at `https://www.mongodb.com/docs/manual/indexes/`.

Designing efficient indexes

Indexes are a cornerstone of MongoDB's performance optimization strategy, enabling fast, efficient querying and sorting over large datasets. However, designing effective indexes requires more than understanding their basic function; it demands careful consideration of query patterns, field cardinality, and operational needs. Common misconceptions about low-cardinality fields and inequality queries often mislead developers, but the right indexing strategies can drastically improve performance. Compound indexes, index compression, covered queries, and partial indexes provide powerful tools for optimizing database operations, and the **Equality, Sort, Range (ESR)** guideline simplifies complex decisions around field ordering.

In this section, we'll explore the foundational principles of index design, covering critical topics such as cardinality versus selectivity, compound index design, prefix compression, partial indexes, and how indexes support aggregation pipelines, giving you the tools to design indexes that maximize performance for your application.

Cardinality and selectivity

There is a common misunderstanding that low-cardinality fields (fields with few unique values) should not be included in indexes. This is simply not true.

Cardinality in databases refers to how many distinct values a particular field can have. A `boolean` field has a cardinality of two: `true` or `false`. A unique ID field has cardinality equal to the number of documents in the collection. Last name has a higher cardinality than first name. Cardinality is not as important to query effectiveness as selectivity, the number of documents in the collection that match a specific value in your query.

As an example, imagine an `orders` collection with a `status` field, which can either be `"processing"` or `"done"`. At any given time, less than 0.01% of orders have `status: "processing"` because most orders are `"done"`. An index on `status` would be excellent for querying for processing orders because it's highly selective, even though the field has low cardinality. On the other hand, using that index to find all orders that have been carried out is of limited help because it matches 99.99% of all documents in the collection.

This brings us to a related misunderstanding that inequality queries (such as $ne) cannot use indexes effectively. That's false! If you query for {status:{$ne:"done"}} against the same orders collection, it will be just as *selective* as querying for {status:"processing"}. The MongoDB query engine handles it slightly differently (it's processed as a range query), but being highly selective, it is still very efficient, even though it will use a different query plan:

```
// For {status:{$ne:"done"}}, the index scan uses:
"indexBounds": {
  "status": [
    "[MinKey, \"done\")",
    "(\"done\", MaxKey]"
  ]
}
// For { status: "processing" }, the index scan uses:
"indexBounds": {
  "status": [
    "[\"processing\",\"processing\"]"
  ]
}
```

These are examples of output from the explain method, which we will talk about more later, in *Chapter 12, Advanced Query and Indexing Concepts*, where we start trying to debug our queries and validate how well our indexes help with performance. Knowing whether an operation is an equality or range query matters a lot to our next topic of ordering fields in compound indexes.

Constructing compound indexes

Optimal compound indexes require understanding how different queries use them. A compound index indexes multiple fields in a defined order, and that order significantly affects how MongoDB uses the index.

A compound index in MongoDB includes multiple fields, and sorts documents first by the value of the first indexed field, then by the second, and so on. Internally, it's organized like a sorted tree structure, enabling efficient traversal when the query matches the beginning of the index key pattern. For example, a compound index on {a:1,b:1,c:1} allows MongoDB to efficiently locate documents that match queries filtering on the following:

```
{ a: <value> }
{ a: <value>, b: <value> }
{ a: <value>, b: <value>, c: <value> }
```

This is known as **prefix matching**. The query must match the prefix of the index fields in order to be eligible to use the index. A query that skips over the first field, such as {b:<value>} or {c:<value>}, cannot use this index. In those cases, MongoDB performs a full collection scan.

Let's take a look at a more practical example. Suppose you create a compound index such as this: {category:1,price:1,stock:1}.

This index works well for queries such as {category:"books"} or {category:"books",price: {$lt:20}}. Using a sorted list can help us to visualize how the index can be utilized:

```
"books",10,399
"books",13,205
"books",15,11
"books",22,0
"pens",2,175
"pens",5,42
"pens",12,109
"pens",15,98
```

When the list is sorted by category and then price, it's easy to quickly find all books or all pens, and once we find a single category, it's easy to find the "price less than $20" range and return those records in order by price.

However, you can see that if I just asked for all items less than $20 without specifying a category, we would have to go through every category value, which would make the index far less useful. This is because the query skips over the category field. Since the index is sorted first by category, MongoDB has no efficient way to isolate the relevant range of documents by price alone. And the index is completely unusable to answer a query such as "what items have stock 0". We may as well do a collection scan for that query.

Understanding how prefix matching works is important for designing compound indexes that align with your application's most common query patterns.

Equality queries

A common query pattern involves using equality on multiple fields. For example, suppose you're storing addresses, mostly in the United States, where the following applies:

- country is usually "US" (low cardinality)
- state has about 50 possibilities (medium cardinality)
- zipString has over 42,000 unique values (high cardinality)

Let's say we always query with equality on all three fields:

```
db.collection.find({country: "US", state: "NY", zipString: "10001"})
```

Which compound index would perform better?

- Option 1: `{ country: 1, state: 1, zipString: 1 }`
- Option 2: `{ zipString: 1, state: 1, country: 1 }`

Conventional wisdom, or your gut, might say *Option 2* because the most selective field is ordered first. But it turns out that it wouldn't make the queries run any faster. For queries with equality conditions on all fields, both indexes will perform equally well. This is an important concept to understand: when selecting on all fields, the B-tree for *Option 1* and *Option 2* will be the same size because they have to index the same number of documents; therefore, they will be the same depth, and finding a specific value will be the exact same *O(log n)* for both.

That said, you should still prefer *Option 1* if all else is equal. When low-cardinality fields (such as country, which might only be "US" or "CA") appear first, MongoDB can compress long runs of repeated values more effectively. Because of **prefix compression**, placing low-cardinality fields first will significantly reduce the index size on both disk and in RAM:

```
"country_1_state_1_zipString_1": 620 KB
"zipString_1_state_1_country_1": 804 KB
```

That's almost a 30% difference in size! Smaller indexes mean less disk usage, faster loads, and more efficient memory usage.

There may still be valid reasons to order fields a certain way. For example, the *Option 2* index can serve queries on just zipString or on both zipString and state. So, there might be good use cases for choosing *Option 2* over *Option 1*, but expecting "faster queries" with equality on all three fields is **not** one of them.

Things get more interesting (and more complex) when we start adding range queries and sort operations into the mix.

Sorts and range queries

Indexes allow us to efficiently answer range queries because we can quickly find the value at one end of the range and then proceed through the index, getting documents in order till we reach the first value above our upper bound, as follows:

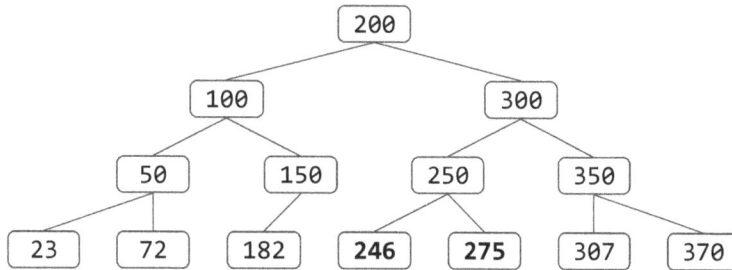

Figure 3.3: Using indexes for efficient range queries and sorting

For a query on {field:{$gt: 205, $lt:290}}, we find our lower range, 205, and then traverse along the leaf nodes until we encounter a value greater than our upper range, 290. Note that we are getting these values in order from the index, so if the query had sort:{field:1}, we would get the values in sorted order "for free." If the sort expression was on {field:-1}, we would just start by looking for 290, the upper value of the range first, and then scan the index right to left (i.e., backward rather than forward) till we got past 205, the lower boundary, which would give us the values in descending order.

What happens if we have an equality query on one field and a range query on another field? Let's look at the index on {category:1,price:1} and the {category:"books",price:{$lt:20}} query. We already saw that we can easily find documents with equality on category and range (or sort) on price:

```
"books",10
"books",13
"books",15
"books",22
"pens",2
"pens",5
"pens",12
"pens",15
```

Since the equality field comes first, we can navigate directly to the part of the sorted tree matching that value, and the second field remains in order, so applying a range filter is just as straightforward. But what happens if the index is on {price:1,category:1}, which means the range filter is on the first field, and equality is on the second field?

The index would now look like this:

```
2,"pens"
5,"pens"
10,"books"
12,"pens"
13,"books"
15,"books"
15,"pens"
22,"books"
```

In this index, when we navigate to the index range where `price` is less than `20`, we'll find that `category` is all mixed. This means we'll have to scan more index entries with a price less than 20, throwing away ones that don't match the equality predicate, than we would with a different index structure. And what if we needed a sort on the second field after applying range on the first field? Again, because the values are not in order, we would need to do a lot more work in memory.

The same concept applies if we have equality and sorting. If the equality is on the first field in the compound index, then the second field values are still "in order" in the part of the index we have navigated to. But if sort is on the first field in the index, then while we can get those values in order while scanning the full index, we have to keep checking and throwing away the entries where the second field is not equal to our predicate.

What if we have all three: equality, range predicate, and a sort on another field? Let's return to our example with three fields in the `{category:1,price:1,stock:1}` index and these values:

```
"books",10,399
"books",13,205
"books",15,11
"books",22,0
"pens",2,175
"pens",5,42
"pens",12,109
"pens",15,98
```

We can see that if we query on the "books" category, the prices are in order, but the stock is not. If the index switched the order of price and stock to become {category:1,stock:1,price:1}, we would have this:

```
"books",0,22
"books",11,15
"books",205,13
"books",399,10
"pens",42,5
"pens",98,15
"pens",109,12
"pens",175,2
```

Now, we can quickly find specific category items that have zero stock, or sort specific categories by stock, but we no longer have our price values in order. So, if we had range and sort or two range queries, while we would be able to determine whether the document matches from the index, we would not be able to limit the number of index entries we examine to just the ones that match.

All this leads us to some general principles we can apply.

The ESR guideline

You may have heard of the ESR guideline for compound indexes:

- **E**: Equality fields first
- **S**: Sort fields next
- **R**: Range fields last

While this isn't a hard rule, it serves as a helpful guideline, and one part of it is absolute: **put equality fields first**. Applying equality to the leading field(s) of the compound index allows us to still take advantage of the rest of the field values being in sorted order. However, whether sort or range fields should come next depends on your specific needs:

- If avoiding in-memory sorts is critical, then put sort fields before range fields (ESR)
- If your range predicate in the query is very selective, place it before sort fields (ERS) to reduce the number of documents to sort and allow for efficient in-memory sorting

So, equality must come first because the structure of a sorted index with multiple fields allows us to apply an equality filter while still preserving the sorted order of the remaining fields.

Maximizing resources with partial indexes

Sometimes, we don't need to index every document, especially if a query only ever targets a small, well-defined subset of your collection. In some cases, your multiple equality query might always specify a particular field with only a single value. For example, in a collection of orders that are being processed, there will likely be far fewer orders with a "processing" status than those marked "done". On the other hand, those are the orders you are more likely to be querying frequently. In such a case, creating an index that supports queries on "processing" orders (and ignores "done" orders) can be much more efficient than a regular index on every document.

To support queries for orders being processed where we get zip, state, and country, we can create the following index:

```
{status:1, zipString:1,state:1,country:1}
```

This index will already benefit from prefix compression, but it would not benefit from being right-balanced, even though we are only querying documents with status processing, because when the status is updated to "done", we now have to update pages in the part of the index that's not usually read. We would save more space and resources by indexing only the documents with status: "processing", like this:

```
db.coll.createIndex(
    {zipString:1,state:1,country:1},
    {partialFilterExpression:{status:"processing"}})
```

Now, only a small subset of your entire collection is stored in the index, and when an order is updated to have status set to "done", it will automatically be *unindexed* or removed from the index, keeping its size small.

Covered queries: the performance holy grail

A **covered** query is one where all the fields needed to satisfy the query are in the index, so MongoDB doesn't need to look at the actual documents at all. These queries usually require the least resources. Here is an example of what it would take to have a covered query:

```
// We create this index:
db.orders.createIndex({ orderId: 1, status: 1 })

// This query is covered, the index already contains status field:
db.orders.find({ orderId: 295 }, { _id: 0, status: 1 })
```

```
// This query is not covered, we need to fetch documents to get the total
field
db.orders.find({ orderId: 295 }, { _id:0, total: 1 })
```

There are some limitations, though. Covered queries generally can't work with multikey indexes when the field you need to return could be an array. This is because MongoDB needs to look at the document to see whether the value to be returned is a scalar or an array. Some null queries cannot be covered because the index doesn't differentiate between fields that contain null and fields that don't exist.

No form of the $exists clause can be determined from a regular index at all because of the same null semantics, so if you hope to have an efficient indexed query, stay away from $exists clauses as a rule, unless you are using a sparse index. We'll look at this topic in more detail in *Chapter 12, Advanced Query and Indexing Concepts*.

Ascending versus descending index order

If you noticed, all the examples used {field:1} as opposed to {field:-1}. This is because we don't usually need to have our index stored in descending order. The query engine can scan the B-tree from left to right or right to left, depending on whether it needs the results in ascending or descending order. There is only one exception to this, and that's when you have a sort on multiple fields in opposite directions. Let's say we have the following query:

```
db.coll.find({category:"books"}).sort({genre:1, price:-1})
```

To create an index that will support this fully, we would have to make the index one of the following:

```
{category:1, genre:1, price:-1}  OR {category:1, genre:-1, price:1}
```

This is because the sort order specified in the query uses two sort fields in opposite directions (one ascending, and one descending); therefore, the index on those two fields should also be in opposite order to support sort. Since the index can be scanned in forward or backward order, we can reverse the order of either of the two sort fields.

Indexing and aggregation pipelines

Indexes are eligible for use by all MongoDB commands that need to find a subset of documents in a collection: find, update, delete, and even aggregate. But the last one often causes some confusion: when can it use indexes to filter data, and when can it not?

Think about what indexes do: they help locate documents by their record IDs. Once an aggregation pipeline transforms documents into new shapes, those indexes no longer apply because we're dealing with new, in-memory documents that don't correspond to our indexed collection structure. But when aggregation needs to get documents from a collection that actually exists, then indexes are just as critical as for any `find` operation.

Indexes are used in the `$match` and `$sort` stages of aggregation when they apply to documents in the collection being aggregated. Indexes are also used by any stage that goes to another collection, such as `$unionWith` (which executes a new pipeline) or `$lookup` (which executes a query on another collection based on a value in the current pipeline). We'll take a closer look at how to determine which indexes are being used in *Chapter 4, Aggregations*, and *Chapter 12, Advanced Query and Indexing Concepts*.

Summary

Indexes are powerful tools that can significantly speed up your MongoDB queries when used correctly. While they improve read performance, they come with a slight trade-off: slower writes. In most cases, this trade-off is well worth it for the performance gains. It's important to understand how different types of indexes behave. For example, right-balanced indexes, such as those based on `ObjectID` or other sequential values, are more efficient in their use of memory.

When choosing which fields to index, focus on selectivity (the ability of a field to narrow down results) rather than cardinality alone. In compound indexes, placing low-cardinality fields first can improve prefix compression, but it's also essential to consider prefix matching to minimize the number of indexes you create. Partial indexes can be a game-changer by dramatically reducing index size when only a subset of documents needs to be indexed. Additionally, covered queries (where all the required fields are in the index) are usually the most efficient, so keep them in mind when designing your indexes.

By applying these best practices, you'll be well equipped to build a high-performing MongoDB database that meets your application's demands. In the next chapter, we'll explore MongoDB's powerful aggregation framework and delve into more advanced topics, such as how the query optimizer selects indexes.

4

Aggregations

If you've ever tried to wrangle data into meaningful insights, you know that raw documents alone won't cut it. You need to slice, dice, transform, and summarize. This is where MongoDB's aggregation framework shines. Think of it like a data assembly line: documents enter from one end, undergo a series of transformations as they pass through various stages, and emerge transformed on the other end. It's powerful and flexible, but if you're not careful, it can become a performance bottleneck.

In this chapter, we'll explore how to build aggregation pipelines that are both powerful and performant. We'll look at pipeline optimization strategies, memory management techniques, stage-specific considerations, and approaches for handling large datasets, all with performance as our North Star.

This chapter will cover the following topics:

- The fundamentals of MongoDB's aggregation framework
- Optimization techniques for aggregation pipeline performance
- Best practices for working with large datasets
- Aggregation in distributed environments and sharded collections
- Monitoring, profiling, and troubleshooting aggregation performance

MongoDB's aggregation framework

MongoDB's aggregation framework is the Swiss Army knife of data transformation and analysis in the database world. But before we dive into optimization techniques, let's understand what makes this tool so special.

In the early days, MongoDB's aggregation options were, let's say, *minimalist*. Developers relied on the mapReduce command or handling aggregations in client code to perform data summarization. While functional, these approaches were often clunky, slow, and not particularly easy to use.

Enter the aggregation pipeline, a game-changer introduced in MongoDB 2.2. Suddenly, developers could chain together a series of stages, each transforming the data in some way, much like an assembly line in a factory or a Unix command-line pipe. Over subsequent releases, the aggregation framework has grown more powerful, adding new stages, operators, expressions, and performance optimizations to meet increasingly sophisticated data processing needs.

If you're coming from a SQL background, you might be used to writing SELECT ... GROUP BY ... HAVING ... queries with multiple JOIN operations and subqueries. The aggregation pipeline offers similar capabilities but with a twist: instead of a monolithic query, you build a pipeline of stages, each performing a specific task or transformation. Documents flow from a collection into the first stage, then from there into subsequent stages, and eventually are returned to the client as the result.

This modular approach makes complex data-processing tasks more readable and maintainable, especially when working with complex document structures that are common in MongoDB. Additionally, you can do things in MongoDB aggregations, including working with complex arrays of documents, that could make a traditional SQL query blush with the complexity.

Core concepts of the aggregation pipeline

Think of your data as a river, and each pipeline stage as a dam, filter, or turbine that changes the flow in some way. Documents enter the pipeline, are transformed by each stage, and emerge at the end as the result set you want. This is very similar to using the Unix command-line pipe to do multiple transformations on a large text file:

```
grep xxx file.log | cut .. | sed | sort | head -20
cat file.log | awk '{print $2, $NF}' | ... >> newfile.log
```

The order of stages matters... a lot! Filtering early will dramatically reduce the amount of work downstream. Each stage works exclusively on the documents it receives from the previous stage, and its output becomes the input for the next stage in the sequence.

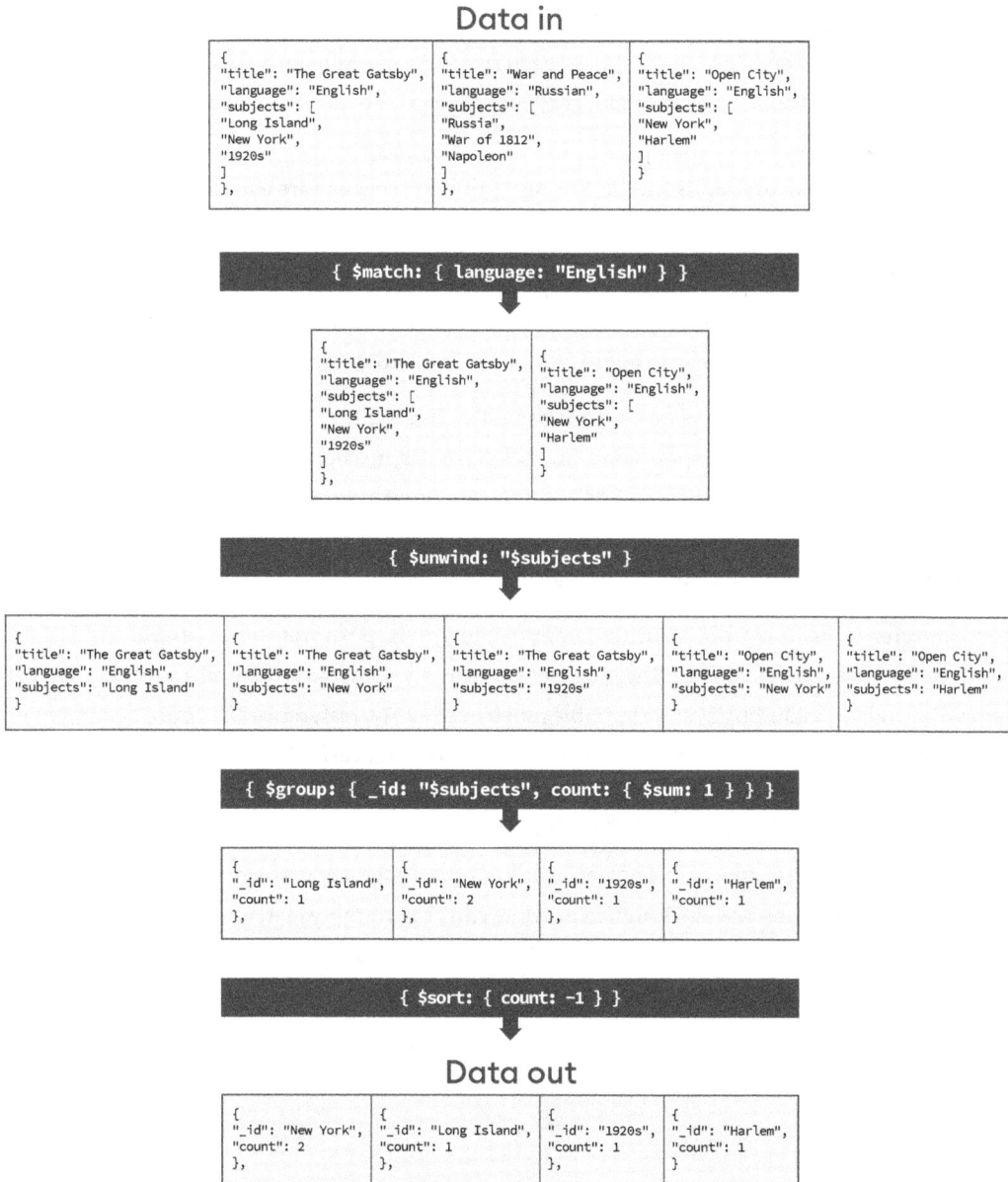

Data in

```
{                              {                            {
"title": "The Great Gatsby",   "title": "War and Peace",    "title": "Open City",
"language": "English",         "language": "Russian",       "language": "English",
"subjects": [                  "subjects": [                "subjects": [
"Long Island",                 "Russia",                    "New York",
"New York",                    "War of 1812",               "Harlem"
"1920s"                        "Napoleon"                   ]
]                              ]                            }
},                             },
```

`{ $match: { language: "English" } }`

```
{                              {
"title": "The Great Gatsby",   "title": "Open City",
"language": "English",         "language": "English",
"subjects": [                  "subjects": [
"Long Island",                 "New York",
"New York",                    "Harlem"
"1920s"                        ]
]                              }
},
```

`{ $unwind: "$subjects" }`

```
{                              {                              {                              {                            {
"title": "The Great Gatsby",   "title": "The Great Gatsby",   "title": "The Great Gatsby",   "title": "Open City",        "title": "Open City",
"language": "English",         "language": "English",         "language": "English",         "language": "English",       "language": "English",
"subjects": "Long Island"      "subjects": "New York"         "subjects": "1920s"            "subjects": "New York"       "subjects": "Harlem"
}                              }                              }                              }                            }
```

`{ $group: { _id: "$subjects", count: { $sum: 1 } } }`

```
{                        {                    {                  {
"_id": "Long Island",    "_id": "New York",   "_id": "1920s",    "_id": "Harlem",
"count": 1               "count": 2           "count": 1         "count": 1
},                       },                   },                 }
```

`{ $sort: { count: -1 } }`

Data out

```
{                      {                        {                  {
"_id": "New York",     "_id": "Long Island",    "_id": "1920s",    "_id": "Harlem",
"count": 2             "count": 1               "count": 1         "count": 1
},                     },                       },                 }
```

Figure 4.1: Documents transform as they flow through stages of the pipeline

Everything in the pipeline uses specific syntax to perform its magic:

- **Stages** define what kind of transformation happens, such as the `$match` stage for filtering documents, `$group` for grouping or aggregating them, `$set` for adding new fields or changing existing field values, and `$sort` for changing the order of documents in the flow. MongoDB offers many such stages, each serving a specific purpose. You can explore the full list at `https://www.mongodb.com/docs/manual/reference/operator/aggregation-pipeline/`.

- **Aggregation expressions** such as `$eq`, `$gt`, `$in`, and `$convert` are used to evaluate, compute, and assign new values.

- **Path expressions** give you a way to use existing values in current fields.

- **Accumulator expressions** such as `$sum`, `$avg`, `$push`, `$min`, and `$max` are used within grouping stages to perform aggregations on grouped data.

Expressions in the aggregation framework use JSON-like syntax. You'll see lots of dollar signs ($); they indicate operators, expressions, or field paths. Expressions can be nested, allowing for powerful and flexible computations. For example, you might use `$add` to sum two fields, `$cond` or `$switch` to implement conditional logic, or a wide range of built-in operators for arithmetic, string manipulation, date handling, and logical operations.

You can refer to fields within your documents using field path notation (simple fields with `"$fieldName"`, nested fields with `"$object.nestedField"`). The framework also supports several types of variables, including system variables such as `$$ROOT` to reference the entire document or `$$NOW` to get the current time, and allows you to set your own variables for readability.

Performance considerations

While the aggregation framework is powerful, it's not magic. A lot of performance depends on how you build your pipelines. A well-designed pipeline can be incredibly fast, while a poorly designed one can bring your database to its knees. The key is to think about how data flows through your pipeline and how each stage will impact performance.

For example, filtering documents early with $match can dramatically reduce the amount of data that subsequent stages need to process. Using indexes effectively is also crucial. Just like with regular queries, a pipeline that can use an index to quickly find the documents it needs will be far more performant than one that has to scan the entire collection.

As we'll see in the next section, MongoDB's query optimizer does a lot to improve performance automatically, but understanding the principles behind these optimizations will help you write better pipelines.

Aggregation pipeline flow

After parsing the pipeline, MongoDB's query optimizer analyzes it and tries to make it as efficient as possible. It may reorder stages to improve performance (making sure it won't change the results), combine compatible operations, push filters closer to the data to use available indexes effectively, and create an optimal execution plan based on your pipeline structure. It also analyzes which fields from original documents your pipeline is using to limit the amount of data it brings into the pipeline from the collection.

Under the hood, MongoDB sends batches of documents through the pipeline in a streaming fashion. Each stage receives a batch of documents from the previous stage, applies its transformation, and passes the results to the next stage. This design minimizes memory usage and allows for efficient processing of large datasets.

However, not every stage can pass each batch to the next stage because some stages need to see *all* the input coming to it, before any of it can be passed on. Think of $sort, which doesn't know what the highest or lowest value is until it's seen the last document, or $group, which cannot know each grouping is complete till it has seen every document. You'll hear those stages referred to as *blocking* stages, as opposed to *streaming* stages. Streaming stages can keep each batch of documents streaming when their own work is done, but blocking stages must receive all the documents before any documents can be passed on to the next stage.

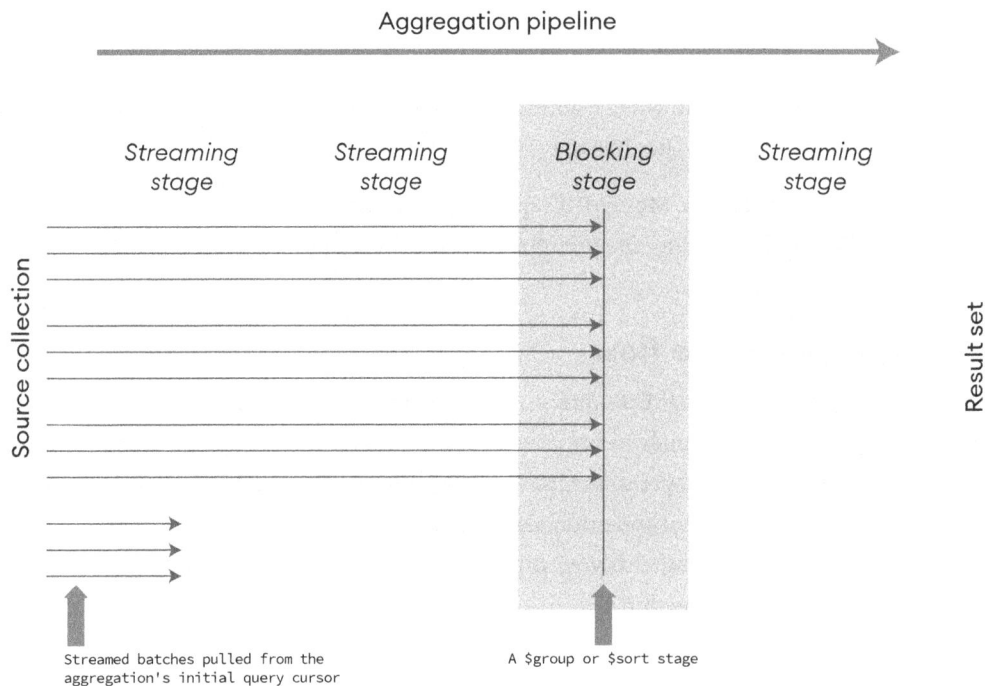

Figure 4.2: Aggregation pipeline with streaming and blocking stages

In sharded clusters, when the pipeline involves documents from more than one shard, MongoDB executes as much of the pipeline as possible on the individual shards to distribute the workload before merging the results. For example, filtering and transformation stages are performed on shards, reducing the amount of data sent across the network, while operations such as grouping or sorting only do initial work on the shards, but then may require merging intermediate results and finishing the work on the mongos router.

MongoDB is doing a lot of work to speed up your pipeline. What optimizations does that leave for you?

Optimizing aggregation pipelines

The order of stages in your aggregation pipeline can significantly impact performance. While MongoDB's query optimizer is quite intelligent and can automatically reorder stages, understanding these optimizations can help you design better pipelines.

MongoDB's query engine executes a slightly different pipeline than the one passed to the query optimizer. You can compare the actual pipeline that will be executed with what you wrote by using the explain() method, which reveals how MongoDB has transformed your pipeline for

efficiency. Run your aggregation with explain("executionStats") or explain("queryPlanner")
to examine the transformed pipeline MongoDB executes. Using "executionStats" will also show
you the number of documents that flow from stage to stage, as well as the total amount of time
that has been taken up to this point. This allows you to see which stages are time-consuming
and should be examined for possible reworking and which are contributing so little to the overall
latency that trying to fine-tune them will not be noticeable when running the full pipeline:

```
db.collection.explain("executionStats").aggregate([ {$match:{a:1} },
{$match:{b:{$gte:2}}}, {$set:{x:"$y"}}, {$set:{a:"$b"}},{$project:{a:1,
c:{$add:["$d","$e"]}, _id:0}}])
{
  stages: [
    { '$cursor': { queryPlanner: {
        parsedQuery: {'$and':[ {a:{'$eq':1}}, {b:{'$gte':2}} ]}
        winningPlan: {
          stage: 'PROJECTION_SIMPLE',
          transformBy: { b: 1, d: 1, e: 1, y: 1, _id: 0 },
          inputStage: {
            stage: 'IXSCAN',
            keyPattern: { a: 1, b: 1 },
            // ...
        },
        executionStats: {
          executionSuccess: true,
          nReturned: 45,
          executionTimeMillis: 2,
          totalKeysExamined: 45,
          totalDocsExamined: 45,
          executionStages: {
            stage: 'PROJECTION_SIMPLE',
            nReturned: 45,
            executionTimeMillisEstimate: 0,
            transformBy: { b: 1, d: 1, e: 1, y: 1, _id: 0 },
            // ...
        }
      },
```

```
      nReturned: Long('45'),
      executionTimeMillisEstimate: Long('2')
}, {
  '$set': { x: '$y' },
  nReturned: Long('45'),
  executionTimeMillisEstimate: Long('2')
}, {
  '$set': { a: '$b' },
  nReturned: Long('45'),
  executionTimeMillisEstimate: Long('2')
}, {
  '$project': { a: true, c: { '$add': [ '$d', '$e' ] }, _id: false },
  nReturned: Long('45'),
  executionTimeMillisEstimate: Long('2')
} /* ... */ ]}
```

Here, you can see the stages executed. The first stage is called $cursor, though it looks like it's executing the $match stage. It shows you which fields it's returning in the transformBy field, and you can see that the $set and $project stages took basically no time at all, as each stage shows cumulative time spent up to itself, which means each of the non-$cursor stages took 0 milliseconds to execute.

Optimization techniques

Let's look at various optimization techniques and how they can help your pipeline run faster.

Filter data early

While MongoDB automatically reorders stages, understanding the principles behind these reorderings can help you write more performant pipelines. The general idea is to reduce the volume of data as early as possible:

- Place $match as early as possible and make sure it can be supported by an index, which will ensure that only necessary documents will be brought into the pipeline to begin with, reducing the number of documents that need to be read from the cache (or worse, from disk) and processed

- Place $sort as early as possible in the pipeline and make sure it can be supported by an index

Avoid early $project stage to preserve pipeline optimization

It's not necessary to manually remove fields that won't be used. This is something that the pipeline optimization stage already does automatically for you by examining which fields your pipeline is using and avoiding fetching unused fields. This automatic pipeline optimization can be unintentionally defeated by adding an unnecessary early explicit inclusion $project stage, so don't use $project till the end of the pipeline to rename or otherwise reshape the results into the form that the client expects.

MongoDB can combine certain stages into a single, more efficient stage. This coalescence reduces overhead and speeds up execution. As a best practice, you can group similar operations yourself and avoid unnecessary stages to help the optimizer do its job, but don't spend too much time on it as some of these stages may already be very fast. On the other hand, some stages can be significantly sped up by doing *the right thing*:

- When the $sort stage is immediately followed by a $limit stage, MongoDB optimizes this by combining them and only tracking the top *N* sorted documents, significantly reducing memory usage for the sort. This is referred to as a *top-N sort*, and it's infinitely more performant than sorting the entire dataset and later only keeping the top *N* values.

- Multiple adjacent $match stages are typically merged into a single $match stage, combining their filter conditions with an implicit AND, so you shouldn't need to combine them yourself. But make sure you have a compound index to support conditions in the combined filter.

In general, when stages that the MongoDB query system can optimize are placed early in the pipeline, they are pushed down to the query subsystem, and only documents that the query returns are processed in the pipeline. When looking at explain output, this will usually manifest by the first stage being $cursor and will absorb all the early stages, such as $match, $sort, and $limit, into it. In cases where there are no further aggregation stages and the full aggregation pipeline could have been expressed as a find command, it will actually get executed the same as the equivalent find command, and explain will not show any additional aggregation stages.

In this section, you saw how certain stages can be pushed down to the query subsystem when they are placed early in the pipeline. They should be optimized the same way as equivalent queries would be. Let's now look at some of the other potentially challenging stages and scenarios.

Avoid unnecessary $unwind and $group

The $unwind stage is used to flatten arrays, and it is often misunderstood as a performance villain, but in reality, it is not inherently slow or problematic. The challenge arises from what is done with its results. When unwinding or flattening an array is done to apply some stages to resultant documents, but then the results are grouped again (using $group) with "$_id" as the group key (reconstructing them back into original documents), it's always the case that it was a mistake to use $unwind + $group. Instead, one or more array-processing expressions should have been used on documents without deconstructing them.

The $map expression allows you to manipulate each element in an array and returns an array of the results, allowing transforming array elements in place. Other array expressions include $filter, which returns only array elements that satisfy a given condition, $sortArray for sorting elements of the array, and $reduce for aggregating array elements within a document without unwinding.

Sometimes, of course, unwinding before $group is the only correct option, particularly when you need to group on individual array elements across multiple documents. In such cases, if you don't intend to keep all the elements, you can use $match with $elemMatch on the array element before $unwind. This allows you to use an index on the array field to improve performance.

Design efficient $group operations

The $group stage can be memory-intensive, especially with high-cardinality grouping keys or when each group document is going to be large. $group must maintain the current state for each unique group it encounters. If the field you are grouping by (the _id field inside $group) has many unique values, this stage might need to store more data in memory than it's allowed (by default, 100 MB is the in-memory limit for any individual stage, which we discuss shortly).

To control group size, only keep fields and values that are necessary in grouping, and avoid using $push of entire incoming documents unless it is absolutely necessary.

Different accumulators may also have different performance characteristics. Accumulators such as $sum, $avg, $min, $max, $first, and $last are generally efficient as they only need to maintain a single running value per group. In contrast, $push and $addToSet will be more memory-intensive when they accumulate many items into arrays, especially when these are large items.

If the input to $group is already sorted by the group key and another value, the engine can optimize some groups without storing all distinct group keys in memory simultaneously. For instance, using a descending $sort followed by $group with $first to find the highest value per group is significantly more performant than having a $group stage use $max to compute the same highest value. Of course, this optimization relies on having the index on $group + $first values to use:

```
db.coll.explain("executionStats").aggregate([
      {$sort:{state:1, groupId:1}},
      {$group:{_id:"$state", firstGroup:{$first:"$groupId"}}} ])
{
    "stages" : [
        {
            "$cursor" : {
                "queryPlanner" : {
                    "namespace" : "test.coll",
                    "optimizationTimeMillis" : 0,
                    "winningPlan" : {
                        "isCached" : false,
                        "stage" : "PROJECTION_COVERED",
                        "transformBy" : {
                            "groupId" : 1,
                            "state" : 1,
                            "_id" : 0
                        },
                        "inputStage" : {
                            "stage" : "DISTINCT_SCAN",
                            "keyPattern" : {
                                "state" : 1,
                                "groupId" : 1
                            },
                            "indexName" : "state_1_groupId",
        // ...
```

The explain output shows the DISTICT_SCAN plan being used to find the first value of each group.

Avoid common $lookup performance issues

The $lookup stage enables *joins* between collections, but it can be a performance bottleneck if not used with care. Understanding two *types* of $lookup is crucial:

- **Local/foreign field lookups** (the *standard* form using localField and foreignField) compare fields between collections using regular find semantics. MongoDB executes these the same way as if you had a $match stage as the first *inner* pipeline stage, which uses the value of localField in find with the {foreignField:{$eq:<localField-value>}} condition when localField is a scalar, or {foreignField:{$in:<localField-array>}} when the localField value is an array. This allows all indexes on the from or foreign collection to be used the same way they are used in normal find commands with the $eq or $in operators.

> ### Using the pipeline option for enhanced joins
>
> The pipeline option can be used with *local/foreign* syntax to add more stages to implement additional join conditions, reduce the size of returned documents (that go into an as array), and do any other processing that the join requires.

- **Expressive lookups** (not using localField and foreignField and only using the pipeline option) usually specify the join conditions in an explicit $match stage that should be first in the pipeline, and can reference fields from the input documents (assigned to variables in the let option) in the sub-pipeline. When there is no condition depending on field(s) from the input documents, this results in an *uncorrelated* subquery, which is only executed once and then its results cached, rather than executing it once for each incoming document in the pipeline. This syntax should only be used when there is *no* equality join condition.

> ### Standard versus expressive $lookup
>
> The only difference between standard and expressive lookups is that one of them includes localField and foreignField while the other one does not. They can both specify pipeline to add stages to the $lookup execution.

For the localField and foreignField forms, the most critical optimization is to have an index on the foreignField in the foreign (from) collection. This allows MongoDB to efficiently find matching documents. If the foreign documents are large but you will only need a few fields, use $project as the last stage within the aggregation defined in the pipeline field to only keep the necessary fields. If you expect only one value to be returned in the as field and you don't want to keep it as an array of one, it's totally free from a performance point of view to immediately follow $lookup with the $unwind stage on the as field as the optimizer will absorb the $unwind stage into the $lookup execution. There are additional optimizations that are available if you plan to use $unwind on the as array; for example, a $match stage on "as.field" that follows the $lookup, $unwind combination will also be pushed down into $lookup as an additional filter:

```
db.a.explain().aggregate([
    { $lookup:{
        from: "b",
        localField: "a._id",
        foreignField: "_id",
        as: "details"        }},
    {$unwind:"$details"},
    {$match:{"details.date":{$gt:ISODate("2025-05-20T00:00:00.000Z")}}}
])
{    "stages" : [
        {"$cursor" : {
                "queryPlanner" : {
                    // ...
                },
                // ...
        }},
        {"$lookup" : {
            "from" : "b",
            "as" : "details",
            "localField" : "a._id",
            "foreignField" : "_id",
            "let" : { },
            "pipeline" : [
                {"$match" : {
                "date" : {"$gt":ISODate("2025-05-20T00:00:00Z")}
                }}
```

```
                ],
                "unwinding" : {
                    "preserveNullAndEmptyArrays" : false
                }
            }}
    ]}
```

The `explain` output shows that the `$unwind` and `$match` stages are both absorbed into the `$lookup` stage.

Only use the expressive pipeline option with `$lookup`, when there is no equality condition on the join at all. In this case, make sure the first stage in the sub-pipeline will be a `$match` stage that uses indexed fields on the foreign collection. The `$match` stage will likely use the `$expr` syntax to bring in variables from each input document that you set via `let`, so make sure the referenced field or fields in the foreign collection is/are in an index.

Efficient use of $project and $addFields

`$project` and `$addFields` serve different purposes and have different performance implications. Use `$project` for inclusion when you need to reshape documents by explicitly controlling which fields to include and what to name them, usually only as the last stage of the pipeline. Use `$project` for exclusion when you want to unset several fields. You can use its alias `$unset` in this case for clarity.

Use `$addFields` (or its alias `$set`) when you want to add new fields or update/compute existing fields while keeping all other existing fields unchanged. `$addFields` can also be used to remove fields at the same time, by assigning the unneeded field the value `$$REMOVE`.

For very complex calculations, it may be clearer to break the work into several stages, each performing a part of the calculation. This can also improve readability and maintainability. It's not strictly necessary to do that, since using the `$let` expression and creating temporary variables in your `$addFields` stage can make writing very complex expressions easier, but multiple sequential `$set` stages won't significantly increase execution time on your pipeline, and likely won't increase it in a measurable way.

Keeping all these techniques in mind will be extra-helpful when your dataset size grows significantly.

Working with large datasets

MongoDB's aggregation framework is designed to handle everything from bite-sized collections to datasets that would make a data scientist sweat. But as your data grows, so do the challenges. Let's explore strategies for working with large datasets and keeping your pipelines running smoothly.

Aggregation pipeline limits

MongoDB imposes several limits to keep your aggregations from running amok:

- **Result size restrictions**: Each document in the result must adhere to the 16 MB limit. The document maximum size limit also applies to documents that flow between stages. The $facet stage can only return a single document, which cannot be larger than 16 MB.
- **Number of stages limit**: Pipelines can have up to 1,000 stages. If you hit this, it's probably time to rethink your approach!
- **Memory limit**: Individual aggregation stages are limited by default to 100 MB of RAM. If a stage exceeds this, the aggregation operation will leverage temporary files on disk automatically since allowDiskUse has been enabled by default since MongoDB version 6.0. This option can be disabled if needed for performance reasons, but then pipelines with stages that exceed this threshold will fail and return an error.

These limits are designed to protect your system from runaway workloads, not to restrict thoughtful development. By understanding and working within them, you can design aggregation pipelines that are both efficient and reliable, even at scale.

Managing memory constraints with allowDiskUse

Blocking stages such as $group or unindexed $sort can be memory hogs, and because of that, there is a 100 MB memory limit on them by default. When you hit that limit, data being kept in memory automatically spills to disk using temporary files. This behavior is controlled by the allowDiskUse option, which by default is set to true. You have two options to avoid using disk for sorts:

- **Optimize your pipeline** to reduce memory usage (the better approach for performance)
- **Explicitly disable disk usage** with allowDiskUse:false, if you prefer operations to fail with an error rather than slow down by having to read and write to disk

While having allowDiskUse enabled by default provides a safety net for memory-intensive operations, it's important to be aware that disk I/O is significantly slower than in-memory operations. You may want to explicitly disable it by setting allowDiskUse:false in scenarios where low latency is critical and it's preferable for operations to fail fast rather than potentially becoming slow due to disk usage.

Only certain aggregation stages are subject to this limit; they are all blocking stages:

- **Unindexed $sort operations on large datasets**: Sorting a large number of documents *without the benefit of an index* and without an immediate $limit following it requires all documents to be sorted to be maintained in memory
- **$group with high cardinality keys and/or large result documents for each key**: If the field(s) used in the _id of a $group stage have many unique values and/or if each grouping has to maintain a large amount of data, the stage needs to maintain a large amount of data for each distinct group in memory
- **$bucket, $bucketAuto, and $setWindowFields**: These stages are variants of $group and can consume significant memory in the same circumstances as $group

Blocking stages and memory usage considerations

Not all blocking stages are able or likely to exceed this stage limit. For instance, $count is a blocking stage that needs to count all the incoming documents, but since it only outputs a single document as its result, its memory use is trivially tiny. The $sortByCount stage is a blocking stage that groups all of its input into small documents containing only two fields, but then it has to sort them in memory. If you don't specify a $limit stage after the $sortByCount and you have well over 1 million distinct group key values, then the result could possibly exceed 100 MB, but that scenario is not very likely. You would likely use $limit rather than returning millions of results to the client.

Aggregation in distributed environments

Sharding, which we cover in *Chapter 6, Sharding*, is MongoDB's secret sauce for scaling horizontally, but it adds a layer of complexity to aggregation pipelines. When your data is spread across multiple shards, understanding how aggregation works in this distributed environment is key to maintaining performance and avoiding bottlenecks.

Optimizing aggregation for sharded collections

In a sharded cluster, aggregation pipelines can be executed in parallel across shards. MongoDB tries to push as much work as possible to each shard that holds the data needed for aggregation, minimizing the amount of data that needs to be transferred over the network.

If an aggregation query can be satisfied by data residing on a single shard (or a subset of shards), mongos will route the query only to the relevant shard(s). This is the most efficient scenario as it minimizes cross-shard communication and coordination overhead. This typically happens when the query includes a filter on the shard key, or the collection being aggregated only lives on one or a small subset of shards.

If the aggregation cannot be targeted (e.g., no filter on the shard key and data lives on multiple shards), mongos performs a scatter-gather operation. It sends the first part of the pipeline to all shards that hold data for the target collection. mongos then gathers the results and merges them by running the rest of the pipeline itself. There are also scenarios where the merge stage must happen on a selected shard rather than on mongos.

The choice of shard key can make or break your aggregation performance. A well-chosen shard key can enable many aggregation queries to be targeted to a single shard, dramatically improving performance. Conversely, a poorly chosen shard key can lead to most aggregations becoming scatter-gather operations, increasing latency and load on the cluster.

Understanding shard-local versus merged operations

Not all pipeline stages are created equal. Some can be executed on individual shards, while others must be merged on mongos. Use the explain() command to determine where each stage runs. The output will show how the pipeline is split, and which parts are executed on the shards and which on mongos.

All streaming stages can run on shards, as well as the first parts of blocking stages. In some special cases, even $group can run entirely on a shard, if you are grouping by the shard key. The final part of the first blocking stage that cannot run entirely on the shard, and *all* stages that follow, will have to run on the merging location, which is usually mongos.

Keep as much processing as possible on the shards to reduce network traffic and speed up your pipeline. If an aggregation can run entirely on a single shard, it avoids network latency and the merging overhead on mongos.

If you have a $group stage, and the group key is (or includes) the shard key, each shard can perform the full group operation locally, with the pipeline continuing locally, and mongos only needs to return the results to the client without additional processing. If the group key is different, or if there is another blocking stage, then the shards perform the initial part of that stage, and mongos does a final merge and all the following stages, which is more work for mongos.

Merges are frequently unavoidable, but you can minimize their impact. The earlier stages in your pipeline ($match) should aggressively filter out documents. The less data each shard sends to mongos for merging, the faster the merge operation will be.

Monitoring and profiling aggregation performance

Even the most carefully crafted aggregation pipeline can run into performance issues. That's why monitoring and profiling are essential skills for any MongoDB practitioner.

You saw briefly how the explain() method is your window into the inner workings of an aggregation pipeline. It reveals the execution plan, showing how each stage is processed, which indexes are used, and where the heavy lifting happens. We'll show a lot more about explain in *Chapter 12, Advanced Query and Indexing Concepts*.

To get the explain output for an aggregation, append .explain() to your collection name before the aggregate() command, use the {explain:true} option inside aggregate, or in mongosh, append .explain() to the end of your aggregate method. Common verbosity modes include the following:

- explain("queryPlanner"): Shows the plan selected by the query optimizer, including stages as they will be executed and how indexes are utilized
- explain("executionStats"): Executes the query and returns detailed statistics about the execution, such as the number of documents returned (nReturned), total documents examined (totalDocsExamined), total execution time after each stage (execTimeMillis), and index usage
- explain("allPlansExecution"): Same as executionStats but includes additional information and statistics about rejected query plans in the $cursor stage

The primary goal of using explain() is to find opportunities for improvement. Look for COLLSCAN (collection scan) as an inputStage for $match or $sort operations where you expected an IXSCAN (index scan). COLLSCAN means MongoDB had to read all documents in the collection to find the relevant ones, which is usually inefficient.

Stages such as $group or $sort that show a high increase in execTimeMillis over the previous stage and process many documents might be memory-intensive. High totalDocsExamined values compared to nReturned for a $match stage suggest that the filter is not very selective or isn't using an index effectively.

You can see whether the $lookup stage used indexes, and if so, how efficient it was. You can also make sure the indexes used are the ones you expected to be selected, and if they are not, you can see whether you have indexes that are redundant and can be dropped. You can also see whether a blocking stage spilled to disk and how much disk space it used. If the operation was fully in memory, you can see how much memory was used and whether it may be getting close to the 100 MB limit, when things will slow down a lot.

Experience and profiling often reveal common patterns that lead to performance issues.

Utilizing materialized views

Sometimes a complex aggregation will be slower than the required SLA to return its results, in which case you can run the aggregation periodically to cache its results in another collection, which the clients can query directly.

Use $out or $merge to store intermediate results as these stages write the results of the aggregation pipeline to a specified collection, which can then be queried, indexed, or used as input for further aggregations.

Summary

Let's distill what you've learned in this chapter into key principles that will help you build aggregation pipelines that are both powerful and performant. First, filter early. The most impactful optimization you can make is often the simplest. Every document you can exclude early means less work for every subsequent stage. This isn't just about adding a $match stage at the beginning, although that's the most impactful optimization you can make. It's also about adding $limit when you know you won't be using all the documents to minimize data flow, not creating fields you won't be using, and reviewing your pipeline with explain to check that only the necessary data is being passed from stage to stage.

Next, leverage indexes strategically. Indexes aren't just for find() operations; they're vital for aggregation performance. For instance, initial $match stages can use indexes just like regular queries; early $sort operations will use indexes, when possible; $lookup will use indexes on from collections; and some $group operations can leverage indexes. The key is ensuring your pipeline structure allows MongoDB to use those indexes. For example, when you need both filtering and sorting, make sure you have a compound index that supports both operations.

Also, design with sharding in mind. In a sharded environment, understanding how aggregation stages distribute across shards can make or break performance. For best results, filter on the shard key early to target only specific shards, minimize the number of shards involved, and be aware of which stages force a merge (that is, stop parallel execution). Finally, monitor and measure performance. Keep experimenting, keep measuring, and keep refining your approach. The most elegant pipeline isn't necessarily the one with the fewest stages; it's the one that balances readability, maintainability, and performance to deliver insights accurately and efficiently.

With your data processing optimized, it's time to turn our attention to the pathways that carry your data.

The next chapter explores replication, read preference, and write concern, which are essential for maintaining data availability, consistency, and performance across distributed systems.

5

Replication

In this chapter, you'll learn how MongoDB uses replication for continuous operation and automatic failover. Replica sets orchestrate data synchronization across multiple nodes, ensuring your application stays online when hardware or network issues arise. You'll see why the right combination of nodes is crucial for reliability, and how features such as read preference and write concern let you tune your system for performance, consistency, and durability.

You will learn about processes such as elections and failover, and dive into advanced replica set configurations that provide workload isolation, reduce network strain, and keep analytics from interfering with operational queries. By the end of this chapter, you'll have the tools to design, configure, and monitor replica sets for robust MongoDB deployments.

This chapter will cover the following topics:

- How replica sets ensure high availability and automatic failover
- The roles of primary, secondary, and arbiter nodes
- Strategies for balancing performance, consistency, and durability with read/write settings
- Monitoring replication health, diagnosing lag, and handling failover
- Advanced features such as chained replication, analytics nodes, and optimal oplog sizing

Understanding MongoDB replica sets

MongoDB replication ensures data availability and system resilience by maintaining copies of data across multiple servers, organized into a replica set. Within this set, a single primary server handles write operations, while secondary servers maintain copies of the data, enabling read requests and providing failover capabilities. Read preference controls which servers are utilized for read operations, giving you greater control over which nodes handle those reads.

Write concern determines the level of confirmation the database provides after a write operation, allowing you to fine-tune the trade-off between write speed and data durability.

These elements combined create a system that can tolerate server failures and manage heavy read loads. Put simply, **replication** makes data copies, **read preference** chooses where to read from, and **write concern** dictates the confirmation level needed after writing data, resulting in a robust database system.

Components of a replica set

A typical MongoDB replica set includes an odd number of nodes to provide fault tolerance and high availability, and consists of one primary node and one or more secondary nodes:

- **Primary**: The primary node is responsible for handling all write operations. It maintains the latest state of the data and propagates changes to the secondary nodes.

- **Secondaries**: Secondary nodes continuously replicate the primary's data to maintain updated copies. They can also serve read operations if the application is configured to allow secondary reads.

- **Arbiters (optional)**: An arbiter node participates in elections but does not store data. Arbiters are not recommended for use in production configurations; however, if system limitations prevent storing data, they can be used to break ties in voting scenarios when you have an even number of data-bearing nodes.

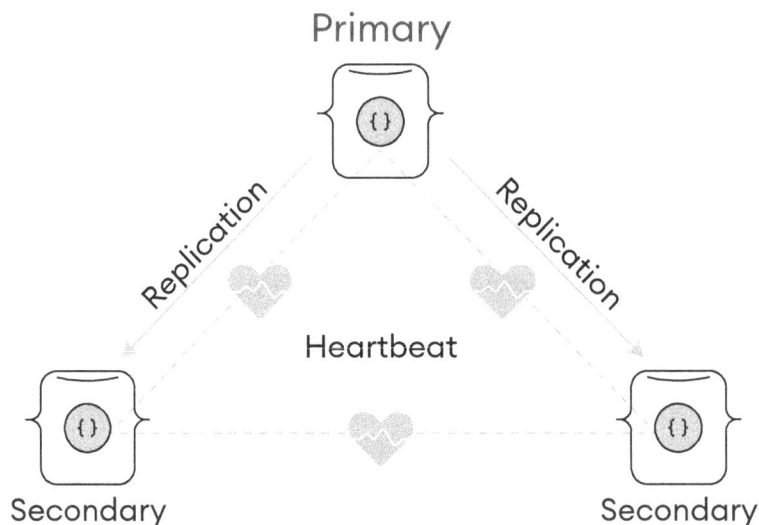

Figure 5.1: MongoDB replica set architecture

Replica sets use an election process to ensure high availability. If the primary node becomes unavailable, an election is triggered to select a new primary. The election process follows these steps:

1. A node calls for an election if it believes it can become the primary (for example, if a secondary cannot see a primary).
2. Nodes cast votes based on factors such as priority settings, replication state, and availability.
3. The node that receives the majority of votes is elected as the new primary.

When designing a MongoDB replica set for optimal performance, you need to carefully consider the number of nodes, their placement, and how to configure election and read preferences. A well-designed replica set configuration can help you balance throughput, fault tolerance, and latency requirements while ensuring high availability for your application.

Having an odd number of voting members in a MongoDB replica set is essential to ensuring that the election process can be completed successfully. When only an even number of voting members are available, it's more likely that a quorum cannot be reached and the successful election of a new primary may be delayed.

In some deployments, additional secondary nodes may be added to distribute read workloads or support analytics without impacting the primary's performance. This configuration ensures the high availability of data while also enabling workload isolation through read targeting.

> **Secondaries are for redundancy, not scalability**
>
> Though read preference enables you to target secondaries for reads, this is not meant to be a mechanism for scaling reads across the cluster. Secondaries provide the cluster with high availability and resilience.

Replication and high availability

As long as a cluster has a minimum of three nodes (the default in MongoDB Atlas), it will be fault-tolerant and resilient out of the box. In the case of a primary member outage, a replica set election process automatically detects the failure, elects a secondary member as a replacement, and promotes that secondary member to become the new primary.

The entire election and failover process happens within seconds, without manual intervention.

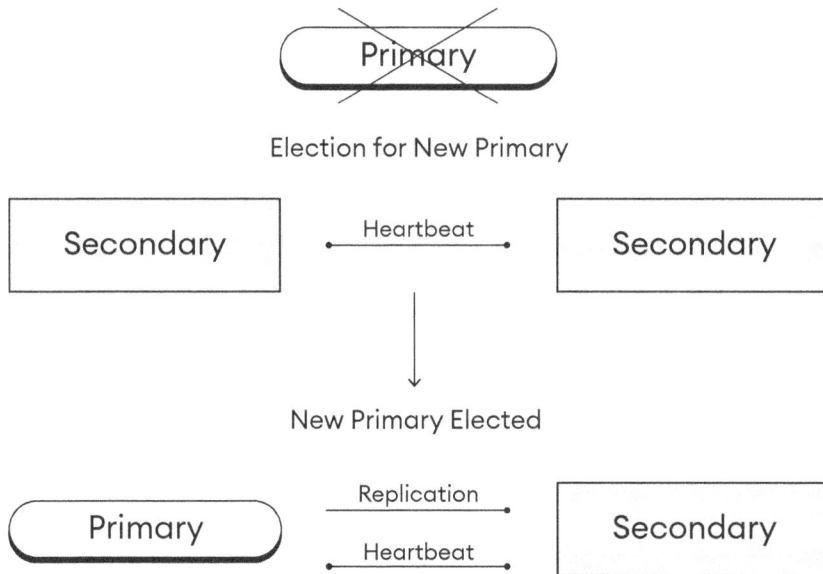

Figure 5.2: MongoDB replica set failover process

Failover time is dependent on several factors, including network latency. The MongoDB election process is designed to avoid unnecessary failover and provide flexibility for different deployment needs.

To minimize downtime during failovers, proper election configuration, including appropriate priorities and timeouts, is crucial for ensuring a swift and seamless transition of leadership among replica set members:

- **Node priority**: Assign higher priority values to nodes to influence election outcomes.
- **Election timeouts**: Configure `electionTimeoutMillis` to balance between quick failover and avoiding unnecessary elections due to temporary network issues. The default of 10,000 (10 seconds) should be suitable for most configurations.

Replica set members exchange heartbeat messages every 2 seconds to monitor each other's status. If the connection fails due to a network error, depending on the member being monitored, a primary that doesn't receive a heartbeat from a majority of voting members will step down, whereas a secondary that doesn't receive a heartbeat from the primary can call for an election. If there isn't a network failure, and a response isn't received within the `electionTimeoutMillis` threshold, the same action will also be taken.

Understanding the MongoDB election process

As just mentioned, a MongoDB replica set uses a fully automated election process to determine which set member will become the new primary member. Replica sets can trigger an election in response to a variety of events, such as the following:

- Losing connectivity to a primary member for more than the configured time-out (for MongoDB Atlas, the default is 5 seconds, or 10 seconds otherwise)
- Adding a new node to the replica set
- Performing replica set maintenance

During any of these events, sophisticated algorithms control the member election process. The election algorithm processes a range of parameters, including a historical analysis to identify those replica set members that have applied the most recent updates from the primary, heartbeat (ping or connectivity) status, and user-defined priorities assigned to replica set members. This process ensures that the most suitable secondary member is promoted to primary. Once the new primary replica set member has been elected, the remaining secondary members automatically start replicating from the configured sync source, as explained in the upcoming *Chained replication* section. If the original primary comes back online, it will recognize that it is no longer the primary and reconfigure itself to become a secondary member of the replica set and begin catching up.

Replica set configuration

In this section, we delve into specialized replica set configurations that extend beyond basic primary-secondary setups. These advanced techniques can help you optimize performance, reduce operational overhead, or cater to specific workload requirements. While each feature introduces additional complexities, they can prove invaluable for teams looking to fine-tune their MongoDB deployments.

> **Note**
>
> Replica set reconfiguration is not available in MongoDB Atlas.

Chained replication

By default, secondaries can pull data changes (oplog entries) from the primary or another secondary. Chained replication enables a secondary to fetch oplog data from another secondary. This approach can help reduce network load on the primary in large or distributed deployments. Chained replication works as follows:

1. MongoDB determines the nearest or best secondary to serve as the sync source.

2. The syncing secondary continuously fetches oplog entries from this secondary source instead of the primary.

3. Changes propagate through the replica set with reduced bandwidth usage on the primary node.

Though there are many advantages to chained replication, there can be some disadvantages as well:

Benefits	Drawbacks
Assists globally distributed deployments: Secondary nodes in remote regions can pull from a geographically closer source, reducing latency	Increased lag in chains: If a downstream secondary falls behind, nodes that depend on it in the chain will also lag
Optimizes network traffic: Particularly beneficial in multi-region deployments where network bandwidth between regions may be limited or costly	Complexity of troubleshooting: Longer replication paths may complicate diagnosing replication issues
—	Cascading delays: Network issues affecting intermediate nodes can impact multiple downstream secondaries

Table 5.1: Advantages and disadvantages of chained replication in MongoDB replica sets

You can allow (or disallow) chained replication by adjusting the replica set configuration from a MongoDB Shell connection to your cluster:

```
cfg = rs.conf();
cfg.settings = cfg.settings || {};
// true allows secondaries to replicate from other secondaries
// false restricts them to replicate only from the primary
cfg.settings.chainingAllowed = true;
rs.reconfig(cfg);
```

> **Note**
>
> Chained replication is enabled by default; however, it is disabled for single-region replica sets in MongoDB Atlas.

When using chained replication, monitoring becomes even more critical. The following script, which can also be run from a MongoDB Shell connection to your cluster, will print sync source and state information about each replica set member:

```
// Check the sync source for each member
rs.status().members.forEach(function(member) {
  print("Member: " + member.name +
        ", Sync Source: " + (member.syncSourceHost || "none") +
        ", State: " + member.stateStr);
});
```

Ensure you monitor replication lag and majority write concern latency more closely if chaining is enabled, especially in high-latency environments.

Replica set tags and analytics nodes

MongoDB Atlas offers analytics nodes, which are specialized read-only nodes used to isolate queries that you do not want to affect your operational workload. They are useful for handling analytic data, such as reporting queries executed by BI tools. Within the context of a replica set, analytics nodes are similar to other secondary members but have a priority of 0 and cannot be elected primary. However, through replica set tag configuration, they can be excluded from typical operational workloads and targeted specifically for others using an appropriate read preference.

For example, to configure a member for analytics, the following replica set reconfiguration could be applied:

```
conf = rs.conf();
conf.members[0].tags = { "usage": "production" };
conf.members[1].tags = { "usage": "reporting" };
conf.members[2].tags = { "usage": "production" };
rs.reconfig(conf);
```

The analytics node, which we've identified as having a tag of usage: reporting, can be targeted by specific workloads by using the appropriate read preference configuration, such as in the following example:

```
db.collection.find({}).readPref("secondary", [{ "usage": "reporting" }]);
```

Replica set tags cannot be directly configured in MongoDB Atlas; however, Atlas offers a set of predefined replica set tags that can be used for workload isolation, some of which are as follows:

Predefined tag name	Description	Example
nodeType	Node type. Possible values are as follows: • ELECTABLE • READ_ONLY • ANALYTICS	{"nodeType" : "ANALYTICS"}
provider	Cloud provider on which the node is provisioned. Possible values are as follows: • AWS • GCP • AZURE	{"provider" : "AWS"}
region	Cloud region in which the node resides.	{"region" : "US_ EAST_2"}

Table 5.2: Common predefined tag names for MongoDB replica set members

For a full list of the predefined replica set tags and possible region values available in MongoDB Atlas, see https://www.mongodb.com/docs/atlas/reference/replica-set-tags.

If an application performs complex or long-running operations, such as **extract**, **transform**, and **load** (**ETL**) or reporting, you may want to isolate the application's queries from the rest of your operational workload by exclusively directing those queries to analytics nodes. This can be configured based on the preceding predefined tags for an application connecting to a MongoDB Atlas cluster, as follows:

```
mongodb+srv://<db_username>:<db_password>@abc123.mongodb.net/
test?readPreference=secondary&readPreferenceTags=nodeType:ANALYTICS
```

Configuring your application with the preceding connection string will ensure all reads target only secondary members that have the `nodeType:ANALYTICS` tag applied.

> **Note**
>
> Analytics nodes in MongoDB Atlas are configured with a priority of 0, which prevents them from being elected primary.

Replication internals and performance

Replication in MongoDB involves mechanisms to keep data synchronized across nodes while managing delays and resource use. Factors such as oplog, control of write rates, and addressing delays between nodes all influence overall performance. Balancing these elements is important for maintaining data consistency and availability. In this section, we will look at the key aspects of replication internals and performance considerations in MongoDB.

Flow control

Flow control is a feature in MongoDB that limits the rate at which the primary applies new operations when secondaries fall too far behind. This helps prevent excessive replication lag at the cost of slightly more latency as it relates to the acknowledgement of writes.

MongoDB provides internal parameters to fine-tune flow control behavior. For example, the `flowControlTargetLagSeconds` parameter defines the acceptable lag threshold before flow control is triggered, as shown here:

```
// Check current flow control settings
db.adminCommand({ getParameter: 1, flowControlTargetLagSeconds: 1 });

// Configure flow control settings
db.adminCommand({
  setParameter: 1,
  flowControlTargetLagSeconds: 10
});
```

The default setting of 10 seconds should be optimal for most use cases, and adjusting it is not recommended.

> **Note**
>
> The setParameter administrative command is unavailable in MongoDB Atlas.

Replication and the oplog

The **operations log (oplog)** is a central component of MongoDB replication. It is a special capped collection where the nodes record all write operations. Secondary nodes use the oplog to replicate changes and stay in sync with the primary.

Here are some key characteristics of the oplog:

- **Capped collection**: The oplog by default has a fixed size, which operates on a **first-in, first-out (FIFO)** basis. Older entries are automatically removed when the oplog reaches its size limit.
- **Replication process**: Secondary nodes continuously apply oplog entries from the primary to replicate changes.
- **Performance considerations**: Proper sizing of the oplog is crucial. If the oplog is too small, secondary nodes may fall behind and require a full resync. Conversely, an oversized oplog may consume unnecessary storage.

Suppose your workload generates 2 GB of updates per hour. To ensure smooth replication, the oplog should be sized to store several hours' worth of operations, typically upward of 24 to 48 hours. This reduces the risk of prolonged resyncs if a secondary node goes offline temporarily.

For instance, if you configure an oplog size of 10 GB, this will provide approximately 5 hours of operation history. This buffer allows secondary nodes to catch up after brief network interruptions or maintenance periods without requiring a full data resynchronization, but may be too short if the node fails in a way that takes longer than 5 hours to bring back online.

A larger oplog provides a longer window for secondaries to catch up if they fall behind due to network issues, resource constraints, or maintenance. This is particularly important in high-throughput environments or during planned downtime for secondary nodes.

To determine the appropriate oplog size for your deployment, consider the following:

- Your application's average and peak write volume
- The expected maximum duration of potential outages
- Network reliability between data centers (for geographically distributed deployments)
- The number of secondary nodes (more secondaries may require a larger window)

MongoDB provides tools to monitor oplog usage and estimate your current window:

```
// Check oplog size and replication window
db.printReplicationInfo();

// Sample output:
// configured oplog size: 5120MB
// log length start to end: 86400secs (24hrs)
// oplog first event time: Wed Apr 02 2025 10:03:25 GMT+0000
// oplog last event time: Thu Apr 03 2025 10:03:25 GMT+0000
// now: Thu Apr 03 2025 10:05:01 GMT+0000
```

The oplog boundaries can be set in one of two ways, size and time, as follows:

- `size`: The maximum size of the oplog in megabytes, which can be configured to any value between 990 MB and 1 petabyte
- `minRetentionHours`: The minimum number of hours to preserve an oplog entry

As the oplog is a capped collection, when these configured boundaries are met, the oldest entries in the oplog will be deleted.

Changing the configured size of the oplog from its current value to 16 GB could be done as follows:

```
db.adminCommand({ "replSetResizeOplog": 1, size: Double(16384)})
```

Similarly, if instead of a fixed size you wanted to ensure exactly 48 hours of oplog content was always available, the command would be the following:

```
db.adminCommand({ "replSetResizeOplog": 1, minRetentionHours: 48})
```

> **Risk of disk space exhaustion with `minRetentionHours`**
>
> When `minRetentionHours` is configured, the oplog can grow without constraint so as to retain oplog entries for the configured number of hours. This may result in a reduction or exhaustion of system disk space due to a combination of high write volume and large retention period.

Changing the oplog size or minimum oplog retention period of a given replica set member with `replSetResizeOplog` does not change the oplog size of any other member in the replica set. You must run `replSetResizeOplog` on each replica set member in your cluster to change the oplog size or minimum retention period for all members.

Managing replication lag

Replication lag occurs when secondary nodes cannot keep up with the rate of operations being processed by the primary. This can lead to stale reads and longer failover times if the lagging node needs to become primary. To minimize replication lag, consider implementing the following strategies:

Strategy	Action	Considerations
Optimize networking	Place secondaries closer to the primary or upgrade network links.	Consider dedicated network links between replica set members. Implement bandwidth prioritization for replication traffic.
Scale resources	Increase CPU, memory, or disk I/O capacity.	Upgrade hardware on existing nodes.
Improve read workload targeting	Offload intensive queries to dedicated secondaries tailored for analytics, keeping the rest of the replica set balanced.	Configure read preferences to direct specific workloads to appropriate nodes.

Table 5.3: Strategies to reduce replication lag in MongoDB replica sets

By proactively addressing replication lag through these strategies, you can ensure faster failovers, more consistent read performance, and overall greater stability within your MongoDB replica set. Regular monitoring and fine-tuning based on workload patterns will help maintain optimal replication health as your deployment scales.

Read and write strategies

MongoDB offers flexible strategies for optimizing reads and writes across replica sets. Read preference settings determine which nodes handle read queries, balancing consistency, availability, or latency. Write concern defines how many nodes must acknowledge a write, affecting data durability versus write latency.

Carefully tuning these strategies helps manage latency and maintain resilience. In this section, we will look at the key approaches and considerations for read and write operations in MongoDB.

Read preference

A replica set will contain more than one server that can service an operation, and MongoDB's client libraries can perform server selection based on a configured read preference to ensure operations are routed to the desired server.

By default, an application directs its read operations to the primary member in a replica set (that is, read preference mode is `"primary"`); however, clients can specify a read preference to send read operations to secondaries.

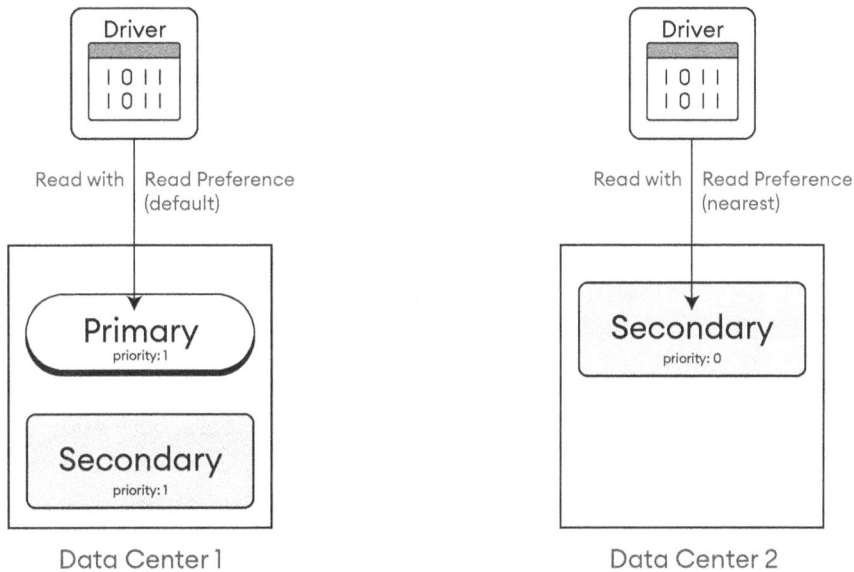

Figure 5.3: MongoDB read preference behavior across data centers

Read preference consists of the read preference mode and optionally, a tag set list, and the `maxStalenessSeconds` option. Since replica set members can lag behind the primary (due to factors such as network congestion, low disk throughput, long-running operations, etc.), the read preference `maxStalenessSeconds` option lets you specify a maximum replication lag, or *staleness*, for reads from secondaries.

When a secondary's estimated staleness exceeds `maxStalenessSeconds`, the client stops using it for read operations. By default, there is no maximum staleness, and clients will not consider a secondary's lag when choosing where to direct a read operation; however, when configuring this option, you must specify a value of 90 seconds or longer.

There are many read preference modes available, which provide varying degrees of flexibility as it relates to maximizing availability and consistency, or minimizing latency.

Read preference mode	Description
primary	The default read preference, where all operations read from the current replica set primary. To maximize consistency and avoid stale reads, this read preference mode should be used.
primaryPreferred	In most situations, operations read from the primary, but if it is unavailable, operations read from secondary members. This read preference mode allows for maximum availability, as consistent read operations will be delivered so long as a primary is available. If the primary is unavailable, however, you can still query secondaries.
secondary	All operations read from the secondary members of the replica set.
secondaryPreferred	Operations typically read data from secondary members of the replica set. If the replica set has only one primary member and no other members, operations read data from the primary member.
nearest	To minimize latency, operations read from a random eligible replica set member, irrespective of whether that member is a primary or secondary, based on a specified latency threshold. The operation considers the following when calculating latency: • The localThresholdMS connection string option • The maxStalenessSeconds read preference option • Any specified tag set lists

Table 5.4: MongoDB read preference modes

For applications that are geographically distributed, a read preference of nearest can further improve read performance as operations will be routed to any member with the smallest latency window, as defined by localThresholdMS (default 15 milliseconds).

If a replica set member or members are associated with tags, you can specify a tag set list (array of tag sets) in the read preference to target those members.

For example, consider the following tag set list with three tag sets:

```
[ { "region": "South", "datacenter": "A" },  { "rack": "rack-1" }, { } ]
```

First, MongoDB tries to find members tagged with both `"region"`: `"South"` and `"datacenter"`: `"A"`. If a member is found, the remaining tag sets are not considered. Instead, MongoDB uses this tag set to find all eligible members.

If a member isn't found, `{ "rack": "rack-1" }` is tried next, followed by the final tag of `{ }`, which will match any eligible member.

> **Note**
>
> Tags and `maxStalenessSeconds` are not compatible with a read preference mode of `primary`.

Read preference configurations allow applications to target the primary or secondary replica set members based on specific needs. This can enhance performance and availability by distributing read loads across multiple nodes, reducing latency, and ensuring continued access to data even if the primary node is unavailable.

Write concern and durability

In MongoDB replica sets, **write concern** is an important configuration option that determines the level of acknowledgment a client requires from the database when performing a write operation. This mechanism directly impacts the delicate balance between data durability and system performance.

Starting in MongoDB 5.0, the implicit default write concern is `w`: `"majority"`. With this write concern, writes request acknowledgment that the calculated majority of data-bearing voting members have durably written the change to their local oplog. The calculated majority is determined by taking the smaller of the following:

- The majority of all voting members (including arbiters)
- The number of all data-bearing voting members.

Write concern for replica sets describes the number of data-bearing members (i.e., the primary and secondaries, but not arbiters) that must acknowledge a write operation before the operation returns as successful.

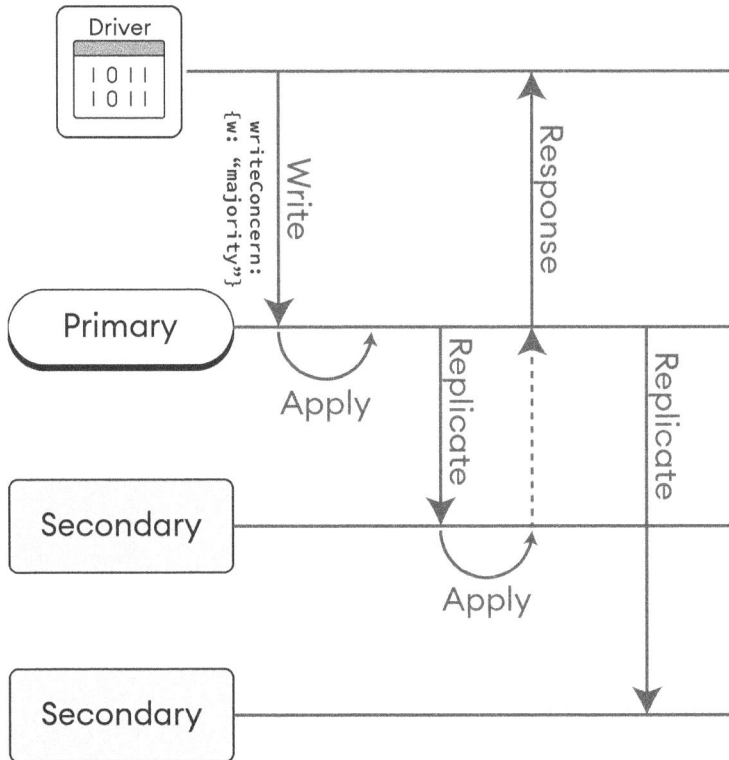

Figure 5.4: Write concern with majority acknowledgment in MongoDB

An application that issues a write operation waits until the primary receives acknowledgment from the required number of members for the specified write concern. For a write concern of w greater than 1 or w : "majority", the primary waits until the required number of secondaries acknowledge the write before returning write concern acknowledgment. For a write concern of w: 1, the primary can return write concern acknowledgment as soon as it locally applies the write, since it is eligible for contributing to the requested write concern.

The more members that acknowledge a write, the less likely the written data is to roll back if the primary fails. However, specifying a high write concern can increase latency as the client must wait until it receives the requested level of write concern acknowledgment.

Write concern is specified using two primary parameters: w and wtimeout. The first parameter (w) determines the number of nodes that must acknowledge the write, and can accept value configurations:

- Number values (1, 2, 3): Specific number of replica set members
- "majority": (Default) A majority of voting members must acknowledge
- Replica set tags: Custom-defined subset of replica set members

The second parameter (wtimeout) specifies a time limit, in milliseconds, for a write operation to propagate to enough members to achieve the write concern after the operation succeeds on the primary. If the wtimeout value is exceeded and a write concern error is returned to the client, the write operation will likely still succeed; however, the client will not be waiting longer than this period for acknowledgement. By default, wtimeout is "infinity", so if you want your application to return an error rather than wait until replication to a calculated majority of the cluster succeeds, you should provide your own appropriate wtimeout value.

The following example demonstrates setting a custom write concern on an insert operation that ensures the write has been acknowledged by the calculated majority of nodes and will return a write concern error if the write hasn't been acknowledged within 5 seconds:

```
db.collection.insertOne(
  { item: "example" },
  {
    writeConcern: {
      w: "majority",
      wtimeout: 5000
    }
  }
);
```

All MongoDB drivers provide the ability to specify write concerns at both the connection level and on a per-operation basis, allowing fine-grained control.

You can modify the global default write concern by issuing the `setDefaultRWConcern` command. From the MongoDB Shell, assuming you have the appropriate privileges to do so, you could modify this value as follows:

```
db.adminCommand({
  "setDefaultRWConcern" : 1,
  "defaultWriteConcern" : {
    "w" : 2
  }
})
```

The preceding example sets the global write concern to `w: 2`. If you issue a write operation with a specific write concern, the write operation uses its own write concern instead of the default.

We recommend leaving `w` at its default `"majority"` value, even though it may seem that latency would be better without waiting for replication. Keep in mind that if the secondaries start falling behind, flow control will kick in and start throttling your writes.

Summary

MongoDB's replication system provides a robust foundation for building highly available and fault-tolerant database deployments. Replica set architecture, combined with automatic failover through elections, ensures that your database can withstand node failures while maintaining data integrity. The oplog serves as the backbone of the replication process, allowing secondary nodes to stay in sync with the primary.

When designing your replica set, consider factors such as the geographical distribution of data and the appropriate oplog size for your workload characteristics. These decisions will significantly impact your database's resilience, performance, and ability to meet your application's specific needs.

Remember that proper configuration is not a one-time task but an ongoing process that should evolve with your application's growth and changing requirements. Through continuous observation and iterative improvements, you can maintain optimal replication behavior even as your MongoDB deployment scales.

In the next chapter, we'll explore how MongoDB's sharding works with replication to provide horizontal scalability for deployments with large datasets and high throughput requirements.

6

Sharding

As modern applications generate and store increasingly vast amounts of data, ensuring high performance and scalability becomes a key concern for any database system. MongoDB's sharding architecture is a solution designed to provide horizontal scalability for applications with massive datasets and demanding throughput requirements. Unlike traditional vertical scaling, which often results in expensive and size-limited hardware upgrades, sharding offers a more efficient and cost-effective way to scale by distributing data across multiple servers. Understanding sharding architecture will help you handle spikes in user activity, global expansion, and growing data complexity.

This chapter delves into the foundational principles of MongoDB's sharding architecture, enabling you to understand how sharding interacts with replication for high scalability and reliability. We'll begin by examining the core components of a sharded cluster and their roles in routing and data distribution. From there, we'll explore critical aspects such as selecting an optimal shard key. Finally, we'll address practical considerations such as shard key refinement, strategic data placement, and techniques for handling large-scale imports and resharding operations. By the end of this chapter, you'll have a strong grasp of MongoDB's sharding ecosystem, enabling you to design scalable architectures that support your application's evolving data demands.

This chapter will cover the following topics:

- How sharding enables horizontal scalability by distributing data across replica sets
- The roles and functionalities of shards, mongos processes, and config servers in a sharded cluster
- Strategies for selecting an efficient shard key to optimize data distribution and query targeting
- Comparing range-based, hashed, and zone-based sharding methods for varying workloads

- Using resharding to redistribute data and address performance bottlenecks without downtime
- Techniques for colocating related data to improve transaction and aggregation query performance
- Configuring and monitoring the balancer to manage chunk migrations effectively
- Approaches to refine shard keys to resolve issues such as jumbo chunks or poor granularity

Understanding core sharding architecture

MongoDB's sharding works with replication to provide **horizontal scaling** for deployments with large datasets and high-throughput requirements. Traditionally, when a workload exceeded the capabilities of the database server, it had to be upgraded to a bigger server. This is known as **vertical scaling**, and it's limited in terms of both the maximum size of any particular server and the price-performance ratio; supercomputers tend to be very expensive! Instead, if you can distribute the workload to multiple smaller servers, you can theoretically scale your workload horizontally nearly infinitely, with, ideally, the costs rising linearly with the number of servers. This is what MongoDB sharding allows you to do when your workload outgrows the capabilities of a single replica set.

If your workload has multiple distinct databases that are relatively isolated from each other, there is nothing wrong with deploying a separate replica set for each one of them. For instance, you might have a separate replica set for users, another for accounts, and a third one for user activity. However, over time, even a single cluster may no longer be able to handle a distinct subset of your overall application workload. That's when it becomes necessary to shard or partition the workload across multiple shards, each one of which is itself a replica set.

So, when your data grows beyond what a single replica set can handle, sharding distributes it across multiple replica sets, each containing a subset of your data. This horizontal scaling allows MongoDB to handle massive datasets and high throughput requirements. This section reviews what the architecture of a sharded cluster is and its important performance elements.

Architectural components of a sharded cluster

A sharded cluster consists of several components: **shards** (each a replica set responsible for a subset of data in the cluster), **mongos processes** (which are primarily responsible for routing operations to different shards and returning results back to the client), and **config servers** (a special replica set that maintains metadata about sharding configuration and location of data in the cluster). Starting from MongoDB version 8.0, config servers don't need to be separate servers and can be embedded with one of the shards.

mongos is the most interesting component here because from the point of view of the driver or client application, it acts as if it's the database, accepting CRUD operation requests and returning results to the driver. On the flip side, it acts as the proxy for the driver when it's talking to shards, sending them CRUD operations, and then forwarding the result back to the driver. Normally, there are multiple mongos processes in a production sharded cluster. *Figure 6.1* shows all the components of a sharded cluster and how the application connects to it.

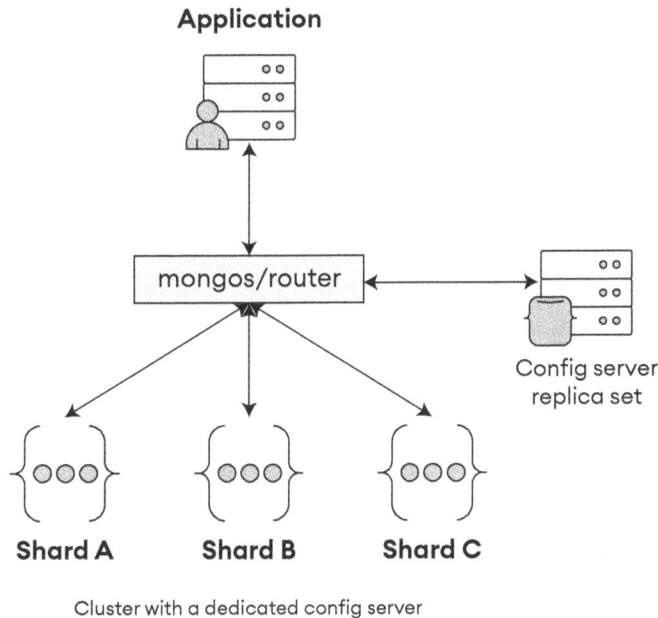

Cluster with a dedicated config server

Figure 6.1: Sharded cluster architecture

But how does mongos know which shards to forward the operations to? Based on the information persisted in the config servers, mongos keeps a current *routing table*, meaning for each collection, it knows where its data lives, and if the collection is sharded, it tracks where each part of the collection is located. It then forwards the operations it receives to one or more shards, as needed, and if it's more than one shard, then it also has to merge or combine results from each of the shards to return a single result to the client.

Sharding a collection and selecting a shard key

When you first deploy a sharded cluster, you have to decide how you want to distribute the data across the shards. This is critical for achieving horizontal scalability because a scalable sharded cluster distributes data in a way that operations are divided equally across all the shards. This means you want all your read and write operations to be spread roughly equally across all the shards.

While you can choose to isolate different collections to different shards, most commonly, sharding is employed when you have a large enough collection that can't be handled by a single shard. At this point, you have to shard or partition the collection, and you get to decide how it will be partitioned by selecting a shard key.

The shard key value is used to split the collection logically into ranges, called chunks. These chunks are then distributed across shards in a way that aims to balance the data evenly across all the shards. In older versions of MongoDB, this typically meant that each shard had roughly the same number of chunks, but in newer versions, chunks are only split when necessary. As a result, while data is still distributed evenly, this doesn't necessarily translate into the same number of chunks on each shard.

Consider a simple example: if your shard key is username and the values of username range from aaaa to zzzz, then your chunks may be divided into ranges such as a-b, c-d, e-f, and so on. The balancer, a background process that runs on the sharded cluster, will automatically distribute data corresponding to these chunk ranges to all the shards, ensuring approximately equal distribution of data.

> **Balancer limitations in assessing shard key activity**
>
> The balancer acts based on data size alone and cannot determine which ranges of shard key values may be more *active* than others.

Now, mongos will route operations that include username starting with a specific letter to the shard that *owns* the chunk range that includes this username.

You must be wondering, what happens to a request that doesn't include a username? In such cases, mongos has to send the request to all the shards. This type of request is called a **broadcast** or **scatter-gather** operation, and it doesn't scale horizontally nearly as effectively as targeted single-shard operations.

Why scatter-gather is bad

It's a common misconception that scatter-gather queries are efficient simply because each shard only has to process a small subset of the data. While this may seem intuitively true, and indeed mirrors how the original map-reduce data process worked (by splitting huge amounts of work across many servers), this approach doesn't scale well horizontally in most cases. Let's explore why that is.

When a query request goes to a single shard, that shard executes the operation and sends the results back to mongos, which forwards them to the client. But when a query request targets all the shards (a scatter-gather operation), each shard has to execute the operation on its own portion of the data and send the result back to mongos to merge and forward it to the client. Notice something about these two scenarios? In targeted queries, only one shard has to execute the operation. In scatter-gather queries, every shard has to execute the operation.

So, in a cluster with 20 shards, a single scatter-gather operation is translated into 20 operations. Even though it may seem like a *cheaper* operation, processing only 1/20th of the total data, the operation execution overhead is still the same for each shard, and mongos has to do the extra work of merging the results. In some cases, mongos cannot start returning data to the client until it has heard back from every shard that received the query.

Suppose your cluster is processing tens or hundreds of thousands of queries. Here's how a single request going to one shard versus a scatter-gather query scaling across a 20-shard cluster will look:

Client queries	Targeted queries only	Scatter-gather queries only
100	100	2,000
1,000	1,000	20,000
10,000	10,000	200,000
100,000	100,000	2,000,000

Table 6.1: Table showing total queries executing across all 20 shards

Now, imagine if you were to double the number of shards in *Table 6.1*. The targeted queries column will remain the same, but the scatter-gather queries column will double! So, you don't get the benefit of linear scaling because increasing the number of shards in your cluster will increase the total number of queries too. As an additional detriment, scatter-gather queries that need to hear from all the shards increasingly get slower as the number of shards grows. This is because the chances of one shard experiencing a latency hiccup (such as a network misconfiguration, an election, or a crash) also increase. This contributes to additional latency to every broadcast query, unlike targeted queries, which only impact a subset of queries directed to the impacted shard.

Strategic shard key selection

Shard key selection is a critical decision that directly impacts the performance and scalability of a sharded cluster. A good shard key can target the operations to specific shards, provide appropriate granularity to evenly distribute data, and minimize the risk of creating hot shards. Let's look at some important elements of a good shard key.

Shard key for targeting operations

To understand how data partitioning influences the distribution of operations, let's look at another example of how collections can be partitioned across shards based on the defined shard key.

Suppose you have an `orders` collection. You might partition it by `order_id`, which is unique and will allow many chunk ranges to be created, allowing fine distribution of data across shards. However, if `order_id` is monotonically increasing, then the *last* chunk (the one from a high `order_id` to `maxInt` range) will always get all the new inserts.

That may or may not be a problem. If new order creation is the bottleneck in your system, this could be problematic, but if new orders are created relatively infrequently and the majority of the load is from orders being updated, read, or aggregated, it may not be a big issue.

Now, let's consider an operation that reads all recent orders for a particular customer. Since you don't know which *range* the customers' orders are in, you will have to broadcast the query to all the shards that have chunks for the orders collection, as shown in *Figure 6.2*, and that's problematic for horizontal scalability.

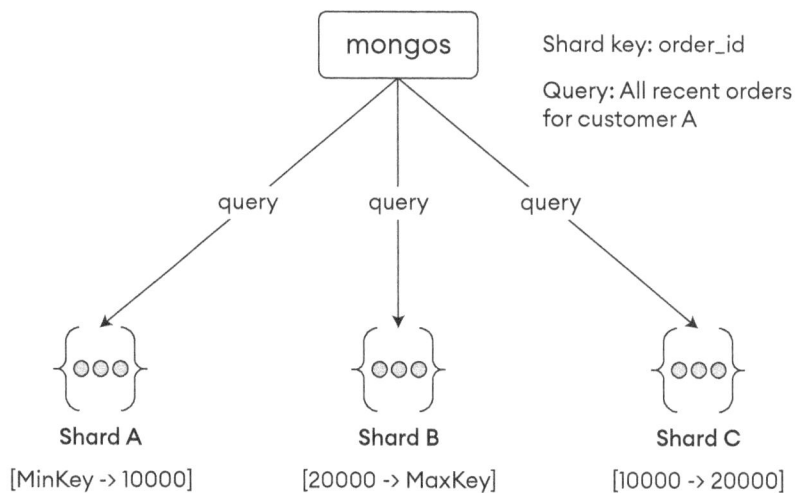

Figure 6.2: Broadcasting query

If you know that your application will always have the `customer_id` value when it's dealing with an order (a reasonable assumption), it would be better to use a compound shard key such as `{customer_id:1,order_id:1}`. This will keep each customer's orders on a single shard (since they will tend to fall within a single chunk), and queries about a particular customer's orders will be targeted to a single shard instead of scattered to all shards.

In *Figure 6.3*, all the orders for customer A are within the chunk covering from the lowest customer_id (inclusive) to customer I (exclusive), which is on shard A. As such, the query for all the recent orders for customer A will only be sent to shard A. As an additional benefit, new orders will no longer be created on the same shard. However, in this case, all your operations on orders must include both customer_id and order_id values in the query to ensure they're targeted to a single shard.

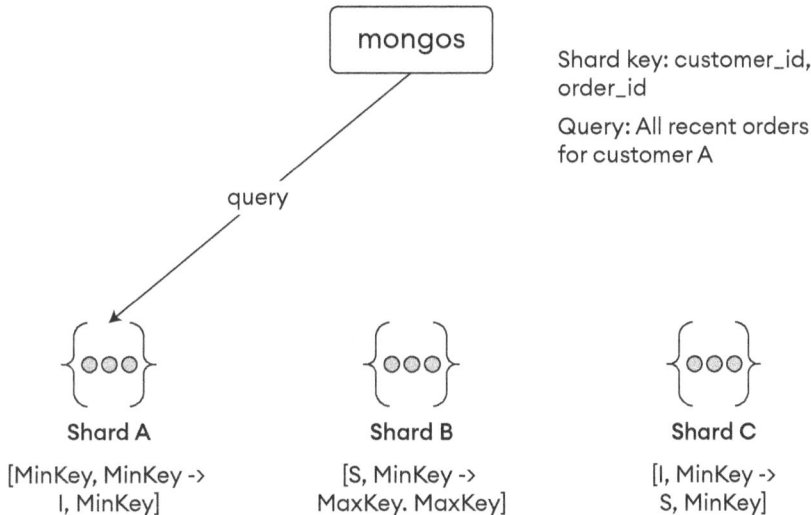

Figure 6.3: Targeting query

Scaling sharded clusters is all about targeting operations to as few shards as possible. A great shard key will allow the majority of the operations to be targeted to a single shard.

Shard key with good granularity

You've probably heard that it's important to choose a shard key that gives you good granularity, primarily because it allows chunks to split effectively. The example we looked at in the previous section illustrated this well. Since order_id is unique, any shard key that includes it as a component can be easily split into smaller chunks. But why is granularity so important, and what will happen if your shard key isn't granular enough?

Imagine a multi-tenant system where the shard key is tenant_id. At first glance, it seems like a good idea because every tenant operation *always* includes the tenant_id value, which is great for targeting the operations for a specific tenant to one shard, and new tenants are not created fast enough for you to worry about all the inserts going into a single chunk range. However, what if one single tenant became a power user, generating so much data in the collection that it is just too big to fit on one shard?

The way that you can locate data on two shards is by deciding which values of the shard key will live where. However, in our case, all of the tenant's data has the same shard key value, making the data *unsplittable*, and the chunk that contains the data is now labeled a *jumbo* chunk. In *Figure 6.4*, tenant_I has a lot of data, and the chunk from tenant_I (inclusive) to tenant_J (exclusive) is labeled jumbo. Shard B has more data than shard A, however, since the chunk is unsplittable, the balancer is unable to move data from shard B to shard A to balance the data. This is where refining or extending the shard key can help by adding another field as a component of the shard key *after* tenant_id.

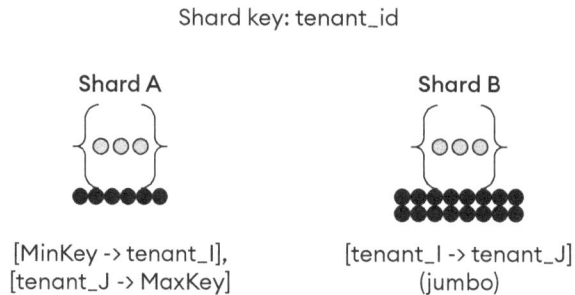

Figure 6.4: Shard key on tenant_id

Luckily, there is a command to refine the shard key without any downtime, and it allows you to extend your shard key when it's not granular enough. This is an inexpensive operation as it allows you to add a field or multiple fields without having to move any data. Once the shard key is extended with another field (for instance, _id or another field that makes sense in your data model), MongoDB can then split the chunk for the big tenant on the _id value, and some of its data can be balanced or moved to another shard. In *Figure 6.5*, after refining the shard key, the previous jumbo chunk can now be split, and some of the data can be moved to the other shard.

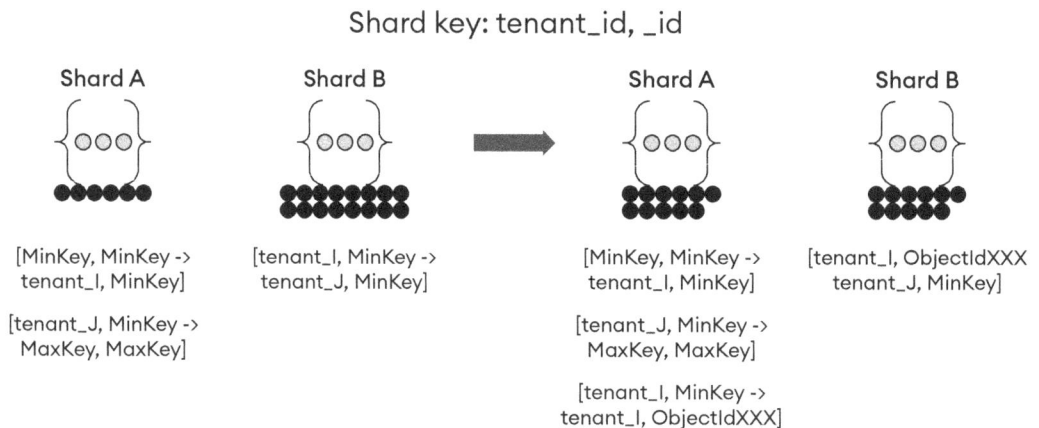

Figure 6.5: Refine the shard key and wait for the data to be balanced

The best shard key will be granular enough to allow splitting ranges of data for better distribution across shards.

Avoid increasing or decreasing shard key values

You may have read that a monotonically increasing shard key is a bad idea. In fact, as highlighted in the earlier example, it is something you should be concerned about if there is likely to be a bottleneck of new document inserts. Let's look at an example where that would likely be the case and why it would be a problem.

Think back to the *Socialite* app example from *Chapter 2*, *Schema Design for Performance*. Consider the content collection, which receives user posts. This collection experiences a high number of writes, primarily from users inserting new posts into the collection. Now imagine sharding the content collection by the _id value of each post, using the default ObjectId type. Since the first four bytes of ObjectId represent the current timestamp, you might think it is useful to have it as a proxy for created time, and that it's not a bad idea to have all recent posts on the same shard for targeting purposes. After all, users usually only want to read the most recent posts, right? However, what this results in is every insert going into the *highest* chunk range.

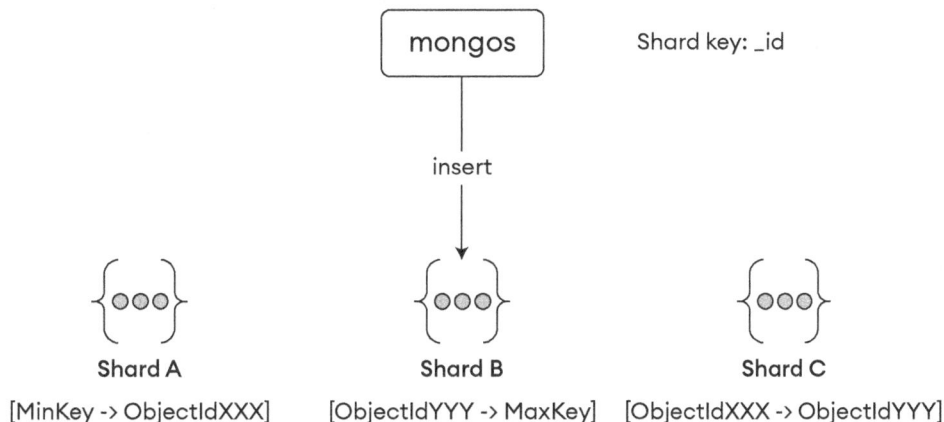

Figure 6.6: Hot shard caused by a monotonically increasing shard key

As you can see in *Figure 6.6*, new inserts are going to turn whichever shard has the top chunk into the hot shard, while the other shards won't receive any writes at all (since posts are usually neither updated nor deleted). Even if your schema design includes updating posts with something such as the count of likes, the activity will be concentrated on only recent posts (because how often do users go back months to like someone's post from back then?). So, the only writes that aren't going to the *top chunk* would be the deletes (when users decide to clean up or archive old content), right? But even those would also create a hot chunk by going to the lowest range values!

You also wouldn't get any benefit from targeting the reads, because when you query for posts to show to someone, they are usually either your friends' posts or your own posts. The query would look something like this:

```
// Query to get latest 20 posts for a subset of users
// This query may result in a scatter-gather operation

db.posts.find({userId:{$in:[ "..." ]}}).sort({_id:-1}).limit(20)
```

This kind of query, to get the latest 20 posts to show for a subset of users, is likely to result in a scatter-gather query. Not only that, but such a query requires waiting for all shards to sort their results, merge them on mongos, and start returning any results to the client. Since the most important thing in a social media app with a feed is to start showing results as quickly as possible, this is not acceptable.

The solution would probably be to use a better shard key. The most obvious one would be to shard by {userId:1, _id:1}, which will likely colocate every user's content in the same chunk, meaning that as hundreds or thousands of users are creating new posts, they will likely be distributed to all the shards that own the chunks for those users. If your userId is random (as any user-selected name would be), your distribution will be random as well. But even if you use some sort of system-generated, unique, monotonically increasing value, and even if your new users tend to be more active at first, this would be balanced out by all the already-existing users creating content and distributing the writes more or less evenly across the shards.

This is a similar approach to one we saw in the earlier example of orders, where prefixing customer_id to order_id makes a better shard key than just order_id alone. In multi-user or multi-tenant systems, always consider making the leading field of the shard key your user or tenant ID to maximize query targeting for each user or tenant.

Note that it's not necessarily a good idea to randomize a monotonically increasing shard key value by hashing it. We will look at some trade-offs to consider before deciding to hash your shard key in the next section.

If you're still not confident in your shard key choice before sharding or resharding a collection, you can always use the configureQueryAnalyzer command to collect a sample of queries on your collection, then run the analyzeShardKey command to evaluate a shard key for this collection.

Types of sharding

Fundamentally, MongoDB supports one core mechanism for distributing data across shards: **range-based sharding**. However, it also offers two special flavors that are best for different use cases: **hashed sharding** and **zone-based sharding**. Let's explore how they work, how they are related to each other, and when each would be an appropriate choice.

Range-based sharding

Range sharding is the default and most intuitive approach. This is what we have been describing in this chapter so far. Range sharding splits data by the natural order of shard key values and then distributes the ranges of data to different shards. This is the right method for most use cases; just be sure to pick a good shard key for your read and write patterns. All the examples we've discussed so far use regular range sharding. All other sharding methods use range sharding as their foundation, but they give you additional abilities on top to either change the values used for ranges or to influence how the ranges are balanced across your cluster.

Hashed sharding

Hashed sharding takes your shard key, runs it through a hash function, and then applies ranges to those hashed values. The result is similar to shuffling all your pages before placing them into volumes, which is great for spreading things out randomly. All the operations automatically do this hashing, so your application doesn't need to change anything in the way it queries the data.

Imagine storing logs or events in a huge collection where the _id value of each event is always increasing. With range sharding, all those records have to be inserted into the same shard. But if you use { _id: "hashed" }, the system will distribute them randomly, avoiding insert hotspots.

There are multiple pitfalls and extra costs with hashing the shard key value. Range queries on the hashed shard key are inefficient, and there is an additional random access index to maintain on every insert. Most importantly, you need to remember that you don't gain any additional *granularity* by hashing the shard key value. If your distribution is bad because of poor granularity of the shard key (not enough distinct values), then hashing them won't change that at all. You'll still have poor distribution with the added overhead of a hashed key.

In cases where a hashed shard key is still the best option for your use case, MongoDB version 7.0 introduced the ability to drop the hashed index, provided you have a different index to support the shard key and your collection is already balanced. Once you drop the hashed shard key index, no more balancing takes place, but you save on having to maintain the hashed index on every insert.

Zone-based sharding

Zone sharding is a way to control which ranges of data reside on which sets of shards based on a policy that you create. It's a way to introduce geography into the picture, or just a way to limit a sharded collection to a subset of shards. There are two steps to follow to use zone sharding. You assign zone tags or labels to a shard or set of shards, and then specify shard key ranges to be associated with these specific zones, giving you control over where the data is physically stored.

Consider a global SaaS company that wants to store user data for European users in the EU for compliance. By zoning shard ranges for the "EU" region to Frankfurt-based shards and the "NA" region to North America-based shards, it keeps data local, fast to access, and policy-compliant.

Here is what those steps look like in database commands that shard the collection, assign appropriate zones to shards, and add shard key ranges to zones:

```
// Shard a collection and assign zones for geo-based data placement
sh.shardCollection("db.coll", {country:1, userid:1})
sh.addShardToZone("shard0", "NA")
sh.addShardToZone("shard1", "EU")
sh.addTagRange("db.coll",
{country:"DE",userid:MinKey},{country:"DE",userid:MaxKey},"EU")
sh.addTagRange("db.coll",
{country:"US",userid:MinKey},{country:"US",userid:MaxKey},"NA")
```

You can find more examples in the MongoDB documentation:

- *Segmenting Data by Location*: https://www.mongodb.com/docs/manual/tutorial/sharding-segmenting-data-by-location/

- *Segmenting Data by Application or Customer*: https://www.mongodb.com/docs/manual/tutorial/sharding-segmenting-shards/

- *Distributed Local Writes for Insert Only Workloads*: https://www.mongodb.com/docs/manual/tutorial/sharding-high-availability-writes/

- *Distribute Collections Using Zones*: https://www.mongodb.com/docs/manual/tutorial/sharding-distribute-collections-with-zones/

Once the number of shards in your cluster grows, you will want to exercise more control over where each sharded (and unsharded) collection is located. For instance, you may have two huge sharded collections across 10 shards, but rather than having each collection on each of the 10 shards, you may prefer to have each collection only on 5 of its own shards. This can help in a number of ways:

if the workload generated by each collection is different, you could allocate different resources via asymmetrical shard scaling, and any scatter-gather operations that are sent to every shard the collection lives on would only be sent to half as many shards. Since decreasing the number of total operations in the cluster helps scalability, this is a simple way to achieve that. As a bonus, if you have unexpected trouble with one of your shards, only one of the two collections will be impacted rather than both.

To distribute two collections to a subset of shards, the database commands might look like this:

```
// Example of distributing collections to subsets of shards using zones
sh.addShardToZone("shard0", "C1")
sh.addShardToZone("shard1", "C1")
sh.addShardToZone("shard2", "C2")
sh.addShardToZone("shard3", "C2")
sh.addTagRange("db.coll1",{"<shKey>":MinKey},{"<shKey>":MaxKey},"C1")
sh.addTagRange("db.coll2",{"<shKey>":MinKey},{"<shKey>":MaxKey},"C2")
```

These commands first label each shard with either a C1 or C2 label, and then assign the coll1 collection to shards labeled C1 and the coll2 collection to shards labeled C2. You would use your actual shard key field names for <shKey>. This control adds complexity. You need to manage zones and range boundaries and how they map to zones, monitor balance across shards, and plan for uneven growth.

While there are advantages of isolating each sharded collection to its own subset of shards, there are two cases where doing so should be avoided, and instead, collections should be colocated on the same shards with shard key ranges that keep related data together. One is to support multi-document transactions across two collections staying on a single shard; the other is keeping $lookup operations between two collections from needing to work across the network. We'll discuss this further in the *Colocating sharded collection chunks together* section, later in this chapter.

Advanced sharding administration

When working with sharded clusters, there are a handful of operational considerations that, while not part of the core sharding mechanics, are important to understand if you want to keep your deployment efficient and responsive over time. These include resharding when things go sideways, pre-splitting for large data loads into new collections, managing the balancer, moving unsharded collections, and understanding how to best distribute your data for best performance.

Resharding: Whether, when, and how

Picking the right shard key the first time is ideal, but let's face it, sometimes we make the wrong decision the first time, and other times, real-world usage patterns evolve. What started as a good key might become a bottleneck. Maybe you chose a hashed shard key on a field that was already randomized without realizing the extra overhead caused by it, and now you want to change it to a regular ranged shard key. Or maybe you used `order_id` for your orders collection and now you realize that the majority of your queries for a particular customer's orders are scatter-gathered and not targeted, and you want to change the shard key to `{customer_id, order_id}` because it allows better targeting of queries.

MongoDB's resharding feature gives you a second chance. Without downtime, you can change the shard key to something more appropriate that lets your data be rewritten across shards without downtime. Resharding is a background operation; it reads and rewrites all your data behind the scenes, but when it completes, you're left with a better-distributed collection and a system that can breathe again.

Resharding is not just for changing your shard key; it can be used with an existing shard key to redistribute or rewrite your collection to existing shards faster than it might take the balancer to move chunks and clean up orphans. Starting from MongoDB version 8.0, you can run the `reshardCollection` command on your collection using the same shard key by setting the `forceRedistribution` option to `true`. Consider using it if you are adding or removing multiple shards at once, or after sharding an existing unsharded collection. In *Figure 6.7*, there are three shards in this cluster, and there is an unsharded collection on shard A. Now, the data in this collection has grown and you want to shard it. As a shard can only be involved in one chunk migration at a time, the balancer can only move the data from shard A to either shard B or shard C at a time. The balancing speed could be slow. Also, after a chunk is migrated, shard A would need to delete its original copy of the data in this chunk, and the disk space is not reclaimed automatically. If you reshard this collection immediately after sharding it, the resharding mechanism then creates a temporary collection, and all three shards can read the data from shard A and rewrite it to the temporary collection in parallel. When resharding completes, it will rename the temporary collection and drop the original collection. The disk space is reclaimed automatically on shard A.

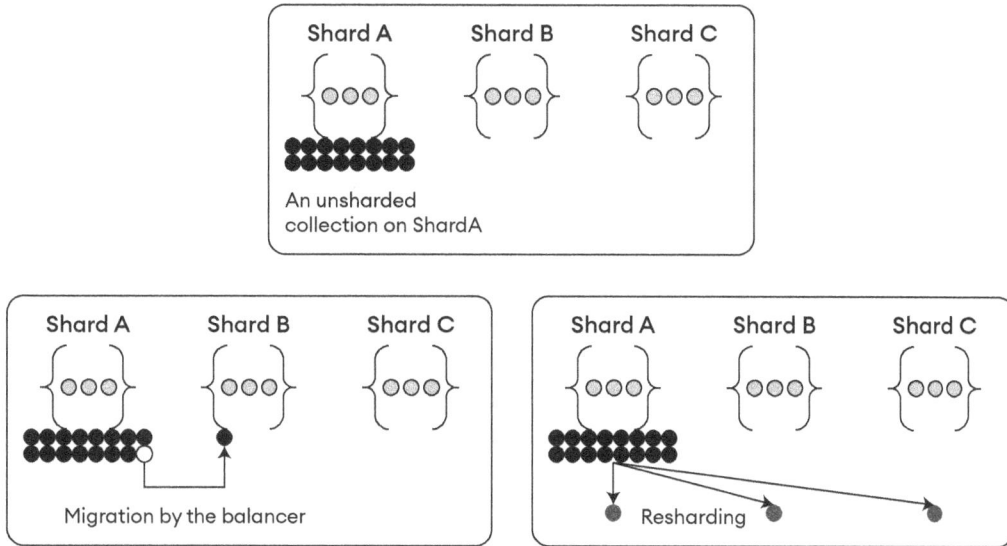

Figure 6.7: Chunk migration versus resharding

See the documentation for more details, restrictions, and examples: https://www.mongodb.com/docs/manual/core/sharding-reshard-a-collection/.

The command to refine (or extend) your shard key that we mentioned in the *Shard key with good granularity* section is different from the resharding command, since extending the shard key with additional fields does not require moving any data from their current shards. Read more about refining the shard key in the documentation: https://www.mongodb.com/docs/manual/core/sharding-refine-a-shard-key/#std-label-shard-key-refine.

Balancer considerations

Behind the scenes of a MongoDB sharded cluster, the balancer works to ensure that data is evenly distributed across shards. Its job is to monitor data distribution and move chunks when things get uneven, keeping the system balanced. But while it's turned on by default and it's easy to forget about it, the balancer isn't free, and understanding its behavior can be key to avoiding unintended side effects.

First, there is overhead. Each chunk migration triggered by the balancer involves copying data from one shard to another, updating the metadata in the config servers, and deleting the original copy of the data. While these operations are efficient and safe, they still consume I/O, CPU, and network bandwidth. On a lightly loaded cluster, you might never notice it happening. On a busy production system, especially during peak demand hours, those background moves can compete with your application's operations for resources and slow things down.

This is why MongoDB allows you to set balancer windows, specific hours during which chunk migrations are allowed. For instance, you might restrict balancing to overnight hours or off-peak periods when traffic is lowest. This lets you maintain optimal performance during the day while still allowing the system to redistribute data when it's safer to do so without noticeable impact.

But even with balancing windows set, you'll want to keep an eye on things. The balancer can act based on data size, not on access frequency. That means it might not catch *hot* shards that serve more traffic, even if they hold fewer documents. Regularly reviewing the distribution of not just data but load is essential to avoiding silent performance degradation. The `balancerStatus`, `currentOp`, and `sh.status()` commands are your friends here, as well as monitoring charts showing you the number of operations on each shard. The last thing to remember is that the balancer is great at moving small chunks of data around to restore balance in a somewhat-unbalanced sharded collection. When you need entire shards to be populated with data, resharding may be faster.

Pre-splitting: Whether, when, and how

Most of the time, MongoDB's balancer does a great job of reacting to growing data and keeping it distributed. But in some scenarios, such as large initial imports, you don't want to insert everything into one shard and then wait for the balancer to catch up. That's where pre-splitting comes in.

Pre-splitting depends on your shard key value range. You'll need to create a script that splits the full range of shard key values into several chunks and distributes them evenly among the shards that will receive new data using the `moveRange` command. If your shard key value is a string, use ranges such as `MinKey-k`, `k-s`, and `s-MaxKey`, if you want to start with chunks on three shards. If your values are of other types, figure out the approximate range of values in your dataset and then split them accordingly. Remember that you don't have to be very precise as the balancer will easily handle smaller imbalances once enough of your data is loaded. What you want to avoid is having all the data going to a single shard at the beginning.

Generally, you want to use pre-splitting before a bulk import into a brand-new empty collection, or during the early stage of setting up a new cluster. Pre-splitting is simplest when you understand how your data is distributed ahead of time, and you want to start off on the right foot.

Pre-splitting is proactive. It shifts your mindset from reactive load management to deliberate data planning, and in the right hands, it's one of the most effective ways to ensure your cluster starts and stays healthy.

Moving unsharded collections

Not every collection in your database will be sharded. In fact, all smaller collections will be unsharded, and only collections too large to fit on one shard should be sharded. Just like not every sharded collection needs to live on every shard, unsharded collections don't need to live together on one primary shard. In fact, it would usually be better to distribute them evenly among your shards, because even unsharded data can cause issues if it causes your cluster distribution to be uneven. Imagine small daily collections for events where each day you dump the data into a separate unsharded collection (and eventually drop old ones). If all the days are on the same shard, that shard will eventually become overwhelmed, not because of sharding, but because of an imbalance of unsharded collections.

In these situations, the moveCollection command (supported starting in MongoDB version 8.0) should be your tool of choice. It lets you manually move an entire unsharded collection from one shard to another. It's not automatic, and it does briefly block writes during the move if you are running it on an active collection (usually for just a few seconds), but it can be a lifesaver in rebalancing workloads without going through the complexity of sharding a collection that doesn't need to be sharded. As a bonus, if you anticipate this and execute moveCollection right at the beginning when you first create the collection, moving an empty collection is going to be fast and low cost.

In *Figure 6.8*, originally, the unsharded A-H collections in the testdb database are all on shard0. We can run the following commands to move some of them to shard1 to distribute the data in this cluster:

```
// Move unsharded collections to specific shards
// Useful for balancing unsharded data across the cluster
db.adminCommand({moveCollection:"testdb.E", toShard:"shard1"})
db.adminCommand({moveCollection:"testdb.F", toShard:"shard1"})
db.adminCommand({moveCollection:"testdb.G", toShard:"shard1"})
db.adminCommand({moveCollection:"testdb.H", toShard:"shard1"})
```

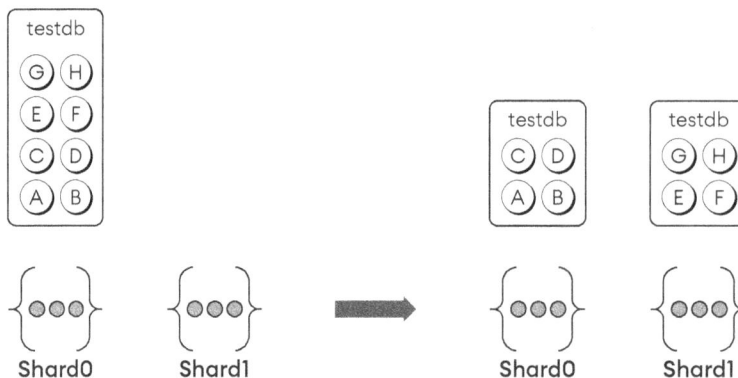

Figure 6.8: Moving unsharded collections

Colocating sharded collection chunks together

As was mentioned in the *Zone-based sharding* section, there are two cases where it may be beneficial for performance to disable the balancer and manually (via scripting) colocate two or more collections on the same shards with shard key ranges that keep related data together. The first case where it can significantly help is multi-document transactions, where single-shard transactions are significantly more performant than multi-shard ones, and the other is aggregations with $lookup operations between two collections, where keeping related ranges on the same shards allows the pipeline to execute locally rather than needing to send data across the network to another shard.

An example of that is the case of the TPC-C benchmark commerce data, which has collections for warehouses, districts, customers, and orders. We can use range sharding on each of these collections, which share prefixes to locate the same values on the same shards:

Collection	Shard key
WAREHOUSE	w_id
DISTRICT	w_id, d_id
CUSTOMER	w_id, d_id, c_id
ORDERS	w_id, d_id, c_id, o_id

Table 6.2: Collections and their shard keys for the TPC-C benchmark

To achieve colocation, we would disable the balancer for these collections, then split them on the same prefix (w_id) values, and move the chunk ranges with the same values to the same shards. Alternatively, we can associate the zone ranges on the same prefix (w_id) values with the same zone using the following commands, and let the balancer split and move the chunk ranges accordingly:

```
// Colocating sharded collection chunks together for TPC-C benchmark
sh.shardCollection("db.WAREHOUSE", {w_id:1})
sh.shardCollection("db.DISTRICT", {w_id:1, d_id:1})
sh.shardCollection("db.CUSTOMER", {w_id:1, d_id:1, c_id:1})
sh.shardCollection("db.ORDERS", {w_id:1, d_id:1, c_id:1, o_id:1})


// Associate each shard to a unique zone
sh.addShardToZone("shardA", "ZoneA")
sh.addShardToZone("shardB", "ZoneB")
sh.addShardToZone("shardC", "ZoneC")


// For each collection, associate the range with the same prefix to the
same zone
sh.addTagRange("db.WAREHOUSE",{w_id:MinKey},{w_id:33},"ZoneA")
sh.addTagRange("db.DISTRICT", {w_id:MinKey,d_id:MinKey},
{w_id:33, d_id:MinKey},"ZoneA")
sh.addTagRange("db.CUSTOMER", {w_id:MinKey,d_id:MinKey,c_id:MinKey},
{w_id:33,d_id:MinKey,c_id:MinKey},"ZoneA")
sh.addTagRange("db.ORDERS", {w_id:MinKey,d_id:MinKey,c_id:MinKey,
o_id:MinKey}, {w_id:33, d_id:MinKey,c_id:MinKey,o_id:MinKey},"ZoneA")


sh.addTagRange("db.WAREHOUSE", {w_id:33},{w_id:66},"ZoneB")
sh.addTagRange("db.DISTRICT", {w_id:33,d_id:MinKey},
{w_id:66,d_id:MinKey},"ZoneB")
sh.addTagRange("db.CUSTOMER", {w_id:33,d_id:MinKey,c_id:MinKey},
{w_id:66,d_id:MinKey, c_id:MinKey},"ZoneB")
sh.addTagRange("db.ORDERS", {w_id:33,d_id:MinKey,c_id:MinKey,o_id:MinKey},
{w_id:66,d_id:MinKey,c_id:MinKey,o_id:MinKey},"ZoneB")


sh.addTagRange("db.WAREHOUSE", {w_id:66}, {w_id:MaxKey},"ZoneC")
sh.addTagRange("db.DISTRICT", {w_id:66,d_id:MinKey},
{w_id:MaxKey, d_id:MaxKey},"ZoneC")
sh.addTagRange("db.CUSTOMER", {w_id:66,d_id:MinKey,c_id:MinKey},
{w_id:MaxKey, d_id:MaxKey, c_id:MaxKey},"ZoneC")
sh.addTagRange("db.ORDERS", {w_id:66,d_id:MinKey,c_id:MinKey,o_id:MinKey},
{w_id:MaxKey,d_id:MaxKey,c_id:MaxKey,o_id:MaxKey},"ZoneC")
```

Figure 6.9 shows that after the zone ranges are defined, the balancer splits and moves the chunks to the corresponding shard associated with the zone.

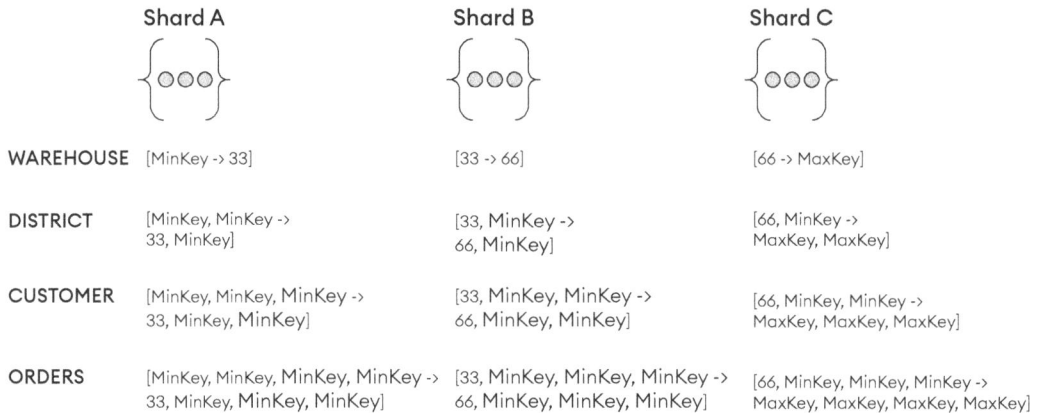

	Shard A	Shard B	Shard C
WAREHOUSE	[MinKey -> 33]	[33 -> 66]	[66 -> MaxKey]
DISTRICT	[MinKey, MinKey -> 33, MinKey]	[33, MinKey -> 66, MinKey]	[66, MinKey -> MaxKey, MaxKey]
CUSTOMER	[MinKey, MinKey, MinKey -> 33, MinKey, MinKey]	[33, MinKey, MinKey -> 66, MinKey, MinKey]	[66, MinKey, MinKey -> MaxKey, MaxKey, MaxKey]
ORDERS	[MinKey, MinKey, MinKey, MinKey -> 33, MinKey, MinKey, MinKey]	[33, MinKey, MinKey, MinKey -> 66, MinKey, MinKey, MinKey]	[66, MinKey, MinKey, MinKey -> MaxKey, MaxKey, MaxKey, MaxKey]

Figure 6.9: Same ranges for different collections on the same shard

While this may seem operationally complex, in reality, this would be scripted, and after being tested in a staging environment, the process in production would just be to run the script to initialize the data distribution automatically.

By partitioning the same warehouse ID values to the same shards, we maximize the likelihood that transactions that involve the same customer, orders, districts, and warehouses will happen on a single shard. This is the same way that we would minimize cross-shard $lookup for aggregation queries that need to look up the details for related entities.

Just like every decision about your MongoDB schema and indexes depends on your requirements and the trade-offs you're able to make, so does the decision to shard for performance and scalability of your cluster. Selecting the shard key with your SLAs in mind is imperative to ensure that you are optimizing for what's most important. There's usually no perfect answer, just trade-offs. The key is to understand your application's dominant access patterns. Are you reading data by entity or writing it in bulk? Do you expect some entities to dominate the workload? Balance is possible, but it starts with modeling intentionally, and it continues with monitoring, iterating, and sometimes... yes, resharding.

Summary

MongoDB's sharding architecture is a powerful and flexible tool for achieving horizontal scalability in deployments with massive datasets and demanding throughput requirements. By understanding the core components of a sharded cluster, the importance of shard key selection, and the variety of sharding methods available, you can design a system that efficiently distributes and targets operations. Additionally, the advanced techniques discussed, such as refining shard keys, using zoning for strategic data placement, pre-splitting during bulk imports, and balancing workloads across shards, all contribute to maintaining an efficient and responsive cluster as your data and workload scale. Effective sharding is not just about distributing data, but also about anticipating and managing the nuances of query patterns, operational overhead, and evolving needs. With this knowledge, you're well positioned to create scalable and robust architectures that can support the growing demands of your application.

In the next chapter on storage engines, we'll shift our focus from data distribution to data storage, diving deeper into the WiredTiger storage engine, the default and most commonly used storage engine for MongoDB.

Get This Book's PDF Version and Exclusive Extras

UNLOCK NOW

Scan the QR code (or go to packtpub.com/unlock). Search for this book by name, confirm the edition, and then follow the steps on the page.

Note: Keep your invoice handy. Purchases made directly from Packt don't require an invoice.

7

Storage Engines

As we saw in *Chapter 1, Systems and MongoDB Architecture*, WiredTiger is a component within the MongoDB server and the most common storage engine for MongoDB. Storage engines act as the interface between the logical structure of the data (as seen by users, applications, and higher layers of the database) and the physical storage of that data. As such, they are a critical factor when diagnosing and resolving performance issues. This chapter aims to equip you with a high-level understanding of the WiredTiger storage engine, enabling you to make informed decisions about its configuration. By the end of this chapter, you will have a solid grasp of WiredTiger's performance-related inner workings and the knowledge to fine-tune it for efficiency.

The topics covered in this chapter include the following:

- An overview of storage engines and their role in MongoDB
- The architecture of WiredTiger, including its storage format, concurrency control, and caching strategies
- How WiredTiger manages its cache, ensures data durability, and handles recovery from unexpected failures
- The compression algorithms supported by WiredTiger, and the trade-offs between compression efficiency and resource usage
- Key configuration options for WiredTiger and how to tune them for your specific workload and hardware setup

Exploring storage engines

Different storage engines employ various data structures, algorithms, and techniques to optimize performance, scalability, reliability, and other characteristics of the database system.

Some common types of storage engines include the following:

- **Row-oriented storage engine**: These engines store data in rows, where each row represents a record and contains multiple columns or fields.
- **Column-oriented storage engine**: These engines store data in columns, where each column represents a field and contains values from multiple rows.
- **Key-value storage engine**: These engines store data as collections of key-value pairs, where each unique key is associated with a single corresponding value. The application can access a value using its key. For example, a key could be a string or a user ID, and the value could be a complex nested data structure.

WiredTiger is a key-value storage engine that can be configured to store data in rows or columns. Other popular examples of database storage engines are InnoDB, MyISAM, and RocksDB. The choice of storage engine can significantly impact the performance, scalability, and functionality of a database system. Different storage engines are optimized for different workloads and use cases, and may offer trade-offs between various factors, such as read/write performance, data compression, transaction support, and data consistency.

For example, InnoDB is currently the default storage engine for MySQL. It provides features such as transactions, row-level locking, and foreign key support. MyISAM, an older storage engine, is known for its simplicity and speed for read-heavy operations, but it does not support transactions or row-level locking.

In theory, WiredTiger could be used as a storage engine for other databases, and MongoDB could use other storage engines. MongoDB has defined a storage engine API that enables developers to implement adapters for other storage engines. For example, MongoRocks is a RocksDB storage engine module for MongoDB.

A specific database might only use a subset of a storage engine's features and allow users to configure a subset of its configuration parameters. For example, at the time of writing, MongoDB doesn't use features such as WiredTiger's column storage or data structures such as log-structured merge trees. This is because MongoDB doesn't currently implement features that use these capabilities, but it may do so in the future. The MongoDB server configuration options support a subset of the WiredTiger configuration options.

Overview of WiredTiger

WiredTiger is the default and most commonly used storage engine for MongoDB. It has been available since MongoDB version 3.0. Before that, the default storage engine for MongoDB was MMAPv1, which used memory-mapped files to manage data. While MMAPv1 was functional, it had some limitations.

The fundamental data structure underlying WiredTiger is the B-tree, which maintains sorted data and allows search, sequential access, insertions, and deletions in logarithmic time. Each node in a B-tree can contain multiple keys (data entries), where the number of keys a node can hold is determined by the degree or order of the tree. Searching for a key in a B-tree involves navigating from the root to a leaf, following the pointers that represent ranges of keys. This is efficient because the height of the tree is logarithmic relative to the number of keys. When compared to binary search trees, B-trees are shallower because they allow more than two children per node. This reduces the number of disk accesses required when walking the tree, which is crucial for databases where I/O operations are expensive.

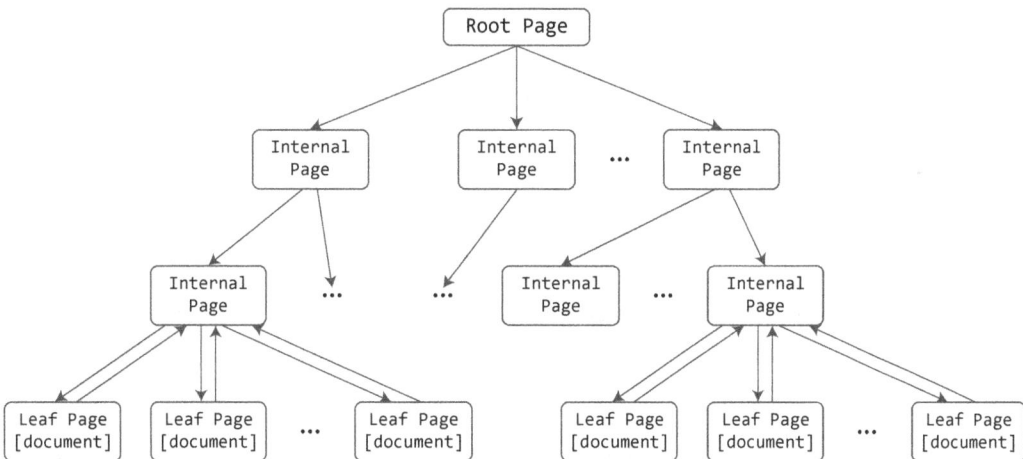

Figure 7.1: The WiredTiger B-tree

Each node of the B-tree contains keys and values. Leaf nodes store actual data, while internal nodes guide the search process through the tree. The fundamental building block of WiredTiger is the key-value pair. Multiple key-value pairs can be combined into pages, and every piece of data is associated with a unique key, enabling efficient retrieval and updates. The internal keys are called record IDs.

Pages in the Linux kernel versus WiredTiger storage engine

The concept of pages exists in both the Linux kernel and the WiredTiger storage engine. While the term *page* is used in both, it represents distinct concepts in each. A page in the Linux kernel is the fundamental unit of memory management.

For example, when trying to retrieve a document with a specific indexed field, such as _id, first an index B-tree is searched using the _id key to get the record ID value. Then, this record ID is used as the key to search the collection and return the value, which corresponds to a MongoDB document.

WiredTiger employs **multiversion concurrency control** (**MVCC**) to manage concurrent access to data in B-trees and pages. This allows multiple readers and writers to operate simultaneously, offering more concurrency than simpler schemes.

Data is persistently stored in files that contain the B-tree structures along with metadata. These files can grow dynamically as needed. On disk, you'll find a separate file for each index and MongoDB collection.

Another set of WiredTiger files is used to store the **journal**, which is often called the **write-ahead log** (**WAL**) in other database systems. Every operation that modifies the database is first written to the journal to ensure the durability of writes, should the server crash or lose power.

When a collection or index is first accessed, the root and first layer of internal nodes are loaded into a cache. As read and write operations occur, the in-memory cache is populated with pages on demand. By default, the WiredTiger cache uses 50% of the available memory minus 1 GB. For example, on a system with a total of 8 GB of RAM, the WiredTiger cache would use 3.5 GB of RAM (0.5 * (8 GB - 1 GB) = 3.5 GB).

The current implementation does not allow explicit pinning of documents or collections in the cache. The cache is shared across all databases and collections in a MongoDB server. WiredTiger periodically creates consistent checkpoints that capture a persistent snapshot of the database at a specific point in time.

WiredTiger supports fully ACID transactions, ensuring data consistency and integrity even in the face of failures. The following sections will tie all these concepts together by describing lookup, update, and insert operations.

A lookup operation

When an application runs a query on the database, it is translated into one or more storage engine lookup operations, each of which does the following:

1. Assuming we're reading a document identified by an indexed field, WiredTiger walks the index B-tree from root to the leaf containing the key.

2. If any pages are not in cache, they are loaded from storage into both the operating system filesystem cache and the WiredTiger cache. Eventually, WiredTiger finds the record ID corresponding to the indexed field.

3. The record ID from the previous step is used to walk the collection's B-tree.

4. If any pages are not in cache, they are loaded from storage both into the operating system filesystem cache and the WiredTiger cache, where they are decrypted and uncompressed.

5. When WiredTiger finds the record ID, it returns the document from the page.

This operation ensures pages are used from memory if they are in the cache and avoids unnecessary storage I/O.

An update operation

When the application updates a document, the database translates this into an update operation on the storage engine. Here's what typically happens:

1. The document is read into cache as described in the previous section.

2. The page is marked as dirty, and the new values of the document are stored in an update list in memory.

3. If the write is part of a transaction, it waits until the transaction is committed.

4. An entry is written to the WiredTiger log that contains enough information to redo the operation should a crash occur. This log write is flushed to the storage device.

5. Later, when either a checkpoint runs or the page needs to be evicted from cache, WiredTiger walks through the page's update list and writes the in-memory page to storage. Older versions of the document are written to a separate history store file.

This mechanism provides durability, crash recovery, and version tracking, all of which are essential for reliable database operations.

An insert operation

For insert operations, WiredTiger performs the following:

1. It traverses the B-tree to find the appropriate leaf node to insert a key for the record/document.

2. When writing the node to storage, if it is full, it is split. The split operation may cascade back up the tree if the parent node is full.

Like reads and updates, inserts rely on efficient B-tree traversal and dynamic node management to maintain the performance and structural integrity of the data. All of the operations on the data involve traversing the B-tree data structures of the indexes and the collection data.

Eviction, checkpointing, and recovery

The cache is limited in size, so WiredTiger needs to evict pages from the cache when it needs space for newer data. WiredTiger uses background threads to manage the eviction process. These threads continuously assess the cache state and perform eviction tasks, running alongside other database operations.

Pages are selected for eviction based on a variation of the *least recently used* algorithm, where the least recently accessed pages are candidates for eviction. This means frequently accessed pages should stay in memory/cache longer.

WiredTiger tracks three types of cache data: total data, dirty data, and updates. For each, it has two thresholds to manage eviction from the cache:

*   **Target**: When the cache reaches this level, WiredTiger begins eviction activities to gradually bring the cache usage back down.

*   **Trigger**: If this level is exceeded, WiredTiger enlists database operation threads to quickly free up space and prevent the cache from becoming full. This reduces the number of threads that can run simultaneous database operations.

These thresholds are configurable when running MongoDB self-managed. We'll see examples later in the *Configuration for improving performance* section of this chapter. When using Atlas, MongoDB selects these thresholds based on the instance size you are running.

A checkpoint takes all of the in-memory data structures and writes any modifications to storage. You can configure how frequently checkpointing occurs. We'll look at an example of this later in the chapter. The rest of the database server continues to read and write to pages during the checkpoint process.

The checkpoint process involves the following steps:

1. WiredTiger ensures all transactions that have been committed up to that point are durably stored in the disk image of the database by writing all the dirty pages from the cache.

2. All pending writes to files are flushed.

3. The journal files that contain the transaction logs are rotated.

4. WiredTiger marks the checkpoint end in its logs and metadata. This allows safe recovery from this point onward.

From a performance perspective, if a large volume of data is written between two checkpoints, many storage and file operations will take place during the second checkpoint. On IOPS- or bandwidth-constrained systems, this can result in periodic performance dips.

Recovery is required if the computer running the MongoDB server crashes or loses power without a proper shutdown. When the server restarts, it begins the recovery process by first loading the database state from the last completed checkpoint. If the previous shutdown was not clean, additional changes stored in the WiredTiger log (journal) are replayed on top of the last checkpoint. As a result, the longer the interval between checkpoints, the longer the recovery time will be.

Compression and encryption

While compression helps save storage space, it comes at the cost of higher CPU usage. If your workload is already constrained by CPU usage on a server running MongoDB, you may choose to disable compression in either of the following cases:

- You are not concerned about the size of the files on your storage devices

- The data you are storing is not very compressible

Alternatively, you can switch to a different compression algorithm to reduce CPU usage, although this typically results in larger file sizes due to less effective compression. MongoDB currently supports three compression options:

Compression algorithm	CPU usage	Compression efficiency	Notes
Snappy	Lowest	Lowest	Fastest option with minimal CPU cost; less effective compression
zstd	Medium	Better than Snappy	A balanced choice between speed and compression ratio
zlib	Highest	Best	Slowest, but offers the highest compression

Table 7.1: Compression algorithms and their performance characteristics

The main compression option is used to compress both the journal and the collection data. Indexes use a form of *prefix compression*. This is effective for data with indexed fields that have common initial sequences.

As mentioned earlier, every workload and dataset is unique, so it's important to run your own experiments to determine the best configuration. For example, if you're using zlib with a highly compressible, large dataset, each storage read may expand into more pages inside the WiredTiger cache. This can lead to increased evictions and potentially more cache misses when re-reading or updating documents.

MongoDB Enterprise uses industry-standard algorithms such as **Advanced Encryption Standard (AES)** for data-at-rest encryption, specifically AES-256 in **Cipher Block Chaining (CBC)** mode configured with PKCS#7 padding. MongoDB Atlas uses encryption at rest by default for all data stored within its clusters. This means someone with physical access to the storage devices can't read the data. Modern processors have hardware acceleration for these algorithms, which means security adds little overhead.

If you are self-managing your MongoDB deployment and you suspect AES hardware acceleration is not being used, you can confirm it by profiling MongoDB and analyzing flame graphs.

Configuration for improving performance

This section outlines several configuration options for the WiredTiger storage engine that can help improve performance. In general, Atlas does not allow direct manipulation of many WiredTiger settings. It automatically manages and optimizes these settings based on the instance tiers. Thanks to Atlas's simplicity and efficiency, you can rely on its advanced automation to optimize performance in response to demand. If your particular needs aren't addressed, you can consult MongoDB support for guidance tailored to your specific application.

However, if you're running a self-managed MongoDB cluster, you can configure and experiment with WiredTiger settings. When you start the MongoDB server, default values will be selected. As you can imagine, it is impossible for MongoDB to pick defaults that are optimal for all datasets and workloads. If you know WiredTiger is the current limiting factor for your workload, then here are some experiments you can run to diagnose and improve performance.

Changing the size of the WiredTiger cache

If you know your workload is I/O bound, you can increase the size of the WiredTiger cache to reduce the amount of I/O needed. For example, if you are running MongoDB on a cloud instance, you can use the cloud provider's metrics dashboards to see how much IOPS your workload is using. With 4,200 IOPS provisioned, a dataset larger than cache, and a workload consisting of 95% read and 5% updates, you might observe steady state metrics such as the following:

- 3,500 storage read requests per second
- 700 storage writes per second (including both journal/log and data files)
- 15,000 database read queries per second
- 800 database update operations per second

Increasing the size of the WiredTiger cache can reduce the number of I/O operations needed per database operation, so while the workload is still limited to 4,200 storage operations per second, more database operations can run because they access data in cache rather than reload it from storage.

To adjust the cache size to 20 GB, you can use the following command:

```
db.adminCommand({setParameter: 1,
wiredTigerEngineRuntimeConfig: 'cache_size=20G'})
```

This command can be used on a running MongoDB instance from the shell.

However, there are also situations where reducing the size of the cache can improve performance. For example, if you have a read-intensive workload that accesses random, compressible documents in a dataset larger than the cache, reducing the size of the WiredTiger cache allows more space for the filesystem cache, where the data remains compressed. Each random read is more likely to miss the WiredTiger cache but hit the filesystem cache, reducing the number of I/O operations and increasing the number of database operations per second.

For example, in some cases, reducing the size of the WiredTiger cache by a factor of three can improve database performance, in operations per second, by as much as 60%. However, this change also has its downsides, such as reducing the performance of an insert workload by nearly 20%.

Changing syncdelay

Reducing `syncdelay` increases the frequency of checkpointing and is beneficial when you need consistent, smaller, and frequent disk write operations to avoid performance spikes. It also reduces the recovery time if a server crashes and restarts.

If you have a write-intensive workload and you notice periodic performance drops that coincide with spikes in storage operations, it could indicate that reducing `syncdelay` might help.

In *Figure 7.2*, we see an illustration of this situation. Periodically, during checkpoints (marked with **C** in the diagram), storage I/O operations increase, and the number of database operations drops.

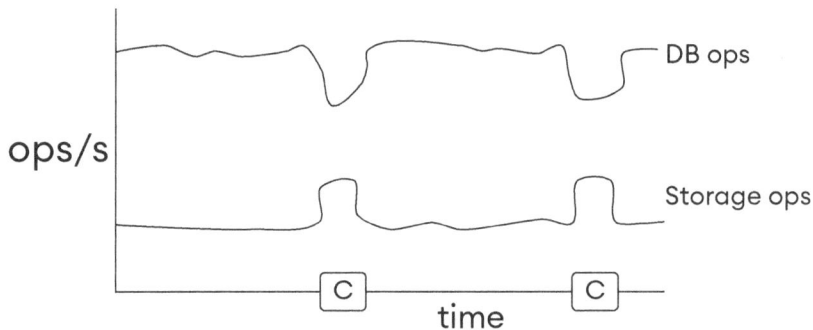

Figure 7.2: Periodic drops in performance during checkpoints

You can reduce `syncdelay` (seconds) by changing the value in the configuration file. It defaults to 60 seconds. If it is already running, you'll need to restart the MongoDB server after changing the configuration file:

```
storage:
  syncdelay: 30
```

Alternatively, you can set `syncdelay` with a command-line option:

```
mongod --syncdelay 30
```

This should change the performance graphs to something similar to *Figure 7.3*. The performance drops and I/O spikes are not as pronounced during checkpoints.

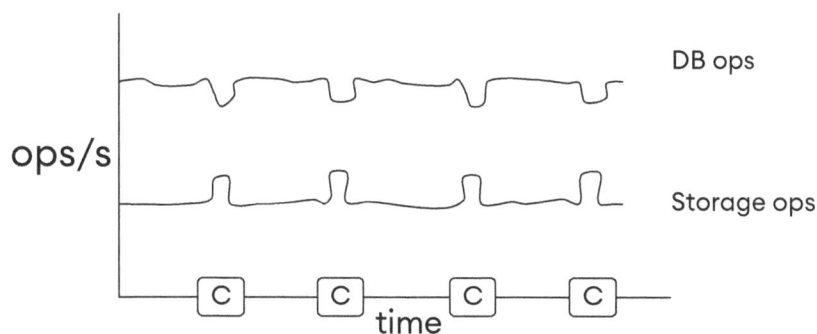

Figure 7.3: Smaller performance drops with more frequent checkpoints

On the other hand, increasing syncdelay can be beneficial for write-intensive workloads when you want to reduce the total number of disk I/O operations, particularly during bulk data processing. For example, in nightly batch workloads that update many documents multiple times, fewer I/O operations may be needed if a document is updated more than once between checkpoints. This reduces the impact of checkpoints on the main workload and may also lower overhead from less frequent transaction management and storage flush operations.

Changing minSnapshotHistoryWindowInSeconds

The minSnapshotHistoryWindowInSeconds parameter in MongoDB specifies the minimum time window (in seconds) for which the storage engine retains snapshot history. A larger window allows you to query the value of a document at a specific point in time using the snapshot read concern over a longer period.

However, maintaining a longer snapshot history, especially for frequently updated documents, requires more storage and may impact write performance, as the system must track more historical versions of the data.

This parameter can be set both at runtime using the setParameter command and at startup using the setParameter setting. For example, to set the parameter to 5 seconds at runtime, you can use the following:

```
db.adminCommand({setParameter: 1, minSnapshotHistoryWindowInSeconds: 5})
```

> **Avoid modifying the snapshot history window on config server nodes**
>
> In sharded clusters, avoid changing the default value on config server nodes, as this can cause internal operations to fail.

Changing how eviction works

While Atlas does not allow direct manipulation of internal WiredTiger eviction settings, such as eviction_dirty_target or eviction_trigger, these settings control how eviction begins gradually (target) and then uses database operation threads (trigger) to bring cache usage back down. Atlas automatically manages and optimizes these settings based on the instance tier.

When self-managing MongoDB, you might observe periodic drops in performance, as illustrated in *Figure 7.4*. During a checkpoint, a large number of write IOPS may occur on the storage device, sometimes exceeding the provisioned capacity, resulting in a dip in database operations per second.

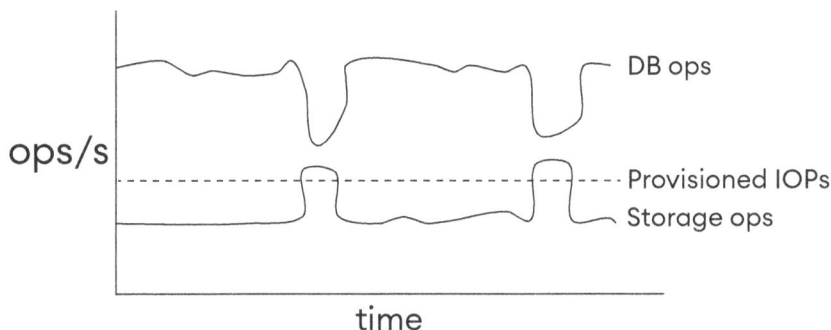

Figure 7.4: Periodic drops in performance during checkpoints

Reducing syncdelay, as discussed earlier, can help shorten the interval between checkpoints, but it may not be sufficient to reduce storage spikes. Instead, a more effective approach is to adjust two eviction settings to clean and evict data from the cache faster. This involves lowering eviction_dirty_target from its default of 5% of cache to 2% and increasing the number of eviction worker threads:

```
"storage": {
  "wiredTiger": {
    "engineConfig": {
      "configString": "eviction_dirty_target=2, eviction=(threads_max=6)"
    }
  }
}
```

Now, when you monitor performance, you'll see a higher number of storage operations per second, but smaller spikes during checkpoints, and the impact on database operations per second is less pronounced. This is because more worker threads are running and evicting dirty pages at a lower threshold before the checkpoint, so less data needs to be written during the checkpoint.

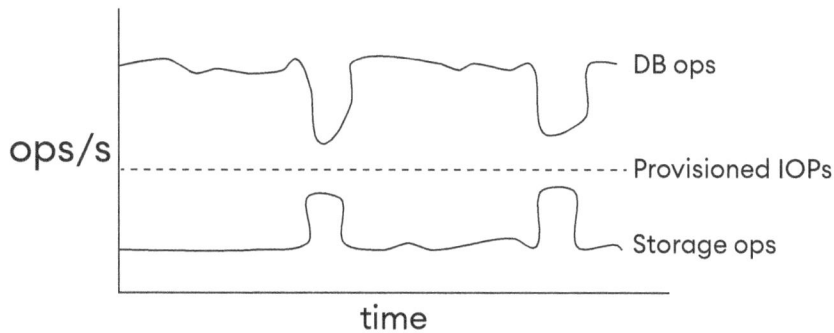

Figure 7.5: Less pronounced drops and spikes with changes in eviction settings

As with many performance-tuning recommendations, it's important to experiment with your workload and dataset. For example, we've seen workloads with a large number of insert operations where increasing `eviction_dirty_target` and reducing the number of eviction worker threads (as low as 1) can significantly improve performance.

Switching to the in-memory storage engine

The in-memory storage engine allows you to avoid disk I/O, giving you higher performance and lower, more predictable latency for database operations. Other than some metadata and diagnostic information, the in-memory storage engine does not write any data to disk. In effect, you can use it as a cache, loading and storing data from another database.

> **Note**
>
> The in-memory storage engine is available only in self-managed deployments and is not supported on MongoDB Atlas.

By default, the in-memory storage engine uses 50% of physical RAM minus 1 GB. However, since your data isn't being written to disk (and you don't need as much filesystem cache), you can increase the allocated size to use more memory. This can be configured in the configuration file (see the following) or set via the command line:

```
storage:
    engine: inMemory
    dbPath: <path>
    inMemory:
        engineConfig:
            inMemorySizeGB: <newSize>
```

Write operations that would cause the data to exceed the specified memory size will return an error. If you're running a self-managed deployment, you can configure shards or replica sets to include a mix of in-memory and WiredTiger storage engines.

A mixed storage engine setup within a replica set should be designed carefully, as it introduces nuances in data persistence, failover behavior, and performance characteristics. This configuration is typically suitable for scenarios where the benefits of rapid access from in-memory members significantly outweigh the added complexity of a hybrid persistence model.

Changing the max leaf page size

As we saw in *Chapter 1, Systems and MongoDB Architecture*, storage devices have throughput and bandwidth limitations. If you're bandwidth-constrained rather than throughput-constrained, you may be able to improve performance by reducing the maximum leaf page size for WiredTiger.

The current default page size is 32 KB for collections and 16 KB for indexes. This means that if you're running an application that performs random reads on a dataset much larger than the cache, each operation that misses the cache only reads one document. If your documents are only 1 KB in size and only one is used per page, you're effectively wasting 31 KB of disk bandwidth (and cache space) per database operation that accesses storage.

For example, in a self-managed cloud deployment, you could use performance monitoring tools or `iostat` to check whether your storage bandwidth is frequently at the limit.

You can change the `leaf_page_max` setting (for new collections) via the configuration file or command line:

```
storage:
  engine: wiredTiger
  wiredTiger:
    collectionConfig:
      configString: "leaf_page_max=8192"   # 8kB
```

You can also specify it when creating a collection:

```
db.createCollection("myCollection", {
  storageEngine: {
    wiredTiger: {
      configString: "leaf_page_max=8192"   # 8kB
    }
  }
})
```

The benefits of such a change can vary depending on factors such as instance size, dataset size, average document size, and the compressibility of your data. For example, in experiments on large instances, we've seen up to a 2x improvement in read-intensive workloads with relatively small documents (1 KB) and a dataset twice the size of available memory. However, when the dataset grows to 10 times the size of memory, the improvement drops to around 1.4x. On smaller instances, the gain might be just 1.1x.

As with any change, there are potential downsides. For example, if insert performance matters to your application, smaller leaf pages can result in more I/O operations since pages fill up faster as you insert documents. Also, smaller pages mean the following:

- Fewer compression possibilities, so the dataset on disk might be larger
- For workloads that scan a lot of data, you need to issue more I/O operations to scan through the same number of documents

On many cloud storage devices, the optimal block size is 256 KB, so smaller pages might be less efficient from a full system perspective.

Changing leaf_page_max requires data rewrite

You can't change the `leaf_page_max` value for existing data, so to change `leaf_page_max` for a collection, you'd need to read the data and rewrite it.

Summary

In summary, WiredTiger is a sophisticated storage engine that blends efficient data structures, advanced concurrency control, and robust data management to deliver a high-performance, scalable, and flexible storage solution for modern applications.

MongoDB chose the current WiredTiger defaults to strike a good balance across a wide range of workloads and datasets. However, your workload and dataset are unique, and running experiments before moving your application into production can help you identify more efficient configurations that unlock better performance.

In the next chapter, we delve deeper into MongoDB's reactive capabilities by exploring advanced patterns, best practices, and real-world considerations for using change streams in production environments. You'll gain insights into scaling event-driven architectures, managing high-throughput scenarios, and integrating change streams with external systems to build robust applications that respond dynamically to changes in your data.

Get This Book's PDF Version and Exclusive Extras

UNLOCK NOW

Scan the QR code (or go to packtpub.com/unlock). Search for this book by name, confirm the edition, and then follow the steps on the page.

Note: Keep your invoice handy. Purchases made directly from Packt don't require an invoice.

8

Change Streams

Change streams represent one of MongoDB's most powerful capabilities for building reactive, event-driven applications. Think of them as a live data stream, constantly sending notifications of updates as they occur within your collections and databases and across your entire MongoDB deployment. This chapter explores the architecture, implementation strategies, and performance considerations for change streams, providing practical guidance to help you leverage this feature effectively in high-performance MongoDB deployments.

We will begin by examining the architecture behind change streams and the evolution from manual **operation log (oplog)** tailing. You'll learn how MongoDB transforms write operations into change events, what those events look like, and how they move through their life cycle. We will then cover how to implement change streams effectively by selecting the right observation scope, applying server-side filtering with aggregation pipelines, and using document lookup strategies that balance performance and completeness. Finally, a hands-on example will demonstrate how to build a real-time price monitoring service using change streams.

The second half of the chapter focuses on performance and durability: strategies for resource optimization, designing resilient consumers, and handling high-volume streams. We also address special considerations for sharded clusters, document size constraints, and collection life cycles. The chapter concludes with guidance on monitoring and replica set nuances and a recap of tuning techniques to ensure your change stream implementation is production-ready.

This chapter covers the following topics:

- Understanding the architecture of change streams and how they work
- Using change streams efficiently
- Managing performance and durability
- Advanced patterns and production readiness

Understanding change streams architecture

At its core, a **change stream** is a cursor that remains open and delivers database change events to applications as they occur. To fully utilize change streams, it's essential to understand how they operate beneath the surface. Before change streams were introduced in MongoDB 3.6, developers who needed change events either relied on polling, built application-side notification systems, or manually tailed MongoDB's oplog collection.

These approaches had several drawbacks. Polling from the application could add unnecessary load to the database server if the polling interval was more frequent than the changes. On the other hand, if the polling interval was less frequent, the application risked missing some changes or introducing delays, requiring additional complexity to handle such scenarios. Parsing raw oplog entries also demanded knowledge of MongoDB internals, adding further complexity. Moreover, the implementation was fragile, since the oplog format is an internal detail that could change between MongoDB versions. Finally, manually tailing the oplog offered limited guarantees: there was no built-in resumability if network connectivity was lost, and no consistent ordering guarantees. These limitations made oplog tailing a brittle solution that required significant expertise to implement correctly and left applications vulnerable to internal breaking changes between MongoDB versions.

Change streams solve these problems by providing an official, supported interface that abstracts away underlying complexities. With it, you can take advantage of features such as the following:

- **Reliability**: There are no duplicate or missed event notifications
- **Structured event documents**: A well-defined format with detailed information about each change
- **Resumability:** Built-in resume tokens enable reliable recovery after disconnections
- **Ordering guarantees**: Ensure consistent global ordering of events, even across sharded clusters
- **Filtering capabilities**: Server-side filtering using aggregation pipelines
- **More secure:** While the oplog exposes all changes on the server, change streams only deliver updates that the user or code has permission to access
- **Simpler**: Events are sent only for majority-committed writes, so your application doesn't need to handle rollbacks
- **Optional images:** You can get a copy of the changed document before and/or after the change

Together, these features offer a robust and reliable foundation for building real-time applications that respond to data changes, while maintaining consistency and resilience, even in the face of disconnections or server failures.

How change streams work: From write operations to events

Change streams are built on MongoDB's replication infrastructure. Understanding this connection helps explain both their capabilities and limitations. At a high level, a client application is notified of a change through the following steps:

1. Part of the client application performs a write operation on a MongoDB collection.
2. The operation is recorded in the primary's oplog.
3. The change stream feature monitors the oplog for majority-committed entries.
4. Raw oplog entries are transformed into a more developer-friendly format.
5. Events are delivered to client applications through an open cursor.

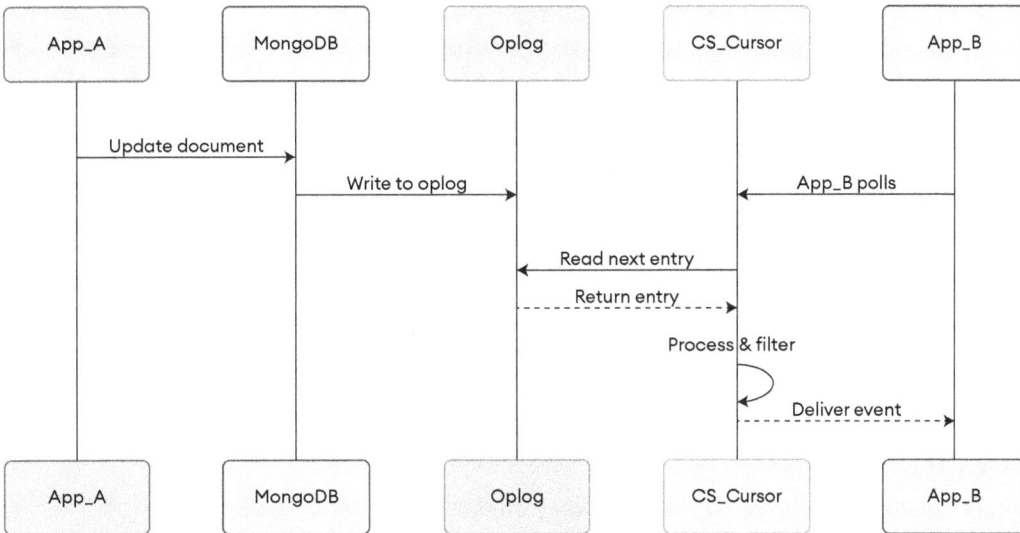

Figure 8.1: Sequence of how document changes are notified through change streams

Figure 8.1 shows a high-level view of the steps involved in delivering change notifications from MongoDB to client applications using change streams. **App_A** and **App_B** could represent the same application. The oplog is part of MongoDB, while the change stream cursor (**CS_Cursor**) exists both within the MongoDB server and on the client side in **App_B**.

This process ensures that all database changes are captured reliably and delivered in a consistent order to applications that need to respond in real time. In sharded clusters, the process becomes more intricate, as the router must coordinate across multiple shards while preserving the global ordering of events.

Event structure and life cycle

Each change stream event contains information about what changed and provides tools for maintaining continuity. For example, here is a change stream event for a change to the price field in a document in a products collection:

```
{
  "_id": {
    "_data": "825F65A78B000000012B022C0100296E5A1004..."  // Resume token
  },
  "operationType": "update",
  "ns": {
    "db": "inventory",
    "coll": "products"
  },
  "documentKey": {
    "_id": ObjectId("5f65a78b00000000000000001")
  },
  "updateDescription": {
    "updatedFields": {
      "price": 29.99,
      "lastModified": ISODate("2023-09-15T14:22:01.123Z")
    },
    "removedFields": ["promotion"]
  },
  "fullDocument": {  // Only present with fullDocument option
    // Complete current state of the document
  }
}
```

As you can see, the change stream event can include the full document, if requested during the change stream setup. However, this can significantly impact performance, so it should be used judiciously. A change stream cursor progresses through the following states during its life cycle:

1. **Opening**: Establishing its position in the oplog

2. **Waiting**: Remaining idle until changes occur

3. **Delivering**: Sending events to the client

4. **Resuming**: Re-establishing the stream after a disconnection

5. **Invalidation**: Terminating after certain operations

Understanding this life cycle is key to building resilient applications.

Implementing change streams effectively

Now that you're familiar with the architecture of change streams, let's look at how to implement an application that uses them effectively for optimal performance across different scenarios.

Choosing the right scope and filtering strategy

MongoDB provides flexibility in both observation scope and filtering capabilities. The combination of these two factors has a significant impact on performance. The observation scope can be limited to a collection, span a database, or extend across the entire deployment. In general, the broader the scope, the greater the performance impact, since more resources are consumed and a higher volume of change events must be processed.

Table 8.1 outlines each scope, its resource usage, the expected event volume, and a typical use case for when you might choose it in your application:

Scope	Resource usage	Event volume	Use cases
Collection	Lower	Focused	Specific business events, targeted synchronization
Database	Medium	Moderate	Cross-collection workflows, database-wide auditing
Deployment	Higher	Highest	Global audit logging, multi-tenant event broadcasting

Table 8.1: Change stream scopes and characteristics

As shown in *Table 8.1*, choosing the appropriate observation scope is a balancing act between visibility and performance. A collection-level scope offers the most efficient resource usage and is ideal for targeted use cases. Expanding to a database or deployment-wide scope increases observability but also demands more from the database and your application.

Best practice

Choose the narrowest scope that meets your requirements. This will maximize performance by reducing resource consumption on the database server and minimize the number of events your application needs to process.

However, you need to balance this with the number of change streams because each, in effect, is parsing and filtering the oplog. For example, if a database has 20 collections and you want to process changes from 16 of them, it's better to have one change stream on the database than 16 change streams on each collection.

Server-side filtering with aggregation pipelines

One of the most effective performance techniques for change streams is server-side filtering using aggregation pipelines. This approach dramatically reduces network bandwidth consumption and application client-side processing overhead.

For example, if you're only interested in price changes on product documents, you can set up a change stream with an aggregation pipeline that matches only changes to the price field:

```
// MongoDB Node.js driver code snippet
// Opening a change stream with a filter pipeline
const pipeline = [
  // Only capture update operations on the products collection
  { $match: { 'ns.coll': 'products', operationType: 'update' } },

  // Further filter to only include price updates
  { $match: { 'updateDescription.updatedFields.price': { $exists: true } }
},
];

const filteredStream = collection.watch(pipeline);
```

This filtered change stream emits only events for updates to the price field in the products collection, significantly reducing the amount of data sent over the network and processed by the client application.

Document lookup strategies and performance

Change streams offer several options for accessing document data, each with different performance implications:

- **Delta-only**: Default behavior; includes only change information.
- **Current state lookup**: `fullDocument: 'updateLookup'` fetches the current document.
- **Before and after images (MongoDB 6.0+)**: Provides the document state before and after changes. This optional feature can affect performance because the database has to capture and store the document before or after the change.

The best approach depends on your specific use case. Ask yourself the following questions to guide your decision:

- Is the value delta in `updateDescription` sufficient for your application use case?
- How much additional network bandwidth can you afford?
- Is the latency of an additional document lookup acceptable?

Choosing the right option depends on your application's need for accuracy, performance, and resource efficiency. For example, the `'updateLookup'` option will fetch the `fullDocument` sometime after the update has occurred. This can have a clear performance impact if the document is large. However, it may also require careful handling in your application. For instance, if the document is changing frequently and there is a queue of changes to be processed, you could end up reading a version that is three changes later. This could also happen if you replay the change stream; the `fullDocument` your application receives (when using `'updateLookup'`) is the current version of the document, not the one at the time of the change.

Building a price monitoring service

To illustrate these concepts in action, let's implement a service that monitors product price changes and notifies interested parties. The following code sets up an aggregation pipeline to watch for updates to the `price` field and notifies other parts of the application when the change exceeds a defined threshold:

```
// Code snippets for MongoDB Node.js driver
// Configure the collection to using preImages (before the changes happen)
db.runCommand({ collMod: "yourCollectionName",
            changeStreamPreAndPostImages: { enabled: true }
        });
```

```
// Setup the change stream with lookups and filtering
const priceMonitor = async (minimumPriceChange) => {
  try {
    const pipeline = [
      { $match: { operationType: 'update' } },
      { $match: { 'updateDescription.updatedFields.price': { $exists: true
} } },
      { $project: { documentKey: 1, 'updateDescription.updatedFields.
price': 1 } }
    ];
    options = { fullDocumentBeforeChange: 'required' };
    const stream = collection.watch(pipeline, options);

    // Process each change as it occurs
    for await (const change of stream) {
      const newPrice = change.updateDescription.updatedFields.price;
      const oldPrice = change.fullDocumentBeforeChange.price;
      const priceDiff = Math.abs(newPrice - oldPrice);

      // Only process significant price changes
      if (priceDiff >= minimumPriceChange) {
        await notifyPriceSubscribers(change.documentKey._id, oldPrice,
newPrice);
      }
    }
  } catch (error) {
    console.error("Change stream error:", error);
    // Implement reconnection logic here
  }
};
```

This example demonstrates several key performance practices. By implementing server-side filtering through the aggregation pipeline, the application reduces network traffic between MongoDB and the client. Additionally, the application applies a business-specific filter (the minimumPriceChange threshold) on the client side. However, keep in mind that capturing the document state (preImage) before the update introduces some overhead.

This can have subtle performance impacts. In effect, enabling `changeStreamPreAndPostImages` causes write amplification because the copies need to be stored. However, they are likely to be in cache when accessed by the application. If you use `'updateLookup'`, you don't need `changeStreamPreAndPostImages`, so these extra writes don't happen. When the read occurs later, it is relatively less likely to hit cache. From a performance point of view, ideally you would use `$match` on fields in `updatedFields`. If that's not possible, experiment with both `changeStreamPreAndPostImages` and `'updateLookup'`.

Managing performance and durability

Building high-performance applications with change streams requires careful consideration of both resource usage and data durability. Let's explore strategies to optimize both.

Resource optimization strategies

Change streams consume resources across your entire stack. In some cases, performing additional processing on the server can reduce the workload on your application. In other situations, extra processing on the client side can enhance overall system performance. *Table 8.2* summarizes these trade-offs:

Resource area	Impact factors	Optimization approaches
Server-side	• CPU usage for oplog processing • Memory usage for cursor state • Network bandwidth consumption	• Filter aggressively. • Use the smallest appropriate scope. • Multiplex several change streams into one and let the application filter to reduce the number of cursors consuming the oplog. • Size the oplog to avoid streams falling too far behind the updates. Ultimately, the oplog is the buffer if the application change stream processing falls behind.
Application-side	• Connection pool usage • Event processing capacity • Memory used for buffering • Network bandwidth usage	• Dedicate connections • Use batch processing

Table 8.2: Trade-offs between server and application processing

As with most performance decisions, there's no one-size-fits-all solution. Optimizing change stream processing requires careful consideration of where resource usage is most critical in your architecture. By understanding the trade-offs between server-side and application-side processing, you can tailor your approach to balance efficiency, scalability, and responsiveness.

> **Best practice**
>
> In high-volume deployments, consider setting up a dedicated service to process change streams. This approach consolidates multiple consumers into a single stream connection, improving efficiency and reducing resource usage.

Handling high-volume event streams

In applications with extremely high write rates, change streams will produce a high volume of events. To help such applications scale effectively, consider the following tactics:

- Implement aggressive server-side filtering
- Deploy dedicated application infrastructure for change stream processing
- Use batching strategies that strike the right balance between throughput and latency

If your oplog is too small, the oplog *rolls over* and overwrites older entries before your application has had a chance to process their change stream events. This will result in a change stream error. This risk is especially high for applications where the change stream processing can go offline for extended periods.

To diagnose this, monitor the `oplog.rs` collection's size and current oplog window. You can check this using the `db.getReplicationInfo()` command in the MongoDB Shell. If your oplog window is short (e.g., just a few hours), there's a higher chance of falling off the oplog and incurring an error. To address this, increase the oplog size. In replica sets, this typically involves adjusting the `oplogSizeMB` parameter in the configuration or reinitializing the replica set with a larger oplog. As a rule of thumb, aim for an oplog that can retain several days, or even a week, of operations, depending on your **recovery point objective (RPO)**.

If you suspect your change stream application is lagging behind actual database changes, this can result in delayed processing or stale data in downstream systems. To prevent this, consider the following methods:

- Monitor network I/O on both the MongoDB primary node and your change stream service. Look for spikes in network utilization that correspond to periods of high database activity.

- Consider the physical proximity of your application to the database. Ensure optimal network connectivity between your MongoDB cluster and your change stream application. This might involve co-locating them in the same data center or cloud region.

- If possible, provision more network bandwidth for both the database server and the consumer application.

- Consider processing events in batches rather than individually.

Your application also needs enough compute resources to process events effectively. If it's resource-constrained and it can't keep up with the volume of changes, it will fall further and further behind before eventually falling off the oplog and receiving an error. Similarly, the MongoDB server must have adequate resources to generate and send change events. Monitor CPU, memory, and disk I/O on the system running your application. Look for high CPU usage, memory pressure, or I/O bottlenecks. Try to minimize expensive operations inside the change stream processing loop. On the database side, high CPU or I/O usage can indicate write bottlenecks. For example, heavy indexing can slow down writes, which in turn affects the speed at which the oplog is written, and consequently, change stream performance.

If your change stream application frequently receives `invalidate` events, forcing it to close and reopen, this can be disruptive and lead to increased latency or missed events if not handled correctly. An `invalidate` event signifies that the collection or database being watched by the change stream no longer exists or has undergone a structural change (such as dropping or renaming) that prevents the stream from continuing.

To troubleshoot, count the types of events your change stream receives. If you see `invalidate` events, identify the specific operation that triggered them. If possible, avoid dropping or renaming collections or databases that are actively being watched by change streams, especially in production environments, where continuous processing is critical. If these operations are necessary, ensure your change stream application is designed to gracefully handle `invalidate` events by re-establishing the stream.

Special considerations for sharded deployments

In sharded clusters, change streams require coordination across multiple shards while maintaining a consistent global ordering of events. This introduces several unique performance considerations:

- **Global ordering overhead**: Maintaining consistent ordering across all shards requires coordination. This is handled by mongos and adds load to that infrastructure.
- **Cold shard impact**: Shards with no write activity still participate in change stream coordination.
- **Geographical latency**: Distributed shards introduce network latency in event delivery.
- **Chunk migration handling**: Changes during chunk migrations require special handling.
- **System-level performance**: If a sharded collection has high levels of write activity, then mongos or the application server processing the stream may not be able to keep up with changes across all shards.

To tune performance in sharded environments, the following code configures two such parameters, maxAwaitTimeMS and batchSize:

```
// MongoDB Node.js driver code snippet
// Configuring change streams for optimal performance in sharded clusters
const shardedStreamOptions = {
  fullDocument: 'updateLookup',
  maxAwaitTimeMS: 1000,   // Adjust based on latency requirements
  batchSize: 100          // Balance between throughput and processing time
};

// Use collection-level streams where possible to reduce coordination
// overhead
const productStream = db.collection('products').watch([],
shardedStreamOptions);
```

The batchSize parameter sets the maximum number of documents that can be returned in each batch of a change stream (up to a limit of 16 MB). It is similar to the batchSize parameter on cursors. This often requires experimentation because if the batch size is too large, the cursor may allocate more resources than needed; if too small, it may lead to increased network round trips.

The maxAwaitTimeMS parameter sets the maximum time in milliseconds that the server waits for new data changes before returning an empty batch to the change stream cursor. It is analogous to the maxAwaitTimeMS parameter on cursors.

Here are some recommended sharded cluster optimization techniques:

- **Configure `periodicNoopIntervalSecs` appropriately** (default: 10 seconds) **to reduce latency** from cold- or low-write shards. These no-op operations ensure that oplog entries are regularly created, even when no real writes occur on the primary, allowing members of the shard to update their logical clocks and replication positions, thus reducing coordination traffic to colder shards.
- **Target change streams at specific collections** whenever possible. This significantly reduces cross-shard communication overhead, especially for high-write collections.
- **Apply server-side filtering** using `$match` pipelines for high-activity collections.
- **Place change stream consumers geographically close** to your primary shards to minimize network latency.
- **Monitor each shard's oplog window independently** to detect potential issues that may impact change stream-based services.
- **Limit the number of document-specific change streams**. For example, instead of creating hundreds of change streams to watch individual documents, create a single change stream and filter the relevant events in your application.

In summary, running change streams efficiently in a sharded cluster requires careful attention to both the configuration and deployment strategy. By tuning parameters such as `batchSize` and `maxAwaitTimeMS`, targeting streams at specific collections, and reducing unnecessary coordination across shards, you can significantly improve performance and reliability. As with most distributed systems, continuous monitoring and iterative tuning are key to maintaining optimal behavior at scale.

Advanced patterns and production readiness

Taking change streams to production requires understanding advanced options and monitoring needs. In this section, we'll explore key considerations for production deployments, based on the official MongoDB documentation.

Transaction visibility and event batching

When working with transactions in MongoDB, change streams follow specific visibility rules that affect event delivery. All changes made within a transaction only become visible to change streams after the transaction commits. At that point, all changes from that transaction appear at once as separate events in the stream while maintaining their logical order within the transaction.

This behavior ensures data consistency but requires your consumer applications to handle these *bursts* of events efficiently when large transactions are committed. Consider implementing batching and throttling mechanisms in your processing logic to handle these surges gracefully.

Document size limitations and collection life cycle

Change stream response documents must adhere to MongoDB's 16 MB BSON document limit. If you use options such as fullDocument: 'updateLookup' (which performs a lookup to fetch the entire current state of a document after an update operation) or work with large documents, you might reach this limit, causing events to fail. For larger documents, in MongoDB 6.0.9+, consider using the $changeStreamSplitLargeEvent aggregation stage to split large change events into multiple smaller fragments that can be processed individually without exceeding size restrictions.

When collections or databases are dropped or renamed while change streams are watching them, the change stream cursors will close when they reach that point in the oplog. After these invalidation events, you must use startAfter (not resumeAfter) with a valid resume token if you want to restart the stream.

Monitoring and health checks

Production deployments should include comprehensive monitoring of several key metrics. For change streams, you may begin by tracking the active cursor count through the db.serverStatus(). metrics.changeStream.currentOpen command. The change events could arrive a significant time after the change is made in the database. Additionally, monitor your event processing latency and throughput to ensure optimal performance. Resume token persistence metrics provide insight into your recovery capabilities, while the oplog window size (measurable via rs.printReplicationInfo()) indicates how far back in time your historical operations extend.

Replica set considerations

When using self-managed MongoDB, and for replica sets with arbiter members, be aware that change streams may remain idle if not enough data-bearing members are available to achieve a majority commit. For example, in a three-member replica set with two data-bearing nodes and an arbiter, if the secondary goes down, writes cannot be majority committed, and the change stream remains open but won't send events.

If you anticipate significant downtime of a service using change streams, for maintenance or disaster recovery, increase the oplog size to retain operations for longer than your estimated downtime period. This ensures your application can catch up with all changes once connectivity is restored.

Performance-tuning recap

When optimizing change streams for production, several key strategies should be implemented. Server-side filtering with aggregation pipelines significantly reduces the event volume, minimizing network traffic and processing overhead. Select an appropriate document lookup strategy based on your specific application requirements, carefully choosing between the various `fullDocument` options to balance completeness with performance.

Size your oplog appropriately for expected maximum downtime scenarios, ensuring it can retain operations long enough to bridge maintenance windows or recovery periods. Always configure your connection pool size to exceed the number of open change streams, preventing resource exhaustion.

Limit the number of specifically targeted change streams, as these cannot leverage indexing optimizations, potentially increasing server load. For applications with particularly high event volumes, consider dedicated infrastructure to isolate change stream processing from your main database workload, preventing performance impact on critical operations.

Summary

Change streams transform MongoDB from a traditional database into a reactive data platform, enabling real-time responses to data changes. When implemented thoughtfully with performance considerations in mind, they provide a powerful foundation for building responsive, event-driven applications.

The next chapter shifts the focus to transactions, an important part of building reliable and consistent applications. We'll delve into the mechanics of multi-document ACID transactions and discuss key considerations for optimizing their performance in various MongoDB architectures.

9

Transactions

In this chapter, we'll dive into MongoDB's multi-document ACID transactions, a feature that dramatically expanded MongoDB's capabilities when it was introduced. Transactions are an important tool in your database toolbox, but just like you wouldn't use a screwdriver to drive in a nail, it's essential to use them only when they are the right tool for the job. While powerful in their capabilities, transactions have the potential to create performance bottlenecks when used incorrectly.

It might surprise you to hear that transactions in MongoDB aren't always the solution you need. In fact, sometimes they're the exact opposite of what you should be using! Throughout this chapter, you'll gain a comprehensive understanding of MongoDB's transaction capabilities that goes beyond basic implementation. You'll learn how to balance the need for data consistency with performance requirements, making informed decisions about when transactions are truly necessary. We'll explore practical examples showing both the Core and Callback APIs, analyze the performance implications of different transaction patterns, and provide you with strategies to optimize your transactional workloads. By the end of this chapter, you'll be equipped to implement transactions that maintain data integrity without sacrificing the performance advantages that make MongoDB such a powerful database platform.

This chapter will cover the following topics:

- Learn how MongoDB supports multi-document ACID transactions
- Use the Transactions API and manage sessions effectively
- Optimize transaction performance through best practices
- Identify and avoid common transaction anti-patterns

Understanding multi-document ACID transactions

Let's dig into MongoDB's multi-document ACID transactions, a capability that marked a significant milestone in MongoDB's evolution from a basic document-oriented database to a platform capable of handling complex, mission-critical workloads. While MongoDB has always provided powerful document-level atomicity, multi-document transactions extend these guarantees across multiple documents, collections, and databases.

Even though many applications can utilize a rich document structure to ensure related writes happen together, there are still use cases that require the coordination of writes between multiple different documents that may be in the same or different collections. Because of this, it's important to understand what MongoDB ACID multi-document transactions guarantee and how to best use them.

In this section, we'll first explore the history and evolution of transaction support in MongoDB, from single-document atomicity to distributed transactions across sharded clusters. Then, we'll break down the core **ACID** properties, that is, **atomicity, consistency, isolation, and durability**, and how they apply within MongoDB's transaction model. Finally, we'll compare document-level atomicity with multi-document transactions, helping you understand when each approach is appropriate and how to balance data integrity with performance.

History and evolution of transactions in MongoDB

MongoDB's journey with transaction support tells an interesting story of how the database has evolved to meet increasingly complex application requirements:

- **The single-document era (pre-MongoDB 4.0)**: From its inception, MongoDB provided atomicity at the single-document level. This was sufficient for many use cases, especially when leveraging MongoDB's flexible document model to embed related data within a single document. Developers would often design schemas specifically to take advantage of this single-document atomicity.

- **The replica set milestone (MongoDB 4.0, 2018)**: This release introduced multi-document ACID transactions for replica sets, a game-changer that brought MongoDB into parity with relational databases for applications requiring strong consistency across multiple documents. This initial implementation supported transactions within a single replica set.

- **The distributed transactions breakthrough (MongoDB 4.2, 2019)**: Building on the previous release, MongoDB 4.2 extended multi-document transaction support to sharded clusters. This significant advancement enabled distributed transactions across shards, providing a comprehensive solution for complex, large-scale applications.

- **Continued refinements (MongoDB 4.4 and beyond)**: Recent releases have focused on performance improvements, operational manageability, and broader API support for transactions.

This evolution reflects MongoDB's commitment to meeting diverse application needs while maintaining its core strengths in flexibility, scalability, and performance.

Introduction to ACID properties in MongoDB

ACID represents the fundamental properties that ensure database transactions are processed reliably, even in the face of errors, crashes, or power failures. Let's break down what each of these properties means in the context of MongoDB:

- **Atomicity**: This guarantees that a transaction is all or nothing; that is, either every operation in the transaction succeeds or none do. If any part of the transaction fails, the entire transaction is rolled back, leaving the database in its original state. While MongoDB has always provided atomicity at the single-document level, that is, if any change to a document fails, then all changes to that document fail, multi-document transactions extend this guarantee across multiple documents.

- **Consistency**: This property ensures that a transaction brings the database from one valid state to another, maintaining all defined rules and constraints. In MongoDB, consistency validations primarily exist on a per-document basis through document and schema validation features. Both single-document operations and multi-document transactions guarantee consistency. Other consistency validations, such as unique index constraints, are also guaranteed the same way inside and outside of transactions.

- **Isolation**: Think of isolation as each transaction operating in its own little bubble. It ensures that concurrently executing transactions don't interfere with one another's outcomes, as if they were executed sequentially. MongoDB provides snapshot isolation for transactions, meaning each transaction sees a consistent snapshot of the data as it existed at the start of the transaction, regardless of changes made by other transactions that commit during its execution. If two transactions try to make a conflicting modification, one of them will fail and retry the entire transaction.

- **Durability**: Once a transaction is committed, its changes are permanent and will survive subsequent system failures such as power outages or crashes. In MongoDB, durability is achieved through journaling on multiple nodes and write concern mechanisms. When a transaction is committed with an appropriate write concern (such as the default `{w: "majority"}`), the changes are guaranteed to be durable across the majority of replica set members. This is a stronger guarantee than a single node committing a write to disk.

Together, the ACID properties provide a foundation for predictable and reliable behavior in MongoDB transactions. They ensure that multi-step operations are either fully completed or have no effect, helping maintain data integrity even in the presence of concurrent workloads, application errors, or system failures. This can be particularly important for applications that coordinate changes across multiple collections, such as processing orders, updating inventory, or managing user accounts.

Document-level atomicity versus multi-document transactions

Understanding the difference between MongoDB's default document-level atomicity and multi-document transactions is crucial for effective data modeling and optimizing performance.

Document-level atomicity

MongoDB has always guaranteed that operations on a single document are atomic. When you update multiple fields within a document, either all changes are applied or none are; there's no in-between state where only some fields are updated. These changes are also only ever visible to other threads together or not at all. This built-in atomicity, combined with MongoDB's rich document model that allows for embedding related data, means many use cases don't actually need multi-document transactions at all.

For example, if you're tracking an order with its line items, embedding the line items within the order document ensures that updates to both the order status and its items happen atomically:

```
{
  "_id": "order123",
  "customer": "jane_doe",
  "status": "shipped",
  "items": [
    { "product": "widget", "quantity": 5, "price": 10 },
    { "product": "gadget", "quantity": 1, "price": 20 }
  ]
}
```

This approach keeps data tightly coupled and ensures consistency without the overhead of coordinating changes across multiple documents.

Multi-document transactions atomicity

Multi-document transactions extend atomicity guarantees across operations involving multiple documents, which can span different collections, databases, or shards. Multi-document transactions are essential when related data cannot reasonably be embedded within a single document. For example, processing an e-commerce order may involve updating inventory levels, customer history, and order records together to maintain data integrity:

```javascript
// Start a session and transaction
const session = client.startSession();
session.startTransaction();

try {
  // 1. Create and insert the order document
  const order = {
    customerId: "customer123",
    items: [
      { productId: "product456", quantity: 2, price: 25.99 },
      { productId: "product789", quantity: 1, price: 49.99 }
    ],
    totalAmount: 101.97,
    status: "processing",
    createdAt: new Date()
  };

  const orderResult = await db.orders.insertOne(order, { session });
  const orderId = orderResult.insertedId;

  // 2. Update inventory for multiple products
  await db.inventory.updateOne(
    { _id: "product456" },
    { $inc: { stockCount: -2 } },
    { session }
  );

  await db.inventory.updateOne(
    { _id: "product789" },
    { $inc: { stockCount: -1 } },
    { session }
  );
```

```
  // 3. Update customer purchase history
  await db.customers.updateOne(
    { _id: "customer123" },                                         `
    {
      $inc: { totalSpent: 101.97, orderCount: 1 }
    },
    { session }
  );

  // If all operations succeed, try to commit the transaction
  await session.commitTransaction();
} catch (error) {
  // If an error occurred, abort the transaction
  await session.abortTransaction();
  console.error("Transaction aborted due to error:", error);
  throw error;
} finally {
  // End the session
  session.endSession();
}
```

The key trade-off to understand is that while multi-document transactions provide stronger consistency guarantees, they typically come with higher performance overhead compared to single-document operations. As a general rule, leverage single-document atomicity when possible and use multi-document transactions judiciously when truly necessary.

When to use multi-document transactions in MongoDB

While MongoDB supports multi-document transactions, that doesn't mean you should use them by default. Transactions come with performance trade-offs, and in many cases, MongoDB's native design offers better, more efficient alternatives. So, when is it a good idea to use multi-document transactions? And when are you better off without them?

Let's look at some scenarios where multi-document transactions are not just helpful but necessary:

- **Financial operations** often require strict consistency to avoid discrepancies that can lead to serious errors. For example, when recording a payment, it's critical to update both the payments collection and the corresponding customer document to subtract the funds owed. If one update succeeds while the other fails, the system could show incorrect balances or incomplete records, outcomes that multi-document transactions are designed to prevent.

- **Inventory and order management** often involve updating stock levels for multiple products simultaneously while creating an order. It's crucial that all these updates succeed or fail as a single unit to prevent overselling or inventory inconsistencies. For example, if the order is recorded but the inventory updates fail, the system may show incorrect stock availability, leading to customer dissatisfaction and logistical issues. Multi-document transactions ensure that the order creation and all related inventory adjustments are applied atomically, maintaining data integrity throughout the process.

- When managing **version updates**, it's important to clearly designate which version of an entity is currently active while simultaneously marking the previous version as inactive. This ensures there is never ambiguity about which version should be used by the application or users. If these changes are applied separately and one update fails, it could lead to conflicting data, such as multiple active versions or none at all, causing errors or inconsistent behavior. Multi-document transactions allow both updates to be made atomically, maintaining a clear and reliable version state.

However, not every multi-step process needs a transaction. MongoDB's document model was designed from the ground up with performance in mind, and this is most evident when we compare single-document operations to multi-document transactions. The performance gap between the two exists because transactions require additional locking to ensure isolation, maintaining snapshots of data, coordination across multiple servers (in sharded clusters), and a two-phase commit protocol (in sharded clusters).

When performance matters, follow this rule: If you can design your data model to keep related data in a single document, you'll almost always get better performance than using multi-document transactions. Therefore, consider avoiding multi-document transactions in the following instances:

- **Related data can be modeled within a single document**: If all the information that needs to be updated atomically fits within a single document, it's more efficient to leverage MongoDB's built-in single-document atomicity. This approach reduces the complexity and overhead associated with multi-document transactions, resulting in better performance and simpler error handling. Using single-document atomicity also avoids the additional locking and coordination costs that come with transactions spanning multiple documents or collections.

- **Weaker consistency is acceptable**: Not every application requires strict consistency guarantees. In some cases, allowing relaxed consistency can improve performance and scalability by reducing locking and coordination overhead. For example, analytics dashboards or social media feeds can tolerate slight delays or temporary discrepancies in data without impacting user experience. Choosing a weaker consistency when appropriate can help optimize resource use and system responsiveness, avoiding the additional cost of multi-document transactions when they aren't necessary.

- **Large-scale write operations**: Transactions have practical limits on the number of documents that can be modified. For example, don't use transactions to load thousands of documents for generating reports or analytics dashboards. This creates unnecessary overhead and can lead to timeout errors. Instead, use snapshot reads with the {readConcern: "snapshot"} option for point-in-time consistency, or create MongoDB views that present a consistent perspective of your data without the transaction overhead.

Remember that effective schema design can often eliminate the need for transactions altogether. Before reaching for a transaction, ask yourself: *"Is transactional consistency absolutely necessary here?"* and *"Could I model this data differently to take advantage of single-document atomicity?"*

Transactions API and session management

MongoDB provides two approaches to working with transactions: the Core API and the Callback API. Each has its place, depending on your requirements and coding style.

Core API

The Core API gives you explicit control over each step of the transaction life cycle. You're responsible for starting the session, beginning the transaction, committing or aborting it, and ending the session. Here's a typical pattern that starts a session, starts a transaction, performs a number of operations, and tries to commit the transaction. It has to handle either the success or failure of the commit, and if there is to be another attempt, it has to be explicitly written in the code, like in the following:

```
// Start a session
const session = client.startSession();

// Start a transaction
session.startTransaction();
```

```
try {
  // Perform operations within the transaction
  await collection1.updateOne({ _id: 1 }, { $set: { status: "active" } },
{ session });
  await collection2.insertOne({ refId: 1, details: "..." }, { session });

  // Commit the transaction
  await session.commitTransaction();
} catch (error) {
  // If an error occurred, abort the transaction
  await session.abortTransaction();
  throw error;
} finally {
  // End the session
  session.endSession();
}
```

Let's go over each part to understand what's happening:

1. **Session creation**: First, we create a new session with `client.startSession()`. A session is required for all transactions in MongoDB.

2. **Transaction initialization**: We start a new transaction within the session using `session.startTransaction()`.

3. **Database operations**: Inside the `try` block, we perform multiple operations (updating one collection and inserting into another). Each operation includes the session object to associate it with our transaction.

4. **Transaction commit**: If all operations succeed, we commit the transaction with `session.commitTransaction()`, which makes all changes visible.

5. **Error handling**: If any error occurs during the operations or commit, we catch it, abort the transaction with `session.abortTransaction()`, and rethrow the error.

6. **Cleanup**: The `finally` block ensures that regardless of success or failure, we always end the session with `session.endSession()` to release resources.

Using the Core API gives you full control, but it also means you're responsible for managing every detail of the transaction life cycle. While powerful, this approach requires careful error handling and cleanup to ensure reliability and consistency.

Callback API

The Callback API (also known as the Convenient API) simplifies transaction management by handling much of the boilerplate code for you. Rather than explicitly having to write out all the steps, each driver provides a less verbose way of doing the same thing, as well as handling the retries on some errors automatically. To get a better idea, let's take a look at an example:

```
// Using the Callback API
await client.withSession(async (session) => {
  return await session.withTransaction(async () => {
    // Perform operations within the transaction
    await collection1.updateOne({ _id: 1 }, { $set: { status: "active" }
}, { session });
    await collection2.insertOne({ refId: 1, details: "..." }, { session
});
  });
});
```

This example demonstrates MongoDB transactions using the Callback API, which offers several advantages over the Core API:

- **Simplified session management**: The `client.withSession()` method automatically creates a session and ensures it's properly closed when the operation completes, regardless of success or failure.

- **Automated transaction handling**: The `session.withTransaction()` method manages the entire transaction life cycle. It starts the transaction, attempts to commit it when your callback completes, and automatically aborts it if an error occurs.

- **Built-in retry logic**: Unlike the Core API example, the Callback API includes automatic retry logic for transient errors, following MongoDB's recommended retry pattern.

- **Cleaner code**: The nested callback structure eliminates the need for explicit `try/catch/finally` blocks, making your code more concise and focused on business logic rather than transaction management.

For most applications, the **Callback API is recommended** due to its simplicity and built-in retries and error handling. However, the Core API might be preferable in situations requiring very specific control over transaction behavior or when you need to interleave transaction and non-transaction operations in complex ways.

Read/write concerns and transaction behavior

Read and write concerns control the durability and consistency guarantees of your operations, including the staleness and durability of the data you read. However, in transactions, read and write concerns have some special behaviors.

Transactions in MongoDB employ speculative majority read behavior to ensure read-your-own write semantics, which means that all or most read concerns behave the same way: they read the latest data available in the snapshot, and the successful ability of the transaction to commit means that data will be majority committed by the time the transaction successfully completes.

A write concern determines the level of acknowledgment requested by MongoDB for write operations. We discussed the various options in *Chapter 5, Replication*, but for transactions, the important thing to know is that the default write concern, majority, is the only one that makes sense to use, and it applies to the transaction as a whole and not to individual writes inside a transaction.

> **Transaction-level read and write concerns**
>
> Read and write concerns are set at the transaction level, not on individual operations within the transaction, so you cannot specify a different read or write concern for individual operations in a transaction.

To set a read or write concern on a transaction, pass the values to the startTransaction method:

```
// Example showing proper transaction read/write concern configuration
session.startTransaction({
  readConcern: { level: "snapshot" },  // Default
  writeConcern: { w: "majority" }      // Default
});
```

As a general rule, it's best to leave the default values for read and write concerns for transactions if you care about their correctness and durability.

Performance considerations with transactions

When it comes to MongoDB transactions, performance is an important consideration that can make or break your application. While transactions provide powerful consistency guarantees, they also introduce overhead that can impact your system's speed, scalability, and resource utilization. In this section, we'll examine the key performance considerations for MongoDB transactions and provide practical advice for optimizing your transactional workloads.

Replica set versus sharded cluster transactions

Transactions behave differently and have different performance implications depending on whether you're running on a replica set or a sharded cluster. In replica sets, transaction performance is relatively straightforward. All operations in a transaction are coordinated by the primary node. The main factors that affect performance are the number of documents affected, the size of documents, and the network latency between clients and the primary. These elements directly impact how quickly a transaction can be executed and committed.

In sharded clusters, things get more complex. Cross-shard transactions, that is, those that touch data on multiple shards, require a distributed transaction coordinator and a two-phase commit protocol. This increases overhead and can impact performance in several ways:

- **Increased latency**: Each cross-shard operation adds network round-trips between the coordinator and the shards
- **Higher resource utilization**: Additional memory and CPU are needed for transaction coordination
- **Potential for cascading performance issues**: If one shard becomes slow, it can affect transaction performance across the entire cluster

However, not all sharded transactions are alike. Transactions that only interact with documents on one shard are the same as replica set transactions performance-wise. Sharded transactions that read from multiple shards but write to only one incur a small performance penalty. The most expensive transactions are those that write to multiple shards. The more shards involved, the higher the latency.

In sharded environments, performance can be significantly improved by designing for shard locality. This means structuring your data and shard keys so that related documents that are frequently updated together in a transaction reside on the same shard. This minimizes the need for cross-shard transactions.

Additionally, if your application is globally distributed, it's important to account for cross-region transaction latency. To mitigate this, consider distributing your collections in such a way that your writes are limited to a single region or explore other techniques to balance consistency and performance.

WiredTiger cache considerations

MongoDB's WiredTiger storage engine uses an in-memory cache to improve performance, but transactions interact with this cache in ways that can sometimes cause performance issues.

Transactions rely on cache by creating snapshots of documents they read or modify. These snapshots must remain in the cache until the transaction is complete. Long-running transactions can prevent cache eviction, leading to memory pressure.

The most serious issue is when this leads to the `TransactionTooLargeForCache` error, which occurs when a transaction's operations and snapshots exceed the available cache size. This commonly happens in the following instances:

- A transaction touches too many documents
- A transaction includes very large documents
- A transaction runs for too long, preventing cache eviction
- The WiredTiger cache is configured too small for the workload

To prevent these scenarios, there are a few strategies depending on the situation:

- **Limit transaction size**: Keep the number of documents per transaction below 1,000
- **Limit transaction duration**: Commit or abort transactions within 60 seconds (the default limit)
- **Configure appropriate cache size**: Ensure the WiredTiger cache is set to at least 50% of RAM for transaction-heavy workloads
- **Monitor cache pressure**: Watch for an increase in metrics such as `wiredTigerCacheSizeBytes` and `wiredTigerCacheMaxBytes`

Ensuring good transaction performance requires using best practices, diligent monitoring, and minimizing transaction use when it's not necessary.

Managing transaction runtime limits and errors

MongoDB enforces a default 60-second transaction runtime limit to prevent long-running transactions from impacting cluster health. This limit exists for several important reasons: extended transactions can lock documents for long periods, preventing other operations from accessing needed data and creating bottlenecks in your application; they increase memory pressure on your servers, potentially affecting overall database performance; they prevent the WiredTiger cache from evicting data from the cache, which can lead to memory exhaustion and degraded performance; and they significantly increase the likelihood of operation conflicts and aborts, forcing your application to handle more error cases.

Given these constraints, effectively managing transaction duration becomes critical for application reliability. You can monitor transaction duration by tracking how long your transactions typically run and setting alerts for those approaching the limit, giving you time to optimize before failures occur. While it's possible to configure the limit by adjusting the `transactionLifetimeLimitSeconds` server parameter, increasing it should be considered a last resort since it doesn't address the underlying performance issues and may worsen the overall system health.

A more sustainable approach is to optimize transactions to complete more quickly. This can be accomplished by splitting large transactions into smaller, more manageable ones that process fewer documents at once; ensuring indexes are in place for all query predicates to speed up document selection; optimizing any queries and aggregation pipelines used within the transaction to reduce processing time; avoiding unnecessary operations within the transaction scope; and performing read-only operations outside the transaction when possible, when they don't require the ACID guarantees that transactions provide.

Beyond the time limit challenge, distributed systems such as MongoDB inevitably experience transient errors that require proper handling for robust applications. MongoDB helps developers identify these situations through specific error labels that suggest appropriate recovery strategies. When you encounter a `TransientTransactionError`, it indicates a temporary issue, such as network glitches, primary elections, or momentary resource constraints, that could succeed if retried. For these cases, implementing a full transaction retry with exponential backoff allows your application to recover gracefully while preventing overloading the system during instability.

Similarly, an `UnknownTransactionCommitResult` error indicates uncertainty about whether a commit succeeded, typically caused by network issues during commit acknowledgment. The proper response here differs slightly: you should retry only the commit operation rather than the entire transaction, as the transaction work itself has already been performed and only the final confirmation is in question.

Importantly, monitoring retry rates provides valuable insight into your system's health. A sudden increase in retries often indicates an underlying performance problem, such as network instability, resource constraints, or configuration issues, that requires investigation. By connecting your retry monitoring with your overall performance metrics, you can identify and address problems before they significantly impact your application's reliability.

Lock acquisition and contention management

MongoDB uses a multi-granular locking system for transactions. Understanding lock behavior is crucial for optimizing transaction performance. MongoDB's locking mechanism operates at multiple levels of granularity, from database-wide to individual document locks, creating a hierarchical system that balances data consistency with operational throughput.

Lock contention typically emerges when multiple transactions compete to modify the same document, during administrative operations such as index or collection creation, or under high-volume write workloads concentrated on a small subset of documents. Effective mitigation requires a multi-faceted approach focused on reducing both the likelihood and duration of lock conflicts.

Keeping transactions small and focused serves as the foundation for minimizing lock duration, allowing other operations to proceed more quickly. Rather than concentrating writes on specific documents, distributing this activity helps prevent the formation of hotspots that become bottlenecks. Administrative tasks should be scheduled during periods of lower activity to avoid competing with regular application workloads.

Proper indexing plays a crucial role in operational efficiency by reducing execution time for operations and therefore minimizing the time they spend holding locks. Regular monitoring through db.serverStatus().locks provides valuable insights into lock wait times, enabling proactive identification of emerging issues before they impact application performance.

Recognition of lock contention problems typically manifests through several key indicators: transaction abort rates and the number of retries begin climbing as operations fail to complete successfully the first time, operation queues grow longer as requests wait for resource availability, lock wait times increase measurably, and clients experience timeouts as operations exceed acceptable response thresholds. By understanding these patterns and implementing appropriate preventive measures, database administrators can maintain optimal performance even under demanding workloads.

Optimizing transaction size and duration

The most effective way to ensure good transaction performance is to keep transactions small and short-lived. In this section, we'll focus on how to optimize your transaction footprint by limiting the transaction size and minimizing the transaction duration.

First, try limiting the size of your transaction. When possible, limit it to fewer than 1,000 modified documents per transaction. Next, there are a few important strategies for minimizing transaction duration:

- **Prepare data before the transaction**: Perform expensive calculations outside the transaction
- **Use efficient queries**: Ensure all operations within transactions use indexes
- **Batch related changes**: Group multiple writes into a single batch operation when possible
- **Split large operations**: Break up very large operations into smaller, more manageable transactions

By applying these optimization strategies, you can significantly improve the performance of your transactional workloads in MongoDB.

Common transaction anti-patterns and their performance costs

Even with the best intentions, it's easy to fall into common traps when using transactions in MongoDB. Understanding how *not* to use transactions is just as crucial as knowing when to use them. In this section, we'll explore the most frequent anti-patterns, explain why they hurt performance, and provide practical guidance on how to avoid them, so you can keep your database humming and your ops team happy.

Long-running transactions and their impact on system performance

When designing transactions for MongoDB, performance should be a primary consideration. Efficient transactions ensure your database remains responsive, maintains high throughput, and provides a good experience for users. Poor transaction design, particularly when operations run for too long, can put excessive pressure on system resources, increase the risk of conflicts, and ultimately lead to failures.

Long-running transactions are like that visitor who overstays their welcome; they tie up resources, block other operations, and can cause significant performance issues. Some examples of overly long transactions are as follows:

- A transaction that attempts to insert or update thousands or millions of documents in a single operation
- Operations that include external API calls, complex computations, or end user interactions causing the transaction to remain open for many seconds or minutes
- Batch-processing jobs that wrap an entire day's worth of data imports within a single transaction

With long-running transactions come several performance costs. These include the following:

- **Increased lock contention**: Locks are held for the duration of the transaction, blocking other operations from accessing the locked documents and significantly reducing concurrency and throughput.
- **WiredTiger cache pressure**: The storage engine must keep all pre-images and post-images of modified data in the cache until the transaction completes. Large transactions can consume substantial cache, forcing frequent evictions of other useful data.
- **Risk of `TransactionTooLargeForCache` errors**: If the modifications exceed a certain threshold of the WiredTiger cache, the transaction will fail completely.
- **Exceeding `transactionLifetimeLimitSeconds`**: MongoDB's default 60-second transaction limit exists for good reason. Long-running transactions risk getting automatically aborted, leading to wasted work and retry storms.
- **Replication lag**: Large transactions can generate a burst of oplog entries upon commit, potentially causing secondaries to fall behind.

The key takeaway is this: break down large operations into smaller, more manageable transactions. Keep transactions short and sweet, ideally completing in milliseconds rather than seconds. This approach helps maintain system performance, reduces resource contention, and decreases the likelihood of transaction failures.

Unnecessary use of transactions where single-document atomicity would suffice

Developers new to MongoDB can fall into the trap of overusing transactions, bringing habits from relational databases that aren't always necessary into the document model. Let's examine some common scenarios where transactions are misapplied:

- **Using a transaction for a single document update**: Wrapping a single document update in a transaction is unnecessary as single-document operations are already atomic in MongoDB. This redundant approach adds processing overhead without providing any additional data integrity benefits.

- **Using transactions instead of better schema design**: Another common mistake is using transactions when the data could be modeled to fit within a single document. Taking time to design your schema properly can eliminate many transaction requirements and significantly improve performance.

- **Splitting logically related data across collections**: Developers also frequently create separate documents for data that logically belongs together, then use transactions to update them atomically. This approach not only complicates your code but also introduces potential performance bottlenecks and increases the likelihood of transaction conflicts.

- **Ignoring single-document atomicity**: MongoDB's single-document atomicity is a powerful feature; don't ignore it! Using multi-document transactions for operations that could be handled with single-document updates adds unnecessary overhead and complexity.

> **Tip**
>
> Where appropriate, embed related data in a single document to reduce the need for multi-document transactions.

Here's an example demonstrating the difference between a transaction-heavy relational approach and a document-optimized MongoDB model:

```
// Instead of separate collections requiring transactions:
// users collection: { _id: userId, name: "Jane", ... }
// profiles collection: { userId: userId, preferences: {...}, ... }
// settings collection: { userId: userId, notifications: {...}, ... }

// Consider a consolidated model:
// users collection
{
  _id: userId,
  name: "Jane",
  profile: {
```

```
      preferences: {"..."}
   },
   settings: {
      notifications: {"..."}
   }
}
```

In the first approach, user information is split across three separate collections: users, profiles, and settings. Each time you need to update related data across these collections, you'd need to use multi-document transactions to ensure consistency. This approach creates unnecessary complexity and performance overhead.

The second approach demonstrates a consolidated model where all user-related information is embedded within a single document in the users collection. With this design, you can update a user's profile preferences and notification settings in a single atomic operation without needing transactions. This approach simplifies your code, improves performance, and leverages MongoDB's document model as it was designed to be used.

Single-document transactions

Making multiple distinct updates to a single document in a transaction can almost always be replaced with a single atomic update. Unless some third-party interaction is involved between the two writes, which is problematic by itself due to the potentially huge increase in latency and risk of exceeding the transaction timeout limit, the correct technique would be to compose a single update (using expressive aggregation syntax if necessary) to make all the modifications in a single operation.

If it's critical that no other thread is reading a document while one thread is making updates to it, it's possible to achieve that without a transaction by placing a logical *lock* field in the document with one update and later when updating the other fields unsetting that field. Take care that the rest of the operations check that no lock exists when they interact with the document.

Transactions for read-only operations

Using multi-document transactions solely for read operations is an unnecessary overhead that can negatively impact performance. To ensure a *consistent snapshot* for a series of reads across many documents, use read concern snapshot rather than starting a transaction. If you need to ensure reads reflect your previous writes, use causally consistent sessions or use the `linearizable` read concern.

Misunderstanding transaction scope and atomicity

A common anti-pattern is either including too little or too much within a transaction, or misunderstanding what operations are truly atomic. Another common misconception is that a single write command is atomic even when it affects multiple documents. An update operation with the `multi:true` option or the `updateMany` method is not atomic as a whole; only each individual write within it is atomic. To make such a multi-update atomic, it would need to be wrapped in a transaction.

Only include operations that must be atomic together in a transaction. Non-critical operations should be performed outside the transaction to reduce scope and improve performance.

Frequent small transactions on hot documents/collections

Small transactions are usually a good thing, but running them too often on the same documents can lead to performance issues. This often happens when different services independently update related documents, such as multiple microservices modifying the order status and inventory for the same products. You might also run into problems when many transactions try to update a single popular document, such as a leaderboard entry during a major gaming event. In some workflows, such as user authentication flows that frequently update session data, logs, and audit records, the same collections get touched over and over again, which can add up.

These situations can cause real slowdowns. Even quick transactions might have to wait in line for document locks, which means operations get processed one at a time instead of in parallel. The more contention there is, the more likely it is that write conflicts will happen, forcing transactions to retry.

In these cases, other approaches often work better. Instead of triggering lots of small transactions, you can batch updates in your application and send them as a single operation. For scenarios that need high throughput, a queue-based system can collect operations and process them in batches.

If you can't avoid contention and need to update multiple documents in a transaction, try updating the most contended document first. That way, if the transaction needs to retry, less work will have to be repeated.

Improper error handling and retry logic

Transactions can fail for a variety of reasons: transient network issues, temporary lock contention, or server-side conditions. If you're using the Core API directly (rather than the Callback API, which handles retries automatically), it's critical to implement proper error handling and retry logic in your application code.

One common mistake is failing to retry a transaction after encountering a `TransientTransactionError`, which is often recoverable with a simple retry. On the flip side, retrying too aggressively, without any delay or backoff, can make the situation worse by increasing contention. Another issue is retrying indefinitely without setting a maximum number of attempts, which can lead to wasted resources and stuck processes. Developers also sometimes mishandle `UnknownTransactionCommitResult`, retrying the entire transaction rather than just the `commitTransaction` command.

These kinds of mistakes can have serious consequences. Poorly managed retries can overload the server during high-traffic periods. Also, if retry logic isn't idempotent or properly scoped, the same operation could be applied more than once.

To avoid these pitfalls, the best approach is to use the Callback API, which automatically retries transactions safely under the hood. If you're using the Core API, make sure to implement retry logic with exponential backoff and jitter to avoid overwhelming the system while still allowing recoverable failures to succeed on a later attempt.

Insufficient monitoring of transaction metrics

As the saying goes, *"If you don't measure it, you can't improve it!"* Failing to monitor transaction performance is a recipe for invisible problems turning into production outages.

To stay on top of transaction health, it's important to track key metrics such as the number of active transactions and total transactions started, committed, and aborted. Monitoring transaction latency, that is, how long transactions take to complete, helps identify slowdowns. Additionally, keeping an eye on WiredTiger cache pressure and eviction rates gives insight into cache utilization. Lock-related metrics such as wait times and acquisition counts reveal whether transactions are being delayed by contention. Finally, tracking error rates, specifically how often transactions abort or require retries compared to total transactions, helps pinpoint instability.

For effective monitoring, set up dashboards in MongoDB Atlas or your preferred system to visualize these metrics. Create alerts for unusual trends such as spikes in abort rates or increasing transaction durations. Logging transaction execution details alongside database metrics can help correlate issues. Regularly reviewing these transaction patterns allows for ongoing optimization and early detection of potential problems.

Summary

Transactions in MongoDB offer powerful consistency guarantees, but they come with trade-offs that need careful consideration. By following the best practices outlined in this chapter, you can use transactions effectively with minimal impact on performance as long as you remember a few key principles. Leverage single-document atomicity over transactions when your data model allows it. Keep transactions small, focused, and short-lived. Monitor and optimize continuously as your application evolves. And, of course, always test transaction behavior under realistic load conditions before production deployment.

The most successful MongoDB applications use transactions judiciously: as one tool in a broader strategy of data consistency that meets your application's requirements while maintaining the performance and scalability your users expect.

Now that you have a solid understanding of MongoDB transactions and their role in maintaining data integrity across multiple operations, let's turn to client libraries in the next chapter. These are what your application uses to interact with MongoDB.

Get This Book's PDF Version and Exclusive Extras

UNLOCK NOW

Scan the QR code (or go to `packtpub.com/unlock`). Search for this book by name, confirm the edition, and then follow the steps on the page.

Note: Keep your invoice handy. Purchases made directly from Packt don't require an invoice.

10

Client Libraries

MongoDB's client libraries, comprising official language drivers and **object-document mappers (ODMs)**, serve as the interface between developers and the database. These libraries abstract low-level database interactions, providing an idiomatic, high-performance experience tailored to each programming language. By encapsulating the complexity of network communications, query optimization, and connection management, client libraries allow you to focus on writing clear, maintainable application code rather than wrestling with database implementation details.

This chapter focuses on understanding, configuring, and optimizing MongoDB client libraries for peak performance and reliability. We will explore the roles of drivers and ODMs, delve into practical configuration best practices, and illustrate how you can leverage their features effectively to build robust, scalable applications that fully utilize MongoDB's capabilities.

The key topics covered in this chapter include the following:

- Defining and explaining the essential role of MongoDB drivers in connecting applications to the database
- Key features of MongoDB drivers, including consistency through shared specifications and idiomatic experiences, as well as performance optimization techniques such as connection management and query efficiency
- Advanced features of drivers, such as error handling, read/write concerns, and monitoring capabilities
- The benefits of ODMs in simplifying application development
- An overview of ODMs, including schema enforcement, query APIs, and relationship management
- Advanced topics such as asynchronous patterns and network performance optimization with client libraries

What are drivers?

MongoDB drivers are software libraries that facilitate communication between your application code and MongoDB clusters. Rather than working directly with low-level networking protocols, **Binary JSON** (**BSON**) serialization, or wire protocol details, you can use these drivers to interact with MongoDB through intuitive, language-specific APIs. Drivers translate high-level operations into database commands, enabling you to perform **create, read, update, and delete** (**CRUD**) operations, manage indexes, execute aggregation pipelines, and implement other MongoDB features without writing raw database commands.

MongoDB provides official drivers for the most popular programming languages, including C#, Go, Java, Node.js, PHP, Python, Ruby, and Rust. Each driver adheres to a shared set of specifications maintained in the MongoDB specifications repository at `https://github.com/mongodb/specifications`, ensuring consistency and feature parity while preserving language-specific idioms, such as method name casing conventions. This structured approach delivers reliability across diverse technology stacks while still feeling natural to developers working in their preferred language.

The effective use of MongoDB's client libraries directly impacts application performance. Properly configured drivers can minimize latency, maximize throughput, and help maintain application scalability. Understanding connection pooling, retryability, read preferences, and read/write concerns allows you to fine-tune database operations for specific workloads and reliability requirements.

As we delve deeper into this chapter, we will explore how these libraries work under the hood, examine configuration best practices, and demonstrate how to leverage their capabilities in real-world scenarios. Whether you're building a simple web application or a complex distributed system, understanding MongoDB's client libraries is essential for creating efficient, robust applications that fully utilize the database's capabilities.

How MongoDB drivers work

When you use a MongoDB driver, you're leveraging a carefully designed interface that handles complex tasks such as the following:

- **Optimizing database access**: Drivers manage connection pools to efficiently reuse database connections. Instead of creating new connections for each operation, the driver maintains a pool of active connections, reducing latency and improving performance. This includes establishing, maintaining, and closing connections as needed, and often allows configuration for pool size and connection timeout parameters.

- **Serializing and deserializing data**: MongoDB drivers handle the serialization of application data into BSON format before sending it to the database, and then deserialize BSON responses back into native data structures. This automatic conversion ensures that data is correctly transmitted and interpreted between your application and the MongoDB server.

- **Automatic retry logic**: To ensure reliability, drivers automatically handle retry logic for network failures. If a database operation fails due to a temporary network issue, the driver can retry the operation, often based on configurable retry policies, ensuring data integrity and application stability.

- **Automatic operations routing**: In replica sets, drivers intelligently route operations to the appropriate servers. Drivers are aware of the cluster topology and can direct read and write operations to the correct nodes, including handling failovers and routing reads to secondaries by read preference configuration.

- **Monitoring server changes**: Drivers continuously monitor server topology changes within replica sets. If a server goes down or a new server is added, the driver updates its view of the cluster and adjusts routing decisions accordingly. This dynamic adaptation ensures application continuity and proper operation in evolving environments.

- **Multi-document ACID transactions**: They provide APIs to initiate, manage, and commit or abort multi-document ACID transactions, ensuring atomicity and consistency across multiple operations (covered in more detail in *Chapter 9, Transactions*).

- **Change streams for real-time data change notifications**: They allow applications to subscribe to change streams, enabling real-time notifications of data modifications, deletions, or insertions, which is essential for building event-driven architectures (covered in more detail in *Chapter 8, Change Streams*).

- **Aggregation pipelines for complex data processing**: Applications can define and execute sophisticated aggregation pipelines that transform, filter, and group data within MongoDB, enabling complex analytics (covered in more detail in *Chapter 4, Aggregations*).

- **GridFS for storing and retrieving large files**: Drivers implement the GridFS specification, allowing applications to store and retrieve large files by splitting them into chunks, overcoming document size limitations.

- **Client-Side Field Level Encryption for enhanced security**: They enable applications to encrypt specific fields before they are sent to the database, protecting sensitive data at rest as well as in flight.

- **Atlas Search and Vector Search**: Drivers expose convenient APIs to enable applications to leverage Atlas Search and Vector Search, providing robust full-text search and vector search capabilities, enhancing the application's search and analytical functions.

In essence, MongoDB drivers are more than simple connectors; they are sophisticated tools designed to streamline database interactions and optimize performance. By handling tasks such as connection management, BSON serialization, and intelligent routing, drivers allow you to focus on application logic rather than low-level database mechanics. Having this understanding of how drivers function enables us to build robust, scalable MongoDB applications and lays the foundation for the effective use of higher-level abstractions such as ODMs.

Key features of MongoDB drivers

MongoDB drivers offer a wide range of features that ensure both functionality and efficiency. Understanding these features is vital for building robust applications. In this section, we'll delve into the key aspects that make these drivers powerful. We'll explore how drivers ensure consistency and reliability through shared specifications, offer an idiomatic experience tailored to each language, optimize for performance, and provide support for advanced features such as transactions and change streams.

Consistency and reliability through shared specifications

One of the defining characteristics of official MongoDB drivers is their adherence to common specifications. By following core specifications, all drivers support the same fundamental features, such as connection pooling, retryable reads or writes, and wire protocol interactions, regardless of the programming language. This consistency is particularly valuable for organizations working in multi-language environments, as developers can expect similar behavior and capabilities across different technology stacks.

When MongoDB introduces new features, these specifications are updated, ensuring that all drivers implement the functionality in a reliable and consistent manner. This specification-driven approach reduces bugs and unexpected behaviors across different language drivers.

Community-maintained MongoDB drivers

Aside from MongoDB's officially maintained drivers, there are community-maintained drivers developed using the shared specifications. These drivers may not implement all specifications or offer all features the official drivers do; however, this should not discourage you from trying them in environments where official drivers don't exist.

Idiomatic experience

Although MongoDB drivers share common specifications, each driver is designed to feel natural within its programming language ecosystem. Take the following examples:

- The Node.js driver leverages JavaScript promises and async/await patterns
- The Python driver follows PEP guidelines and Pythonic principles
- The Java driver provides strong typing and integrates with Java's concurrency tools
- The C# driver embraces .NET idioms and LINQ-style queries

This idiomatic design means that you can work with MongoDB using patterns and practices you're already familiar with, reducing the learning curve and improving productivity. Each driver's API is designed to align with the conventions of its host language, making database interactions feel like a natural extension of the language itself.

Performance optimization

MongoDB drivers are meticulously engineered for performance. They minimize latency and maximize throughput by incorporating numerous optimizations, such as the following:

- **Connection pooling**: Reusing existing database connections instead of creating new ones for each operation, reducing connection overhead and lowering latency.
- **Intelligent operation routing**: Drivers make intelligent server selections by continuously monitoring network latency and server state, dynamically routing read and write operations to the most optimal nodes in a replica set or sharded cluster, ensuring high availability and minimal latency.
- **Network data compression**: Efficiently compress data before it is transmitted across the network, employing algorithms such as Snappy, zlib, or zstd, which reduces the amount of data transferred, thus lowering bandwidth usage and speeding up data transmission. This is particularly beneficial for applications dealing with large, compressible documents or high network loads.
- **Bulk database operations**: Allow multiple actions, such as inserts, updates, or deletes, to be grouped into a single request, which minimizes the number of network round-trips and dramatically reduces overall network overhead. This is especially beneficial for improving the performance of batch data processing tasks.

These optimizations are particularly important for high-throughput applications where database performance directly impacts user experience. The drivers handle these optimizations behind the scenes, allowing developers to focus on application logic rather than performance tuning.

What are object-document mappers (ODMs)?

Beyond the official drivers, ODMs offer an additional abstraction layer that bridges MongoDB's document-based data model with object-oriented programming paradigms. Similar to **object-relational mappers** (**ORMs**) in SQL databases, ODMs allow you to work with native language objects instead of raw BSON documents. Popular ODMs include EFCore for C#, Symphony for PHP, Django for Python, Mongoose for JavaScript, Mongoid for Ruby, and Prisma for TypeScript.

ODMs provide valuable features, including the following:

- Schema enforcement and validation
- Convenient query-building APIs
- Relationship management between documents
- Middleware and life cycle hooks
- Type safety and IDE autocompletion

Similar to the value ORMs bring to developers working with SQL databases, ODMs provide a meaningful abstraction layer between MongoDB's document-based data model and an application's object-oriented programming paradigm.

Understanding ODMs

At their core, ODMs translate between two worlds: MongoDB's flexible document model and the structured, class-based approach of object-oriented programming. This translation layer offers significant advantages for developers seeking to maintain a clean separation of concerns within their applications.

To illustrate the contrast between using MongoDB's native driver directly and leveraging an ODM, the following examples compare retrieving a user document, the first using the PyMongo driver, while the second demonstrates the same operation using MongoEngine:

```python
from pymongo import MongoClient

client = MongoClient()
db = client.my_database
users = db.users
user = users.find_one({"email": "john@example.com"})
print(f"Name: {user['first_name']} {user['last_name']}")
```

While PyMongo gives you full control over queries and data structures, it leaves it to the developer to enforce schema constraints, handle serialization logic, and manually parse or transform results.

```python
# With MongoEngine ODM
from mongoengine import Document, StringField, connect

connect('my_database')

class User(Document):
    first_name = StringField(required=True, max_length=50)
    last_name = StringField(required=True, max_length=50)
    email = StringField(required=True, unique=True)

user = User.objects.get(email="john@example.com")
print(f"Name: {user.first_name} {user.last_name}")
```

With MongoEngine, the schema is declared once using Python classes, making your domain model explicit and easier to reason about. Queries feel more natural in an object-oriented context, and developers benefit from built-in validation, better code completion in IDEs, and reduced risk of runtime key errors. The result is code that can be easier to read, test, and evolve over time.

The key differentiator between a driver and an ODM is that the driver is operation-based, whereas the ODM is state-based. Drivers primarily focus on CRUD operations, or other database operations that you need to perform directly.

ODMs, on the other hand, rely heavily on the state. You load an object into a context, manipulate that object using language primitives, then persist those changes. It is the job of the ODM to translate the current state of the object into the necessary database commands to persist the object's state.

While MongoDB's native drivers provide the foundation for database communication and interaction, ODMs build upon them to offer higher-level abstractions that align more naturally with application code patterns. This approach reduces boilerplate, enhances code organization, and improves maintainability by representing database entities as classes with well-defined behaviors.

Key features of ODMs

ODMs offer numerous benefits that simplify database interactions and enhance application development. In this section, we'll explore the key advantages of ODMs, specifically focusing on schema enforcement and data validation for structured data, the use of intuitive query

APIs for readable database interactions, relationship management to define and handle data associations, middleware and life cycle hooks for executing custom logic at various stages, and finally, type safety and IDE integration, which promotes a more robust development workflow with error detection.

Schema enforcement and data validation

Although MongoDB has a flexible schema by design, many applications benefit from structural consistency. As we saw in *Chapter 2, Schema Design for Performance*, MongoDB offers optional schema validation features that can be enforced server-side. For client-side validation, however, ODMs allow developers to define explicit schemas that ensure documents conform to expected patterns.

MongoDB's inherent flexibility allows data to be stored in JSON-like documents without rigid schemas. While this approach offers great adaptability, it can also lead to inconsistencies if the data structure is not managed. ODMs such as Mongoose provide a solution by enabling developers to define schemas, which act as blueprints to ensure each document conforms to a specific structure and rules by doing the following:

- Defining required fields and default values
- Specifying data types and constraints
- Implementing custom validation logic
- Applying transformations when saving or retrieving data

This degree of control provides safety and predictability while still retaining the flexibility MongoDB is known for, such as with the following example that demonstrates how Mongoose helps enforce data types and validation rules, ensuring data integrity within your MongoDB collections:

```javascript
const mongoose = require('mongoose');

const userSchema = new mongoose.Schema({
  firstName: { type: String, required: true, trim: true },
  lastName: { type: String, required: true, trim: true },
  email: {
    type: String,
    required: true,
    unique: true,
    validate: {
      validator: function(v) {
```

```
        return /^\w+([.-]?\w+)*@\w+([.-]?\w+)*(\.\w{2,3})+$/.test(v);
      },
      message: 'Please enter a valid email'
    }
  },
});
const user = mongoose.model('User', userSchema);
```

In the preceding example, a Mongoose schema is defined that lays out several rules for how fields will be handled for user records. A user's first name, last name, and email are all required. For the first two fields, excess whitespace will be automatically trimmed, and email address uniqueness and composition will be enforced. The custom validator on the email field will show a custom message if validation fails, which makes for a better developer experience than simply failing to modify the document.

Intuitive query APIs

ODMs provide language-idiomatic ways to construct database queries, making them more readable and maintainable. Examples of this include using LINQ in C#, or Builders APIs in C#, Java, and PHP.

To illustrate the intuitive nature of query building in ODMs, this Ruby code example using Mongoid demonstrates how to construct a complex database query using method chaining and language-specific syntax to find in-stock products within a specific category and price range and then sort them:

```ruby
class Product
  include Mongoid::Document
  field :name, type: String
  field :price, type: Float
  field :category, type: String
  field :in_stock, type: Boolean
end

# Find all in-stock products in the "electronics" category
# priced between $100 and $500, sorted by price
results = Product.where(:category => "electronics")
                 .and(:in_stock => true)
                 .and(:price.gte => 100, :price.lte => 500)
                 .order_by(:price => :asc)
```

Most ODMs offer a range of features that make working with MongoDB more intuitive and efficient, including the following:

- Fluent APIs for complex query construction
- Filtering operators that match MongoDB's query capabilities
- Projection and sorting mechanisms
- Pagination helpers
- Aggregation framework abstractions

Therefore, by offering language-native syntax and language idiomatic functionality such as method chaining, ODMs greatly simplify and enhance the query-building process, making it both more approachable and more efficient for developers.

Relationship management

MongoDB's document model inherently supports embedded documents and references. ODMs extend this with explicit relationship definitions.

To illustrate how ODMs facilitate defining relationships, the following Prisma schema example in TypeScript demonstrates how to specify one-to-one, one-to-many, and many-to-many relationships between different entities, such as authors, books, and genres, effectively modeling complex data associations in a structured manner:

```
model Author {
  id       String   @id @default(auto()) @map("_id") @db.ObjectId
  name     String
  email    String   @unique
  books    Book[]   // One-to-many relationship
  bio      Bio?     // One-to-one relationship
}

model Book {
  id       String   @id @default(auto()) @map("_id") @db.ObjectId
  title    String
  isbn     String   @unique
  authorId String   @db.ObjectId
  author   Author   @relation(fields: [authorId], references: [id])
  genres   Genre[]  // Many-to-many relationship
}
```

```
model Genre {
  id          String    @id @default(auto()) @map("_id") @db.ObjectId
  name        String    @unique
  books       Book[]
}

model Bio {
  id          String    @id @default(auto()) @map("_id") @db.ObjectId
  text        String
  authorId    String    @unique @db.ObjectId
  author      Author    @relation(fields: [authorId], references: [id])
}
```

To ensure data conforms to specific patterns, ODMs provide the following capabilities that enable developers to define and enforce rules for document structure and validation:

- One-to-one, one-to-many, and many-to-many relationships

- Embedded document patterns

- Reference patterns with automatic population

- Cascading operations (saves, updates, and deletes)

By providing explicit definitions for various relationship configurations, ODMs empower developers to model complex data associations effectively within MongoDB's document structure, bridging the gap between a flexible database model and structured application design.

Middleware and life cycle hooks

Most ODMs provide hooks to execute code at specific points in a document's access or modification life cycle. The following example demonstrates Mongoose middleware that runs before the 'save' operation, automatically hashing a user's password before it's stored in the database:

```
userSchema.pre('save', async function(next) {
  // Only hash the password if it's modified or new
  if (!this.isModified('password')) return next();

  try {
    this.salt = await bcrypt.genSalt(10);
    this.password = await bcrypt.hash(this.password, this.salt);
```

```
      next();
    } catch (error) {
      next(error);
    }
  });

  userSchema.post('save', function(doc) {
    console.log(`User ${doc.email} has been saved`);
  });
```

ODMs typically provide a variety of hooks within a document's life cycle, allowing developers to execute custom logic at strategic points, such as the following common examples:

- Pre/post validation
- Pre/post save
- Pre/post update
- Pre/post delete

These hooks enable complex behaviors such as automatic timestamps, logging, encryption, and change tracking.

Type safety and IDE integration

Modern ODMs leverage language features to provide compile-time safety and improved developer experience. The following TypeScript example using Typegoose (a library for Mongoose) demonstrates how class decorations can define schemas and their properties, enabling autocompletion and type checking during development, thus reducing errors and improving developer productivity:

```
  class User {
    @prop({ required: true })
    public firstName!: string;

    @prop({ required: true })
    public lastName!: string;

    @prop({ required: true, unique: true })
    public email!: string;
```

```
  @prop({ default: Date.now })
  public registeredAt?: Date;

  public get fullName(): string {
    return `${this.firstName} ${this.lastName}`;
  }
}

const UserModel = getModelForClass(User);

// Autocomplete and type checking works:
const newUser = new UserModel({
  firstName: "Jane",
  lastName: "Doe",
  email: "jane@example.com"
});

// TypeScript would catch this error:
// newUser.nonExistentField = "value"; // Error!
```

The seamless integration with language tooling and type systems offers developers many advantages that enhance productivity and reduce errors by leveraging features such as code completion and type checking:

- Autocompletion for document properties
- Type checking for query operations
- Refactoring support
- Documentation through types

Ultimately, the combination of type safety and tight IDE integration offered by advanced ODMs leads to a more efficient and error-free development process, allowing developers to focus on building features rather than debugging basic data-handling issues.

Impact on developer productivity

ODMs play a crucial role in streamlining the development process and boosting developer productivity. By offering abstractions and tools that align with familiar coding practices, ODMs reduce the time spent managing low-level database details, allowing developers to focus on building application features. The following outlines how ODMs achieve significant productivity gains:

- **Reducing boilerplate code**: Common database operations such as data validation, type conversion, and relationship management can be automated, eliminating the need for developers to write repetitive, verbose code, which frees up time and reduces the chance of errors in those repetitive tasks.

- **Improving code organization**: ODMs facilitate a more structured approach by representing database entities as classes or objects, organizing code logically around business concepts, which simplifies development and maintenance and aligns database interactions with the application's architecture.

- **Enhancing readability**: ODMs use language-idiomatic syntax and intuitive query APIs, making database operations more readable and understandable, as they follow familiar programming patterns rather than requiring knowledge of specific MongoDB commands, thereby improving code clarity and team collaboration.

- **Catching errors earlier**: Using schema enforcement and type checking to catch data-related errors at development time rather than runtime, ODMs can prevent invalid data from reaching the database. This reduces the need for debugging later, which saves time and improves overall code quality.

- **Simplifying complex operations**: ODMs make complex database operations, such as relationship management, nested document handling, and conditional updates, more straightforward by providing high-level abstractions and methods, enabling developers to perform complex tasks with less code and reduced cognitive load.

Through automating routine tasks, streamlining complex operations, and offering clearer code structures, ODMs significantly enhance developer productivity, allowing them to focus more on feature development and less on database plumbing.

When to use ODMs

ODMs offer significant benefits in many development scenarios but aren't always necessary for every project. Deciding whether to employ an ODM depends on several factors, including the complexity of the application, the development team's experience, and the specific requirements for data integrity and consistency. The following situations are where ODMs are particularly valuable and beneficial to your development project:

- Teams transitioning from relational databases to MongoDB will find ODMs helpful in adapting to a non-relational data model, thanks to the familiar object-oriented patterns they provide.

- When consistent data structures are a priority, ODMs make it easier to define and enforce schemas, helping prevent data inconsistencies.

- Applications with complex domain models, where managing relationships between entities is crucial, can greatly benefit from the structure that ODMs provide.

- For code bases that benefit from a clear separation of concerns, ODMs help by abstracting database interactions into distinct layers.

- Development teams seeking to reduce database-related bugs early in the development process will appreciate the built-in type checking and validation features that ODMs provide.

However, ODMs do introduce an abstraction layer that may impact performance or limit access to some MongoDB-specific features. For applications with extreme performance requirements or those using advanced MongoDB capabilities, a hybrid approach or direct driver usage might be appropriate in performance-critical sections.

Ultimately, the decision to use an ODM should be driven by a balanced evaluation of the project's complexity, the team's familiarity with MongoDB, and the need for structured data handling and productivity enhancements.

What are application frameworks?

Application frameworks provide a structured foundation for building software applications, offering a collection of pre-built components and libraries that standardize development patterns and practices. By abstracting common tasks, such as handling HTTP requests, managing database operations, and rendering views, these frameworks allow developers to focus on implementing business logic rather than reinventing low-level functionality for each project.

The value of application frameworks

Application frameworks such as Ruby on Rails, Django, Spring, ASP.NET MVC, and Laravel significantly boost development efforts by offering a structured approach to building software. They provide numerous benefits that enhance both the development process and the final product. Here's a breakdown of the key advantages application frameworks bring to development teams and their solutions:

1. **Standardization:** Frameworks enforce consistent structure and coding style across projects, making it easier for teams to collaborate and maintain code bases. This standardization reduces the learning curve for new team members and ensures best practices are followed throughout the development life cycle.

2. **Efficiency**: By providing reusable components and libraries, frameworks accelerate development time. Developers can quickly integrate features such as authentication, routing, and data validation without writing extensive boilerplate code, allowing teams to deliver functionality faster.

3. **Scalability**: Well-designed frameworks are built to handle the complexities of scaling applications. They offer built-in support for load balancing, caching, and database connection management, enabling applications to grow seamlessly as user demand increases.

4. **Community support**: Popular frameworks have large, active communities that contribute plugins, extensions, and comprehensive documentation. This wealth of resources helps developers solve problems quickly and stay updated with the latest advancements in technology.

In essence, application frameworks empower developers with a structured, efficient, and scalable foundation, fostering standardization, productivity, and, in most cases, robust community support.

Leveraging ODMs and ORMs in frameworks

Most application frameworks integrate with ODMs or ORMs to streamline data modeling and schema management. These integrations provide a consistent approach to database operations, allowing developers to work with data using their native programming language patterns.

The following is a code example illustrating how an ODM, specifically Mongoose, can be integrated within a popular web application framework, Express.js. This demonstrates the seamless connection and interaction between the application's routing layer and the data modeling provided by the ODM, simplifying database operations within the context of a web application:

```javascript
const express = require('express');
const mongoose = require('mongoose');
const app = express();

// Connect to MongoDB
mongoose.connect('mongodb://localhost:27017/myapp');

// Define a schema using Mongoose ODM
const userSchema = new mongoose.Schema({
  name: { type: String, required: true },
  email: { type: String, required: true, unique: true },
  created: { type: Date, default: Date.now }
});
```

```
// Create a model from the schema
const User = mongoose.model('User', userSchema);

// Use the model in an Express route
app.post('/users', async (req, res) => {
  try {
    const user = new User(req.body);
    await user.save();
    res.status(201).send(user);
  } catch (error) {
    res.status(400).send(error);
  }
});
```

The preceding example demonstrates a basic Express application integrated with MongoDB using Mongoose. It connects to a local MongoDB instance, defines a user schema with required name and email fields (the latter also marked as unique), and provides a created timestamp with a default value. A Mongoose model is created from the schema to interact with the database and exposed via a custom route, allowing a basic REST API for creating new users.

By unifying patterns and standards within an application, frameworks enhance developer productivity, code maintainability, and project scalability. They also facilitate collaborative workflows, enabling teams to integrate new features seamlessly while benefiting from established best practices.

Popular MongoDB-compatible frameworks

Several application frameworks offer excellent integration with MongoDB, providing a robust and efficient environment for building modern applications. Each of these frameworks brings its own set of features and advantages tailored to specific programming languages and development paradigms. Here are some of the popular frameworks that seamlessly work with MongoDB:

- **Spring Data MongoDB (Java):** Provides a convenient, annotation-driven approach to managing MongoDB documents within Spring applications. It offers repository abstractions, object mapping, and transaction support, making it a robust choice for enterprise Java applications.

- **Entity Framework (C#)**: Offers a familiar data access paradigm for .NET developers, leveraging the repository pattern and code-first modeling. MongoDB providers allow .NET developers to use the same Entity Framework abstractions they're familiar with while working with document databases.

- **Ruby on Rails (Ruby)**: With Mongoid as its ODM, Rails provides convention over configuration, simplifying setup and automating many routine data operations. Its asset pipeline and scaffolding tools make it particularly efficient for rapidly developing MongoDB-backed applications.

- **Quarkus (Java)**: Designed for cloud-native and containerized environments, Quarkus optimizes performance with a reactive programming model that integrates well with MongoDB's asynchronous drivers. Its low memory footprint makes it ideal for microservices architectures.

- **Django (Python)**: Django provides a comprehensive framework that can integrate with MongoEngine, allowing developers to leverage MongoDB's flexibility while working within a familiar, structured Python ecosystem.

- **Flask (Python)**: Flask is a lightweight alternative that pairs well with PyMongo or ODM extensions, giving developers more flexibility and control when working with MongoDB.

- **FastAPI (Python)**: A modern, high-performance framework for building APIs with Python, FastAPI is ideal for creating RESTful services backed by MongoDB. It supports asynchronous database operations through Motor or Beanie, offering excellent performance characteristics.

- **Laravel (PHP)**: A popular PHP framework that includes artisan commands and scaffolding tools to simplify database management. Its Eloquent ORM can be extended with packages such as `jenssegers/mongodb` for MongoDB integration.

- **Symfony (PHP)**: Another widely used PHP framework offering powerful tools for database management. Symfony integrates with Doctrine MongoDB ODM for working with MongoDB.

Collectively, these frameworks provide a range of options for developers to effectively utilize MongoDB within their preferred programming languages and architectural patterns, fostering efficient and scalable application development.

Best practices when using frameworks with MongoDB

When leveraging application frameworks with MongoDB, consider these important practices:

- **MongoClient reuse**: A MongoClient instance maintains connection pools to all cluster members, as well as monitoring connections. It's important to reuse this instance to prevent the unnecessary duplication of connections, which is commonly achieved via the Singleton pattern or proper configuration of the framework's IoC container.

- **Efficient schema design**: Design your schemas to minimize redundancy while optimizing query performance. Use embedded documents and references appropriately to balance data normalization and denormalization based on application access patterns, as well as to avoid potential N+1 problems.

- **Avoiding N+1 problems**: Be mindful of N+1 query issues, where multiple separate queries are executed to fetch related data. Use techniques such as eager loading, the MongoDB aggregation pipeline, or batch operations to reduce database round-trips.

- **Caching strategies**: Implement appropriate caching layers to reduce database load and improve application performance. Most frameworks offer built-in caching solutions that can be configured to work with MongoDB query results.

- **Lazy versus eager loading**: Choose between lazy and eager loading based on your application's specific needs. Lazy loading defers the loading of related data until it's accessed, while eager loading fetches all related data upfront. Each approach has trade-offs in terms of performance and memory usage.

- **Life cycle callbacks**: Leverage the life cycle hooks provided by your framework's ODM to execute custom logic at various points in a document's life cycle. These callbacks allow you to implement consistent business rules, such as data validation, transformation, or triggering events.

- **Performance monitoring**: Instrument your framework code to monitor MongoDB operation performance. Understanding query patterns and execution times helps identify bottlenecks and optimization opportunities.

Application frameworks significantly enhance MongoDB development by providing structured, reusable components that streamline common tasks. Their integration with ODMs offers a natural development experience in which database operations align with idiomatic programming patterns. By selecting a framework that complements your language expertise and project requirements, development teams can build scalable, maintainable MongoDB applications more efficiently.

As we'll explore in the next section, understanding the specific patterns and pitfalls for popular ODMs and frameworks will help you leverage MongoDB's capabilities while maintaining clean, performant code.

Beyond the basics

In this section, we'll explore advanced techniques and strategies that can dramatically improve your MongoDB application's performance, resilience, and scalability when working with client libraries. These practices represent the difference between basic functionality and production-ready applications capable of handling real-world challenges.

Asynchronous and non-blocking patterns

Modern applications often need to handle multiple operations concurrently while maintaining responsiveness. Asynchronous programming patterns are essential for achieving this, particularly when working with database operations that might otherwise block application execution.

MongoDB client libraries provide robust support for asynchronous operations across various programming languages:

- **Promises and async/await**: JavaScript and Node.js drivers leverage promises and async/await syntax for clean, readable asynchronous code. This eliminates complex callback chains while maintaining non-blocking execution.

- **Event-driven frameworks**: Many MongoDB drivers integrate seamlessly with event-driven architectures, allowing your application to decouple business logic from I/O operations. This approach lets your application continue processing while waiting for database responses.

- **Language-specific implementations**: Different language drivers implement asynchronous patterns according to language conventions, for instance, Java's `CompletableFuture`, Python's asyncio, or C# and Node.js' `async/await`.

By implementing asynchronous patterns effectively, your application can maintain responsiveness even under high load, as illustrated in this Python example:

```python
import asyncio
from pymongo import AsyncMongoClient
async def main():
    uri = "" client = AsyncMongoClient(uri)
    try:
        database = client.get_database("sample_mflix")
        movies = database.get_collection("movies")

        # Query for a movie that has the title 'Back to the Future'
        query = { "title": "Back to the Future" }
        movie = await movies.find_one(query)
```

```
        print(movie)

        await client.close()
    except Exception as e:
        raise Exception("Unable to find the document due to the following
error: ", e)

# Run the async function
asyncio.run(main())
```

Implementing asynchronous patterns within MongoDB client libraries enables you to build highly responsive and performant applications. By leveraging constructs such as Promises, async/await, or, as is the case with the preceding example, language-specific concurrency features, developers can ensure database operations do not block the application's main thread.

Concurrent execution, coupled with non-blocking I/O, prevents applications from freezing or becoming unresponsive, ultimately leading to a smoother and more efficient user experience, especially under high load.

Surfacing and handling failure conditions

To manage transient failures and network issues, you should implement robust error handling. MongoDB drivers provide mechanisms for retryable reads and writes, which can automatically retry operations in case of temporary failures:

- **Retryable writes**: MongoDB drivers support automatic retries for write operations that fail due to transient network issues or replica set elections. This feature is enabled by default but can be disabled using the retryWrites=false connection string option.
- **Retryable reads**: Similarly, read operations are configured to automatically retry on certain failures by default. You can disable this behavior using the retryReads=false option.

As robust as these automatic retries may be, they should be coupled with appropriate error-handling patterns in your application code to gracefully handle database exceptions, such as with the following Node.js code snippet, which illustrates how specific error conditions can be caught and logged when performing an insert operation:

```
try {
  const result = await collection.insertOne(document);
  console.log(`Document inserted with _id: ${result.insertedId}`);
} catch (err) {
```

```
    if (err.code === 11000) {
      console.error('Duplicate key error');
    } else if (err instanceof MongoNetworkError) {
      console.error('Network error occurred');
    } else {
      console.error('An error occurred:', err);
    }
  }
```

If a duplicate key error is detected, one failure condition will have been met, whereas a network issue would trigger another failure condition. The try-catch blocks allow the application to remain resilient to these conditions, which should be handled with appropriate business logic.

Some MongoDB drivers, such as the Node.js driver, have now implemented **Client Side Operation Timeout (CSOT)**. This feature introduces a more predictable operation lifetime control mechanism through the configuration of a timeoutMS value:

```
  const docs = await collection.find({}, {timeoutMS: 1000}).toArray();
```

This example ensures that the initialization of the cursor and retrieval of all documents will occur within 1 second (or 1,000 milliseconds), throwing an error if it exceeds this time limit. This error would need to be handled in the application; however, tighter control over operation lifetimes could be achieved by ensuring control returns to the application within 1 second.

In addition to ensuring the operation will not exceed the timeoutMS threshold, when CSOT is configured and retryable reads are enabled, operations will continue to be retried until timeoutMS elapses. This provides an added layer of resilience to operations that may have failed due to a longer-lasting transient network error and require additional retries to succeed.

By implementing robust handling for failures and retries, developers can ensure their MongoDB applications remain stable and reliable even when facing transient issues or network disruptions.

Connection management

To efficiently manage database connections, use the driver's connection pooling capabilities. Rather than creating new connections for each database operation, connection pools help maintain a set of reusable connections that significantly improve performance. It's important to configure your connection pool size based on your application's concurrency requirements and the resources available on your MongoDB servers.

The following is an example demonstrating how to initialize a MongoDB client in Python using the PyMongo driver, setting specific parameters for the connection pool, such as the maximum and minimum pool sizes, as well as the maximum idle time for connections:

```
client = MongoClient('mongodb://localhost:27017/',
                     maxPoolSize=50,
                     minPoolSize=10,
                     maxIdleTimeMS=30000)
```

Connection management will be discussed in greater detail in *Chapter 11, Managing Connections and Network Performance*; however, the preceding example shows how a connection pool can be created alongside a MongoClient instance. In this case, the pool will always have 10 connections open and available, and can scale up to 50 connections if needed. Each connection will wait for 30 seconds (the value of maxIdleTimeMS) before being automatically closed if left unused.

Effective connection management is foundational for application performance and resource utilization. Covered in the following list is an introduction to some of the concepts and tunables you can set via MongoClient options or the connection string directly:

- **Connection pooling**: Connection pools maintain a set of reusable database connections, eliminating the overhead of repeatedly establishing new connections. Configure the connection pool size based on your workload characteristics. Too small leads to connection wait times, while too large wastes resources.

- **Monitoring connection health**: Implement health checks to identify and replace failed connections. Most MongoDB drivers handle this automatically but may benefit from tuning timeouts and retry logic.

- **Connection options**: MongoDB drivers offer numerous connection string options that can be tuned for specific use cases:

  - maxPoolSize: Maximum connections maintained in the pool
  - minPoolSize: Minimum connections to maintain
  - maxIdleTimeMS: How long connections remain idle before being closed
  - connectTimeoutMS: Maximum time to wait when establishing connections

Effectively configuring and managing your MongoDB driver's connection pool and its options is crucial for maintaining application performance, stability, and efficient resource utilization. Optimizing settings such as pool size, connection timeouts, and idle times ensures your application scales gracefully and responds quickly to user requests, while robust monitoring and life cycle management prevent connection issues from impacting availability.

To illustrate how to fine-tune connection pools, consider the following scenarios and their corresponding recommendations:

Scenario	Recommendation
Slow application-side operation times that are not reflected in the database server logs or the real-time panel.	Use `connectTimeoutMS` to ensure the driver does not wait indefinitely during the connection phase. Set `connectTimeoutMS` to a value greater than the longest network latency you have to a member of the set. For example, if a member has a latency of 10,000 milliseconds, setting `connectTimeoutMS` to 5000 (milliseconds) prevents the driver from connecting to that member.
A misconfigured firewall closes a socket connection incorrectly and the driver cannot detect that the connection closed improperly.	Use `socketTimeoutMS` to ensure that sockets are always closed. Set `socketTimeoutMS` to two or three times the length of the slowest operation that the driver runs.
The server logs or real-time panel show that the application spends too much time creating new connections.	Not enough connections are available at startup. Allocate connections in the pool by setting `minPoolSize`. Set `minPoolSize` to the number of connections you want to be available at startup. The `MongoClient` instance ensures that the number of connections exists at all times.
The load on the database is low and there's a small number of active connections at any time. The application performs fewer operations at any one time than expected.	Increase `maxPoolSize`, or increase the number of active threads in your application or the framework you are using.
Database CPU usage is higher than expected. The server logs or real-time panel show more connection attempts than expected.	Decrease the `maxPoolSize` value or reduce the number of threads in your application. This can reduce load and response times.

Table 10.1: Connection-related performance issues and recommended MongoDB driver settings

By fine-tuning these parameters, you can significantly enhance your application's efficiency and reliability when interacting with MongoDB.

Read/write concerns and read preferences

As discussed in *Chapter 5, Replication*, MongoDB provides configurable read preferences, write concerns, and read concerns that give you fine-grained control over how operations interact with replica sets. These settings can be configured directly through client libraries and play a crucial role in balancing consistency, availability, and performance:

- **Read preferences**: These determine which replica set members handle read operations:

  - `primary`: This is the default setting. All reads go to the primary node.

  - `primaryPreferred`: Try the primary first and use the secondary if unavailable.

  - `secondary`: Read only from secondaries.

  - `secondaryPreferred`: Try secondaries first and use the primary if unavailable.

  - `nearest`: Read from the node with the lowest network latency.

- **Write concerns**: These specify the level of acknowledgment required for write operations:

  - `w:1`: The primary acknowledges writes.

  - `w: "majority"`: The default setting. A write must be persisted on the majority of replica set members.

  - `w:0`: No acknowledgment required (fire and forget – not recommended).

  - `wtimeout`: Option to specify a time limit to prevent write operations from waiting indefinitely.

- **Read concerns**: These control the consistency and isolation properties of the data read from replica sets and sharded clusters:

  - `local`: Default setting. Returns the latest data from the instance.

  - `available`: Similar guarantees as `local`. It is used in sharded clusters for lowest-latency reads at the expense of consistency as an `available` read concern can return orphaned documents when reading from a sharded collection.

  - `majority`: Returns data that has been acknowledged by a majority of the replica set members. The documents returned by the read operation are durable, even in the event of failure.

  - `linearizable`: Returns data that reflects all successful majority-acknowledged writes that completed prior to the start of the read operation. The query may wait for concurrently executing writes to propagate to a majority of replica set members before returning results.

- snapshot: A query with the snapshot read concern returns majority-committed data as it appears across shards from a specific single point in time in the recent past. The snapshot read concern provides its guarantees only if the transaction commits with the majority write concern.

Through the effective use of write concerns and read concerns, you can adjust the level of consistency and availability guarantees as appropriate, such as waiting for stronger consistency guarantees or loosening consistency requirements to provide higher availability.

Compression and network performance

Optimizing data transfer between your application and MongoDB can significantly impact performance, especially with large datasets or high-throughput requirements:

- **Network compression**: MongoDB drivers support several compression algorithms:

  - **Snappy**: Offers a good balance between compression ratio and speed

  - **zlib**: Higher compression ratio but more CPU-intensive

  - **zstd**: Newer algorithm with excellent compression and good speed

- **Minimizing network latency**: Deploy your application and database in the same region or data center when possible. Consider edge deployments or caching strategies for geographically distributed applications.

- **Batch operations**: When inserting, updating, or querying multiple documents, use bulk operations to minimize network overhead, as shown here:

```
// Instead of multiple single inserts
const bulkOp = collection.initializeUnorderedBulkOp();
for (const doc of documents) {
  bulkOp.insert(doc);
}
await bulkOp.execute();
```

- **Projection**: Request only the fields you need, rather than retrieving entire documents, as shown here:

```
// Only retrieve necessary fields
const result = await collection.findOne(
  { _id: documentId },
  { projection: { name: 1, email: 1 } }
);
```

Effectively managing data transfer through network compression, minimizing latency with strategic deployments, optimizing operations with batching, and utilizing projections to reduce data retrieval all play a vital role in enhancing the overall performance of MongoDB applications. By focusing on these areas, developers can significantly improve the efficiency and speed of data exchange, ensuring a smoother and more responsive application experience for end users.

Summary

This chapter has provided a comprehensive exploration of MongoDB's client libraries, including both drivers and ODMs, which serve as the critical interface between applications and the database. We began by defining the essential role of MongoDB drivers in facilitating language-specific, high-performance communication and explored key features such as consistency through shared specifications, idiomatic experiences tailored to different languages, performance optimization techniques such as connection management, and advanced capabilities such as transaction support. We then delved into the world of ODMs, highlighting their benefits in simplifying development through schema enforcement, intuitive query APIs, and relationship management, and examined popular solutions such as Mongoose, Mongoid, Prisma, Spring Data, and Django.

We discussed the importance of best practices, including connection and error management, query optimization, read/write concerns, and monitoring, and explored how application frameworks integrate with MongoDB and leverage ODMs for enhanced productivity. Finally, we ventured beyond the basics to address advanced topics such as asynchronous patterns, network performance optimization, and handling failures and retries. Mastering these aspects empowers developers to build not just functional but performant, scalable, and resilient MongoDB applications, fully utilizing the database's capabilities for real-world deployments.

In the next chapter, we'll build on what you've learned about client libraries by diving into connection management and network performance, key factors that determine how effectively your application communicates with MongoDB behind the scenes.

11

Managing Connections and Network Performance

A proper connection management strategy can make the difference between a lightning-fast, resilient solution and one that crumbles under load. In this chapter, we'll explore the role that connection management plays in achieving optimal performance and reliability.

First, we'll examine connection fundamentals and the network factors that impact database performance, including latency, connection churn, and network saturation. Then, we'll explore the MongoDB connection architecture, from the TCP/IP layer to driver connection pooling, and dive into the connection lifecycle to understand how connections are established, utilized, and terminated. Finally, we'll cover essential strategies for monitoring, troubleshooting, and optimizing connection management to prevent failure cascades and ensure your MongoDB applications maintain peak performance under real-world conditions.

The topics covered in this chapter include the following:

- Key concepts behind how connections work in MongoDB
- What a typical connection lifecycle looks like
- How certain connection failures can lead to broader system issues
- A look at how MongoDB handles connections internally
- Tips for managing connections efficiently

Understanding connection fundamentals

Network performance often becomes a hidden bottleneck in database-driven applications. Even with powerful hardware and optimized queries, poor network connectivity can negatively impact the responsiveness and user experience of your application. There are several factors that contribute to this impact, including the following:

- **Round-trip latency**: Each database operation requires at least one network round-trip, leading to noticeable delays in interactive applications where users expect sub-second responses. This becomes particularly problematic in microservice architectures, where a single user request might trigger multiple cascading database operations.

- **Connection establishment overhead**: Creating new connections requires TCP handshakes, TLS negotiation, and MongoDB authentication. These steps can add hundreds of milliseconds to the first query in a session. The impact of this overhead becomes more apparent in serverless environments or high-concurrency applications where connections are frequently established and terminated.

- **Bandwidth limitations**: Large query results or bulk operations may saturate available network capacity, causing delays for all database operations sharing the same network path. Applications processing media files, generating reports with extensive datasets, or performing data migration or ETL tasks are especially vulnerable to bandwidth constraints.

- **Network stability**: Packet loss or intermittent connectivity issues can cause retries and timeouts, resulting in unpredictable response times and degraded user experience. These issues are particularly disruptive in mobile applications, edge computing scenarios, or when operating in regions with less reliable infrastructure.

- **Distributed system complexity**: In modern distributed architectures, applications may communicate with multiple database instances across different regions or cloud providers, multiplying connection overhead and introducing coordination challenges. This complexity becomes most apparent during global deployments, where cross-region latency can dramatically impact performance, or during partial outages when failover mechanisms are triggered.

While developers often focus on optimizing queries and indexes, the network layer frequently determines the actual performance ceiling. A single poorly managed connection can add hundreds of milliseconds to operation times, creating a noticeable impact for users.

Connection management under production load

Connection management issues often appear only under production loads. A system that performs well during development may still experience severe connection problems when exposed to real-world traffic patterns.

Understanding how network factors and connection processes impact your application helps identify and address potential performance bottlenecks in your MongoDB deployment. There are three key network factors that directly impact your application's throughput and responsiveness: **latency**, **connection churn**, and **network saturation**. Let's examine each of these.

Latency

Latency is the delay between sending a request and receiving a response. This delay affects every operation, no matter how small. Latency in MongoDB operations is influenced by a range of factors, including geographic distance, network conditions, and how operations are structured, making it essential for globally distributed applications to adopt strategies such as data locality or edge caching to maintain responsiveness. Consider the following factors:

- Geographic distance between application servers and MongoDB instances adds unavoidable baseline latency. Deploy MongoDB instances in the same region as your application servers and use multi-region clusters with appropriate read preferences for global applications.

- Network quality issues such as congestion or routing problems increase latency variability. Implement network monitoring with tools such as MongoDB Atlas metrics or custom probes to identify and address network degradation before it impacts users.

- Individual operations sent separately incur cumulative latency penalties compared to batched operations. Use bulk operations when appropriate.

- Applications with globally distributed users may need strategies such as data locality or edge caching to mitigate high latency effects.

In conclusion, latency represents a significant yet often overlooked factor affecting MongoDB performance and user experience. The cumulative impact of even small latency improvements can dramatically enhance application responsiveness, particularly at scale. By strategically addressing geographic placement, network quality, operation batching, and data locality, developers can minimize latency bottlenecks and deliver the responsive experience users expect, even in globally distributed applications. Remember that latency optimization is not a one-time task but an ongoing process requiring regular measurement, analysis, and refinement as your application and user base evolve.

Connection churn

Creating and destroying connections frequently creates significant overhead, which can dramatically impact application performance and resource utilization. Connection churn refers to the rapid establishment and termination of database connections, which introduces several costly operations each time. Here are some examples:

- New connections require TCP handshakes, often with TLS negotiation. Each TCP handshake requires a minimum of one round-trip between client and server, while TLS negotiation adds multiple additional round-trips and complex cryptographic operations that can take hundreds of milliseconds to complete, especially across geographic regions.

- MongoDB's SCRAM authentication requires multiple round-trips. This secure authentication mechanism performs a challenge-response sequence that typically needs 2-3 network round-trips before the connection is authenticated and ready for use, adding latency to every new connection.

- Both client and server must allocate memory and resources for each connection. On the server side, MongoDB allocates memory buffers, creates thread resources, and maintains state for each connection. On the client side, similar resources are allocated, including socket buffers and management structures, which can become significant with hundreds or thousands of connections.

- Modern TLS handshakes involve complex cryptographic operations including key exchange, certificate validation, and cipher negotiation. These operations consume CPU cycles, which at high connection rates can contribute to CPU saturation.

Connection churn is particularly problematic in serverless environments or microservices architectures where services frequently start and stop. In serverless environments, each function invocation might establish a new database connection if not properly managed. At scale, this can result in thousands of connection attempts per second during traffic spikes, overwhelming both the database server and the application infrastructure.

In later sections, we'll explore how we can address connection churn by using connection pooling. We'll also briefly discuss how we can minimize connection churn when using a serverless environment.

Network saturation

When connections or bandwidth reach their limits, performance degrades rapidly, which can result in a number of potential issues emerging:

- MongoDB servers have configured limits on concurrent connections

- Too many active connections can consume available server threads

- When connections are saturated, operations must wait in the queue

- Excessive operations can overwhelm available network bandwidth

Monitor connection utilization to ensure you're not approaching saturation thresholds. Being proactive helps avoid cascading failures that suddenly appear under load.

Now that we've established the importance of managing these network factors, let's dive deeper into how MongoDB connections are actually established, maintained, and terminated throughout their lifecycle. Understanding these mechanics will provide practical insights into optimizing your application's database interactions.

Understanding the connection lifecycle

MongoDB connections have a well-defined lifecycle. Understanding this lifecycle can help you build efficient, scalable applications. The connection lifecycle is grouped into three stages, which we'll explore in the following sections.

Connection establishment

Establishing a MongoDB connection involves a series of low-level and application-level handshakes that prepare the client and server to communicate securely and efficiently. Each step in this process introduces some overhead, but together they form the backbone of a reliable and authenticated session:

1. **TCP three-way handshake creates the network connection**: This initial step establishes communication between your application and the MongoDB server using the standard SYN, SYN-ACK, ACK packet exchange.

2. **TLS/SSL handshake (if enabled) negotiates secure communication**: When network encryption in-transit is enabled, this additional handshake exchanges certificates, verifies identities, and negotiates encryption protocols. Modern MongoDB deployments typically use TLS 1.2 or 1.3 for optimal security.

3. **MongoDB handshake exchanges version and authentication information**: Once the network connection is established, the driver and server exchange protocol information, including supported features, server capabilities, and MongoDB version compatibility. This ensures the driver and server can communicate properly using compatible features.

4. **Authentication process validates credentials**: Depending on your security configuration, MongoDB verifies user credentials using the authentication mechanisms you configured. Failed authentication attempts are logged and may trigger security alerts depending on your configuration.

5. **Server allocates resources for the new connection**: Each connection consumes server resources, including memory for buffers, thread scheduling capacity, and file descriptors. These resources are finite on any server, which is why connection limits exist to prevent resource exhaustion, which could impact database performance or stability.

Together, these steps ensure that every new connection is secure, authenticated, and fully prepared for client-server interaction.

Connection utilization and pooling

MongoDB drivers use connection pooling to optimize performance, reduce latency, and manage resources more efficiently. Here's how pooling works behind the scenes:

- **Connection pooling maintains already established connections**: MongoDB drivers implement connection pools that pre-establish and maintain a set of connections. This eliminates the establishment overhead for subsequent operations and provides immediate access to database resources.

- **Operations acquire connections from the pool when needed**: When your application executes a query, update, or command, the driver automatically obtains an available connection from the pool. If no connections are available, the operation either waits (with a configurable timeout) or the pool creates a new connection if below maximum capacity.

- **Operations release connections back to the pool when complete**: After an operation completes, the connection returns to the pool rather than closing, making it immediately available for the next operation. This recycling approach improves throughput by avoiding the establishment cost for each operation.

- **Proper reuse eliminates repeated establishment costs**: By reusing connections, applications avoid the cumulative overhead of repeated handshakes and authentication. For high-volume applications, this can reduce latency and significantly increase overall throughput.

- **Health monitoring ensures connections remain valid**: Drivers periodically check pool connections for validity using lightweight heartbeat commands. This prevents applications from using stale connections that might have been closed by firewalls, proxies, or network issues, ensuring operations don't fail due to using invalid connections.

Connection pooling enables efficient MongoDB usage, and understanding its role can help you better manage application performance, especially under load.

Connection termination

Whether by design or due to unexpected events, MongoDB connections can and will terminate. Understanding the common causes and best practices for handling termination ensures your application stays stable and responsive:

- **Idle connections may close after configured timeout periods**: To conserve resources, both drivers and servers can close connections that remain unused for extended periods. This cleanup prevents resource leakage but requires re-establishment if activity resumes after a timeout.

- **Application shutdown should properly close connections**: Well-designed applications explicitly close their MongoDB clients during graceful shutdown. This releases server resources promptly and prevents connection leaks. Most modern frameworks provide hooks for registering these cleanup operations.

- **Network errors may force abrupt connection termination**: Unexpected issues such as network partitions, firewall interruptions, or hardware failures can abruptly terminate connections. Robust applications implement retry logic with exponential backoff to handle these scenarios gracefully without user impact.

- **Server restarts or maintenance requires re-establishing connections**: During MongoDB maintenance operations or replica set elections, existing connections may be terminated. Drivers automatically detect these events and establish new connections, but applications should implement appropriate error handling for operations during these transitions.

- **Proper cleanup ensures resources are released promptly**: Each connection consumes memory, file descriptors, and processing capacity on both the client and server. Proper termination frees these resources, preventing memory leaks and exhaustion of system limits such as maximum file descriptors.

By proactively managing idle timeouts, application shutdowns, and unexpected disconnections, you help ensure that resources are released cleanly and your application can recover gracefully.

Closing MongoClient to prevent resource leaks

If the driver you're using supports it, you should always call the `MongoClient.close()` method in your application shutdown routine to properly release all connections and associated resources. This prevents resource leaks and ensures clean application termination. See the *Optimizing connection management* section later in this chapter for more details on proper connection cleanup strategies.

Understanding the MongoDB connection lifecycle is important for building applications that are both performant and resilient. Connection establishment carries some overhead, making efficient pooling and reuse important for high-throughput systems. Proper handling of connection termination prevents resource leaks that could degrade your application over time.

MongoDB connection architecture

Understanding how MongoDB manages connections from the driver to the server is important for designing resilient applications. This section covers the fundamental connection mechanisms and how they interact across your application stack, including **TCP/IP** and the **MongoDB Wire Protocol**, **driver connection pooling**, and **server connection handling**.

TCP/IP and the MongoDB Wire Protocol

MongoDB's client-server communication is built on TCP/IP, but with several MongoDB-specific enhancements and optimizations. Understanding these technical details helps developers diagnose connection issues and optimize network performance.

The MongoDB Wire Protocol is a socket-based, request-response style protocol that defines how clients and servers communicate over standard TCP/IP sockets. It has several defining characteristics:

- **Binary JSON (BSON) format**: Unlike text-based protocols (such as HTTP), MongoDB uses BSON for efficient serialization and deserialization with minimal CPU overhead.

- **Modern message format**: Since MongoDB 5.1, `OP_MSG` has been the primary opcode used for both client requests and database replies, replacing older opcodes such as `OP_QUERY` and `OP_REPLY`.

- **Compression support**: `OP_COMPRESSED` wraps other opcodes using compression algorithms such as snappy, zlib, or zstd to reduce network bandwidth.

- **Message checksums**: Optional CRC-32C checksums ensure data integrity, particularly important for non-TLS connections.

When a client connects to MongoDB, several operations occur sequentially, with potential performance implications at each stage:

1. **DNS resolution stage**: The connection process begins with resolving MongoDB server addresses. DNS resolution translates hostnames into IP addresses, with SRV records enabling intelligent service discovery for replica sets and sharded clusters. TTL settings on DNS records affect how quickly topology changes propagate to clients. Failed resolutions can trigger exponential backoff retry algorithms in drivers, potentially causing connection delays. Once addresses are resolved, the connection proceeds to the TCP establishment stage.

2. **TCP connection stage**: After DNS resolution, the client establishes the network foundation. Keep-alive packets help maintain long-lived connections and detect dead connections and free resources. TCP window scaling enables higher throughput over high-latency connections by allowing larger amounts of in-transit data before requiring acknowledgment. After the TCP connection is established, security layers are applied.

3. **TLS/SSL security stage**: With the TCP connection in place, security encryption is then established. Certificate validation introduces a small delay as the server's authenticity is verified. TLS session resumption can reduce the handshake overhead on reconnections by reusing parameters from prior sessions. With TLS 1.3 (supported in newer MongoDB versions), the handshake round-trips are reduced from two to one, improving the connection speed. The selected cipher suite influences both the security posture and CPU overhead. Once the encrypted channel is established, MongoDB-specific protocol negotiation begins.

4. **MongoDB-specific handshake stage**: The connection now exchanges MongoDB protocol information. The client sends `hello` (or `isMaster`) commands to exchange capability documents (`isMaster` is maintained for backward compatibility). During this stage, drivers detect server versions and adjust feature compatibility accordingly. Topology discovery identifies the primary, secondaries, and arbiters in the cluster. Server parameters such as `maxWireVersion` determine available features and Wire Protocol compatibility. After establishing protocol compatibility, the connection moves to authentication.

5. **Authentication stage**: The final stage verifies client identity before allowing database operations. SCRAM-SHA-256 (default) provides strong security but requires multiple round-trips. X.509 certificate authentication binds identity to TLS certificates for enhanced security. LDAP and Kerberos proxy authentication add additional network hops and latency. Once the authentication is complete, the connection is fully established and ready for use.

Each of these steps contributes to the total connection latency, which can range from a few milliseconds in local deployments to several hundred milliseconds across geographic regions or with complex authentication schemes. This connection overhead underscores why connection pooling is critical for high-performance applications.

Driver connection pooling

MongoDB drivers are language-specific libraries that handle the complexities of communicating with MongoDB servers. One of their most important functions is connection pooling. When your application initializes the MongoDB client, the driver creates a connection pool (or multiple pools, depending on the topology). The driver then borrows an available connection from the pool when your code executes a MongoDB operation. It sends the command over the connection and waits for a response. After the operation completes, the connection is returned to the pool for reuse. The driver also maintains the connection pool by monitoring the health of connections and may periodically test them or replace them.

Connection pools have the following parameters that can be adjusted:

- `maxPoolSize`: The maximum number of connections the pool can maintain (default: 100 in most drivers).
- `minPoolSize`: The minimum number of connections the pool can maintain, even when idle (default: 0 in most drivers).
- `maxConnecting`: Limits how many connections can be in the process of being established concurrently (default: 2 in most drivers). This parameter is not available in the Rust driver.
- `maxIdleTimeMS`: The duration an idle connection remains in the pool before being closed.

Optimizing maxPoolSize for asynchronous applications

For asynchronous applications, setting `maxPoolSize` to match your expected concurrency rather than your thread pool size often results in better performance.

For more information on the above connection pooling parameters, make sure to check out the MongoDB documentation at `https://www.mongodb.com/docs/manual/tutorial/connection-pool-performance-tuning/`.

Connection pool behavior varies significantly depending on whether the driver is synchronous or asynchronous. For synchronous drivers, when no connections are available, the calling thread blocks operations until a connection becomes available or the wait queue timeout expires. On the other hand, asynchronous drivers return a future or promise that resolves when a connection becomes available, instead of blocking.

MongoDB server connection handling

Efficient connection handling supports scalable, high-performance MongoDB deployments. On the server side, MongoDB uses a combination of configurable parameters and operating system-level resources to manage incoming client connections:

- `net.maxIncomingConnections`: Controls the maximum number of simultaneous client connections (default: 1 million on Windows; on Linux, defaults to 80% of the maximum file descriptor limit). Since each connection requires a file descriptor, this limit helps prevent resource exhaustion on the server.
- **Operating system limits**: File descriptor limits (`ulimit -n` on Linux/Unix systems) can also restrict the number of connections.

The specifics of connection management also depend on the deployment topology (whether it's a standalone instance, a replica set, or a sharded cluster):

- **Standalone**: Applications connect directly to a single MongoDB server with a single connection pool
- **Replica set**: Drivers discover all members and maintain separate connection pools for each, routing operations based on read preferences
- **Sharded cluster**: Applications connect to `mongos` routers, which maintain their own connections to shards, creating a multi-tier connection architecture

Now that you're familiar with MongoDB's connection architecture, let's discuss how it facilitates monitoring and troubleshooting connections.

Monitoring and troubleshooting connections

Effective connection management requires ongoing monitoring and the ability to quickly diagnose problems when they occur. By implementing proactive monitoring practices and having clear troubleshooting approaches ready, you can identify potential issues before they impact your application's performance and reliability.

MongoDB drivers expose detailed metrics about their connection pools, giving you visibility into how your application is utilizing database connections.

Most MongoDB drivers implement the **Connection Monitoring and Pooling (CMAP)** specification, though each language driver provides different methods for accessing these metrics. For example, in Node.js, you can use event listeners to monitor connection pool activity:

```
// Node.js example using event listeners for CMAP events
const uri = "mongodb+srv://user:pass@abcdef.mongodb.net/";
const client = new MongoClient(uri);
client.on('connectionPoolCreated', event => console.log(event));
client.on('connectionCheckedOut', event => console.log(event));
client.on('connectionCheckedIn', event => console.log(event));
```

See https://www.mongodb.com/docs/drivers/node/current/monitoring-and-logging/ monitoring/#connection-pool-events to learn more about tracking these connection metrics using the Node.js driver.

While driver metrics capture the application's view of its interactions with the database, MongoDB servers provide complementary metrics about incoming connections from their viewpoint. These metrics can help you understand your deployment's overall connection utilization across all client applications:

- **connections.current**: Number of active client connections to the server. Approaching the maximum indicates potential connection saturation.
- **connections.available**: How many more connections the server can accept before reaching its configured limit.
- **connections.totalCreated**: Total number of connections created since server start. Rapid increases may indicate connection churn.

You can retrieve these metrics through the serverStatus command in MongoDB Shell or through your preferred MongoDB driver:

```
db.adminCommand({ serverStatus: 1 })
```

By correlating client-side and server-side metrics, you can build a comprehensive view of connection health across your entire application stack. Check out the MongoDB documentation for the `serverStatus` command at `https://www.mongodb.com/docs/manual/reference/command/serverStatus/#connections` to learn more.

When connection issues occur, they typically manifest as specific error types. Learning how to recognize these symptoms is crucial for effective troubleshooting:

- **`socketTimeout`**: The operation takes longer than the configured `socketTimeoutMS`. Often indicates network congestion or overloaded servers.
- **`EOF` (End of File)**: The server closed the connection unexpectedly. This may result from server restarts, network interruptions, or idle timeout policies.
- **`Broken pipe`**: The connection was severed while the client was still using it. Typically indicates network failures or proxy interruptions.
- **Authentication failures**: Incorrect credentials or authentication configuration. May occur after credential rotations or configuration changes.

Connection pool exhaustion is a particularly serious condition that can rapidly degrade application performance. Look out for these warning signs:

- Increasing wait queue length in driver metrics
- `MongoWaitQueueTimeoutException` or similar errors in application logs
- Sudden increases in operation latency
- Request failures during traffic spikes

It's important to remember that connection pool exhaustion can quickly cascade into system-wide failures as timeouts trigger retries, which create more connection requests, accelerating the exhaustion.

For deployments using TLS or DNS-based service discovery, additional connection problems may arise from security or network configuration issues. These issues can be particularly challenging because they may appear intermittently or only under specific conditions. Secure connections depend on proper TLS configuration and certificate management. When experiencing TLS-related connection failures, verify the following:

- Certificate chains are valid and trusted by all clients
- Certificate hostnames match the server's configured hostname
- TLS protocol versions and cipher suites are compatible between client and server

- Certificate expiration dates are valid and not approaching expiration
- Intermediate certificates are properly installed on all systems

A common issue occurs when clients and servers have mismatched TLS configurations. For example, if your application requires TLS 1.3 but your MongoDB server only supports up to TLS 1.2, connections will fail despite both systems having valid certificates.

MongoDB Atlas and replica sets often rely on DNS SRV records for service discovery. When connection problems occur in these environments, DNS configuration is a frequent culprit. For DNS SRV resolution issues, you can use standard DNS diagnostic tools to verify proper configuration:

```
dig srv _mongodb._tcp.your-cluster-hostname.mongodb.net
dig txt your-cluster-hostname.mongodb.net
```

These commands help verify that your DNS is correctly configured to support MongoDB's service discovery mechanisms, which are especially important in replica set and sharded cluster deployments. When working with MongoDB Atlas, remember that DNS propagation delays can sometimes cause temporary connection issues after cluster configuration changes. If you've recently modified your Atlas cluster, allow sufficient time for DNS updates to propagate through your network.

Connection monitoring best practices

After understanding how to diagnose specific connection problems, implementing a comprehensive monitoring strategy becomes essential for maintaining system health over time. For effective connection monitoring, you should do the following:

1. **Establish baselines**: Understand normal connection patterns for your application
2. **Set meaningful thresholds**: Configure alerts based on connection usage relative to limits
3. **Correlate metrics**: Connect driver-side and server-side metrics for a complete picture
4. **Monitor trends**: Watch for gradual changes that might indicate evolving issues
5. **Automate alerts**: Set up proactive notifications for high wait queue times or connection counts approaching limits

By combining these monitoring practices with the troubleshooting approaches outlined earlier, you can build a robust connection management strategy that helps prevent problems before they impact your users.

Optimizing connection management

Now that you understand how to achieve and maintain a resilient system via connection management, as well as how to monitor and troubleshoot connection issues, let's take things a step further and talk about how to optimize connection management. Achieving optimal MongoDB performance and resilience requires thoughtful tuning of your connection management strategy. This section covers key approaches for optimizing connection pools and implementing strategies for different workload patterns.

Connection pool optimization

Optimizing the connection pool starts with ensuring the size of the pool is ideal for your application. The ideal connection pool size varies based on your application's workload characteristics:

- **OLTP workloads**: Start with moderate pool sizes (50-100 connections) for many short operations
- **OLAP workloads**: Use smaller pools sized to match expected concurrent analytical operations
- **Batch processing**: Size the pool to match the parallelism of your batch operations

A best practice is to tune your connection pool size based on application performance metrics and observed behavior, rather than relying on a fixed utilization percentage. Monitor key indicators such as wait queue size, operation latency, and server-side connection metrics to determine whether your pool size needs adjustment.

Consider these guidelines when tuning connection pools:

- If your application spends excessive time creating new connections, increase `minPoolSize` to ensure sufficient connections are available at startup
- If the database CPU usage is higher than expected with many connection attempts, consider reducing `maxPoolSize` to decrease the load
- If the load is low but the application throughput is less than expected, you may need to increase `maxPoolSize` or adjust application threading

Remember that each MongoDB driver creates a separate connection pool for each server in your topology, so the total connections from an application will be `maxPoolSize` multiplied by the number of MongoDB servers.

Connection timeout configuration

Building resilient, high-performance applications that gracefully handle network disruptions and service degradation requires the configuration of proper timeout settings. Poorly configured timeouts can lead to cascading failures, resource exhaustion, or degraded user experience. MongoDB provides several configurable timeout parameters that control different aspects of connection behavior:

- `connectTimeoutMS`: How long the driver waits when establishing a new connection. Set this to a value greater than the longest network latency you have to any member of your deployment.

- `socketTimeoutMS`: How long the driver waits for a response for a specific operation. Set this to two or three times the length of the slowest operation that your driver runs.

- `maxIdleTimeMS`: How long idle connections remain in the pool (balance between connection churn and resource utilization).

Properly tuning these timeout parameters requires understanding both your application behavior and your MongoDB deployment topology.

Important

Do not use `socketTimeoutMS` to prevent long-running server operations. Instead, use `maxTimeMS()` or `timeoutMS()` for drivers that support client-side operators timeout with your queries so that the server can cancel long-running operations. For example, if operations time out gracefully at the driver level, the application can attempt meaningful retries without overwhelming the server. Without proper timeouts, retries could flood connection pools, amplify resource exhaustion, and result in system-wide downtime.

Server-side optimization

In self-managed deployments, you need to configure both MongoDB's connection parameters and the underlying operating system limits to ensure optimal performance. These settings work together to determine how many concurrent clients can connect to your database.

```
net:
  maxIncomingConnections: 65536
```

The maxIncomingConnections setting controls the maximum number of simultaneous client connections that MongoDB will accept. Increasing this limit allows more concurrent client applications to connect to your MongoDB server, which is essential for high-traffic applications or environments with many microservices. However, simply increasing this parameter is not sufficient; you must also adjust the operating system's limits.

Operating system configuration

In Unix-based systems, MongoDB uses one file descriptor per client connection. When MongoDB reaches either the maxIncomingConnections limit or the operating system's file descriptor limit (whichever is lower), it will refuse additional client connections. This creates a bottleneck that can severely impact application availability during periods of high demand.

For Linux systems using systemd, you should configure the file descriptor limit in the MongoDB service file:

```
[Service]
# In the MongoDB systemd service file
LimitNOFILE=64000
```

For non-systemd environments, set the limits for the MongoDB service user in the /etc/security/ limits.conf file:

```
mongodb soft nofile 64000
mongodb hard nofile 64000
```

After changing these limits, MongoDB must be restarted for the changes to take effect. To confirm that your configuration changes are benefiting your deployment, you can use these verification methods:

1. Check the current operating system limits with the following:

    ```
    ulimit -n          # For the current shell session
       cat /proc/$(pidof mongod)/limits   # For the running MongoDB
    process
    ```

2. Monitor MongoDB connection utilization through the serverStatus command:

    ```
    db.adminCommand({ serverStatus: 1 }).connections
    ```

The output will show:

```
{
  "connections": {
    "current": 123,        // Current active connections
    "available": 63877,    // Remaining available connections
    "totalCreated": 1578   // Total connections created since
startup
    }
}
```

3. Watch for connection rejection errors in MongoDB logs, which indicate you've hit connection limits:

```
[conn12345] Too many open connections
```

You should see improved stability and performance under load after properly configuring both MongoDB's maxIncomingConnections limit and the operating system's file descriptor limits. Applications will be able to establish connections reliably even during traffic spikes, and you'll avoid cascading failures that occur when connection limits are reached. MongoDB Atlas manages these settings automatically based on the cluster tier, scaling both the database configuration and underlying infrastructure resources to match your workload needs.

Performance optimization leveraging network compression

Network compression is an important optimization technique in MongoDB that reduces the amount of data transmitted between clients and servers. By compressing data before transmission and decompressing it upon receipt, MongoDB can significantly reduce network bandwidth requirements while potentially improving overall performance. This feature is particularly valuable when operating over high-latency connections or in bandwidth-constrained environments.

Benefits and trade-offs of network compression

When implementing network compression in your MongoDB deployment, it's important to understand both the advantages and potential drawbacks to make informed decisions.

One of the primary benefits of enabling compression is the significant reduction in network bandwidth consumption. By compressing data before transmission, MongoDB can significantly reduce the total amount of data transferred across the network.

This is especially effective for text-heavy documents, such as JSON data with lengthy field names or string values, which typically compress very well. Another notable advantage is the potential for reduced latency and faster response times in certain environments. Since less data needs to travel across the network, operations can complete more quickly, leading to a more responsive application experience for users.

However, there are important considerations that must be considered before enabling compression in a production environment. CPU resource utilization is an important factor. Compression and decompression operations require computational resources on both the client and server sides. In environments where CPU resources are already constrained, the additional processing requirements might offset the network benefits.

It is also important to recognize that compression may not always yield meaningful performance improvements, and in some cases, may even introduce inefficiencies. For small operations or when working with already compressed binary data (such as images or videos), the overhead of compression and decompression might outweigh the benefits of reduced network traffic. In these cases, enabling compression could potentially decrease overall performance.

Available compression algorithms

MongoDB provides several compression algorithm options, each with different characteristics that make them suitable for various use cases:

- **snappy** offers an excellent balance between compression speed and ratio. It typically compresses data to about 30-50% of its original size while using minimal CPU resources. This makes it an ideal default choice for most MongoDB deployments, providing meaningful bandwidth savings without significant processing overhead.

- **zlib** delivers higher compression ratios than Snappy, potentially reducing data size to 20-40% of the original. However, this comes at the cost of increased CPU usage for both compression and decompression. zlib may be appropriate when bandwidth is extremely limited and CPU resources are abundant.

- **zstd** (available in newer MongoDB versions) provides excellent compression ratios while maintaining reasonable CPU efficiency. It often achieves better compression than zlib with less computational cost, making it an increasingly popular choice for environments that support it.

Choosing a compression algorithm depends on the specific trade-offs your system can afford between CPU usage and network bandwidth, and should ideally be guided by benchmarking in the context of your workload.

Implementing network compression

Enabling compression in MongoDB is straightforward and requires minimal configuration changes. You can specify your preferred compression algorithms through the connection string when establishing a connection to the database:

```
mongodb://hostname/?compressors=snappy,zlib
```

When a connection is established, the client and server negotiate to select the best mutually supported compression algorithm from the provided list. If multiple algorithms are specified (as in the preceding example), they are evaluated in order of preference from left to right.

By default, MongoDB deployments are configured with compression enabled; however, messages between clients and the cluster will not be compressed unless the client specifies a compressors configuration. Enabling network compression with the appropriate algorithm for your specific requirements can reduce your MongoDB deployment's network utilization while maintaining excellent performance.

Connection strategies for serverless environments

Managing connections in serverless environments presents unique challenges due to their ephemeral nature and distinctive execution model. This section explores comprehensive MongoDB connection strategies for serverless functions (AWS Lambda, Azure Functions, Google Cloud Functions), covering the fundamental challenges of ephemeral execution contexts, cold starts, connection bursts during scaling events, and resource constraints, followed by practical implementation patterns including connection pool optimization, initialization techniques outside function handlers, and methods for maintaining connection persistence across invocations—all designed to help you build resilient, efficient serverless applications with reliable MongoDB connectivity while minimizing costs and maximizing performance.

Serverless functions are ephemeral by design, creating unique connection management challenges:

- **Ephemeral execution**: Functions spin up, process requests, and may be terminated at any time
- **Cold starts**: New function instances must establish fresh connections
- **Connection bursts**: Many concurrent function invocations can create connection spikes
- **Resource constraints**: Function instances have memory and CPU limitations

The most critical pattern for serverless environments is initializing your MongoDB client and connection pool outside the function handler. Let's take a look at the following example so you can get a better understanding:

```
const { MongoClient } = require('mongodb');
// MongoClient now auto-connects so no need to store the connect()
// promise anywhere and reference it.
const client = new MongoClient(process.env.MONGODB_URI);

export const handler = async() => {
  const databases = await client.db('admin').command({ listDatabases: 1
});
  return {
    statusCode: 200,
    databases: databases
  };
};
```

This code demonstrates an implementation of the MongoDB connection pattern optimized specifically for AWS Lambda, but could be adapted for other serverless environments.

The MongoClient instance is created outside the scope of the function handler, which will allow it to be reused. The intentional exclusion of client.close() at the end of the handler should keep the connection pool alive for subsequent invocations, reducing latency for "warm" function calls.

Connection pools for serverless environments typically require different configurations than traditional applications:

- **Smaller pool size**: Start with a small maxPoolSize (3-5 connections) as each function instance has its own pool
- **Lower idle timeout**: Set a shorter maxIdleTimeMS limit to release unused connections more quickly
- **Avoid excessive minimum pools**: Use minPoolSize: 0 to prevent maintaining connections that might not be used
- **Set appropriate wait queue timeouts**: Match with function execution time limits

Employing appropriate connection strategies within serverless environments can help mitigate some challenges typical of these ephemeral functions. By strategically initializing connection pools outside function handlers with optimized parameters, developers can mitigate cold starts and connection bursts, ensuring persistent, low-latency database interactions.

Summary

Effective MongoDB connection management is essential for building high-performance, resilient applications. Throughout this chapter, we've explored how the network stack serves as a critical foundation of your database architecture, from the fundamental network factors of latency, connection churn, and saturation to the technical details of MongoDB's wire protocol and connection lifecycle.

Connection pooling stands as the most impactful optimization technique, significantly improving application performance by reusing TCP connections and distributing authentication costs across multiple operations. Proper implementation requires understanding both client-side pool configuration parameters and corresponding server-side limits. The critical relationship between MongoDB's maxIncomingConnections parameter and operating system file descriptor limits deserves particular attention, as these settings work together to determine connection capacity during peak traffic periods.

Different computing environments demand specific connection management approaches. For serverless deployments, initialize connection pools outside function handlers and use smaller pools with appropriate timeout values. In distributed architectures, adjust timeout settings based on network characteristics and leverage locality-aware routing when possible.

Regular monitoring of client-side metrics such as pool utilization and wait queue times, combined with server-side metrics from serverStatus, creates a comprehensive view of connection health. This observability allows you to prevent cascading failures through early detection and appropriate sizing adjustments.

By implementing these technical principles throughout your technology stack, you'll develop MongoDB applications that maintain consistent performance even under challenging network conditions, ensuring both reliability and efficient resource utilization as your data volumes and user base expand.

The next chapter dives into MongoDB's indexing and query patterns, examining the query execution lifecycle, analyzing explain output, and diagnosing slow queries through logs. It also covers mastering MQL semantics with appropriate index usage and leveraging specialized collections and features to optimize overall database performance.

12

Advanced Query and Indexing Concepts

There are many reasons why your queries might be *slow*, a subjective term that usually means *slower than you expected or needed it to be*. Many factors that can contribute to this include a lack of indexes, suboptimal indexes, insufficient hardware resources, using inefficient operations unnecessarily, or too many other competing operations for the same resources.

In this chapter, we'll look at some advanced concepts in query execution, covering how queries use indexes, how the query optimizer selects an index, ways to dig deeper using the explain command, and techniques to improve performance if there's room for improvement. We will also introduce some special index types and collections that may be a good fit for your use case when regular indexing strategies seem to be inadequate. We will also describe other places where inefficiency may creep into your system and provide other tips for best performance.

The topics covered in this chapter are as follows:

- The query execution life cycle
- The process of evaluating and analyzing explain output
- Using log messages to detect, analyze, and diagnose the root causes of slow queries
- Understanding MongoDB Query Language semantics and index use
- Additional special collections, index types, and features that can enhance performance

Understanding query execution

It's important to understand what happens when an operation is sent from the application to the database. There are many places where performance can be improved, and having a full understanding of what all the stages are makes it possible to reason correctly about where things are not as optimal as they could be and how to fix them.

When a query is sent to the database engine, whether as part of a find, update, delete, or aggregate $match filter, several things happen. First, the query is parsed into a standardized form. Then, the query planner has to figure out whether there's an index that can be used, and if there is more than one, then which one would be best. The initial batch of results is returned to the client. Then, if the client requests more results, the getMore command will return additional batches.

Since there is some overhead in selecting the right index, MongoDB uses a process that ensures that once a plan is chosen for a particular *query shape*, it is stored in a plan cache for future use. A query shape is the query being run with the values ignored, so {x:5} and {x:25} are considered the same query shape. There is also a mechanism to ensure that if an index turns out not to be the best, it will get re-evaluated in case a better one is available.

Figure 12.1 shows the complete query-planning process flow:

Query Planner

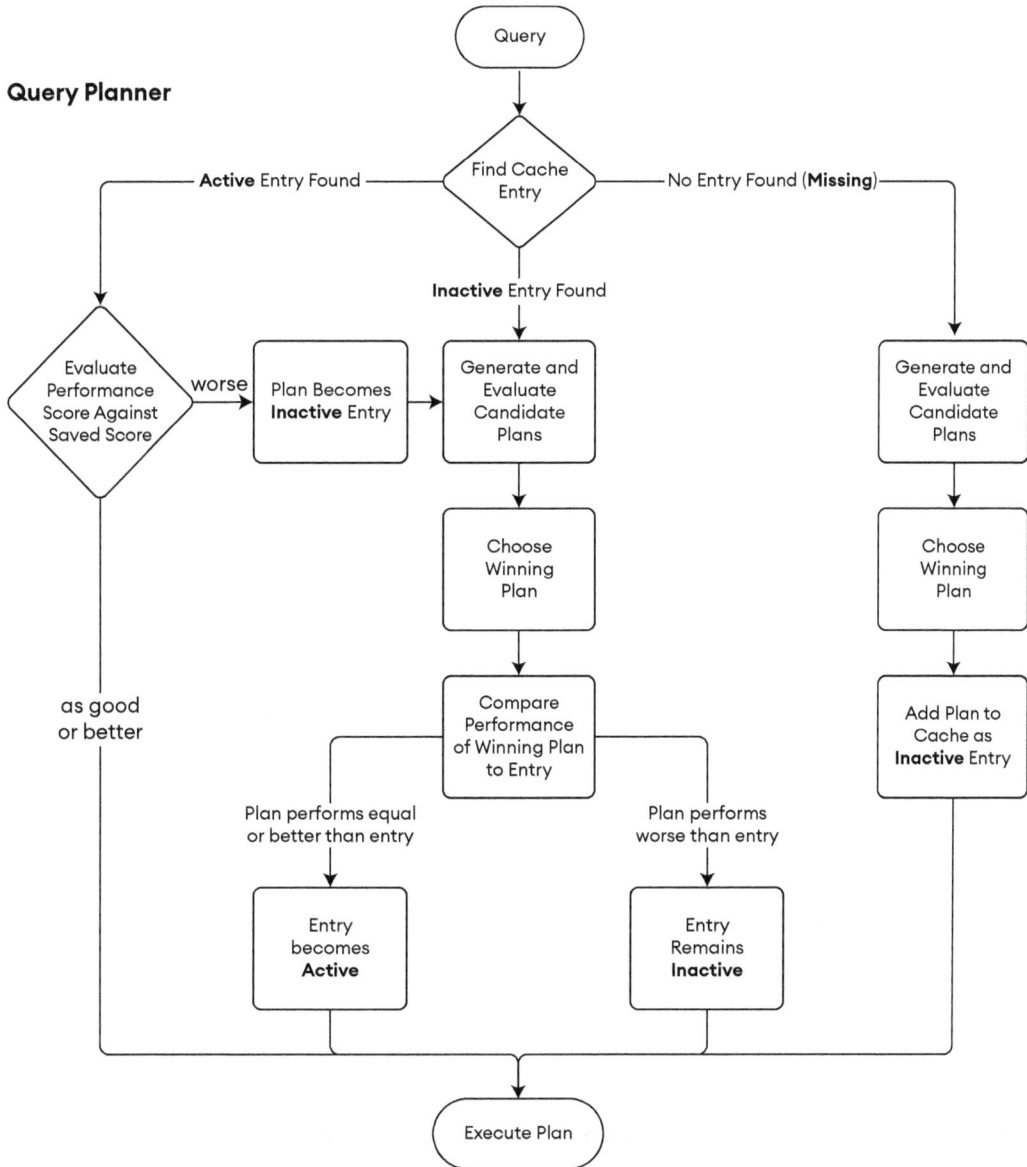

Figure 12.1: Query-planning process

But you can think of this in a slightly simplified way: first, we ask, *"Is there already a plan cached?"* If yes, then use it; if not, then generate and evaluate candidate plans, choose the winning plan, and add it to the cache for future use. This is a slightly simplified flow description as it doesn't take into account that the winning plan is first saved as inactive and then only activated after it's confirmed to have good performance. But as a simplification, this is a good approximation.

What are possible candidate plans for any particular query? We already know that if there is no eligible index, then the plan will be a full collection scan (COLLSCAN). If there is an index or multiple indexes available, then depending on the exact query requirements, they can be used in different ways. We will look at the different ways to use indexes in the next section.

Plan cache usage with single eligible index

If there is only one plan available, for instance, there is only one eligible index, then it will not be stored in the plan cache. The plan cache is strictly for scenarios when multiple indexes can satisfy the query.

Depending on the efficiency of the index, as well as whether it provides covering for the query and/or supports sort and query filters, a score will be assigned. The exact details of how plans are scored are beyond the scope of this book. However, as a general principle, the highest score would represent the most efficient plan during trial execution and become the tentative winner. This plan is then cached along with its score, at least until an inefficient execution of the same query shape using the plan ends up scoring significantly worse than the saved score, in which case, the cached plan is evicted from the plan cache. When this happens, the query is re-planned, meaning it goes through the plan evaluation stage again to try and find a better index to use.

Planning is not independent of returning results to the client. The documents found while planning the query execution get returned to the client as the first batch of results.

Plan stages, or "how indexes can be used"

Even though we've just been saying *"queries use indexes,"* it turns out there are multiple ways that indexes can be used. In a standard case of looking for a field in a document matching a single value in a B-tree, we traverse the B-tree and find the recordId of the matching leaf node. However, there are other ways indexes can be used in cases of queries that are not looking for documents but counts of documents. There are other optimizations in how the index is traversed when we are looking for the first distinct value across the full B-tree or a subsection of it. All of these have different internal names that you may see in the query plan summary in the logs, or in the explain output.

Here are the different **indexed** query plans and what they mean:

- IXSCAN: An index scan means we are traversing (usually a subset of) the B-tree in some order
- IDHACK or EXPRESS_IXSCAN: Special optimized index scan for _id indexes or other unique indexes
- DISTINCT_SCAN: Special index scan to support finding all distinct values in the B-tree
- COUNT_SCAN: Special index scan to support only getting counts from a subset of the B-tree

If there is no eligible index for the operation, then the query plan will be COLLSCAN, meaning a full collection scan.

Index preference over COLLSCAN

If there is at least one eligible index for a query, then COLLSCAN will not be selected unless forced by the user.

Even though the efficiency of the query plan is roughly in the increasing order of this list, that's not an absolute statement as it depends on the size of the B-tree subset that the scan is examining (a COUNT_SCAN of the entire index will likely be slower than an IXSCAN of a tiny portion of the index).

There are other *stages* or steps you will see in the query planner output. Here is what they mean:

- FETCH: Full document had to be read and, optionally, a filter applied to ensure it matches
- SHARD_FILTER: Usually applied last to ensure only documents owned by the shard are returned
- SORT: Indicates an in-memory sort of results
- SORT_MERGE: Used to merge multiple already-sorted streams of documents

There are a few other, more obscure stages, but we won't worry about them for now.

Index-supported sorts omit SORT stage

A sort that is supported by an index does *not* have any SORT stage in the plan as there is no extra step required to return sorted results.

The metrics and diagnostics that come out of query planning and execution show up in multiple places:

- explain output
- Logged messages for slow queries in the mongod and mongos logs
- system.profile collection when you enable profiling
- Dashboards in Atlas, such as Query Insights
- currentOp command output

These metrics include which plan was selected, how many index entries and documents were looked at, whether there was an in-memory sort, and several others that we'll explore through examples later in the chapter.

The most detailed and useful tools for debugging query planner performance will be the explain command.

Using the explain command

We already touched on how to use the explain command to examine your query and aggregation execution. Now, let's look in detail at how it runs and what it shows. Whenever we run any command with a query filter passed to it, we have the option to invoke explain by inserting it between the collection name and the command helper method in mongosh, as in the following example:

```
db.collection.explain(<option>).find({<query>})
```

The <option> to explain determines how verbose the output will be, and it can be one of the following:

- "queryPlanner": The default value. Only runs the query optimizer and returns which query plan would be selected.
- "executionStats": Runs the query optimizer, executes the chosen winning plan, and returns statistics describing the execution.
- "allPlansExecution": The same as "executionStats" but in addition to returning statistics about executing the winning plan, it also returns statistics for the rejected plans captured during plan selection and evaluation.

The output from the explain command includes multiple sections. The queryPlanner section is always present. If you use the executionStats or allPlansExecution option, you will see the very informative executionStats section.

The queryPlanner section

queryPlanner section is where you see basic information about the query, including how it was parsed into canonical or normalized form, queryHash which is a shortcut way of identifying the same query shapes with different values, planCacheKey of the plan will be present if the query plan was in the cache, indication whether the query plan selection was influenced by any special settings, the winningPlan, and rejected plans in the case when there were additional plan options.

The executionStats section

The explain command that actually ran the query will include the executionStats section, where all the actual observed metrics during the run are captured. For the query filter portion, it includes fields such as totalKeysExamined (number of index keys looked at), totalDocsExamined (number of documents looked at), nReturned (number of documents that would be returned to the client if explain was not specified), and the same details for each execution stage that was observed.

For in-memory sorts, the explain command includes a SORT section with information about how much memory was used. This section appears when there's no eligible index to support getting data in sorted order. It also indicates whether the data had to be spilled to disk and, if so, how much disk space was used to aid the sort.

In the case of aggregations, explain also lists every stage after the initial $cursor stage (which is responsible for fetching documents from the collection to stream into the rest of the pipeline). It includes the number of documents that were returned from each stage, as well as the cumulative time taken by all the stages up to this one.

Here is a portion of sample output for an aggregation execution stats section listing stages:

```
stages: [
{
  '$cursor': { queryPlanner: { executionStats: { ... } } }
  nReturned: Long('10805'),
  executionTimeMillisEstimate: Long('21')
},
{
  '$set': { ... },
  nReturned: Long('10805'),
  executionTimeMillisEstimate: Long('21')
},
```

```
  {
   '$unwind': { ... },
   nReturned: Long('14804'),
   executionTimeMillisEstimate: Long('22')
  },
  {
    '$group': { ... },
    maxAccumulatorMemoryUsageBytes: { count: Long('1768') },
    totalOutputDataSizeBytes: Long('3534'),
    usedDisk: false,
    nReturned: Long('13'),
    executionTimeMillisEstimate: Long('23')
  },
  {
    '$sort': { sortKey: { count: -1 } },
    totalDataSizeSortedBytesEstimate: Long('3638'),
    usedDisk: false,
    spills: Long('0'),
    nReturned: Long('13'),
    executionTimeMillisEstimate: Long('23')
  }
```

The first stage is called $cursor, and it indicates that the source of the documents for the pipeline is a collection. Early $match stages and other stages that are executed the same way as the find command can be observed inside the $cursor stage. This stage returned a certain number of documents, which then flowed through the pipeline. The execution time estimate is cumulative, so we see that the query portion took 21 milliseconds, with most other stages taking less than 1 millisecond, except for $unwind and $group, which took 1 millisecond each.

In sharded collections, the mongos router forwards a query with the explain option to each shard, merges their results, and includes its own work in the explain output, which has separate sections for shards' work and mongos work.

Here is an example of the explain output fields for an aggregation query in a sharded cluster:

```
    "mergeType" : "mongos",
    "splitPipeline" : {
    "shardsPart" : [ ... ],
    "mergerPart" : [ ... ]
```

This shows that the merging of outputs from each shard takes place on mongos. It also shows how the overall pipeline is split into two parts. The first part is sent to relevant shards, while the merging part is executed on mongos.

Here is an example of explain on a shard that needs to filter out orphan documents:

```
winningPlan: {
    stage: 'SHARD_MERGE',
    shards: [
      {
        shardName: 'shard01',
        winningPlan: {
          stage: 'FETCH',
          inputStage: {
            stage: 'SHARDING_FILTER',
            inputStage: {
              stage: 'IXSCAN',
              keyPattern: { id: 1 },
              ...
```

This example shows a query on a particular field that efficiently uses an index for the query. However, since the shard key is not in the index, an additional step is needed to fetch the document to check whether its shard key value belongs to this particular shard. This query can be made more efficient by adding a compound index that includes shard key fields (usually as trailing fields) in the index.

> **SHARD_MERGE versus SINGLE_SHARD stages**
>
> SHARD_MERGE indicates that the query is being handled by multiple shards. If the query can target a single shard, the name of the stage will be SINGLE_SHARD.

Analyzing log messages

As useful as the explain output is, there is a lot of information available in the logs from each actual execution of a command that you cannot see in explain. Here is an example formatted for readability and trimmed of fields not specific to query filter execution:

```
"type" : "command",
"ns" : "test.coll",
"collectionType" : "normal",
```

```
        "command" : {
            "aggregate" : "coll",
            "pipeline" : [
                {"$match" : {"$or" : [
                    {"x" : {"$gt" : 5,"$lt" : 10}},
                    {"a" : {"$gt" : 5,"$lt" : 10}}
                ]}},
                {"$sortByCount" : "$b"}
            ],
            "$clusterTime" : { ... },
            "$db" : "test"
        },
        "planSummary" : "IXSCAN { x: 1 }, IXSCAN { a: 1 }",
        "planningTimeMicros" : 2572,
        "keysExamined" : 567,
        "docsExamined" : 567,
        "hasSortStage" : true,
        "nreturned" : 40,
        "planCacheKey" : "DAC1B215",
        "queryFramework" : "sbe",
        "locks" : {"Global" : {"acquireCount" : {"r" : 4}}},
        "storage" : { },
        "workingMillis" : 12,
        "durationMillis" : 12
    }
```

You can see which query plan was used (two indexes, one for each $or clause) and that there was a SORT stage (hasSortStage: true), indicating there was an in-memory sort of results. You can also see how selective the indexes were by the number of keys versus documents examined, and you can see how long the operation took, along with a breakdown of where the time was spent. If the multiple-plan evaluation process were run, then you would also see "fromMultiPlanner":true in the log message.

Messages in the logs are in json format, so if you want to analyze them programmatically, you can load them into their own MongoDB collection, or you can use grep and other command-line tools to look for problematic patterns.

Identifying problematic patterns

Just as not all fast queries are optimally efficient, sometimes well-written, index-supported queries can still be slow. It's important to understand why they are slow to avoid wasting time tuning something that's not the root cause of the performance issue.

Will problematic queries always be slow? Not necessarily. We already know that *slow* is relative, and by default, queries that are slower than 100 milliseconds are recorded in the mongod logs. This threshold can be configured to be higher, lower, or based on something other than an absolute time threshold; see *Chapter 14, Monitoring and Observability*, for more details. However, inefficient queries may still slip under the radar if they fall just below the threshold, even though they could still be significantly faster with optimal indexes. We can look for these slow queries by adjusting the logging threshold and looking at the query targeting ratio, disk use, or other resource contention.

Query targeting ratio

One of the most important metrics for how *efficient* your queries are is called the **query targeting ratio**. Now that we've seen what details are available in explain and log messages, let's look at what goes into this ratio. When you query for all documents that satisfy a particular criterion, the fewer documents the system has to look at to determine which ones to return, the faster the query will complete.

Query targeting ratio refers to either the number of index keys read compared to the number of documents returned or the number of documents read compared to the number of documents returned. The ideal number for either of these would be 1, as we'd like to only look at index entries or only documents that need to be returned to the client. If there is an optimal index for a query and each index entry scanned ends up being in the result set, then the ratio will be 1:1. Covered index queries are a special case where we don't even need to look at any documents and will be indicated by having "docsExamined":0, but let's put those aside for the purpose of understanding the following examples.

The simplest example is query {a: 5} and an index on a. Every index entry we look at will be for the value we want to match, and we will only visit documents that need to be returned to the client. That's an ideal ratio. If there is no index on a, then we have to do a collection scan, meaning we look at every document in the collection. If there are 50 documents that match our condition and need to be returned, and there are 50 million documents in the collection, then our targeting ratio will be 1 million to one, which is not very good, given the ideal ratio would be one to one.

Here are several log message snippets from queries that used an index to satisfy several query predicate clauses but then had to examine additional fields in the document to determine whether it should be returned to the client:

```
"keysExamined":977,"docsExamined":977,"nreturned":4
"keysExamined":69070,"docsExamined":147,"nreturned": 0
```

While the `keysExamined` to `docsExamined` ratio tells you how efficient the indexes were in narrowing down the number of documents the query needed to examine, `nreturned`, being significantly lower still indicates that additional filters had to be applied to the document directly. This only applies to queries, not aggregations, which can return a lower number of documents due to aggregating them into a smaller number of total groups.

Waiting for disk or other resources

One of the most useful metrics in our logs may be `storage`, which will be empty in the case of a fast query. However, if any of the index or data pages were not in the storage engine cache, the metrics related to that will appear in the `storage` field. Very slow queries, even those that use indexes effectively, are often slow because the data isn't already in the WiredTiger cache, and this is the field that will indicate whether that's the case.

Here's what partial log messages might look like for three queries:

```
storage:{data:{bytesRead:8674010,timeReadingMicros:6297}},durationMillis:105
storage:{data:{bytesRead:15353,timeReadingMicros:918415}},durationMillis:919
storage:{data:{bytesRead:31033716,timeReadingMicros:82948}},
durationMillis:145
```

From the database's point of view, this indicates that the data didn't come from its cache. This data could still have been read from the filesystem cache.

In different cases, the root cause may be a problematically very slow disk (second example line), a large amount of data not present in cache, or an in-memory sort that had to spill data to disk. You can track this by finding `"usedDisk":true` in the log message, or by examining the more detailed information in the `explain` output.

In the same way, log messages can indicate that a slow query used an optimal execution plan, but was still slow due to other unavailable resources, such as waiting for other slow operations. There is no point trying to *tune* that query because it's the system overall, or other slow operations, that need to be addressed.

How to influence query execution

Sometimes, no matter how much you try to create a perfect index for a query, the query planner picks a different index. There are two ways you can influence the execution to force your preferred index to be selected, or to block undesirable queries from being able to execute entirely.

Using hint

You can pass a `hint` directive to any query with the name or definition of an index. This instructs the query engine to completely bypass the query cache and planning process, and instead use the specified index for the query. There are a few things to be cautious about when using hints. Specifying a non-existent index will return an error. Specifying a sparse, partial, or otherwise incompatible index can return incomplete results if the index does not include all documents satisfying the query predicate.

When using `hint` within your application code, it's important to proceed with caution: periodically check that it's still necessary. It's usually preferable to remove extra indexes that cause the query engine to make suboptimal choices, but in cases where that's not possible, using hints can provide a quick solution.

Here is an example of code that forces `find` to use an index by its name via a hint:

```
db.coll.find({<filter>}).hint("indexName")
```

Use hints thoughtfully. Always validate their continued relevance as your data and indexes evolve.

Using query settings

MongoDB version 8.0 introduced a new feature called persistent query settings. This feature allows you to control query execution by automatically adding hints on the server without having to make code changes to your application, defining rejection filters, and configuring other fields. Rather than relying on a hint being explicitly added to a particular query shape in the application code (which comes with the risk of missing some places if the query is invoked in multiple parts of the system), you can configure the server to automatically apply a hint whenever a specific query shape is observed.

This command sets an index hint for a specific database, collection, and query shape:

```
db.adminCommand( {
  setQuerySettings: {
    find: "collName",
    filter: {<filter>},
    $db:"dbName"
  },
  settings: {
    indexHints: {
      ns: {db: "dbName", coll: "collName"},
      allowedIndexes: ["indexName"]
    }
  }
})
```

When you want to block a problematic query from running entirely, modify the `settings` field to include the `reject:true` directive. To learn more about the `setQuerySettings` command, visit `https://www.mongodb.com/docs/manual/reference/command/setquerysettings/`.

Other options

Another setting worth noting, which exists as a giant hammer, though generally not recommended for production environments, is the `--notablescan` option when starting `mongod`. This setting can block any and all queries that have a query filter but do not have an eligible index to use. This might be safe to enable in a test or staging system to find out whether any queries are unexpectedly running collection scans, but it may not be such a good idea to use such a non-discriminate tool in production. You can monitor for such queries in production and either decide to block them from the system using query settings or add indexes to support them.

MQL semantics and indexes

As discussed in *Chapter 3, Indexes*, indexes were designed to support **MongoDB Query Language (MQL)** find semantics, but what does that mean? MQL has several components, some specific to aggregation, some specific to updates, and some specific to `find` command filters, which are called match expressions. This is the syntax you use when you specify a query predicate for the `find`, `update`, and `delete` commands, and also the syntax that the `$match` aggregation stage expects. Indexes support some of the peculiarities of match expressions, and this can impact how efficiently your index can be used by a specific query. Understanding this can help you spot, debug, and rewrite hard-to-optimize queries and write more efficient queries from the start.

Challenges with arrays and multikey indexes

Fields that store arrays introduce unique challenges for query planning and index use. Documents with fields that could be arrays need special consideration to avoid becoming a source of unintended performance issues.

Equality is not just equality

In an MQL query specifying equality ($eq) to a value—explicit or implicit—means either *equal* or *array where one of the elements is equal to the value.*

For example, db.coll.findOne({a:5}) matches {a:5} as well as {a:[1, 5, 10]}.

This means that an index on field a that contains the entry 5 must point to documents where a is 5, as well as documents where a is an array containing 5. The entries look exactly the same, but as soon as any array element is indexed, the index acquires the multikey property, which tells the query engine that a might be an array. Therefore, when returning the value a, it cannot be returned from the index alone; the document must be fetched to return the actual value of the field.

Note that in aggregation, the $eq expression does not have this nuance. In {$eq:[v1, v2]}, the result is true if the two values are equal, and false otherwise. Aggregation expressions do not reach inside arrays to match individual values.

$elemMatch

How we index arrays doesn't just have implications for returning potential array fields; it also impacts how we can use indexes to check $elemMatch conditions. The $elemMatch operator checks *whether at least one element in the array satisfies the query criteria.*

For example, the query {a:{$elemMatch:{$eq:5}}} will match {a: [1, 4, 5]} but will not match {a: 5} because 5 here is not an array element.

Similarly, {a:{$gt:5, $lt:10}} will match {a: [1, 4, 11]} because both conditions are true; a has an element that is smaller than 10 and it also has an element that is greater than 5.

In order to look for a *single* element that matches both conditions, we would have to write {a:{$elemMatch:{$gt:5, $lt:10}}}. Now, the meaning becomes: a *must have a single element that is both greater than 5 and less than 10.*

Given that we index array values in the B-tree, there are several situations where the index may not answer the query as efficiently as you might expect. A simple {a:{$elemMatch:{$eq:5}}} query can use the index to find all documents where a is either scalar 5 or an array containing 5.

But without looking at the document, it's not possible to tell whether a is an array element or not, because a flexible schema allows you to include scalars and arrays in the same field in a collection.

Another case where a query's use of indexes may surprise you is when you don't use $elemMatch for multiple conditions, specifically when you don't want a single element to satisfy several conditions, but instead want to find an array where different elements can satisfy these conditions.

An example is the preceding {a:{$gt:5, $lt:10}} query, which can use an index on a, but if the index is multikey (that is, if it's known that a can be an array in some of the documents), then it cannot be used the same way as a *regular* non-array index.

Consider the example we've been looking at and how it could use a non-multikey versus multikey index:

```
db.coll.explain().find({a:{$gt:5, $lt:10}})
```

```
// non-multikey index on a          // multikey index on a
"winningPlan" : {                    "winningPlan" : {
  "stage" : "FETCH",                   "stage" : "FETCH",
                                       "filter" : {"a" : {"$lt" : 10}},
  "inputStage": {                      "inputStage" : {
    "stage" : "IXSCAN",                  "stage" : "IXSCAN",
    "keyPattern":{"a":1},                "keyPattern" : {"a" : 1},
    "isMultiKey" : false,                "isMultiKey" : true,
    "indexBounds":                       "indexBounds" : {"a" :["(5.0,inf.0]"]}
      {"a":["(5.0,10.0)"]}}            },
}                                    "rejectedPlans" : [
                                     { "stage" : "FETCH",
                                       "filter" : {"a" : {"$gt" : 5}},
                                       "inputStage" : {
                                         "stage" : "IXSCAN",
                                         "keyPattern" : {"a" : 1},
                                         "indexName" : "a_1",
                                         "isMultiKey" : true,
                                         "indexBounds":{"a" :["[-inf.0, 10.0)"]}}}]]
```

Table 12.1: Query uses different index bounds depending on whether the index is multikey

On the left, the non-multikey index uses tight bounds to find all documents where the field a is between 5 and 10. On the right, the plan uses the index to find all documents where a is between 5 and infinity and then fetches the document to check that there is also a that's less than 10. Why can't a multikey index use the same index bounds as a non-multikey index, and instead has to choose between using one bound in the index and checking the other bound manually in the FETCH stage? This is because array semantics say, *"one element can match one condition, and a different element can match the other condition,"* and if we used *tight* bounds, we would miss matching documents such as {a:[1, 11]}, where neither of the elements falls between 5 and 10!

Deduplication

Since every element of an array is indexed separately in the B-tree, additional work is required to deduplicate the matched documents when a multikey indexed query looks like {a:{$in:[1, 5, 10]}}. In this case, we perform three lookups in the B-tree, one for each value, but all three may point to the same recordId. The query must always perform extra work with multikey fields of multikey indexes to ensure that duplicate records are not being returned (or counted more than once).

Let's look at the executionStats portion of the explain output for the query {a:{$in:[500, 501, 502]}}, where multiple documents have arrays with several of these values:

```
executionStats: {
    inputStage: {
        stage: 'IXSCAN',
        nReturned: 1,
        works: 4,
        advanced: 1,
        isEOF: 1,
        keyPattern: { a: 1},
        isMultiKey: true,
        multiKeyPaths: { a: [ 'a' ] },
        indexBounds:  { a: [ '[500, 500]', '[501, 501]', '[502, 502]' ] },
        keysExamined: 3,
        seeks: 1,
        dupsTested: 3,
        dupsDropped: 2
```

The single document returned had all three values in the search list in array "a", which is why we see that out of the three tested results, two were dropped as duplicates. This shows the extra work performed, which you can already see because nReturned is 1 while keysExamined is 3. The extra work is not because the index doesn't efficiently store all the values we want to return; it's because of the extra work done to eliminate duplicate results. While arrays are a powerful way of representing complex structures in your documents, it's important to be aware of the extra cost some queries can have when dealing with indexed array fields.

Challenges with null and $exists

In MQL, the query {a: null} matches all documents where a is either absent or a is present and equal to null. This includes cases where a is an array that contains null as well as some more complex scenarios.

But in all of these cases, because both missing and null are returned by this query, the B-tree indexes store the value null to indicate that a value is *either* explicitly null or it's missing; that is, it is not there at all. So, indexes can be used to easily check that a field is *not* equal to null, but it cannot be used to answer $exists:true or $exists:false queries. That's because the document would still need to be checked to see whether the field exists with a null value, or whether it's not there at all. The only exception to this is sparse indexes, which only index values that exist (including null) and, therefore, can answer the $exists:true predicate directly from the index without needing to check additional details in the document itself.

Here are several explain fields when an index on a is used to check db.coll.find({a:{$ne:null}}):

```
        stage: 'IXSCAN',
        keyPattern: { a: 1 },
        indexBounds: { a: [ '[MinKey, null)', '(null, MaxKey]' ] }
```

The index bounds show that the query is handled as a range query, which matches values less than null and greater than null.

All of this is essential to understand to write queries that are correct, but it's also important to understand when indexes can and cannot be used as effectively as you might expect. In summary, if your application has a query that must check for the existence of a field, a sparse index can be used.

Additional best practices

Here are a few additional tips on the best ways to write your applications and knowing what to be aware of, as well as what to avoid as a general rule if you want to have a performant and scalable system. Some of the features to avoid are already planned for deprecation and removal by MongoDB, while others are meant for very specific use cases, and using them outside of those cases can introduce unnecessary overhead to your system.

Updates

When composing your update modifications, it is always preferable to use individual field modifications rather than replacing the full document. From the application developer's point of view, using updateOne is generally better than using replaceOne because replacing the full document when only a handful of fields have changed will be less efficient for the replication subsystem.

In some cases, when the new version of a document is received from outside your application, and determining the exact changes would be prohibitively expensive or impractical, there is a trick you can use. Don't use the following syntax:

```
db.coll.replaceOne({_id:X}, {entire-new-document})
```

Instead, use this updated syntax to achieve the same effect:

```
db.coll.updateOne({_id:X}, [ {$replaceWith:{$literal:entire-new-
document}}])
```

While at a glance this seems to use the aggregation syntax to tell the system to perform the same *"replace existing document with this new document"* process, in practice, what happens internally is that MongoDB compares the existing and new documents and generates *deltas* to record in the replication oplog, resulting in a much smaller oplog entry. In cases where our computation finds that those deltas are actually more verbose to record than the entire new document, we will write the entire new document to the oplog.

For correctness, in multi-threaded systems, make sure you compose your updates using update modifiers, which allow multiple threads to make changes to the same document simultaneously without overwriting each other's work. That means using $inc to increment counters rather than reading the document, modifying it in code, and then writing it back out. If the read-modify-write pattern is unavoidable for application-specific reasons, use versioning to ensure no other change has been made to the document between your read and write, or use the previous value of the field you are modifying in the filter for the write, so your write only succeeds if the value hasn't been changed since you read it.

findAndModify

The findAndModify command is known in driver methods as findOneAndUpdate, and its purpose is frequently misunderstood. It is essentially the exact same command as updateOne, but instead of returning the result document that informs the client exactly what the update did (for example, was there an update, did it match any document or not, etc.), findOneAndUpdate performs the same update operation but returns the document that was updated (if any), either the version before the update or the one after it.

Why does this functionality even need to exist? This is because sometimes you need to know what effect your update had, or which document was updated, and your update filter is structured in such a way that you don't know and cannot determine this information any other way. Consider an example where there is a single document collection that just tracks a counter that's being incremented by 1 every time a value is used:

```
{_id:1, count: 35}
```

If a client wants to use the next available count value and increment the counter so that it's in the correct state for the next thread, it cannot do it with two separate update and find commands as there is no guarantee that another thread won't sneak in there between the two operations. This is where findOneAndUpdate is useful: it lets the client send an update with {$inc:{count:1}} to increment the counter and, at the same time, retrieve the correct value the document had before or immediately after the update.

Another example would be a client that's looking for the next *item of work* in a collection that represents a queue. In addition to retrieving the _id value of the next document to be processed, it also needs to write to the document to indicate that it's now being worked on, preventing another thread from trying to work on the same item. Here, returning the document, while at the same time atomically setting a field to logically *lock* it from other threads that are trying to find their own next piece of work, can be easily achieved with the findOneAndUpdate (aka findAndModify) command. It applies a filter and sort to find the document that's *ready for work* (typically with the lowest or highest timestamp value) and isn't already locked by another thread, sets the field to indicate "*I'm going to work on this document,*" and returns the document so the client knows what it's working on. Using a separate updateOne operation followed by a findOne operation would not only introduce an unnecessary extra round trip but also leave no reliable way to know how to find the document that was just modified in a separate call.

So, why is `findAndModify` more expensive than `update`, since both commands update one document and return one document (either the result document or the modified document)? It turns out that the main reason is a feature described in *Chapter 10, Client Libraries*, called *retryable writes*, where a MongoDB driver automatically retries a write operation that may or may not have succeeded during primary failover in a replica set. MongoDB internally tracks whether each write operation has succeeded, and can easily return a duplicate copy of the *result* if an operation is retried after already succeeding. However, to return the correct version of the document when a `findAndModify` operation is retried, the system has to do the extra work of writing a copy of the pre-change modified document to a special side collection. This introduces overhead that can make your system slower if you routinely use `findOneAndUpdate` unnecessarily instead of `updateOne`, and the impact is even greater and more problematic if your documents are quite large.

Therefore, it's perfect to use `findAndModify` when it's necessary to correctly implement your application logic, but best to avoid it when a simple `updateOne` can do the job.

Aggregation and query

Some aggregation stages and expressions are fine when used sparingly and only in specific cases they were designed for, but you should not overuse them when a simpler, more efficient alternative would suffice. This section will list some of those stages, operators, and commands that should be avoided or used sparingly, along with their potentially more performant alternatives.

$sample

The `$sample` stage is meant to return some number, N, of randomly selected documents from the point in the pipeline where it appears. However, it performs efficiently in only one very specific scenario: when it is the *first stage* of the pipeline on a collection with *more than 100 documents*, and the number of documents requested is *less than 5%* of the total documents in the collection. In that one scenario, it uses a pseudo-random cursor to select those N documents. In all other scenarios, `$sample` does an expensive random sort of all the documents just to return the first N. If you genuinely need a truly random subset of documents, then of course, use `$sample`, but in most cases, where you simply want to limit the number of returned documents, it's a lot quicker to use `$limit`.

$facet

$facet processes multiple aggregation pipelines within a single stage on the same set of input documents. There is a misconception that the $facet stage does some aggregation magic to parallel-process a pipeline into multiple branches. That's not really what happens at all. The simplest way to think about $facet is this: every document flowing through the pipeline up to that point is sent to each branch of $facet. This means that if one branch needs only the first 10 documents, but another needs 1 million, then all 1 million documents will be sent to every $facet branch.

$facet is an excellent candidate when you want to do extremely similar processing in each branch, for instance, when computing both counts by category and counts by price range of all incoming documents. It is not at all a good candidate when the processing you want to do in its branches is very different. One example would be wanting to return the first 10 documents as well as the total count of documents. In such cases, it's much better to use $unionWith, which runs two (or more) pipelines while preserving all the optimizations that can be performed on each of them.

$where, $function, $accumulator, and mapReduce

When run on the server, JavaScript will always be slower than expressing the same logic using native MQL syntax. In addition, JavaScript is inherently a security risk for MongoDB servers and has been deprecated with the intention of eventually removing it altogether to eliminate that risk.

For faster execution and better security, avoid using any JavaScript in your MongoDB queries or aggregations.

> **JavaScript execution: Server versus mongosh shell**
>
> This doesn't apply to the mongosh shell, which expands and interprets all the JavaScript before sending it to the server. This warning is specifically for any and all JavaScript that is meant to be executed on the database server itself.

$text

If you wanted to do a full-text search before the MongoDB Atlas full-text search feature was introduced, your options were either using a $text operator, which relied on legacy MongoDB text indexes, or sending your data to another system. Since the launch of Atlas Search, development on native legacy text indexes has been stopped, and it's fully expected that this feature will eventually be deprecated in favor of Lucene-based search. This newer search capability will be available in the MongoDB Community version as well as MongoDB Atlas.

$regex and indexes

Because indexes store values in sorted order, it might not come as a surprise that when you use a $regex operator to match part of a string, the index can only be used efficiently if $regex is the equivalent of the *starts with* pattern, what we call a *left-rooted* or *anchored* regular expression. Additionally, the index can only be used efficiently if the regular expression *does not* specify the *case-insensitive* option. For example, if your query is something such as {s:{$regex:/^Abc/}}, which says, "*all strings that start with exactly Abc*," then an index on s will be used as an efficient range query. For case-insensitive string matching, consider using indexes with appropriate collation.

Aggregation versus match expressions

There are a few expressions that share the same name in both find and aggregate but behave slightly differently. Always be cautious and ensure that you are expressing the exact semantics your application needs, and check that indexes are being used the way you want them to be. For example, $eq in aggregation literally means *equal*; it does not look inside arrays. On the other hand, $in in aggregation means "*are any array elements equal to this value?*" whereas in find, $in is checking whether any of the specified values are equal to the field we are searching (with *equals* in find meaning "*is equal to the value or contained within an array*").

$expr and indexes

Because using $expr in find or $match means "*I'm about to use an aggregation expression*," it implies aggregation semantics, and the use of indexes, which are designed to support find semantics, becomes tricky. This is why many queries that use $expr don't use indexes when you might have expected them to, or they use indexes but have additional steps to ensure that the correct semantics are applied to your query. If it's possible to express the query without using $expr, then make sure that's how it's written, and only use $expr when it's the only way to achieve the exact query semantics you need.

$or clause and indexes

Normally, a single query can only use one index. In this context, *query* refers to a single query filter passed to the find command or $match stage; a pipeline with many stages or subpipelines can use different indexes for different components. For instance, each subpipeline in a $unionWith stage is planned independently of the rest of the pipeline, and $lookup pipelines do their own planning using appropriate indexes regardless of the top-level pipeline.

The only exception in the current MongoDB versions is when you have a query with a top-level $or. In this case, each branch of $or can use a different index since the results are a union of all of the branch results. In some cases, an $or might even be inside an $and clause and can be rewritten to be at the top level so that multiple indexes can be used. Sometimes the query optimizer rewrites this automatically, but to make things simpler, put the $or clause at the top level if it's possible. What you learned about query planning still applies, as each clause of the $or statement is planned separately, but each clause's plan will show up in the explain output as a special SUBPLAN stage.

Special collections, index types, and features

There are use cases that are challenging to implement using basic documents and regular B-tree indexes. For very specific patterns, such as time series, geospatial coordinates, or vector embeddings, MongoDB offers specialized collections and indexes. MongoDB's special collection types and advanced indexing features can substantially boost your application's performance for specific use cases.

Time-series collections

Imagine you're building an IoT platform that collects temperature readings every second from thousands of sensors, or tracking stock prices that change by the millisecond. You'll have a constant stream of data points, each with a timestamp. Updates are rare, and queries are usually over slices of time.

In MongoDB, any set of documents where every document includes a timestamp and all documents share some metadata fields can be stored in a special time-series collection. For more details, see https://www.mongodb.com/docs/manual/core/timeseries-collections/.

Rather than treating each timestamped document separately, MongoDB time-series collections group them internally into buckets, so that data from the same source is stored alongside other data points from a similar point in time. This reduces storage requirements and write amplification, as well as making typical range queries over time slices much faster.

The performance gains come from several factors. MongoDB automatically compresses and organizes time-series data into an internal columnar format, which is incredibly efficient for the repetitive measurements typical of sensor or financial data. This leads to massive storage savings, often between 70 and 90%. A clustered index on the time field is created automatically, making time-range queries highly efficient without any extra setup. This translates to query speeds that are often 3-5x faster than what you'd get with the same queries on a standard collection. The reduced storage footprint also means less memory usage, smaller backups, and lower infrastructure costs.

For instance, one fintech start-up saw their query times drop from 5 seconds to just 200 ms after migrating to a time-series collection, while a manufacturing customer cut their data storage costs by over 80%.

Geospatial indexes

MongoDB supports query operations on geospatial data. By storing data as GeoJSON objects or coordinate pairs and then building geospatial indexes on it, you unlock access to multiple geospatial query operators to find objects within particular geometry, intersecting shapes, and points nearest to a specific location. You can find a full overview of geospatial queries and capabilities at https://www.mongodb.com/docs/manual/geospatial-queries/.

When working with geospatial data, a well-configured 2dsphere index can improve query performance by orders of magnitude, especially for large datasets where queries without indexes would be painfully slow. However, keep in mind that geospatial indexes are larger than standard B-tree indexes, so it's wise to monitor their memory usage, particularly if you're indexing large polygons. The density of your data also matters; if your query area contains many points, MongoDB will have more work to do. In such cases, it's a good idea to use additional filters to narrow down the results. For queries that frequently combine location with other criteria, such as finding restaurants within a 5 km radius that are currently open, a compound index on both the geospatial field and the other filter fields is the best approach for optimal performance.

Atlas Search

While MongoDB's regular query capabilities are powerful, sometimes you need more advanced full-text search functionality. Atlas Search integrates Apache Lucene directly into your MongoDB cluster. You can learn more at https://www.mongodb.com/docs/atlas/atlas-search/.

Atlas Search delivers highly optimized text search, a significant step up from what's possible with regular indexes. It excels at natural language searches, fuzzy matches, and autocomplete functionality, with results ranked by relevance to help users find what they need faster. This not only improves the user experience but also boosts infrastructure efficiency. Without Atlas Search, you would likely need to maintain a separate search engine alongside MongoDB, which adds operational complexity and data synchronization headaches. Because Atlas Search is built on Lucene, it maintains consistent performance even as your dataset grows.

Atlas Vector Search

Atlas Vector Search enables efficient similarity searches using vector embeddings, a task that is computationally expensive and slow with standard query methods. By storing your vector data alongside your other MongoDB data, you can use it as a vector database. This enables you to query data based on its semantic meaning and power your AI applications. To learn more, visit `https://www.mongodb.com/docs/atlas/atlas-vector-search/vector-search-overview/`.

When implementing Vector Search, there's a trade-off between query speed and accuracy and your choice of similarity algorithm (such as `cosine`, `euclidean`, or `dotProduct`) will impact both. Cosine similarity often provides a good balance between the two. For very large collections, using **approximate nearest neighbor** (**ANN**) searches can be dramatically faster than exact searches with only a minimal trade-off in accuracy.

Collations

Different languages have different rules for sorting and comparing strings. Collation lets you specify language-specific rules for string comparison. Rather than jumping through complex hoops of storing your strings normalized to simple binary comparison, you can store data as it is and use appropriate collation to influence how sorting and comparisons behave in your application without sacrificing performance. Collation is an option on regular B-tree indexes. It is not just for supporting different characters in languages such as French or German; it also allows you to use case-insensitive string comparison, among other options. You can read more about how it works at `https://www.mongodb.com/docs/manual/reference/collation/`.

For the best performance, it's crucial that your queries use the same collation settings as your indexes. A mismatch will prevent MongoDB from using the index, forcing a much slower collection scan instead. While indexes with collation may use slightly more memory than standard ones, the trade-off is usually worth it. Sorting large result sets in memory with or without complex collations is very CPU-intensive, so relying on indexed sorts is always the better option when possible.

The main benefit of using a specialized tool for a particular use case is that it can save you a significant amount of time compared to supporting the features yourself using base MongoDB features as building blocks. MongoDB special collections and indexes are optimized at the storage engine level to perform better than what can be implemented in your application. Don't start thinking about these features only when you anticipate that you will reach enterprise scale. The ease of use of ready-made implementation means you can leverage it for small time-series collections, or limited geo or full-text search, as well as petabyte-sized workloads.

Summary

Optimizing database performance starts with a thorough understanding of how the MongoDB query engine processes queries and utilizes indexes. Knowing the life cycle of query execution, that is, how queries are parsed, planned, executed, and returned, provides developers with the foundation needed to design efficient operations. Diagnostic tools such as the explain command and log messages are invaluable for examining query results and identifying inefficiencies caused by suboptimal query plans, resource constraints, or other issues. These insights allow developers to pinpoint whether performance problems stem from the query itself or external factors such as disk I/O or memory contention. Proper evaluation of metrics such as query targeting ratios and execution statistics further equips developers to design smarter queries that minimize unnecessary overhead and reduce latency.

Beyond the execution life cycle, avoiding inefficient operations and leveraging MongoDB's specialized features can significantly improve system performance while reducing development effort. Using time-series collections for IoT or financial data, geospatial indexes for location-based queries, and tools such as Atlas Search or Atlas Vector Search for full-text and semantic similarity searches offers tailored solutions for unique use cases. These features, optimized at the storage engine level, provide efficiency and scalability without requiring custom implementations. Additionally, implementing strategies such as query hints, persistent query settings, and well-tuned indexes ensures a fine-grained control over execution plans and keeps systems running optimally. By combining thoughtful query design and robust diagnostic practices and selecting the right tools for the right workloads, developers can create high-performing, scalable applications that meet diverse requirements with less effort and fewer resources.

In the next chapter, we will describe how operating systems and system resources can influence the performance and cost of your production systems.

13

Operating Systems and System Resources

When running a self-managed MongoDB deployment, you have the flexibility to configure kernel and operating system settings to suit your specific needs. However, this flexibility also introduces additional variables and potential performance bottlenecks that must be carefully considered during tuning.

This chapter is primarily relevant to self-managed environments, as MongoDB Atlas does not permit direct access to the underlying operating system. In Atlas, configuration is handled based on instance tier, and operating system upgrades are managed automatically to prevent unexpected performance issues due to kernel or system changes. Additionally, Atlas can auto-scale compute and storage in response to workload changes, which is a capability that we'll explore later in the chapter.

In this chapter, you'll learn how to do the following:

- Optimize system performance by understanding the impact of infrastructure choices
- Fine-tune operating system and storage configurations for improved reliability and throughput
- Identify and address performance bottlenecks in both self-managed and managed (Atlas) environments

Technical requirements

This chapter will mainly focus on Linux and high-level operating system concepts. For details on specific operating systems and MongoDB versions, see the documentation operations checklist at `https://www.mongodb.com/docs/manual/administration/production-checklist-operations/` and the production notes at `https://www.mongodb.com/docs/manual/administration/production-notes/` for self-managed deployments.

To monitor utilization of all kinds of system resources, you can use operating system commands, MongoDB Atlas monitoring, and other GUI tools that are designed specifically for monitoring multiple servers. More details will be provided in *Chapter 14, Monitoring and Observability*.

For system resources, Linux commands such as `top`, `vmstat`, `iostat`, and `netstat` can be used to monitor CPU, memory, storage, and network, respectively, at a point in time on a single server. Tools such as `dstat` and `sar` can be used to combine data from simpler tools and view it over a period of time.

MongoDB Atlas monitoring provides historical and real-time system resource data, which is integrated with database-specific metrics.

For self-managed deployments, you can use graphical tools such as Netdata, Prometheus + Grafana, Zabbix, Munin, or Observium. Finally, you can use commercial **application performance monitoring (APM)** tools such as AppDynamics, Datadog, Dynatrace, LogicMonitor, New Relic, SolarWinds, and Splunk Observability.

To try the configuration changes or commands mentioned in this chapter, you will need to use a Linux server and install MongoDB locally. You can download the MongoDB Community Edition from `mongodb.com`. You will also need to download the official drivers for the language of your choice (Ruby or Python): `https://www.mongodb.com/docs/drivers/`.

Managing resources for optimal performance

So far, throughout this book, we've explored situations where performance is limited by a resource being used to its full capacity. For example, these resources can include CPU cycles, memory, storage, or network bandwidth. To improve performance, we either need to increase the availability of the limiting resource or reduce its usage. This section provides an overview of each type of resource and describes how it can impact MongoDB performance.

CPU utilization

If the CPU on the primary MongoDB server is the current bottleneck for your application, you may need to scale up to faster instances with more cores. If you're running MongoDB as a replica set and have already scaled the instances or systems as much as possible, it might be time to shard. This was covered in detail in *Chapter 6, Sharding*.

Alternatively, you can optimize your application's queries and database operations to minimize their CPU footprint. This includes using appropriate indexes, designing efficient data models, and avoiding inefficient aggregation pipelines or sort operations that can consume excessive CPU cycles. These techniques were discussed in more detail in *Chapters 2, 3, 4*, and *12*.

By default, the MongoDB server is configured to use all available CPU cores on the system it's running on. This is a deliberate choice to maximize the database's ability to process multiple simultaneous queries, handle concurrent connections, and manage internal operations efficiently. The WiredTiger storage engine, for instance, benefits significantly from multi-core parallelism.

If you're self-managing MongoDB, it's recommended to deploy the MongoDB servers on dedicated machines. Running other CPU-intensive software on the same system is strongly discouraged. Diagnosing performance issues becomes significantly more complex when multiple applications are competing for the same resources.

At MongoDB, the efficiency of the database server is continuously being improved by tuning code and adopting modern compilers, linkers, and optimizers that make better use of CPU cycles. This process involves careful code tuning to reduce overhead, eliminate bottlenecks, and streamline critical operations. MongoDB also evaluates new hardware architectures, instruction sets, and tools to generate more optimized machine code, leading to lower resource consumption. This two-pronged approach (software-level and technology-level optimization) is central to MongoDB's mission of delivering a high-performance, resource-efficient database.

Later in the chapter, in the *Configuring systems for MongoDB performance* section, we'll explore practical examples of how to ensure CPUs are being utilized effectively and how to identify whether other applications are impacting CPU availability for the MongoDB server.

Memory management

Figure 13.1 shows a high-level diagram of the memory layout of a system running a MongoDB server. It's useful to keep this in mind as you work on performance tuning, because some features will use more data than others, which, in turn, reduces the amount of memory available for the filesystem (page) cache, leading to more I/O requests being directed to storage devices.

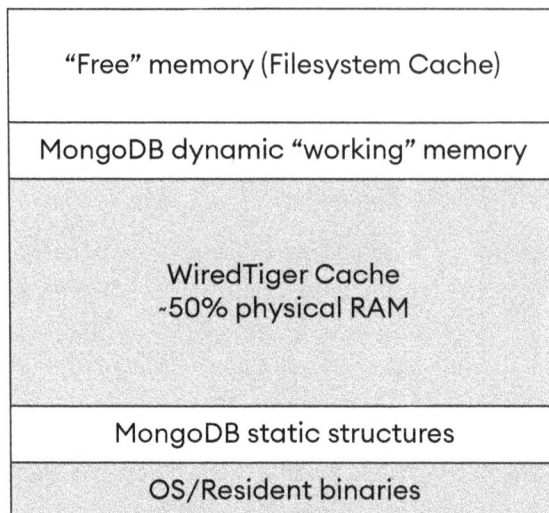

Figure 13.1: Memory layout of a system running the MongoDB server

At a fundamental level, the server's memory usage can be broadly categorized into several key components, each playing an important role in its overall functionality.

Starting from the bottom of the diagram, we have the following:

- **OS/resident binaries**: This is the code in memory for the operating system and the MongoDB server binary.

- **MongoDB static structures**: Metadata that the server uses and allocates when it first starts.

- **WiredTiger cache**: By default, this is 50% of memory (minus 1 GB). The WiredTiger cache holds frequently accessed data and indexes in RAM to minimize disk I/O. We covered this cache in some detail in *Chapter 7, Storage Engines*. Some Atlas instances may use different relative sizes for the WiredTiger cache.

- **MongoDB dynamic "working" memory**: MongoDB uses memory buffers to construct, parse, and manipulate BSON documents during operations. When queries are executed, MongoDB allocates memory for various operations, including sorting, aggregation pipeline stages, and projection operations. Complex queries or those involving large sorts or aggregations can temporarily consume significant amounts of memory. Very large sort operations may spill to disk. Each active client connection to the MongoDB server consumes a certain amount of memory, and a large number of concurrent connections can cumulatively use a substantial portion of RAM.

- **"Free" memory (page cache)**: This refers to the remaining memory, typically used by the kernel to cache filesystem data in RAM to avoid repeated disk I/O. It provides a second layer of caching beyond WiredTiger's cache and is particularly beneficial in scenarios where the WiredTiger cache is heavily utilized.

Understanding this memory distribution helps you better diagnose performance issues and make informed decisions about where to optimize system resources.

Storage

Different types of storage devices typically have their own set of performance limitations. Physical storage devices generally fall into two main categories: mechanical HDDs and SSDs. Networked disks and virtual drives in cloud environments have other limitations.

The performance of physical storage devices is constrained by the following factors:

- **Bus interface speed**: The bandwidth of the device's connection, such as SATA, PCIe, or NVMe, can cap the maximum available throughput.
- **Memory and cache size**: Most modern storage devices contain internal memory and cache. Insufficient caching can lead to bottlenecks when handling large amounts of data.
- **Fragmentation**: Data scattered across sectors or blocks can increase seek times and reduce performance for both HDDs and SSDs.
- **Read vs. write operations**: Write operations often require more processing than read operations, especially for SSDs, due to erase-before-write requirements.

> **Erase-before-write**
>
> SSDs use NAND flash memory, which requires data to be erased before new data can be written to the same location. This can slow down successive write operations, especially if many blocks need erasing. To mitigate this, SSD firmware and the operating system's TRIM functionality can preemptively clean up unused cells to ensure available space, avoiding erase delays for future writes.

- **Sequential vs. random I/O**: Sequential reads and writes typically have higher throughput compared to random I/O due to reduced mechanical movement (for HDDs) or reduced overhead (for SSDs).

- **Concurrent access**: High levels of concurrent I/O requests can overwhelm the capabilities of the storage device, especially if it lacks efficient queue management or optimizations for parallel access.

- **Medium degradation**: Both HDDs and SSDs can experience reduced performance over time—HDDs due to mechanical wear, and SSDs due to wear on NAND flash memory cells.

- **Overfilling storage**: Storage devices typically perform worse when they're close to full capacity. This is particularly true for SSDs, where over-provisioning space is required to sustain consistent write performance.

HDDs are less frequently used now in high-performance systems. At the time of writing, the cost per GB of HDDs is still lower than SSDs, but the gap is closing. For HDDs, the performance-limiting factors include the following:

- **Disk speed**: The spinning speed of platters (measured in **revolutions per minute (RPM)**) affects latency and sustained throughput

- **Read/write head movement**: The movement and positioning of the read/write head introduce mechanical delays (seek time)

SSDs offer various advantages over HDDs in performance, durability, and power efficiency. For SSDs and flash storage arrays, the limiting factors include the following:

- **NAND limitations**: NAND cell programming time and the number of simultaneous operations in a NAND array can limit performance

- **Wear leveling**: Performance can degrade if wear-leveling algorithms become inefficient or fail to manage writes effectively across NAND cells

- **Firmware optimizations**: SSD controllers use internal algorithms (such as garbage collection, wear leveling, and over-provisioning) that can impact performance, especially under heavy workloads

- **Overheating**: Excessive heat can throttle the performance of modern SSDs, as internal thermal management mechanisms reduce performance to prevent damage

For networked disks and virtual drives in a cloud environment, the following factors can constrain or limit performance:

- **Bandwidth**: The speed at which data can be transmitted over the network can limit storage performance in **network-attached storage (NAS)** or **storage area networks (SANs)**

- **Latency**: Network latency can introduce delays that are critical for applications requiring low-latency I/O

- **Concurrent network I/O**: High volumes of simultaneous network traffic accessing storage can lead to contention and bottleneck issues

A filesystem connects the operating system and block storage devices, providing a unified abstract interface across physical disks, networked disks, and virtual drives in a cloud environment. Choosing the right filesystem is critical, as it can have significant performance implications. With a self-managed MongoDB deployment, you have the option to use separate storage devices for the journal and data files. By separating journal files and data files onto different storage devices, you minimize I/O contention between journal writes and data reads/writes. This can improve performance for high-write workloads.

> **Tip**
>
> Place journal files on a fast SSD or NVMe drive. This enables MongoDB to handle frequent sequential writes much faster, without competing for I/O bandwidth with the main data files.

Data files, which are typically larger and require bulk storage, can be placed on higher-capacity, cost-effective storage solutions (e.g., slower HDDs). However, there are some downsides to consider. Managing separate storage devices for journal and data files introduces complexity and increases the probability of failure:

- You have two devices to configure, monitor, and investigate for potential bottlenecks.
- Using two devices increases the probability of failure. For example, the typical **annualized failure rate (AFR)** for enterprise SSDs is currently 0.3%–0.8% per year. If we use the midpoint of that range (0.55%), and the server is using two SSDs independently for journal and data, the AFR for the storage would be 1.1%. As a safety net, the MongoDB replication mechanism protects against the risk of such failures.
- In cloud environments, separating journal and data files onto different virtual disks may still lead to hidden contention.
- It can make it challenging to perform a consistent snapshot of both the journal and data files. Snapshots are often used to take instantaneous backups of the database, and consistent snapshots depend on atomicity across both the journal and data files.

A data services platform, such as a database, depends on the underlying storage technology. This means it's important, from both a performance and lifecycle point of view, to understand the characteristics of the technology you're using.

Network

Networking plays a crucial role in the performance of a MongoDB deployment. The following are key networking factors that can limit MongoDB performance:

- **High network latency**: This causes delays in communication between the application and the MongoDB database, or between cluster nodes in a sharded or replicated setup.

- **Insufficient network bandwidth**: This limits the flow of data between MongoDB components, especially in high-throughput environments, affecting read and write operations.

- **Packet loss**: This occurs when data packets fail to reach their destination due to network congestion, hardware faults, or misconfiguration. This can lead to the following:

  - Increased retries on failed operations, slowing down overall database performance
  - Potential replication lag on secondary nodes of a replica set
  - Interruptions in communication between shards in a distributed cluster

- **Slow or unreliable DNS resolution**: This causes delays in connecting to MongoDB servers, particularly during initial connections or failover events.

- **High network traffic**: Competition for shared resources can degrade MongoDB's ability to transmit or receive data efficiently.

- **Misconfigured firewalls**: Overly restrictive security policies may block or delay legitimate traffic, affecting MongoDB performance.

- **Inconsistent network topology**: A poorly designed network infrastructure can cause asymmetric routing, inconsistent latency, or inefficient data flow.

- **Geographic latency**: Deploying MongoDB nodes across geographically distant regions can introduce significant communication delays.

Slow or unreliable network connections can severely affect database throughput, latency, and scalability.

In summary, performance bottlenecks often arise from using a resource to its full capacity. The most common examples are CPU cycles, memory, storage, and network. It's worth noting that with MongoDB Atlas, many of these resources are managed for you.

Configuring systems for MongoDB performance

In this section, we will look at actions you can take to diagnose and fix example issues with CPU cycles, memory, storage, and network.

Understand the ideal ratio of simultaneous operations per CPU core

The MongoDB server runs multiple operations concurrently and distributes them across threads running on multiple CPU cores. As we saw in *Chapter 1, Systems and MongoDB Architecture*, the application server can become a bottleneck if it doesn't send enough operations in parallel to fully utilize the MongoDB server.

For example, if you were to run a series of experiments using your application's critical performance workload and chart the results in a spreadsheet, you might see a graph similar to *Figure 13.2*, which shows CPU utilization and performance trends as the number of threads or parallel operations increases.

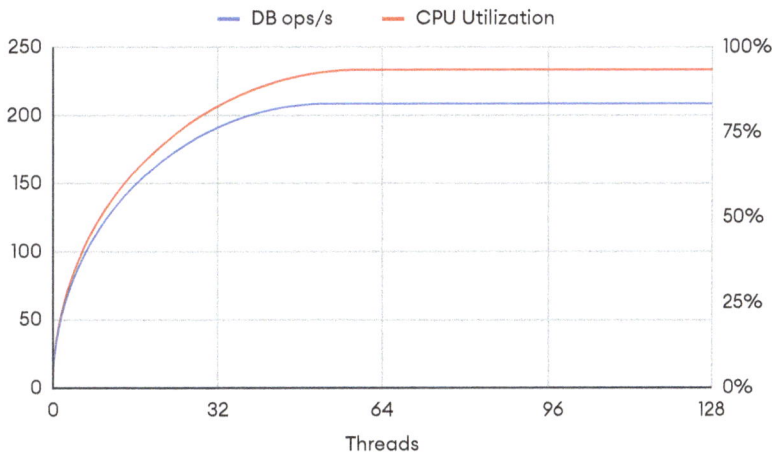

Figure 13.2: The effects on CPU utilization and performance trends as you increase parallelism

In this example, the database server is running on a 16-core CPU. Performance peaks at 64 threads, and may even decline slightly beyond that point as more threads are added. This is a typical pattern for many applications. In this case, optimal performance is reached with 64 threads on 16 cores, suggesting a ratio of 4 active threads or connections per core. It's important to test with a production workload and dataset to determine the ideal threads-to-core ratio for your critical performance workloads. For instance, you don't want to find yourself running only 8 operations in parallel on a 16-core machine, leaving half the cores idle, as this can lead to unnecessary resource costs.

Search for other CPU-intensive processes during performance dips

Periodic performance dips can be caused by other CPU-intensive processes competing for system resources. To diagnose these issues, you can use various tools and commands to identify which processes are consuming significant resources. You can use Linux tools such as top, htop, ps, pidstat, iotop, and perf to see what's running on the system during performance dips.

For example, running the top command shows the top processes by resource usage:

```
top - 18:09:15 up 10 min,  1 user,  load average: 1.01, 0.02, 0.00

%Cpu(s):  87.0 us,  13.0 sy,  0.0 ni, 0.0 id,  0.0 wa,  0.0 hi,  0.0 si,  0.0 st
MiB Mem :  31373.4 total,  30190.5 free,    428.5 used,    754.3 buff/cache
MiB Swap:      0.0 total,      0.0 free,      0.0 used.  30616.0 avail Mem

    PID USER      PR  NI    VIRT    RES    SHR S  %CPU  %MEM     TIME+ COMMAND
   1927 ubuntu     5 -15  531488 139020  70108 R  47.3  0.4   1:08.63 mongod
   1910 ubuntu     5   0  500288  99191   6436 R  16.1  0.1   0:25.98 python
      1 root      20   0  167004  11108   7464 S   6.0  0.0   0:01.06 systemd
      4 root       0 -20       0      0      0 I   0.0  0.0   0:00.00 rcu_par_gp
    589 root      20   0   82100   3204   2796 S   0.3  0.0   0:00.03 irqbalance
   1968 ubuntu     5 -15    7148   3296   2448 R   0.3  0.0   0:00.04 top
      2 root      20   0       0      0      0 S   0.0  0.0   0:00.00 kthreadd
```

In this output, you can see that there are no idle CPU cycles (0.0 id), and a Python process is using 16.1% of the CPU, time that MongoDB (mongod) might otherwise be able to use.

If MongoDB is running on a virtual machine, periodic dips might also result from processes outside the virtual machine, such as other virtual machines or hypervisor tasks. In this case, check host-level resource usage using hypervisor tools such as vmstat, virt-top, or your cloud provider's monitoring tools.

Select the right filesystem for your application

This section focuses on Linux filesystems. We'll cover the two most relevant options, **eXtent File System (XFS)** and **fourth extended filesystem (ext4)**, in more detail, and touch on other filesystems in a later section.

Extent file system (XFS)

The MongoDB production notes recommend XFS for production deployments. XFS generally delivers better performance for workloads with high throughput and concurrent read/write operations. It handles large files and fragmented data more efficiently than ext4 and tends to better manage large numbers of flush operations, exhibiting fewer I/O stalls during checkpoints. XFS also supports larger file and filesystem sizes.

Originally developed by **Silicon Graphics, Inc. (SGI)** in 1994, XFS was ported to Linux in 2001 and integrated into the mainline kernel in 2004 (version 2.6). Red Hat adopted XFS as the default filesystem for RHEL 7 in 2014, citing its scalability and performance for enterprise workloads.

Fourth extended filesystem (ext4)

If the Linux distribution you are using supports XFS, use that. If not, ext4 remains a solid choice. ext4 is a mature, widely used filesystem and has long been the default on many Linux distributions. While ext4 used to be more widely available than XFS, the gap has closed in recent years. The performance gap between ext4 and XFS has also narrowed over time as operating systems, kernels, and MongoDB itself have evolved.

Other file systems

While MongoDB can run on other filesystems, their features sometimes overlap with those already provided by MongoDB and WiredTiger, leading to inefficiencies:

- **Network File System (NFS)**: Not recommended for MongoDB. See the MongoDB production notes for more information.
- **B-tree File System (Btrfs)**: Can struggle with write-heavy workloads. Its **copy-on-write (CoW)** design can cause write amplification, where a 100B document at the database level could result in many times more data being written to the storage device. Btrfs also implements mechanisms that already exist in WiredTiger.
- **Zettabyte File System (ZFS)**: Better suited for large, sequential data such as backups or media. For MongoDB's small, random reads/writes, ZFS can be slower than XFS or ext4.
- **Ceph File System (CephFS)**: Designed for distributed storage clusters and cloud-native apps. MongoDB already supports these use cases via sharding and replication.

In general, XFS or ext4 are the most reliable choices for MongoDB deployments, offering the best balance of performance, stability, and compatibility.

Filesystem settings

By default, before kernel 2.6.30, Linux updated the **access time (atime)** metadata for files every time they were read. This meant read-intensive workloads also triggered a write operation each time a file was accessed on disk. Since 2.6.30, **relative access time (relatime)** became the default behavior. This reduces the frequency of atime updates and avoids unnecessary disk writes, significantly improving file I/O performance while retaining sufficient atime information for most use cases.

You can disable all atime update behavior by adding the noatime option to the filesystem mount settings. The /etc/fstab file is a Linux configuration file that defines how filesystems, partitions, and storage devices should be mounted during boot.

To disable atime writes, add the noatime option in /etc/fstab, as in this example:

```
/dev/sdX /path/to/mongodb_data xfs defaults,noatime 0 0
```

Other filesystem options can also improve performance, but many of them reduce the durability of writes. In general, MongoDB doesn't recommend using such options unless you clearly understand the risks and trade-offs.

Avoid RAID with parity

A **redundant array of independent (or inexpensive) disks (RAID)** storage device refers to a system that uses multiple physical HDDs or SSDs combined to improve performance, data redundancy, or both. RAID is commonly used in servers, workstations, and storage systems to provide better reliability or performance compared to a single disk. However, RAID is being used less frequently as the industry moves toward more modern, distributed, and software-defined storage solutions that offer better scalability, redundancy, and fault tolerance.

MongoDB doesn't require RAID for fault tolerance. If your organization mandates the use of RAID, it's recommended to use RAID 0 or RAID 10. RAID 0 splits (stripes) data across multiple drives. It writes data simultaneously to all drives in the array, improving read and write performance by leveraging parallelism.

However, RAID 0 does not store mirrored or parity data, meaning it provides no data protection. If one drive fails, all data is lost. RAID 10 (also called RAID 1+0) combines mirroring and striping. It creates mirrored pairs of drives (RAID 1) for redundancy, then stripes data across the mirrored pairs (RAID 0) for better performance.

The MongoDB production notes recommend avoiding RAID 5 or RAID 6 for write-heavy databases because their parity calculations can slow down write operations.

Adjust readahead settings

The Linux readahead feature is a kernel-level optimization designed to enhance the efficiency of sequential disk reads. It anticipates future data access by reading additional data blocks beyond what's requested and caching them in memory. For workloads where disk access and data layout are sequential, the next block may already be in the cache by the time the database issues an I/O request. This can improve performance by reducing disk I/O latency.

With MongoDB, the impact of readahead tuning depends on the nature of the workload, data layout on disk, and the kernel version. MongoDB queries typically access data in a random pattern. However, if your workload accesses documents in the order they were written, a higher readahead value can be beneficial.

By default, MongoDB's WiredTiger engine reads ~28 KB data blocks most of the time (with the default leaf_page_max=32KB setting). In Linux, the readahead value is specified in blocks, with each block being 512 bytes. For example, a readahead value of 32 means the kernel will prefetch 32 blocks, which translates to 16 KB.

In Linux kernels 5.x and 6.x, the handling of readahead with a value of 0 was improved to avoid the performance penalties seen in 4.x kernels. Kernel 6.x also includes better scaling heuristics, which more efficiently determine readahead size based on workload behavior and device characteristics. It also simplifies readahead logic by removing redundant code paths. Changing kernel versions can significantly impact performance, so it can be useful to rerun readahead tuning experiments after a kernel change or upgrade.

It's recommended to start with a readahead value of 32, then test with 16 and 64. If performance improves with either, continue tuning in that direction. Values of 0 or above 256 are generally not recommended.

Change filesystem cache settings

Tuning system settings such as vm.dirty_background_ratio can improve MongoDB's performance and reliability by controlling how the Linux kernel handles dirty (modified but not yet written to disk) pages in memory.

The vm.dirty_background_ratio setting defines the percentage of total system memory that can be filled with dirty pages before the kernel starts flushing them to disk in the background. Dirty pages represent changes to the filesystem (e.g., from MongoDB writes) that haven't yet been persisted to storage.

MongoDB frequently writes to disk and relies on the operating system for write buffering. If vm.dirty_background_ratio is set too high, the kernel may delay flushing, allowing a large number of dirty pages to accumulate. This can trigger sudden, intensive I/O spikes that increase latency. Lowering this value results in smaller, more frequent flushes, smoothing out disk writes.

Another related setting, vm.dirty_ratio, defines the maximum percentage of memory that can be filled with dirty pages. Once this threshold is exceeded, processes generating new writes are blocked until dirty pages are flushed to the disk.

Write-ahead journal versus data file writes

These settings affect writes to data files. Write-ahead journal operations are flushed immediately by MongoDB for durability (rather than relying on kernel-level mechanisms).

You might consider tuning vm.dirty_background_ratio in the following scenarios:

- **I/O spikes or high latency**: If you see irregular bursts of disk I/O when large batches of dirty pages are flushed at once, lower the dirty background ratio to trigger smaller, more frequent flushes. Use the iostat command to look for high values of await. The await measurement is the total response time (in milliseconds) seen by applications making I/O requests. It includes both the time waiting in the I/O scheduler queue and the time spent accessing the disk itself. Measure await before and after a change to see whether it makes a difference.

- **Excessive memory usage by dirty pages**: If dirty memory consistently occupies a significant portion of the memory, greater than 10–20% of RAM, lower vm.dirty_background_ratio to trigger earlier background flushes. You can use the following command to monitor the dirty memory on Linux:

  ```
  $ cat /proc/meminfo | grep -E "Dirty|Mem"
  ```

  Here is the example output:

  ```
  MemTotal:       32126312 kB
  MemFree:         3067873 kB
  MemAvailable:    3134261 kB
  Dirty:           6425262 kB
  ```

  The grep part of the command looks for the Dirty and Mem substrings in the output. In this example, the system has ~10% of free memory and nearly 20% dirty.

- **Slow checkpoints or high write latency**: Long MongoDB checkpoint durations or latency during write operations may indicate poor synchronization between MongoDB and kernel flush behavior.

- **Write stalls due to dirty ratio exceeded**: If MongoDB writes are blocked when dirty memory exceeds the threshold defined by vm.dirty_ratio, adjustments to both vm.dirty_ratio and vm.dirty_background_ratio are needed. You can use the following command on Linux to see write operations and blocked processes:

  ```
  dstat -c --top-io
  ```

- **System performance drops during high write activity**: High CPU usage or disk performance degradation during write spikes suggests inefficient dirty page flushing.

These scenarios highlight when tuning vm.dirty_background_ratio becomes necessary, but understanding the adjustment is just the first step; applying it thoughtfully, alongside complementary settings and monitoring, is key to improving overall write performance.

To do this, start by moderately lowering vm.dirty_background_ratio to control the accumulation of dirty pages and trigger earlier flushes. The default is often 10%. It's recommended to start with a lower value, ranging between 5–7%:

```
sudo sysctl -w vm.dirty_background_ratio=7
```

Dial down vm.dirty_ratio to reduce blocking risk. The default is often 20–30%. It's recommended to lower this value to 15–18%:

```
sudo sysctl -w vm.dirty_ratio=18
```

The previous two commands make changes to the running system. If you want the changes to persist when the server reboots, you need to make edits to /etc/sysctl.conf. When experimenting with these configuration settings, we recommend:

- Monitoring performance after making each adjustment
- Using iostat or sar to ensure smooth and predictable I/O without bursts
- Measuring MongoDB write latency using mongostat
- Searching the database logs for checkpoint completion times to ensure predictable durations

If your workload exhibits write latency spikes, large memory usage by dirty pages, or blocked writes, lowering vm.dirty_background_ratio can help smooth out disk flush operations and reduce performance bottlenecks. Combine this with monitoring and adjustments to other settings, such as vm.dirty_ratio, MongoDB checkpoint frequency, and WiredTiger cache size, for maximum optimization.

Check SSD health

SSDs use sophisticated firmware techniques such as wear leveling, garbage collection, over-provisioning, and TRIM to reduce the performance impact of erase-before-write. At the operating system level, make sure TRIM and garbage collection are enabled. These features make modern SSDs fast and reliable across a wide range of use cases. However, it's important to monitor their health to detect when wear is starting to impact performance or when the drive is nearing the end of its lifespan.

On Linux, most SSDs support SMART data reporting, which provides detailed health and diagnostic metrics such as wear leveling status, remaining life, and bad block count. Many SSD vendors offer proprietary tools to monitor their drives. These tools often expose wear-related data and let you set alerts for health issues or performance degradation. If you're using enterprise-grade SSDs in a server or data center, additional monitoring tools may be available, such as Nagios, Datadog, Dynatrace, Zabbix, or Prometheus with Node Exporter.

SSDs also log system-level warnings or errors when health or performance begins to degrade. On Linux, check `/var/log/syslog`, use `journalctl`, or run `dmesg` to look for I/O-related errors tied to your SSDs.

Avoid double encryption and compression

Some storage technologies include support for compression or encryption, and some support both. For example, enterprise storage arrays and SSDs often include both. Cloud storage services typically don't support compression but do support encryption to protect data at rest, in transit, and within snapshots.

Compressed or encrypted data is harder to compress. If the database compresses and/or encrypts the data, the storage device's compression logic may find fewer redundant patterns, resulting in little to no further compression. In some cases, attempting compression on already compressed data may cause storage overhead, increasing the required compute resources.

Data processed by both the database and the storage device could be compressed and encrypted twice. This is often inefficient and may impact performance while offering no significant benefits. To prevent this, you should determine where compression and encryption are most effectively applied, either at the database layer or at the storage layer.

In some industries, double encryption may provide an extra layer of defense by ensuring encryption is enforced independently at multiple layers (e.g., database encryption for logical security and storage device encryption for physical security).

Ensure resident memory usage stays below 80%

As a general rule, you should try to keep resident memory usage below 80% because low memory can have a big impact on performance. For example, code could be paged out (evicted from physical RAM) because it can be reloaded from its original source. However, if it needs to run again, it will need to be paged back in and wait for I/O. If swap is configured, the system moves less frequently used memory pages to disk to free up RAM for active processes. This causes a write and subsequent read from storage when the memory is accessed again. If memory gets critically low, the **out-of-memory (OOM)** "killer" could terminate the server process.

If you are self-managing a MongoDB system and can't add memory, you should regularly monitor the memory usage of your cluster for insights on whether adjustments are needed. You could experiment with reducing the size of WiredTiger's cache, as we discussed in *Chapter 7, Storage Engines*.

In Atlas, you can set up fine-grained alerts to notify you when resident memory approaches critical thresholds. You can remediate this by scaling to a higher tier or enabling auto-scaling, which is described in more detail in the *Using autoscaling for Atlas performance* section later in this chapter.

In both Atlas and self-managed deployments, if a large amount of memory is being used by complex aggregations running analytical workloads, you could use MongoDB's features for workload isolation.

Workload isolation minimizes contention for memory and ensures each workload runs efficiently. When creating an Atlas cluster, you have options to create analytics nodes or search nodes for workload isolation.

Use analytics nodes to isolate queries that you do not wish to contend with your operational workload. For example, analytics nodes can handle data analysis operations, such as reporting queries from BI Connector for Atlas. The cluster tier for your analytics nodes can be different from the operational nodes. If you select an analytics node on a significantly lower tier, you need to monitor replication lag to make sure it's not under-resourced.

Similarly, you can use dedicated search nodes to isolate search workloads from your operational workload. Finally, if you are not using sharding yet, this could be a good reason to start. See *Chapter 6, Sharding*, for more details on when and how to add sharding.

Networking best practices

As with all distributed systems, following networking best practices is essential for stable and high-performance MongoDB deployments. If you've determined that the network is the current limiting factor, the following checklist may help:

- Deploy MongoDB clusters close to your application servers (e.g., in the same region if using cloud infrastructure).

- Utilize low-latency network connections with high-speed interconnects.

- Use network compression and monitor/optimize query patterns to reduce data transfer. This is a feature that MongoDB drivers support but is not enabled by default.

- Allocate sufficient bandwidth for MongoDB servers, especially in high-traffic production environments.

- Use network interfaces optimized for higher throughput (e.g., gigabit or multi-gigabit Ethernet).

- Rely on a stable, well-maintained network infrastructure to minimize packet loss.

- Prioritize MongoDB traffic using **quality-of-service (QoS)** settings.

- Set short and consistent **time-to-live (TTL)** values for DNS entries to prevent stale cache issues.

- Deploy MongoDB clusters with fixed IPs or DNS names that resolve quickly; use local DNS servers for faster resolution.

- Isolate MongoDB traffic from non-critical workloads using VLANs or QoS.

- Scale network infrastructure or migrate MongoDB to a less congested environment if needed.

- Avoid deep packet inspection of MongoDB traffic where possible.

- Use **virtual private clouds (VPCs)**, trusted networks, and VPNs to secure traffic without overloading packet filtering systems.

- Implement consistent routing policies across all nodes.

- Test network topology regularly to ensure balanced and efficient traffic distribution.

- Deploy MongoDB clusters within the same geographic region when possible.

- Leverage MongoDB Atlas's global clusters for distributed workloads while minimizing latency.

- Choose cloud providers with optimized regional interconnects.

Additionally, consider tuning the following operating system-level networking parameters:

- **somaxconn**: In Linux, this parameter defines the maximum number of pending connection requests that can be queued on a socket. Increasing the somaxconn value allows MongoDB to queue more incoming connections, reducing the likelihood of connection errors during periods of heavy network traffic.

- **tcp_max_syn_backlog**: Controls how many pending SYN requests are queued during the initial TCP handshake.

- **tcp_syncookies**: Prevents SYN flood attacks when the SYN backlog is full.

- **tcp_fin_timeout**: This parameter controls the amount of time (in seconds) a socket remains in the TIME_WAIT state after the connection has been closed. The TIME_WAIT state is a safety mechanism ensuring that all packets related to the closed connection have been properly transmitted and acknowledged before the socket is released for reuse. While this is critical for preventing packet retransmission errors, an unnecessarily high tcp_fin_timeout value can cause resource exhaustion in busy environments, as the system holds onto a large number of closed connection states for an extended period.

Although networking bottlenecks are typically less common than those related to CPU, memory, or storage, it's still wise to monitor network health actively and address issues proactively with the right tools and configuration.

Using auto-scaling for Atlas performance

MongoDB Atlas offers auto-scaling, a powerful feature designed to streamline resource management and ensure optimal performance for your cluster workloads. By dynamically adjusting both cluster tier and storage capacity, auto-scaling helps you maintain high availability and performance while minimizing manual intervention. It can scale compute up or down; storage is auto-scaled up only. Users benefit from Atlas's simplicity and efficiency. If your particular needs aren't addressed, consult MongoDB support for guidance tailored to your specific application.

When workloads change and data grows, scaling resources manually can be challenging and inefficient. Automatic scaling addresses these challenges by leveraging automation, ensuring that your cluster resources align with your application's demands in real time. This eliminates over-provisioning or underutilization, resulting in cost efficiency and consistent performance.

Key performance benefits of auto-scaling include the following:

- **Seamless workload management**: Automatically adjusts resources to accommodate sudden spikes or drops in workload without requiring downtime
- **Enhanced reliability**: Ensures that sufficient resources (CPU, RAM, and storage) are available to avoid bottlenecks during peak usage
- **Cost optimization**: Prevents unnecessary provisioning when workload demands are low, reducing operational expenses
- **Proactive scaling**: Prepares your application for rapid usage spikes or large data ingestion events to deliver uninterrupted service

With auto-scaling, MongoDB Atlas automatically monitors your cluster's performance and utilization metrics, such as CPU usage and disk space.

Here are the two main components of auto-scaling in MongoDB Atlas:

- **Cluster-tier auto scaling**: Adjusts the cluster tier (e.g., M10, M20, or M40) to ensure sufficient resources for CPU and memory utilization
- **Storage auto-scaling**: Scales disk capacity to accommodate data growth, preventing errors related to insufficient storage

Automatic scaling is enabled by default when you provision a new cluster, which can be disabled if needed. To stay informed about scaling events, set up alerts in the Atlas Monitoring suite. Alerts will notify you of resource changes, allowing you to track activity and ensure that adjustments align with your expectations. Automatic scaling is not a substitute for other performance best practices, such as optimizing queries. It is a temporary safety net, but in the long term, you should periodically review your cluster's performance and scaling history to identify patterns and apply other optimizations.

Summary

This chapter has provided an in-depth guide to optimizing MongoDB performance by configuring the operating system and other system resources, with a primary focus on self-managed deployments. While MongoDB Atlas automates many of these tasks, understanding the underlying principles remains valuable.

We covered key resource categories (CPU, memory, storage, and networking) and offered practical guidance on topics such as core-to-operation ratios, choosing the right filesystem (with a recommendation for XFS), and tuning filesystem cache settings. We also cautioned against using double encryption/compression and exceeding 80% resident memory usage.

Additionally, we outlined a checklist for network optimization, including ensuring cluster proximity, maintaining low-latency connections, and planning for bandwidth allocation. Finally, we explained how MongoDB Atlas's auto-scaling dynamically adjusts cluster tiers and storage capacity to meet demand.

The next chapter examines monitoring and observability in MongoDB, showing how to track critical metrics, leverage both built-in and external tools, and establish practices that ensure reliability and performance at scale.

14

Monitoring and Observability

In high-performance database environments, understanding what's happening under the hood isn't just beneficial, it's essential. Monitoring and observability form the foundation of maintaining and optimizing MongoDB deployments, especially as systems scale and workloads become more complex.

This chapter provides a practical guide to monitoring and observability in MongoDB, equipping you with the knowledge to maintain high performance and reliability as your systems grow. You'll learn how to interpret key metrics, leverage built-in and external tools, and respond proactively to early signs of trouble before they impact your applications. Whether you're running MongoDB in the cloud with Atlas or managing your own infrastructure, this chapter will help you build a robust observability strategy tailored to your needs.

Key topics covered in this chapter include the following:

- The difference between monitoring and observability
- Why monitoring and observability both matter for database performance
- The core MongoDB metrics and signals to track for optimal health and troubleshooting
- How to use MongoDB Atlas and self-managed tools for real-time monitoring and alerting
- Best practices for integrating MongoDB metrics into broader observability platforms

Key differences between monitoring and observability

While often used interchangeably, monitoring and observability represent distinct but complementary practices. **Monitoring** answers *Is something wrong?* by collecting and alerting on predefined metrics, opcounters, cache pressure, page faults, and connection counts against known thresholds. It's focused on tracking the known failure modes of a system.

Observability answers *Why is it happening?* by enriching those metrics with contextual data such as logs, traces, and explain plans, so you can drill down from an alert to the root cause. It enables the exploration of unknown issues by providing a comprehensive view of the system's internal state.

In high-throughput environments, whether running a single replica set or a global sharded cluster, subtle performance degradations can cascade into major outages. Without comprehensive visibility into resource utilization, query performance, and system health, identifying bottlenecks becomes a frustrating guessing game.

Observability transforms this guesswork into data-driven insights. By continuously tracking key signals, you can optimize performance and detect early signs of trouble before they impact your applications. Here are some examples:

- **Correlate logged operations** with index usage (or lack thereof) and execution plans to pinpoint missing or inefficient indexes
- **Overlay disk queue depths** with commit times to uncover storage contention under peak workloads
- **Chart replication lag** against write throughput to detect network bottlenecks during failover events
- **Monitor memory pressure** to identify optimal cache sizes and prevent page faults
- **Track connection patterns** to properly size connection pools and prevent queuing

These practices are important because they turn raw monitoring data into actionable insights. By correlating slow queries with index usage, overlaying disk queue depths with commit times, and tracking replication lag, memory pressure, and connection patterns, you can move beyond simply detecting that something is wrong; you can pinpoint the root cause of performance issues. This enables you to proactively optimize your MongoDB deployment, prevent outages, and ensure that your database continues to deliver reliable, high performance as workloads grow and change. In short, these techniques help you shift from reactive troubleshooting to continuous, data-driven improvement.

To truly optimize performance, you need more than just a snapshot of system health; you need clear, timely signals that reveal when and where degradation is occurring. A robust monitoring and observability strategy provides these essential signals, making it possible to identify emerging issues such as slow queries, resource constraints, replication lag, storage bottlenecks, or connection problems. With this visibility, you gain the context and confidence to diagnose, prioritize, and resolve issues before they escalate, turning what would otherwise be reactive firefighting into a process of ongoing improvement and resilience.

Core MongoDB metrics and signals

Understanding the internal state of your MongoDB deployment is crucial for maintaining optimal performance and diagnosing issues. MongoDB exposes a comprehensive set of metrics that provide insights into its health, resource utilization, and operational characteristics. By monitoring and correlating these core signals, you can proactively identify potential bottlenecks, make informed decisions about capacity planning, and ensure that your database effectively supports your application workloads.

These metrics generally fall into two categories: operational metrics, which give a real-time view of the database's current activity, and performance-specific metrics, which delve deeper into workload behavior and potential areas of contention.

Operational metrics

Operational metrics answer the question *How is my database operating right now?*. These are exposed by the serverStatus command and can be collected via the shell, drivers, or external monitoring solutions such as Prometheus, as discussed later in the *Integration with external monitoring systems* section.

The following example demonstrates how to extract a few of the most important operational metrics using the MongoDB Shell. This code retrieves the current server status and prints a selection of key metrics that are essential for monitoring real-time health and workload:

```
// Run from the MongoDB shell
// Example: Extract key operational metrics in the MongoDB shell
const status = db.serverStatus();
printjson({
   opcounters:      status.opcounters,        // reads, writes, commands
   memUsageMB:      status.mem.resident,       // resident memory in MB
   cacheStats:      status.wiredTiger.cache,   // WiredTiger cache
utilization
   connections:     status.connections         // active vs available
});
```

The preceding code reveals several of the most actionable metrics for day-to-day monitoring, but it's important to note that serverStatus exposes a much broader set of metrics covering nearly every aspect of MongoDB's operation. In the following list, we highlight only some of the most relevant fields for practical, ongoing observability. Here's what each field represents, and where to find related metrics not shown in the code:

- **opcounters (from `status.opcounters` in the code)**: These track the number of database operations (reads, writes, commands) since the server started. Monitoring these helps you understand workload patterns and spot sudden spikes that may indicate query storms or application issues. Imbalances between reads and writes may suggest opportunities for scaling or optimization.

- **memUsageMB (from `status.mem.resident` in the code)**: This shows the amount of physical RAM (in megabytes) currently used by the MongoDB process. Keeping an eye on this helps ensure that your working set fits in memory, minimizing disk access and maintaining performance. For a deeper view, the `mem` section of `serverStatus` also includes virtual memory, mapped memory, and page faults.

- **cacheStats (from `status.wiredTiger.cache` in the code)**: This provides details on the WiredTiger storage engine's internal cache usage, including how much data is cached and the ratio of dirty (modified) to clean pages. High cache pressure or frequent evictions can signal the need for more memory or cache tuning. The full `wiredTiger.cache` section contains additional metrics such as eviction rates and maximum cache size.

- **connections (from `status.connections` in the code)**: This reports the number of active client connections and the available connection slots. Monitoring this helps prevent connection saturation, which can lead to application errors or degraded responsiveness. The `connections` section also shows the number of available connections and the total created since startup.

- **Replication metrics (not shown in the code)**: For deployments using replica sets, metrics such as replication lag, oplog window, heartbeat times, and election metrics are available in the `repl` and `oplog` sections of `serverStatus`, or via replica set-specific commands such as `rs.status()` and `rs.printReplicationInfo()`. These are vital for ensuring data durability and failover readiness.

- **Disk I/O metrics (not shown in the code)**: Storage performance metrics, such as queue depth, latency, throughput, and IOPS, are found in the `wiredTiger` and `metrics` sections of `serverStatus`, or through external monitoring tools. These are crucial for identifying storage bottlenecks and ensuring that your disk subsystem can handle the workload.

By regularly collecting and reviewing these metrics, you gain a comprehensive, real-time view of your database's operational health, enabling you to detect emerging issues and optimize performance before problems escalate.

Performance-specific metrics

While operational metrics provide a broad overview of database activity, performance-specific metrics delve deeper into the sources of slowdowns and inefficiencies. These metrics help pinpoint bottlenecks and answer the critical question: *Where exactly are the performance issues occurring?*. Performance-specific metrics include slow query statistics, query execution statistics, and index usage metrics.

To capture and review slow operations, use the MongoDB database profiler (via `db.setProfilingLevel()` and the `system.profile` collection), or Query Insights in Atlas. Locking and contention metrics can be accessed through the `serverStatus` command and visualized through external tools such as Prometheus and Grafana.

For query execution statistics, such as documents examined versus returned and execution time breakdowns, use the `explain()` method in the shell or drivers, the database profiler, and Atlas Query Insights. For programmatic monitoring, extract the relevant fields from the profiler output or `system.profile`. To understand index usage and effectiveness, leverage the `explain()` method, the `collStats` command, Atlas Performance Advisor, and Query Insights to identify usage patterns and optimization opportunities.

For now, familiarize yourself with the built-in tools (MongoDB database profiler, explain plans, `serverStatus`, and the Atlas UI) and external integrations (Prometheus, Grafana, and Datadog) that make this level of observability possible.

Monitoring with MongoDB Atlas

MongoDB Atlas provides a fully managed, cloud-based database service that surfaces critical database signals in real time and guides you toward data-driven optimizations. In high-performance database environments, effective monitoring isn't just about collecting metrics; it's about transforming those metrics into actionable insights that help you maintain peak performance for your clusters.

Atlas UI features

The Atlas UI provides a robust suite of features for monitoring and performance analysis. The Real-Time Performance Panel offers live visualizations of cluster health, including resource consumption, operation rates, and query execution times, ideal for immediate oversight. The

Performance Advisor continually analyzes workloads, suggesting indexes to enhance performance, while Query Insights provides a higher-level view by grouping similar queries, monitoring latency percentiles, and identifying **hot** collections. Lastly, profiler integration within Query Insights simplifies the diagnosis of performance bottlenecks by offering a user-friendly interface for the MongoDB database profiler.

Real-Time Performance Panel (RTPP)

MongoDB Atlas provides a live, high-level visualization of your cluster's health and operational throughput, updating every few seconds. Available for M10+ clusters, RTPP is especially useful for monitoring live environments, load testing, and post-deployment performance validation. It enables you to visually identify spikes, bottlenecks, and trends across a range of critical metrics, helping you correlate performance changes with resource utilization or operational load in real time.

RTPP offers two main views, **Graph** and **Table**, each surfacing a comprehensive set of metrics, including the following:

- **Resource Consumption**: CPU usage, system memory, and disk **I/O operations per second (IOPS)**, as well as network traffic (bytes in/out). These metrics help you spot resource saturation or sudden spikes that often correlate with performance degradation.

- **Operation Rates:** The number of read, write, command, and aggregation operations processed per second, providing insight into workload intensity and patterns.

- **Query Execution Times:** Latency statistics for current read, write, and command operations, allowing you to quickly identify slowdowns.

- **Query Targeting:** The ratio of documents scanned to documents returned across all operations during a sampling period, which helps assess index efficiency and query optimization needs.

- **Replication Lag:** For replica sets, the delay between primary and secondary nodes, critical for data consistency and failover readiness.

- **Reads & Writes:** The number of active and queued read/write operations, indicating potential bottlenecks or resource contention if queues grow.

- **Connections:** Current client connections and network throughput, useful for detecting connection saturation.

- **Hottest Collections:** Collections with the most operations, highlighting potential hotspots for further investigation (leveraging mongotop-like statistics).

- **Slowest Operations:** The slowest currently running operations, with the ability to drill down for details or terminate problematic queries.

You can pause the **Graph** view to inspect exact metric values at a specific point in time, including the slowest operations and hottest collections. RTPP is enabled by default but can be toggled in **Project Settings** by users with *Project Owner* access. RTPP is particularly valuable during load testing, production incidents, or after deployments to quickly correlate performance changes with resource utilization or operational load.

Performance Advisor

The Atlas Performance Advisor continuously analyzes your cluster's workload, specifically looking for inefficient query patterns. It offers actionable insights through the following:

- **Index suggestions**: Recommends specific indexes that could improve the performance of identified slow queries, often providing an estimated impact percentage.
- **Index management**: Allows you to review, create, or drop suggested indexes directly through the Atlas UI. It also highlights potentially unused indexes that could be dropped.

Integrating Performance Advisor checks into development workflows or CI/CD pipelines helps you proactively identify and address potential query performance issues before they reach production.

Query Insights

Query Insights exposes improved observability and granular telemetry with namespace-level and operation-level latency statistics.

Namespace Insights

Monitor collection-level query latency with **Namespace Insights**. The Namespace Insights page displays two charts and a table with information for each top or pinned namespace. The information includes metrics and statistics for certain hosts and operation types. You can manage pinned namespaces and choose up to five namespaces to show in the corresponding query latency charts. This allows you to monitor the performance difference between multiple namespaces using percentile latencies (P50, P95, and P99), revealing not just average performance but also tail latency experienced by users. High P95 or P99 latencies indicate that some users may be experiencing slow responses.

Reviewing this information can help you identify hot collections, which can be combined with other tooling to provide a high-level view of workload distribution.

Query Shapes and Query Profiler

Within Query Insights, Atlas provides a user-friendly interface for surfacing insights about logged operations. Operations are logged to mongos/mongod logs when they exceed the slowms threshold (which defaults to 100 milliseconds).

The Query Shapes tab groups these operations by shape and allows you to see their performance metrics. The Query Profiler can help you see more details to diagnose and resolve performance bottlenecks with greater precision through the following:

- **Slow query identification**: Detects queries that consistently exceed the slowms threshold. This can occur on a collection scan (reading entire collections without using an index) or operations that aren't optimally indexed. If you see a slow query with planSummary: COLLSCAN, consider an appropriate index.

- **Recent slow operations**: List of operations exceeding your configured threshold, along with key details such as execution time, namespace (database and collection), and documents scanned versus returned. If execution time is high and the ratio of documents examined versus documents returned is elevated, optimize the query or add indexes to reduce unnecessary scanning.

- **Execution statistics**: Drill down into individual slow operations to examine their execution plan, index usage, read/write latency, and response size. Add or adjust indexes as needed. Large response sizes may indicate the need for projections to limit returned fields.

- **Filter and drill down**: Narrow down the profiler output by time range, operation type, or namespace to isolate specific issues. Use this to correlate slowdowns with application changes, deployment events, or specific workloads.

In practice, use the Query Insights in tandem with Performance Advisor to confirm that new indexes or query changes yield the expected latency improvements.

Alerts

Atlas issues alerts for the database and server conditions configured in your alert settings. When a condition triggers an alert, Atlas displays a warning symbol on the cluster and sends alert notifications. Your alert settings determine the notification methods. Atlas continues sending notifications at regular intervals until the condition resolves or you delete or disable the alert.

Atlas has a number of predefined alerts at both the organization and project levels; however, you can create custom alerts as well. Let's look at some common alert categories and how the underlying issues can be addressed.

Atlas Search issues

Atlas Search triggers alerts when the amount of CPU and memory used by Atlas Search processes reaches a specified threshold. If the search process (mongot) runs out of memory, indexing and queries fail.

Atlas Search alerts often occur when you try to build a large or complex search index. These indexes remain in the *Initial Sync* phase until you resolve the memory issue.

If the search process runs out of memory or disk space, you can upgrade your cluster to fix the immediate problem. You can select a cluster tier with more memory, storage, and IOPS, or consider a dedicated search node for even greater availability, performance, and workload balancing.

Connection issues

Connection alerts typically occur when the maximum number of allowable connections to a MongoDB process has been exceeded. Once the limit is exceeded, no new connections can be opened until the number of open connections drops below the limit.

Connection alerts are generally a symptom of a larger problem. If these alerts are being triggered often, a proper solution will likely involve the following:

- Examining your database applications for flawed connection code. Situations in which connections are opened but never closed can allow old connections to pile up and eventually exceed the connection limit. Additionally, you may need to implement some form of connection pooling.
- Upgrading to a larger Atlas cluster tier, which allows a greater number of connections, if your user base is too large for your current cluster tier.

By identifying the root cause and addressing it, whether in your application code or cluster configuration, you can prevent recurring connection issues and ensure smoother, more reliable database performance.

Query issues

The query targeting alert typically occurs when there is no index to support a query or queries, or when an existing index only partially supports a query or queries. Examples of these alerts are as follows:

- **Query Targeting: Scanned Objects / Returned**: These alerts are triggered when the average number of documents scanned relative to the average number of documents returned server-wide across all operations during a sampling period exceeds a defined threshold. The default alert uses a 1000:1 threshold. Ideally, the ratio of scanned documents to returned documents should be close to 1. A high ratio negatively impacts query performance.

- **Query Targeting: Scanned / Returned**: These alerts occur if the number of index keys examined to fulfill a query relative to the actual number of returned documents meets or exceeds a user-defined threshold. This alert is not enabled by default.

The most common source of this issue is a missing index, which the Performance Advisor provides the easiest and quickest way to investigate. The Performance Advisor monitors queries that MongoDB considers slow and recommends indexes to improve performance. Identifying issues using these alerts, coupled with the concepts introduced in *Chapter 12, Advanced Query and Indexing Concepts*, can help you more effectively troubleshoot and address underperforming queries.

Oplog issues

In *Chapter 5, Replication*, we learned about the **operations log** (**oplog**) and the role it plays in ensuring write operations are propagated to all replica set members. We also learned that the oplog is a capped collection of a fixed size (either by disk size or window size in time).

If a large amount of write operations are conducted on the primary node of the replica set and the secondary nodes do not have enough time to replay all of the operations contained in the oplog, this will typically result in "falling off the oplog," which requires an initial sync in order to recover and ensure that the data is consistent across all nodes.

Atlas offers monitoring and alerting of events relevant to this scenario in the form of the following:

- **Replication Oplog Window is (X)**: This occurs if the approximate amount of time available in the primary replication oplog meets or goes below the specified threshold. This refers to the amount of time that the primary can continue logging, given the current rate at which oplog data is generated.

- **Oplog Data Per Hour is (X)**: This occurs if the amount of data per hour being written to a primary's replication oplog meets or exceeds the specified threshold.

The most common trigger for these alerts is intensive write and update operations in a short period of time. When this occurs, some common mitigations are as follows:

- Increase the oplog size by editing your cluster's configuration to ensure it is higher than the peak value from the **Oplog GB/Hour** graph in the cluster metrics view.
- Ensure that all write operations specify a write concern of majority to ensure that writes are replicated to at least one node before moving on to the next write operation. This controls the rate of traffic from your application by preventing the primary from accepting writes more quickly than the secondaries can handle.

To get the most value from your alerting system, regularly review and tune alert thresholds to match your workload and business requirements, which helps avoid both alert fatigue and missed incidents. Integrate alert notifications with your team's preferred communication and incident management tools to ensure rapid response. Treat alerts as actionable signals: when triggered, promptly investigate the root cause, take corrective action (such as scaling resources, optimizing queries, or adjusting thresholds), and document the resolution for future reference.

Periodically audit the configured alerts to ensure they remain relevant as your application and infrastructure evolve. Finally, use alert history and trends to inform capacity planning, identify recurring issues, and drive continuous improvement in your monitoring strategy.

For a full list of available alert conditions, see the MongoDB Atlas documentation at `https://www.mongodb.com/docs/atlas/reference/alert-conditions/`.

Self-managed monitoring tools

When operating MongoDB outside of the managed Atlas environment, you are responsible for assembling your own observability pipeline. Fortunately, MongoDB provides a suite of built-in command-line utilities and database commands designed to offer deep insights into the server's real-time activity and historical performance. Mastering these tools is essential for diagnosing issues, understanding workload characteristics, and ensuring the health of your self-hosted deployments.

mongostat: real-time activity snapshot

Think of `mongostat` as a MongoDB-specific monitoring utility that provides a dynamic, real-time view of the status of a running `mongod` or `mongos` instance. By sampling the server status periodically (by default, every second), it presents key metrics in a concise, tabular format, allowing you to quickly assess the current operational load and resource utilization.

To run mongostat, you can connect to your MongoDB instance like so:

```
// Run from the System Command Line
mongostat --host localhost:27017 --rowcount 2
```

You'll see an output similar to the following, updating each second:

```
insert  query update delete getmore command   dirty used flushes vsize  res
     0      8      0      0       0     3|0    3.4% 7.4%       0 1.2G  512M
     1     12      0      0       0     5|0    3.7% 2.5%       0 1.2G  210M
```

Key fields include the following:

- **Operation counters**: Shows the number of operations per second, indicating the shape and intensity of your workload (insert, query, update, and delete).

- **Memory**: Reveals memory utilization details, including mapped memory, virtual size, and resident memory. Significant changes or high resident memory might indicate memory pressure (mapped, vsize, and res).

- **Commands**: Shows the number of commands executed per second (command).

For replica sets, you can use the --discover option to automatically track all members and their status:

```
mongostat --discover
```

Use mongostat for a quick health check, to observe the immediate impact of application changes, or during performance incidents to get a high-level view of database activity.

mongotop: Collection-level read/write timings

While mongostat provides a server-wide overview, mongotop focuses specifically on the time spent performing read and write operations on a per-collection basis. This is invaluable for identifying which collections are experiencing the heaviest activity or potentially causing I/O bottlenecks.

Like mongostat, you connect mongotop to a running instance:

```
// Run from the System Command Line
mongotop --host localhost:27017 --rowcount 2
```

The output looks like this:

```
ns              total   read    write  2025-04-30T16:30:27-04:00
mydb.users      0.1ms   0.1ms   0.0ms
mydb.orders     5.2ms   2.8ms   2.4ms
```

The columns show the following:

- `ns`: The namespace (`<database>`.`<collection>`) being monitored
- `total`: Total time the server spent performing operations on this collection during the interval
- `read`: Time spent on read operations
- `write`: Time spent on write operations

Use `mongotop` to pinpoint hot collections that might benefit from schema optimization, indexing improvements, or sharding if activity is consistently high and impacting overall performance. For example, in the preceding output, you can see that the `mydb.orders` collection experiences significantly higher read and write activity compared to `mydb.users`, which might warrant further investigation.

serverStatus: Comprehensive metrics via the shell

For the most detailed snapshot of a MongoDB server's state, the `serverStatus` command is the definitive source. It returns a large JSON document containing hundreds of metrics covering nearly every aspect of the server's operation:

```
// Run from the MongoDB shell
db.adminCommand({ serverStatus: 1 })

// Or using the shell helper
db.serverStatus()
```

While the output is too extensive to detail fully here, important sections include the following:

- `opcounters`: Granular counts of all database operations since the server started
- `connections`: Information about current, available, and queued client connections
- `locks`: Information about lock contention (database, collection, or global)
- `wiredTiger`: Deep metrics specific to the WiredTiger storage engine, including the following:
    - Cache usage (pages read into cache, pages written from cache, dirty bytes)
    - Transaction checkpoints
    - Block manager statistics
- `mem`: Resident and virtual memory statistics
- `metrics`: Various operational metrics such as document insertion/update/deletion rates, query executor stats, and replication details

serverStatus is less suited for real-time monitoring due to the volume of data, but it is essential for deep analysis, establishing performance baselines, and programmatic monitoring where specific metrics are extracted and tracked over time by external systems.

Database profiler: Deep dive into slow operations

When you need to understand the performance characteristics of individual queries, the database profiler is the tool of choice. It captures detailed information about database operations for a specific database, allowing you to identify slow or inefficient queries that might impact application performance.

To get started, you can enable the profiler for a specific mongod instance using the setProfilingLevel() method from the MongoDB Shell. This method offers three profiling levels, each suited for different needs:

- **Level 0 (off)**: The profiler is disabled by default and does not collect any data
- **Level 1 (slow operations)**: It captures data only for operations slower than a specified threshold (slowms, default 100 ms)
- **Level 2 (all operations)**: It captures data for all operations (use with caution in production due to performance overhead)

Additionally, you can configure slowms, which is the slow operation threshold. Any user operation that completes faster than this will not be logged to the mongod log. sampleRate can also be set, which allows you to control what fraction of slow operations should be logged.

The following command, when run via the MongoDB Shell, will enable the database profiler for the current database with a slow operation threshold of 20 milliseconds and a sample rate of 42%:

```
db.setProfilingLevel(1, { slowms: 20, sampleRate: 0.42 })
```

Once enabled, you can query the profiler data to analyze recent operations. For example, this command finds and displays the five most recent profiled operations:

```
// Run from the MongoDB shell
// Find the 5 most recent profiled operations
db.system.profile.find().sort({ ts: -1 }).limit(5).forEach(printjson)
```

Profiled operations are stored in the system.profile capped collection in each database for which profiling has been enabled. Each document in this collection contains details such as the following:

- `millis`: The duration of the operation in milliseconds

- `ns`: The namespace (`database.collection`) targeted

- `command`: The full command document associated with the operation

- `execStats`: Detailed execution statistics for query operations (similar to the output of an `explain` operation)

Here's an example of a profiler entry for a slow query. Since we specified an `appName` value in the connection string of the application that was connected to the cluster when this operation was logged, the app name is shown alongside the operation:

```
{
  "op": "query",
  "ns": "mydb.orders",
  "command": {
    "find": "orders",
    "filter": { "status": "shipped", "orderDate": { "$gt":
ISODate("2025-01-01") } },
    "sort": { "customerName": 1 },
    "limit": 100
  },
  "keysExamined": 0,
  "docsExamined": 1000000,
  "nreturned": 53,
  "responseLength": 24601,
  "millis": 2543,
  "planSummary": "COLLSCAN",
  "execStats": {
    // Detailed execution statistics
  },
  "client": "192.168.1.50",
  "user": "appuser",
  "appName" : "my-custom-microservice-01"
}
```

In this example from an application we named `my-custom-microservice-01`, we can immediately identify several issues. The operation took 2.5 seconds (`"millis": 2543`), it performed a collection scan (`"planSummary": "COLLSCAN"`), and it examined `1000000` documents (`docsExamined`) to return just 53 documents (`nreturned`).

These profiler details show that the query is scanning the entire collection rather than using an index, which is highly inefficient, especially given the filter on "status" and "orderDate". This pattern clearly indicates that there is no suitable index on these fields. To improve performance, you should create a compound index on "status", "customerName", and "orderDate" in that order, allowing MongoDB to efficiently locate matching documents without scanning the whole collection.

Best practices for MongoDB Profiler in production

Enabling the MongoDB database profiler at level 2 (profiling all operations) in production environments can introduce significant performance overhead. In most production scenarios, it is best practice to use level 1 profiling, set sampleRate, or enable full profiling only for short, targeted periods during troubleshooting. Always monitor system impact when adjusting profiler settings in live environments.

Use profiler data to pinpoint inefficient queries, detect missing indexes, and guide schema refinements. By analyzing patterns in slow operations, you can make targeted optimizations that significantly improve application performance.

Integration with external monitoring systems

While MongoDB provides powerful built-in tools such as mongostat, mongotop, and serverStatus commands, and MongoDB Atlas offers a comprehensive managed monitoring suite, modern application environments rarely operate in isolation. To achieve true end-to-end observability, it's crucial to integrate MongoDB's performance signals into broader external monitoring and observability platforms.

This integration allows you to do the following:

- Correlate database behavior with application performance and infrastructure health
- Create unified dashboards spanning your entire technology stack
- Implement consistent alerting across all components
- Gain historical context for performance analysis
- Support root cause analysis across system boundaries

In essence, by feeding MongoDB's performance data into your organization's wider observability tools, you gain a more holistic view, making it easier to connect database performance with overall application health, manage alerts centrally, and perform comprehensive root cause analysis across your entire technology stack.

Prometheus + Grafana

Prometheus and Grafana together form a popular open source monitoring solution. Prometheus collects and stores metrics, while Grafana visualizes them through customizable dashboards. MongoDB Atlas provides native integration with this stack, allowing you to monitor your MongoDB deployments alongside your other infrastructure components.

> **Note**
>
> The Prometheus integration is available only on M10+ clusters.

Atlas integration for Prometheus

MongoDB Atlas offers a straightforward integration with Prometheus that eliminates the need for third-party exporters. Here's how to set it up:

- **Configure authentication**: In the Atlas UI, navigate to the **Integrations** tab and set up Prometheus credentials specifically designed for metric collection.
- **Choose discovery method**: Select either **HTTP Service Discovery** (recommended) or **File Service Discovery**, depending on your infrastructure and preference.
- **Update Prometheus configuration**: Add the appropriate scrape configuration to your Prometheus server.

In summary, integrating MongoDB Atlas with Prometheus involves three key steps:

1. Configure authentication credentials within the Atlas UI.
2. Select a service discovery method (either HTTP or file-based).
3. Update your Prometheus server's configuration to include the necessary scrape settings.

Here is an example of what the scrape configuration might look like in your prometheus.yml file:

```
scrape_configs:
  - job_name: "<insert-job-name>"
    scrape_interval: 10s
    metrics_path: /metrics
    scheme: https
    basic_auth:
      username: <prometheus-username>
      password: <prometheus-password>
    http_sd_configs:
```

```
- url: <url-of-the-service-discovery-configuration>
  refresh_interval: 60s
  basic_auth:
    username: <prometheus-username>
    password: <prometheus-password>
```

Once configured, Prometheus will automatically discover and scrape a variety of metrics from all your Atlas clusters. These metrics include operation rates (such as queries, inserts, updates, and deletes), resource utilization (such as CPU, memory, and connections), replication metrics (including lag and oplog window), and storage metrics (such as disk usage and IOPS).

Visualizing with Grafana

To complete your monitoring solution and gain deeper insights into your deployment's performance, you can import prebuilt MongoDB dashboards into Grafana:

1. In Grafana, navigate to the **Import** screen (click the + icon, then select **Import**).

2. Upload a sample dashboard JSON file (e.g., mongo-metrics.json or hardware-metrics. json). These can typically be found in the Atlas UI or the official documentation.

3. Ensure that the imported dashboard is configured to use your Prometheus data source.

4. Start monitoring your MongoDB deployment using these purpose-built visualizations.

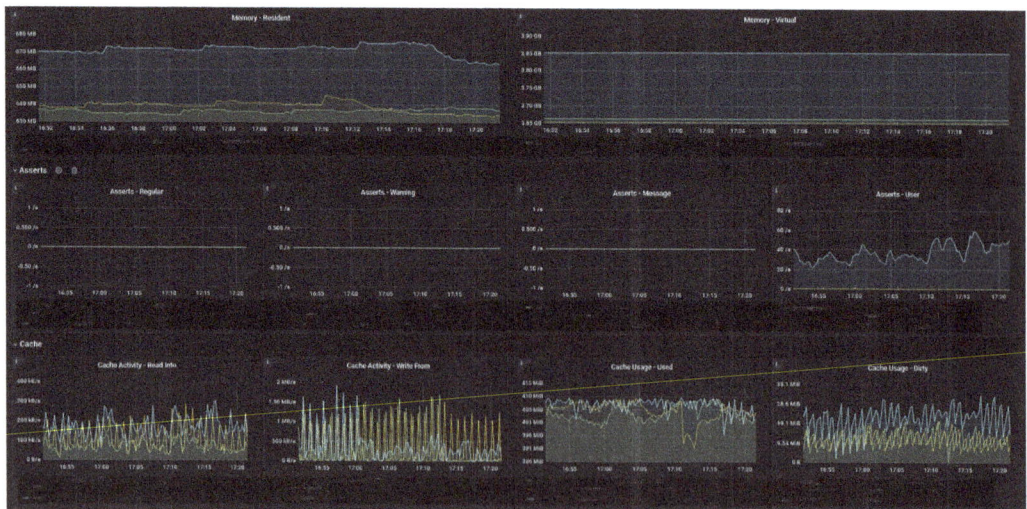

Figure 14.1: Sample MongoDB metrics dashboard in Grafana

For detailed step-by-step instructions and to access the sample dashboard JSON files, refer to the official MongoDB Atlas documentation at `https://www.mongodb.com/docs/atlas/tutorial/prometheus-integration/#import-a-sample-grafana-dashboard`.

This integration works with MongoDB Atlas as well as Cloud Manager and Ops Manager deployments, providing consistent monitoring capabilities whether your MongoDB infrastructure is fully managed or self-hosted.

Datadog

Datadog is a comprehensive commercial SaaS observability platform that offers infrastructure monitoring, SAPM, log management, and more. MongoDB Atlas provides a first-class integration with Datadog that enables seamless monitoring of your database deployments.

The MongoDB Atlas integration with Datadog allows you to monitor your Atlas clusters directly within your Datadog dashboards, providing a unified view of your database performance alongside your other application and infrastructure metrics.

Key features of this integration include the following:

- **Native integration:** Configure the connection between Atlas and Datadog with just a few clicks in the Atlas UI
- **Automatic metric collection:** Once connected, Atlas automatically sends performance metrics to your Datadog account
- **Prebuilt dashboards:** The integration includes preconfigured dashboards showing key MongoDB performance metrics
- **Unified alerting:** Create alerts in Datadog based on Atlas metrics that integrate with your existing notification workflows
- **Cross-platform correlation:** Easily correlate database performance issues with application and infrastructure metrics

> **Note**
>
> The Datadog integration is available only on M10+ clusters. You need a Datadog account and API key.

To set up the integration, follow these steps:

1. Ensure that you have *Project Owner* access in Atlas.

2. In Atlas, navigate to your project, then click on **Integrations**.

3. Click the **Datadog** tile.

4. Enter your Datadog API key. You can find or create this in your Datadog account under **Integrations > APIs**.

5. Configure which clusters and specific metrics you want Datadog to monitor.

6. Optionally, to track high-cardinality metrics, enable `sendDatabaseMetrics` and `sendCollectionLatencyMetrics`. This can be done via the Atlas UI or the Atlas Administration API.

7. Once configured, you can access your MongoDB Atlas dashboard and metrics within Datadog.

For more detailed steps and information, refer to the official MongoDB Atlas documentation on Datadog integration at `https://www.mongodb.com/docs/atlas/tutorial/datadog-integration/#procedure`.

> **Atlas project metrics automatically sent to Datadog**
>
> If you configure your Atlas project to send alerts and events to Datadog, you do not need to follow this procedure separately. Atlas sends project metrics to Datadog through the same integration used for alerts and events.

Once the integration is complete, you can start exploring the prebuilt dashboards in Datadog to get an overview of your Atlas cluster's performance. Consider setting up alerts for key metrics such as CPU utilization, disk space, and replication lag to be notified of potential issues. You can also begin to correlate MongoDB metrics with your application and infrastructure data to get a holistic view of your system. We will delve deeper into performance monitoring strategies and alerting best practices in subsequent sections.

Application performance monitoring platforms

Platforms such as **New Relic**, **AppDynamics**, and **Dynatrace** specialize in **application performance monitoring (APM)**. Their primary strength lies in tracing application requests end-to-end, providing deep visibility into how application code interacts with the database.

APM agents are typically integrated into your application code via language-specific libraries. When your application makes a database call, the APM agent does the following:

1. Intercepts the call

2. Measures its duration

3. Captures relevant context (such as the query itself, often normalized)

4. Correlates this with the broader request context

This integration enables APM platforms to do the following:

- Trace individual requests from the user's browser or API client through multiple services down to specific database queries

- Identify slow database calls within the context of a complete user transaction

- Correlate application errors or latency spikes with specific database operations

- Provide aggregated views showing how database performance impacts overall application performance

Ultimately, APM platforms provide a powerful lens to understand how database interactions fit into the larger picture of application behavior, making it easier to pinpoint database-related bottlenecks that affect the end-user experience.

OpenTelemetry

OpenTelemetry is an open source observability framework providing vendor-neutral APIs, libraries, and instrumentation to capture distributed traces, metrics, and logs. It represents the future of observability instrumentation, with growing adoption across the industry.

OpenTelemetry offers instrumentation libraries for popular programming languages and MongoDB drivers. By incorporating these libraries into your application, MongoDB driver calls are automatically captured as "spans" within distributed traces. Each span records the following:

- The duration of the database operation

- The operation type (query, update, insert, etc.)

- The target collection or database

- Any errors that occurred

These spans provide a detailed record of each database interaction, capturing what operation was performed, how long it took, where it was executed, and whether it succeeded. This granular data is crucial for understanding database performance and diagnosing issues.

For a Node.js application, implementing OpenTelemetry instrumentation for MongoDB might look like this:

```js
// tracing.js
const opentelemetry = require('@opentelemetry/api');
const { NodeTracerProvider } = require('@opentelemetry/sdk-trace-node');
const { MongoDBInstrumentation } = require('@opentelemetry/
instrumentation-mongodb');
const { registerInstrumentations } = require('@opentelemetry/
instrumentation');

// Configure the tracer provider
const provider = new NodeTracerProvider();
provider.register();

// Register MongoDB instrumentation
registerInstrumentations({
  instrumentations: [new MongoDBInstrumentation()],
});

// Export traces using your preferred exporter
// (OTLP, Jaeger, Zipkin, etc.)
```

With this instrumentation in place, MongoDB operations are automatically captured and can be sent to any OpenTelemetry-compatible backend.

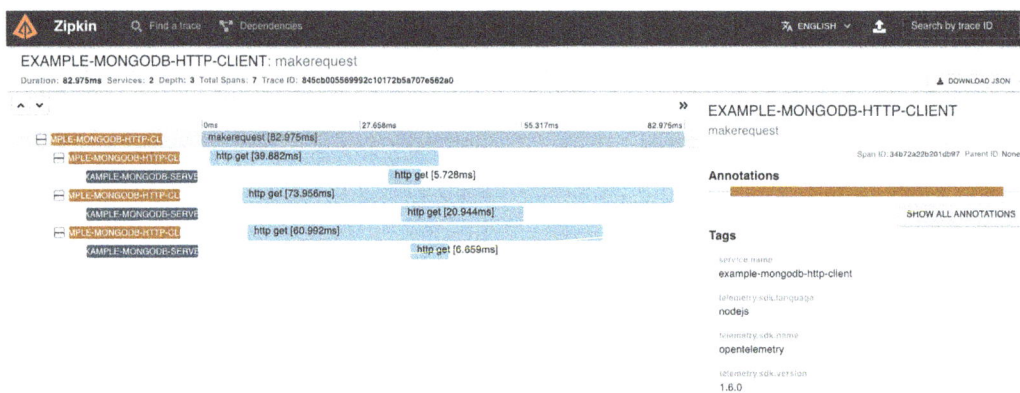

Figure 14.2: Visualization of MongoDB operation spans captured by OpenTelemetry

The preceding screenshot is from the OpenTelemetry MongoDB instrumentation example available at `https://github.com/open-telemetry/opentelemetry-js-contrib/tree/main/examples/mongodb`.

This instrumentation creates detailed spans for each MongoDB operation, capturing crucial information such as operation type, database and collection names, and execution time, enabling precise performance monitoring and troubleshooting across your entire application stack.

Considerations for external tools

When integrating MongoDB with external monitoring systems, several important factors should be considered to ensure effective and secure monitoring. Securing access to your MongoDB instances and the data flowing to monitoring systems is paramount. This involves implementing robust authentication mechanisms, encrypting data in transit, and adhering to the principle of least privilege for monitoring users. Careful attention to these security aspects will help protect your data and maintain the integrity of your monitoring setup.

Key security practices include the following:

- **Dedicated monitoring users**: Create MongoDB users specifically for monitoring tools with minimum required privileges (typically the `clusterMonitor` role)
- **Strong authentication**: Use strong passwords and consider certificate-based authentication, where supported
- **TLS/SSL**: Encrypt communication between monitoring tools and MongoDB
- **Network security**: Restrict monitoring tool access to MongoDB through appropriate firewall rules

Beyond security, another critical aspect of integrating external monitoring tools is managing their resource consumption. Monitoring systems, by their nature, interact with your MongoDB deployment to collect data. This interaction, if not carefully configured, can impose an additional load on your database servers, potentially impacting their performance. Therefore, it's essential to be mindful of how these tools consume resources to ensure that the act of monitoring doesn't degrade the performance of the system you're trying to observe.

Key considerations for managing resource consumption include the following:

- **Scraping/polling frequency**: Configure appropriate intervals for metric collection (typically 10–60 seconds) to balance between timely data and minimizing overhead
- **Resource overhead**: Monitor the resource consumption of the monitoring agents themselves to ensure they don't impact MongoDB performance

- **Payload size:** Be aware of the volume of data being collected, especially from commands such as serverStatus that return large documents

- **Benchmark in staging:** Test monitoring configurations in non-production environments before deploying to production

In summary, integrating external monitoring tools with MongoDB requires a balanced approach, prioritizing both security and performance. By securing access and carefully managing resource usage, you can ensure reliable monitoring without compromising your deployment's stability or integrity.

Common performance patterns and what to monitor

Understanding common performance bottlenecks in MongoDB and knowing which metrics signal their presence is crucial for proactive performance management. By monitoring key indicators, you can detect and diagnose issues before they significantly impact your application's responsiveness and reliability. This section explores recurring performance challenges and the essential signals to track.

Disk I/O bottlenecks

The storage subsystem is frequently a limiting factor for database performance, especially under heavy read or write workloads. When the disk cannot keep up with the demand from MongoDB, operations will slow down as they wait for data to be read from or written to disk.

To identify and diagnose disk I/O bottlenecks, it's instrumental to monitor several key indicators:

- **Disk latency:** Measure the time it takes for read and write operations to complete at the disk level. Consistently high latency (typically above a few milliseconds, depending on the storage medium) is a primary indicator of an I/O bottleneck. This is often monitored via OS-level tools or cloud provider metrics, and Atlas surfaces disk latency in its metrics views.

- **I/O queue depth:** Track the number of pending I/O operations waiting to be serviced by the disk. A persistently high queue depth signifies that the storage system is saturated.

- **Disk throughput (bytes/sec) and IOPS:** Monitor the actual data transfer rate and the number of I/O operations per second. Compare these against the provisioned limits of your storage hardware. Reaching these limits confirms an I/O bottleneck.

Addressing disk I/O bottlenecks may involve optimizing queries to reduce disk access, improving indexing, increasing provisioned IOPS/throughput, upgrading storage hardware, or ensuring the working set fits in RAM to minimize disk reads.

Cache pressure (WiredTiger cache utilization)

MongoDB's WiredTiger storage engine uses an internal cache to hold frequently accessed data and indexes in memory, minimizing the need for slower disk access. Cache pressure occurs when the active working set (the data and indexes required by the current workload) exceeds the size of the configured WiredTiger cache. This leads to increased cache eviction activity and page faults, degrading performance.

Several key metrics can help you detect and diagnose WiredTiger cache pressure in MongoDB. Monitoring these indicators gives you early warning signs of performance bottlenecks caused by memory constraints:

- **Cache utilization**: Track the amount of the WiredTiger cache currently in use (`serverStatus().wiredTiger.cache["bytes currently in the cache"]`). While high utilization is generally good, consistently hitting the maximum limit indicates pressure.

- **Cache eviction rate**: Monitor the rate at which pages are being evicted from the cache to make room for new data (`serverStatus().wiredTiger.cache["unmodified pages evicted"]`). A high or rapidly increasing eviction rate suggests the cache is churning frequently. Atlas often visualizes cache activity, highlighting evictions.

- **Pages read into cache**: Track the rate at which data is being read from disk into the cache (`serverStatus().wiredTiger.cache["pages read into cache"]`). High rates often correlate with high eviction rates and indicate that the required data is frequently not found in memory.

- **Page faults**: While not solely tied to the WiredTiger cache (OS page faults can also occur), frequent page faults (`serverStatus().extra_info.page_faults` or OS metrics) often accompany cache pressure, indicating that MongoDB processes are requesting data not currently in physical RAM.

Monitoring these metrics provides a clear picture of cache health. High utilization isn't inherently bad, but when combined with high eviction rates, increased page reads from disk, and page faults, it signals that the cache is struggling to keep up with the workload, forcing frequent reads from slower disk storage.

The following `db.serverStatus()` command can be used in the MongoDB Shell to retrieve some of these key cache metrics:

```
// Run from the MongoDB shell
// Check WiredTiger cache usage and eviction metrics
const wtCache = db.serverStatus().wiredTiger.cache;
const bytesInCache = wtCache["bytes currently in the cache"];
const maxBytes = wtCache["maximum bytes configured"];
const evictedPages = wtCache["unmodified pages evicted"];


print(`Cache utilization: ${(bytesInCache/maxBytes*100).toFixed(2)}%`);
print(`Evicted pages: ${evictedPages}`);
```

Resolving cache saturation typically involves increasing the available RAM and the configured WiredTiger cache size, optimizing queries and indexes to reduce the working set size, or scaling the cluster horizontally.

Replication lag and oplog window drift

Replication lag is a common metric you may want to monitor, as excessive lag can impact read consistency (if reading from secondaries), increase failover time, and put data durability at risk.

Replica set health can be tracked by monitoring the following key metrics:

- **Replication lag**: Monitor the lag in seconds for each secondary node. This is an important metric available in the `rs.status()` output and prominently displayed in the Atlas UI. Alerts should be configured for lag exceeding acceptable thresholds.
- **Oplog window**: Track the estimated time window covered by the oplog (`rs.printReplicationInfo()` or Atlas metrics). A shrinking oplog window increases the risk of secondaries needing to resync if they fall behind.
- **Oplog rate (GB/hour)**: Monitor the rate at which the oplog is being generated on the primary. High rates can contribute to replication lag if secondaries cannot apply writes fast enough or if the network bandwidth is insufficient. Atlas provides metrics for oplog throughput.

Collectively, these metrics provide a comprehensive view of replication health. Monitoring lag ensures data consistency and readiness for failover, tracking the oplog window helps prevent costly full resynchronizations of secondaries, and observing the oplog generation rate can highlight whether the primary's write load is outpacing the replication capacity.

You can use the following commands in the MongoDB Shell to retrieve the current replication status and oplog information:

```
// Run from the MongoDB shell
// Check replication lag on all secondary nodes
const rsStatus = rs.status();
const primary = rsStatus.members.find(m => m.state === 1);
rsStatus.members.forEach(member => {
  if (member.state === 2) { // secondary
    const lagSeconds = Math.abs((primary.optimeDate.getTime() -
                          member.optimeDate.getTime()) / 1000);
    print(`Secondary ${member.name} lag: ${lagSeconds.toFixed(2)}s`);
  }
});


// Check oplog window size
const oplogInfo = db.getReplicationInfo();
print(`Oplog window: ${oplogInfo.timeDiff / 3600}h`);
```

This script utilizes several key commands and concepts. rs.status() fetches a detailed document for each replica set member, including state and optimeDate (the timestamp of the last applied operation). The script then compares the optimeDate value of the primary with that of each secondary to calculate replication lag in seconds. db.getReplicationInfo() is used to retrieve information about oplog, specifically timeDiff, which indicates the oplog window duration. Finally, the script prints the calculated lag for each secondary and the oplog window in hours, providing a clear snapshot of replication health.

Executing this script might produce output similar to the following:

```
Secondary mongo-secondary-0.example.com:27017 lag: 2.35s
Secondary mongo-secondary-1.example.com:27017 lag: 1.80s
Oplog window: 48.25h
```

This output allows administrators to quickly assess whether secondaries are keeping up with the primary and whether the oplog window is sufficient for the operational needs.

Causes of replication lag include high write volume on the primary, insufficient resources (CPU, RAM, or I/O) on secondaries, network latency between nodes, or long-running operations on secondaries blocking replication.

Summary

Effective MongoDB monitoring and observability transform raw data into actionable insights that keep your deployments healthy, performant, and reliable. Throughout this chapter, we've explored the critical distinction between monitoring (tracking known metrics to see whether something is wrong) and observability (leveraging metrics, logs, and traces to understand why something is happening).

We've examined an array of tools available from the comprehensive suite offered by MongoDB Atlas, which includes the Real-Time Performance Panel, metrics explorers, and the Performance Advisor for automatic optimization recommendations, to self-managed tools such as `mongostat`, `mongotop`, and the database profiler for deep insights into self-hosted deployments. Furthermore, external systems such as Prometheus+Grafana, Datadog, and APM platforms extend these capabilities, allowing for unified observability across your entire technology stack.

By implementing a robust observability pipeline and combining real-time dashboards, tiered alerts, detailed logs, query execution plans, and distributed traces, you can detect emerging issues before they impact users, diagnose root causes efficiently, and make data-driven decisions for performance optimization.

Remember that the most successful teams don't just collect data; they establish a culture where observability drives ongoing optimization. With the principles and practices outlined in this chapter, you'll be well positioned to maintain optimal MongoDB performance, even as your applications scale and evolve.

Having established a strong foundation in monitoring and observing your MongoDB environment, the upcoming chapter will shift focus to another critical aspect of database performance: how to proactively optimize and fine-tune your MongoDB deployment to prevent issues before they arise.

15

Debugging Performance Issues

Performance issues in databases can challenge even the most experienced developers and database administrators. These issues often surface unexpectedly, causing application slowdowns, user complaints, and sometimes even outages. The late MongoDB expert William Zola identified three fundamental reasons for slow MongoDB performance: **inherently slow operations** that consume significant resources by nature; **blocked operations**, where processes are waiting for other slow operations to complete; and **insufficient or poorly tuned hardware resources** that lack the capacity to handle the workload.

Although MongoDB has evolved significantly since Zola first articulated these principles, they remain remarkably relevant. Most performance problems can still be traced back to one of these three root causes, with poor schema design often lurking as an underlying factor.

This chapter provides a structured approach to identifying, understanding, and resolving MongoDB performance issues. We'll explore real-world examples that illustrate common problems and their solutions, building on techniques covered in earlier chapters. By the end of this chapter, you'll be equipped with a systematic methodology for approaching performance issues in your own MongoDB deployments.

Through practical case studies, in this chapter, you'll learn how to do the following:

- Identify the symptoms of different types of performance problems
- Diagnose the root causes using MongoDB's monitoring tools
- Implement targeted solutions to resolve the issues
- Prevent similar problems from occurring in the future

Identifying inherently slow operations

Inherently slow operations are those that require MongoDB to do significant work, often involving reading large amounts of data or performing complex calculations. These operations become particularly problematic as data volumes grow.

The most common inherently slow operations include the following:

- Collection scans (queries without indexes)
- Queries that examine many more documents than they return
- Complex aggregation pipelines
- Queries that return large result sets
- Operations that cause index builds on large collections

When these operations occur frequently, they can consume substantial system resources and slow down overall database performance.

Case study: Troubleshooting cluster performance with Atlas

MongoDB Atlas, our platform for database management, relies on internal clusters to monitor and manage customer deployments. Among these, one key cluster is responsible for gathering server and configuration data from all Atlas deployments. This data is vital for understanding the health, performance, and operational status of customer databases, helping us proactively identify and fix issues.

However, as Atlas scaled rapidly, this central data collection cluster began to show signs of strain. From monitoring, we noticed the following:

- Normalized system CPU on shard 0 rose from a steady 45–55% to around 70%
- Query targeting ratios began to increase
- Latency also climbed
- Query operation counts increased from approximately 21,000 database operations per second to over 30,000 within a five-month period

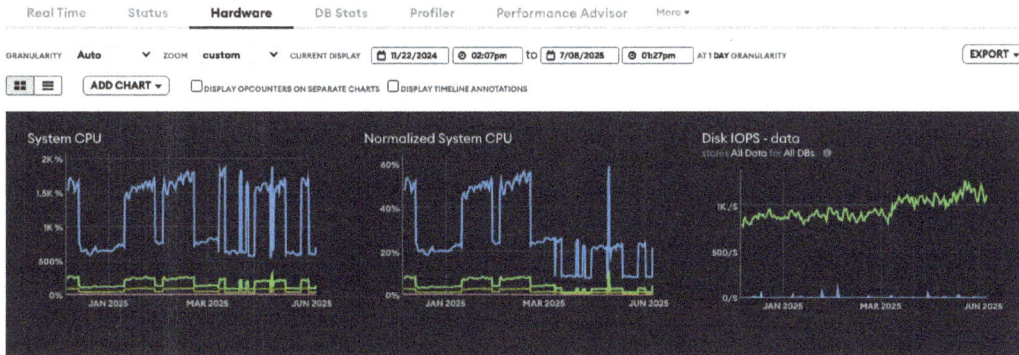

Figure 15.1: Cluster hardware dashboard displaying System CPU, Normalized System CPU, and Disk IOPS

To keep the system working, we scaled the cluster up to a higher tier. At the same time, we initiated a project to figure out how we could tune performance to handle the increased workload while remaining on the previous tier.

This gradual performance degradation manifested in several key metrics that provided clear indicators of underlying problems. While increased CPU usage is expected as applications grow, in this case, the rate was significantly higher than anticipated for the workload. The elevated query targeting metrics were particularly concerning, as they pointed to possibly suboptimal indexes, with queries processing many documents just to return a few results. Such inefficiencies often go unnoticed in over-provisioned systems, masking the underlying design problems. However, as these suboptimal query operations accumulated, they eventually produced measurable latency increases that surfaced the fundamental issues. Resolving these scaling problems became a top priority to ensure the continued reliability, performance, and comprehensive monitoring of customer deployments on Atlas.

Diagnosing the cause

The MongoDB team began an investigation using Atlas monitoring tools as described in *Chapter 14, Monitoring and Observability*. As shown in *Figure 15.2*, there were peaks in **Opcounters** during periods when the server was primary, with drops when it switched to secondary. The spike in **Query Targeting** at the end of March was particularly noteworthy.

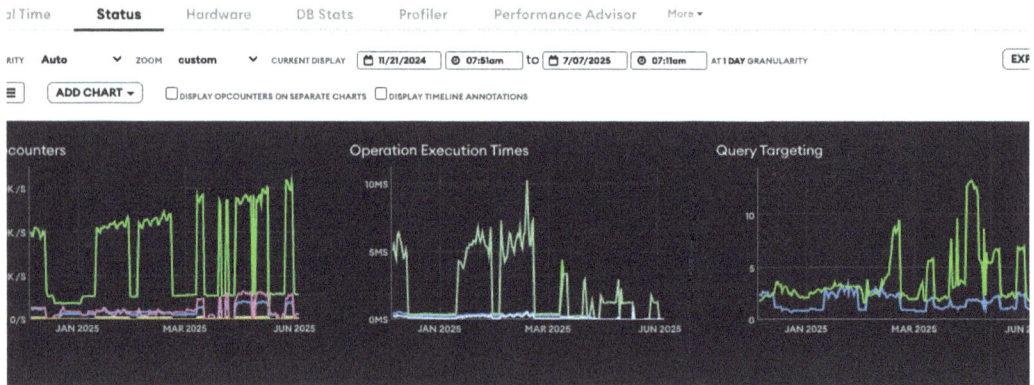

Figure 15.2: Cluster status dashboard displaying Opcounters, Operation Execution Times, and Query Targeting

To mitigate the ongoing strain on the cluster resources, the team temporarily upgraded the cluster tier. This gave us the immediate CPU boost we needed, and as expected, the normalized system CPU metric went down noticeably. While this addressed the performance issue at the time, it was only a temporary measure. The team's main goal was still to identify the underlying cause and implement a more cost-effective, long-term solution to the high CPU usage, ensuring both system stability and financial efficiency.

Root cause identification

With our temporary workaround in place, the engineering team began a root cause analysis of the system's performance issues.

They first used the Atlas **Performance Advisor**, which recommended **19 potential indexes**, a clear indicator that many queries were using suboptimal indexes. Alongside this, **log analysis** revealed slow queries with timestamps that directly correlated with **periods of high CPU utilization**. This combination provided strong evidence that specific query patterns were causing the performance degradation, particularly those performing full collection scans or complex aggregations without proper indexing support.

After confirming that some queries were likely causing the performance degradation, the Atlas **Query Insights** and **Query Profiler** were the natural next steps to understand what was happening. Query Insights and Query Profiler revealed that certain **aggregated and mean query execution times were extremely long**, with some queries taking up to 8 seconds, as shown in *Figure 15.3*.

This detailed information by namespace allowed the team to understand exactly where bottlenecks were occurring, enabling them to develop targeted optimization strategies such as creating new indexes or rewriting inefficient queries. This combined approach provided a clear picture of the system's performance challenges and led to a more efficient database.

The **Query Insights** page presents a list detailing the number of operations and their total execution times for each namespace.

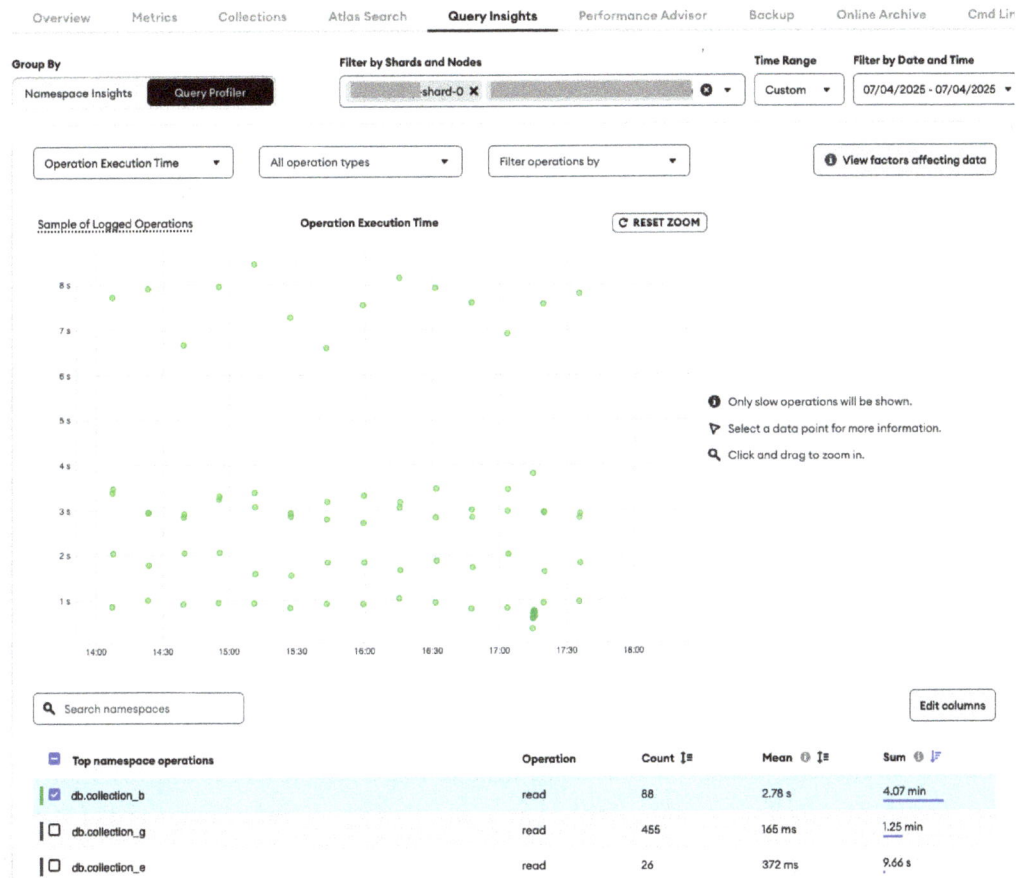

Figure 15.3: Cluster Query Insights dashboard displaying slow queries

Through correlation, using the same technique as above, the team identified that during periods when the database processed approximately 20,000 operations per second, the logs indicated around 13,000 slow queries daily.

By utilizing both the logs and Query Profiler, we were able to correlate slow queries with periods of high CPU usage. This correlation helped us identify the query shapes that were likely contributing most to our performance issues. For instance, the most frequently logged slow query shape, occurring roughly 9,000 times per day, appeared as follows:

```
{
  "find": "db.collection_g",
  "filter": {
    "attribute1_Id": {
      "$oid": "621094e7bdbed43d3f408384"
    },
    "attribute1_Name": "aws-use1-1-v2-1",
    "attribute2_Id": {
      "$oid": "65bd5e7ccff98a5722037dc6"
    }
  },
  "limit": 1
}

"planSummary": "COLLSCAN",
"planningTimeMicros": 259,
"keysExamined": 0,
"docsExamined": 34436,
"nreturned": 1,
"durationMillis": 103,
"cpuNanos": 10987385
```

This query pattern was particularly problematic. It was scanning over 34,000 documents and returning one matching document, consuming significant CPU resources in the process. The team identified that this collection and query had been added as a new feature at the end of March without a corresponding index. This coincided with the spike in query targeting they had observed.

Implementing the solution

With a clearer understanding of the performance bottlenecks, the team focused on targeted, low-risk optimizations. Their goal was to improve efficiency without causing further strain on system resources.

The team implemented several targeted solutions:

- **Created recommended indexes**: They created an index for the most frequent slow query, which immediately improved performance and reduced the Query Targeting metric. To avoid further straining the already taxed CPU resources during this critical time, the team carefully planned the index creation by scheduling it during off-peak hours with continuous monitoring of system resources to prevent additional performance degradation.
- **Set up preventative monitoring**: They created a Query Targeting alert from the **Project Alerts** page to monitor high ratios of scanned objects to returned documents. This would alert them when workloads, applications, or datasets changed to make queries less efficient over time.

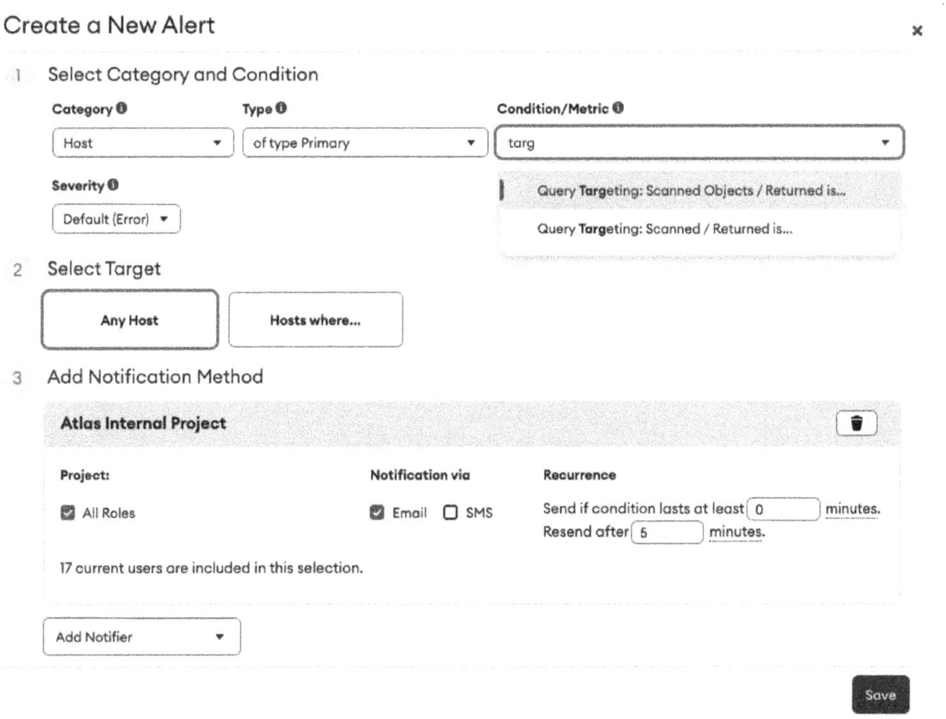

Figure 15.4: Create a new alert to target slow queries

- **Removed redundant indexes**: While reviewing Performance Advisor recommendations, the team identified 9 indexes on fields that were prefixes of another compound index that could potentially be dropped. However, dropping indexes is an operation that requires careful consideration and planning. The team first validated each recommendation in a test environment, assessed potential query impact, and implemented the changes gradually with close monitoring. Only after thorough evaluation did they proceed with removing these redundant indexes by initially hiding the indexes, then confirming no ill effects on the system, and dropping them. This ultimately improved the write performance without impacting the read performance.

These actions collectively reduced CPU usage, improved query efficiency, and stabilized system performance. More importantly, they laid the groundwork for ongoing optimization and proactive monitoring going forward.

Results and learnings

This case illustrates several important principles about diagnosing inherently slow operations:

- Performance issues often coincide with application changes or new features
- Using multiple diagnostic tools such as Performance Advisor, Query Profiler, and logs provides a comprehensive view
- Creating appropriate indexes is often the most effective solution for collection scans
- Removing redundant indexes can improve the write performance
- Setting up alerts for key metrics enables proactive identification of future issues

Ultimately, this risk was first identified by monitoring key metrics over time. This helped us identify gradual performance degradation and act before there was an impact on customers. This performance tuning exercise allowed us to reduce cluster tiers and reduce costs.

Case study: Unexpected admin query causing collection scan

Slow queries are often the first indicator of performance issues in MongoDB deployments. A major issue hit a customer's self-managed MongoDB deployments. Their application monitoring showed a sudden increase in the latency of database operations, impacting users across the entire system. The suddenness of the problem meant we needed to investigate and fix it right away to avoid further disruption and get services back to normal.

Diagnosing the cause

A customer engineer contacted MongoDB support. The support engineer realized the situation was critical and first looked for an immediate but safe remediation to reduce the severity of the impact. Support asked the customer to run a shell command to show operations that had been running for 10 or more seconds:

```
db.currentOp({"secs_running":{ $gte: 10}}).inprog
[
  {
    type: 'op',
    opid: 201,
    host: 'somewhere.net:27017',
    connectionId: 1063017,
    client: '555.111.222.333:47140',
    currentOpTime: '2024-12-31T00:29:08.230+00:00',
    threaded: true,
    secs_running: Long('5410'),
    microsecs_running: Long('5410001296'),
    op: 'command',
    ns: 'admin.$cmd',
    command: {
      /* Redacted */
    },
    "planSummary": "COLLSCAN",
    numYields: 0,
    locks: {},
  }
]
```

This revealed an operation that had been running for over 90 minutes according to the secs_running field. Further investigation showed that a database administrator had logged in and run a complex query. The host field in the logs revealed that this query was executed from another office, while the ns admin field confirmed that the user had administrative rights. This query started a collection scan, causing cached collections to be evicted from memory.

Implementing the solution

The customer, faced with a non-critical operation that was consuming excessive resources and threatening system stability, took decisive action. To regain control and prevent further degradation, they initiated a termination sequence for the problematic process. To do this, the following command was used:

```
db.killOp(201)
```

In this case, the team killed the problematic ad hoc operation, and the issue was resolved. During follow-up analysis, the MongoDB support team discovered the complex query issued by the administrator had caused massive cache eviction. This had occurred because the scan loaded massive amounts of rarely used documents into memory, pushing out frequently accessed data from the limited cache space. This explained why performance remained affected even after terminating the query; the damage to the cache had already been done. After approximately 2-3 minutes, once the frequently accessed data (working set) had been reloaded into MongoDB's cache from disk storage, database performance metrics returned to their baseline levels. While this recovery period might appear as additional performance degradation following the intervention, it's important to note that the system was already blocked by the problematic query, so this brief recovery phase was an unavoidable consequence of addressing the root issue.

Results and learnings

This case highlights several important principles. First, long-running collection scans can dramatically impact performance for all users. Additionally, cached data eviction is a common side effect of large collection scans.

Ad hoc queries by administrators on production databases represent a significant risk that requires careful management and governance. While these impromptu investigations can provide valuable insights, they can also severely impact system performance and availability when executed without proper consideration of their resource requirements. To avoid this, organizations must implement strict policies regarding who can run ad hoc queries on production systems, when they can be executed, and what limitations should be placed on their scope and complexity. Ideally, such exploratory work should be conducted on secondaries or during maintenance windows, with query timeouts and resource limits configured to prevent runaway processes. Without these safeguards, even well-intentioned database administrators can inadvertently trigger cascading performance issues that affect thousands of application users.

Managing blocked operations

Blocked operations can occur when a process must wait for another operation to complete or for a resource to become available, creating a domino effect that can severely impact your application's responsiveness. Understanding what causes operations to block is essential for maintaining optimal database performance. Recognizing these patterns early allows you to implement preventive measures before they impact your users' experience.

Typical causes of blocked operations in MongoDB include the following:

- Long-running operations with exclusive locks, such as index builds or collection drops
- Resource contention, where multiple operations attempt to access the same collections or documents, especially during peak usage
- Connection pool exhaustion, which occurs when all available connections are in use and new operations must wait, creating artificial queuing

Blocking-like symptoms from non-blocking issues

Some conditions, such as cursor leaks or high network latency, can produce symptoms that *resemble* blocking. For example, high latency or slow queries, but they do not involve actual lock contention.

Case study: Cursor leak investigation

A customer experienced slower operations and a high number of queries timing out. The issue directly impacted users, with some experiencing application timeouts. Atlas monitoring revealed a significant spike in open cursors, specifically, over 600,000 starting from 4:00 AM in the customer's local time zone.

Tracking open cursors via serverStatus

For self-managed MongoDB instances, this information is also available in the `cursor.open.total` counter from the `serverStatus` command.

Diagnosing the cause

The MongoDB support team initially focused on optimizing slow operations and suggested creating an index as recommended by Performance Advisor to speed up queries. However, this didn't improve the situation. The continued high number of open cursors, even after index optimization, suggested a more complex underlying issue. This could have been due to inefficient application logic, cursors not being closed properly, or connection pooling issues.

Automatic cursor lifecycle management in MongoDB

MongoDB automatically manages cursor lifecycles in most normal operations. Cursors are closed when they're fully iterated through after timing out (typically after 10), or when a client session ends. In applications that use standard MongoDB drivers and patterns, cursor leaks are relatively rare.

The customer's deployment continued to degrade, with more users experiencing slow response times and errors. Key system indicators such as CPU, memory, and I/O all showed a serious bottleneck. Even after a thorough investigation by our support team, the exact cause wasn't clear, but we needed to stabilize the system fast to avoid an outage. The support team recommended that the customer restart the primary node. This would trigger a planned failover, making one of the secondary nodes the new primary, ensuring services would continue. After the secondary was successfully promoted, system performance immediately improved, confirming that this action temporarily resolved the urgent operational problems.

The support team continued to monitor the system overnight. The open cursor count was rising, but user activity was lower, and operation latencies had not yet reached a critical level. When the customer engineer started work the following morning, the open cursor count had risen to 260,000 and was still climbing.

The support team and the customer worked together to diagnose the issue in real time and identified several key indicators:

- **Profiler Analysis**: The customer enabled the database profiler for 40 minutes to capture queries taking longer than 20 ms.
- **Log Analysis**: Analyzing the logs, the support engineer observed the open cursors spike to 600,000 and then drop back close to zero. From the server status, they observed the following:
  - Large numbers of `cursor.lifespan.greaterThanOrEqual10Minutes`
  - Over 500 `cursor.totalOpened` per second but fewer than 250 `cursor.moreThanOneBatch`
  - Over 300,000 log messages with `{"ctx":"LogicalSessionCacheRefresh", "msg":"Killing cursor as part of killing session(s)"}`

- **Query Pattern Analysis**: Using grep commands, they analyzed the log file patterns:

```
grep 'aCollection' mongodb.log* | grep -v 'getMore' | wc -l
  122784
```

```
grep 'aCollection' mongodb.log* | grep '"cursorExhausted":true' | wc -l
  46954
```

The first command counts all operations on 'aCollection' while excluding 'getMore' operations, revealing 122,784 initial cursor creations. The second command counts only cursors that were properly exhausted (fully iterated through or explicitly closed), showing just 46,954 such cases. This significant discrepancy (only about 38% of cursors being properly closed) confirmed our suspicion of a cursor leak, as the majority of cursors created by the application were being abandoned without proper cleanup, causing them to accumulate until their timeout period elapsed.

Root cause identification

The problem originated from a specific bug in the customer's application that had remained hidden until recently. When queries began returning more than the default 101 documents in a single batch due to data growth, the issue finally became apparent. The application was designed to process small result sets and would properly handle cursors in those cases.

This issue only manifests when a client keeps an active session open while not fully exhausting the cursor (either by not iterating through all results or not explicitly calling close() on the cursor). Under normal circumstances, with properly implemented cursor handling or smaller result sets, this problem wouldn't occur. Most MongoDB driver implementations and standard query patterns automatically handle cursor lifecycle management, making this type of leak relatively uncommon in well-designed applications.

For more information on how cursors behave, visit the MongoDB Documentation on cursors at https://www.mongodb.com/docs/manual/core/cursors/#behavior.

Implementing the solution

While the customer's development team worked on a permanent fix, the MongoDB support team provided a key temporary measure: a shell command to terminate idle cursors on the affected namespace. This helped prevent a build-up of inactive cursors, which could have worsened performance and caused system instability. This command offered immediate relief and gave the development team valuable time to fix the core issue.

The customer developed a complete and proper fix for the bug. The fix was deployed collaboratively with MongoDB support on an active call, ensuring real-time guidance and immediate troubleshooting.

The deployment had an immediate and significant impact. Before the fix, open cursors would routinely spike to over 600,000 before temporary drops. For this particular application, normal operations should have required only around 100 concurrent cursors at any given time. After deployment, the system stabilized. The maximum number of open cursors consistently stayed at a much lower and manageable level of 100. This reduction greatly improved system efficiency and resource utilization.

Further confirming the success of the deployed fix, server status reports showed the issue was resolved. Specifically, the `cursor.lifespan.greaterThanOrEqual10Minutes` metric consistently reported 0. This metric is useful for identifying long-lived, potentially problematic cursors. A value of 0 showed that no cursors were staying open for 10 minutes.

Results and learnings

The customer's situation represented an unusual edge case where their application code was repeatedly creating new cursors without properly closing them.

This example applied a number of troubleshooting principles:

- Gradual performance degradation can be caused by cursor leaks
- Diagnosing the root cause often requires multiple approaches
- While a permanent solution is being developed, temporary mitigation might be necessary
- Monitoring metrics enables early detection

Finally, this situation provides a vivid example of how application code issues from the development phase can appear as database performance problems in production.

Use case: Burst of poorly optimized queries

A customer noticed a sudden burst of timed-out operations. Atlas monitoring showed a spike in normalized CPU utilization to 100% and over 3.7 GB/s of data being read into the storage engine cache, as demonstrated in *Figure 15.5*:

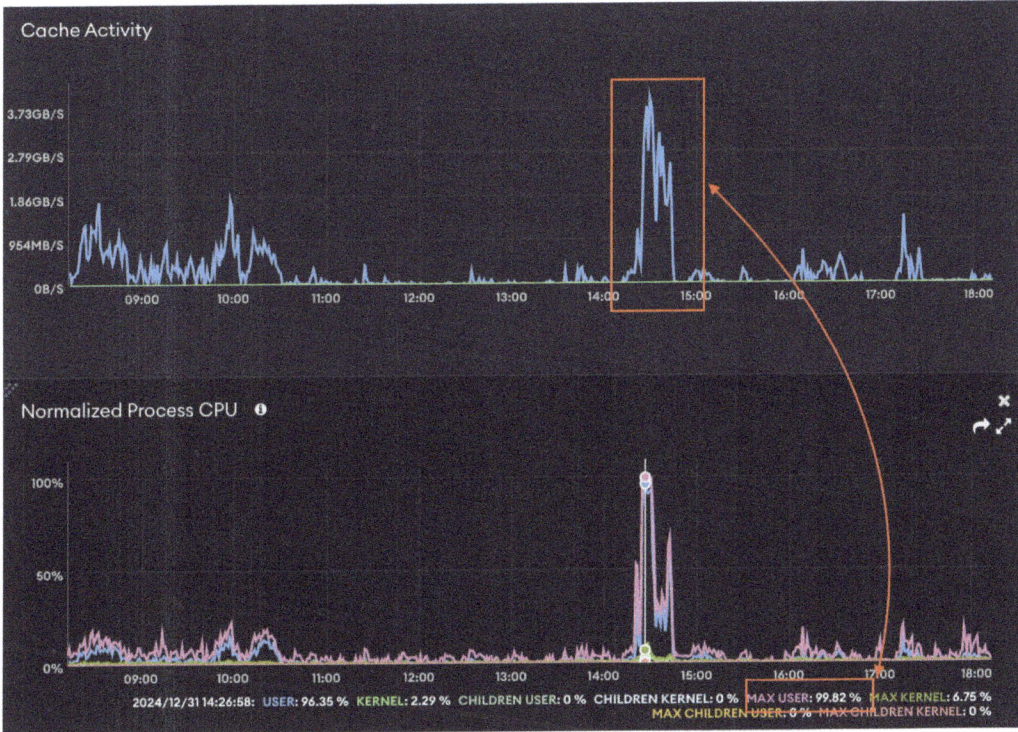

Figure 15.5: Cache Activity and user CPU utilization

Application queries were severely impacted. Users experienced timeouts, slow responses, and in some cases complete request failures. The system was effectively blocked as normal operations couldn't proceed while these resource-intensive processes monopolized the available CPU and I/O capacity. But what caused this sudden, crippling load? Since the database primarily serves customer queries, these performance metrics strongly suggested that one or more problematic queries were likely behind the spike. To identify the specific culprits behind this unusual activity, we needed to look deeper into the query patterns. This led us to examine Atlas Query Insights for a more detailed understanding of what was happening at the query level.

Diagnosing the cause

The Query Insights/Query Profiler revealed a significant number of queries on a collection examining over 1 million documents each, shown in *Figure 15.6*, represented as green dots at the top of the graph. At the bottom of the screenshot, we can also see that, in total, 233 queries scanned approximately 144 million documents during this 16-minute period. We looked at the previous 20 minutes and saw only 8 million documents in total were scanned.

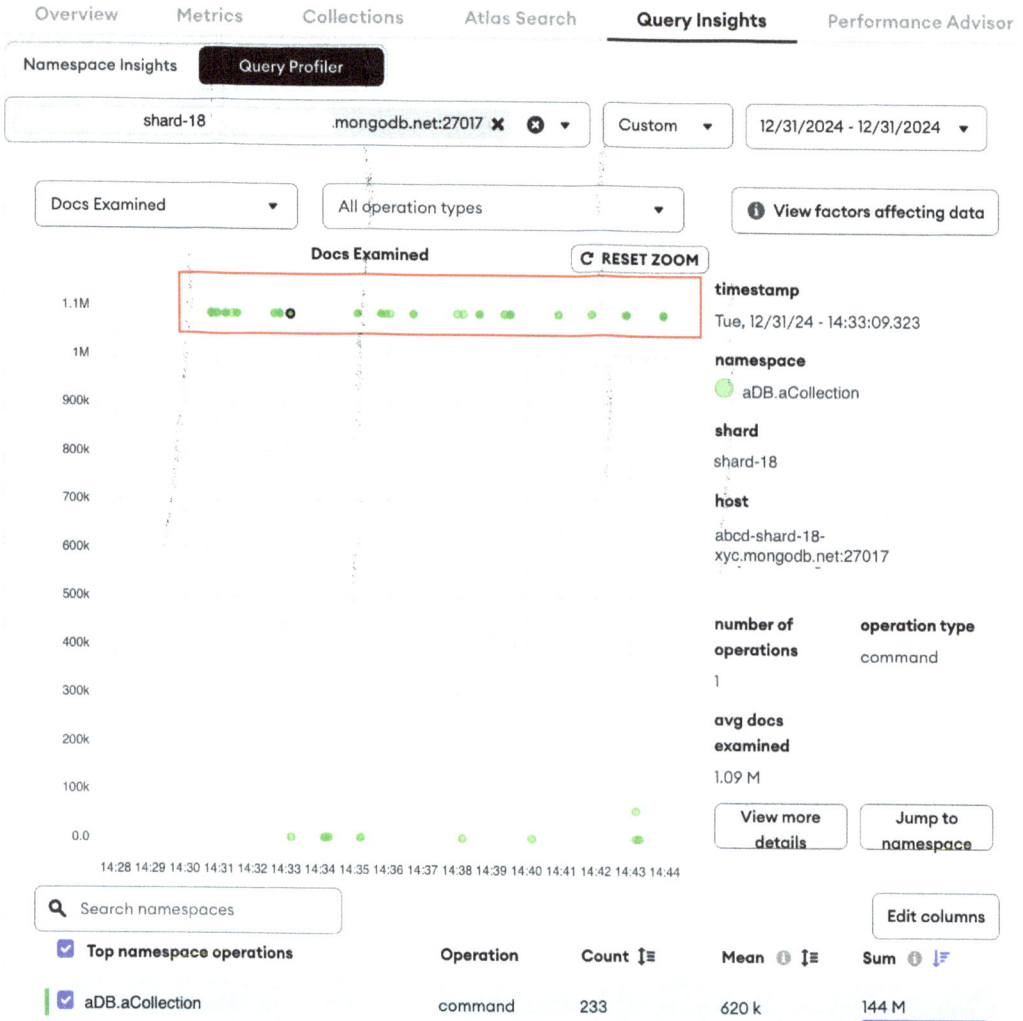

Figure 15.6: Query Profiler showing a large number of documents being examined

Clicking on one of the green dots displayed in the Query Profiler, as shown in *Figure 15.6*, revealed deeper insights into each individual query. When clicking on one of those queries, the profiler showed the following:

```
"replanReason": "cached plan was less efficient than expected: expected
trial execution to take 2 works but it took at least 20 works"
```

This indicated the query planner was struggling to find an efficient execution plan. Upon reviewing the collection, they found 25 indexes that were eligible to be used, but none were a good match for these queries, indicating that a new index might be necessary.

In addition, further log analysis also revealed that some of the slow queries in this collection were trying to match documents over a six-month range.

Implementing the solution

To address the inefficiencies caused by the lack of an optimal index, the team reviewed the Performance Advisor, which, as expected, provided a recommendation for a new compound index tailored to resolve the issue, as shown in *Figure 15.7*. Acting on this advice, the team promptly created the compound index, significantly improving query performance.

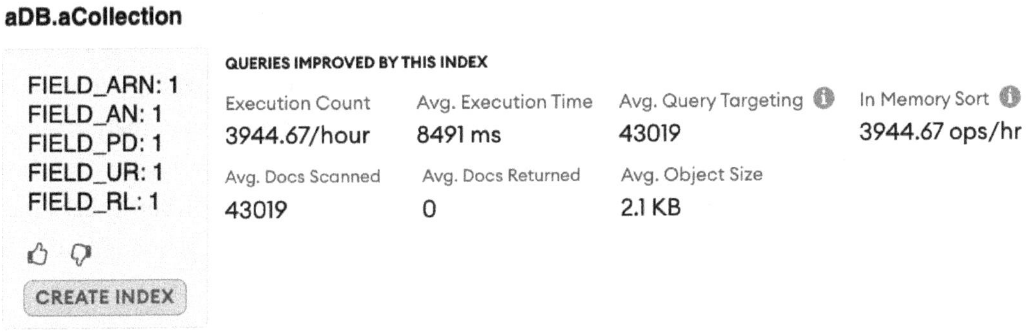

aDB.aCollection

FIELD_ARN: 1	QUERIES IMPROVED BY THIS INDEX			
FIELD_AN: 1	Execution Count	Avg. Execution Time	Avg. Query Targeting ⓘ	In Memory Sort ⓘ
FIELD_PD: 1	3944.67/hour	8491 ms	43019	3944.67 ops/hr
FIELD_UR: 1	Avg. Docs Scanned	Avg. Docs Returned	Avg. Object Size	
FIELD_RL: 1	43019	0	2.1 KB	

👍 👎

CREATE INDEX

Figure 15.7: Performance Advisor recommendations

Additionally, the team enhanced the application by modifying its query logic to match documents within a shorter time span. This adjustment further optimized the query execution, reducing both the size of data returned and query latency, resulting in faster performance and more efficient use of system resources.

Results and learnings

This case underscores several key principles of query optimization. Sudden performance issues often correlate with changes in application behavior, making it essential to monitor application patterns closely. One critical indicator of inefficient queries is when the database examines a disproportionately large number of documents compared to the actual results returned. This can signal an underlying issue with query design or indexing. Additionally, the Query Planner may encounter difficulties when operating over extensive data ranges, highlighting the importance of narrowing the scope of queries whenever possible.

Addressing performance challenges often requires a combination of strategies, including both database changes, such as creating optimized indexes, and application-level adjustments, such as reducing the time span of queried data. Tools such as the Performance Advisor are invaluable in identifying missing indexes, even for infrequent query patterns. It provides actionable recommendations to enhance efficiency and resolve bottlenecks.

Addressing hardware resource constraints

Hardware resource constraints represent a critical challenge in maintaining optimal MongoDB performance. Even with well-optimized queries and thoughtfully designed schemas, the underlying hardware ultimately dictates how efficiently your database can handle workloads. Resource constraints arise when the computational, memory, network, or storage capacity of your deployment is insufficient to support the demands placed on it, leading to cascading performance issues. Imagine a production line where machines are running at their maximum capacity. Any increase in demand or inefficiency pushes systems past their limits, resulting in bottlenecks and delays. Similarly, resource constraints in MongoDB can significantly impair your application's responsiveness and scalability.

These constraints typically surface in four primary areas: CPU, memory, disk I/O, and network. High CPU utilization may limit the processing power available for queries, aggregations, and background tasks, forcing operations to queue and delaying results. Memory constraints occur when the available RAM is insufficient to store the working set, leading to increased reliance on slower disk reads and degraded performance. Disk I/O constraints, such as a slow or overloaded storage subsystem, can drastically impede operations that require frequent or large data reads and writes. Network constraints can significantly impact distributed database operations, causing issues such as increased replication lag, slower initial syncs, extended backup times, and delayed elections in replica sets, all of which can compromise data availability and consistency across your deployment.

The impact of resource constraints is often gradual, emerging alongside growing data volumes, increasing workloads, or changes in usage patterns. However, the problem can also appear suddenly when resources are unevenly distributed across a cluster, creating hotspots or imbalances that exacerbate performance bottlenecks. Recognizing and addressing these hardware limitations is essential for ensuring MongoDB remains responsive and reliable at scale. Understanding how CPU, memory, and storage interact with MongoDB workloads allows teams to proactively mitigate constraints and optimize resource allocation across deployments.

Case study: Atlas cluster resource optimization

Continuing from the previous Atlas monitoring cluster example, the team noticed that even after addressing the inherently slow operations with indexing improvements, resource utilization on shard-0 remained higher than on other shards. This imbalance presented a significant problem because it created a performance bottleneck within the distributed system. When one shard consistently operates at higher utilization levels than others, it effectively becomes the limiting factor for overall cluster performance. This not only risks resource exhaustion on the overloaded shard, potentially leading to operation failures, but also represents inefficient use of the entire cluster's capacity. Additionally, this imbalance undermines the fault tolerance and scalability benefits that sharding is designed to provide, as the system becomes disproportionately constrained by a single shard's performance.

Looking at the unnormalized process CPU on the primaries of each shard, they observed that shard-0 had higher utilization and data size than all other shards, as shown in *Figure 15.8*.

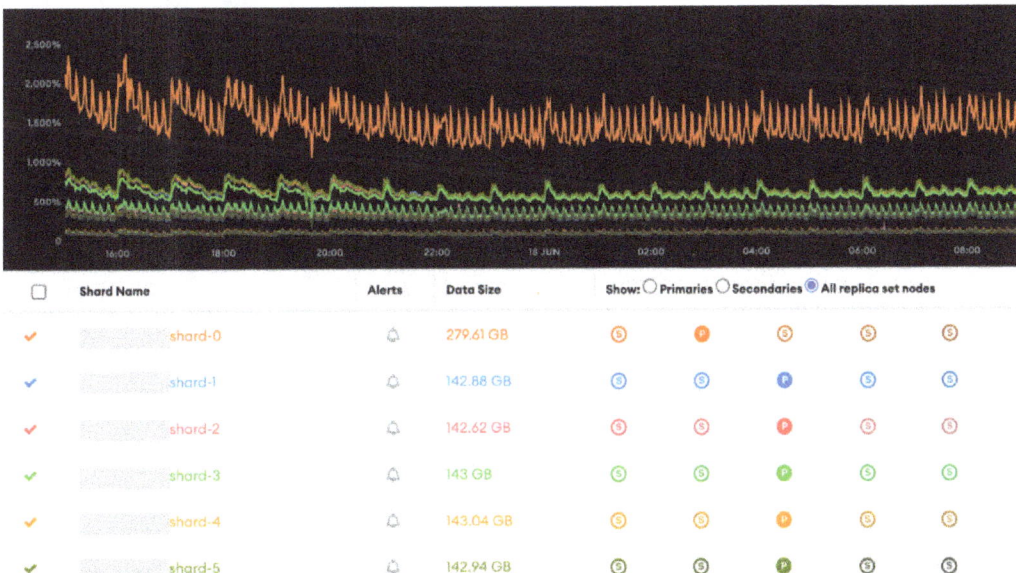

Figure 15.8: Graph showing the unnormalized process CPU on the primaries of each shard

Additionally, *Figure 15.9* illustrates a significant observation: over the past year, write IOPs for shard-0 have increased at a faster rate compared to other shards in the cluster.

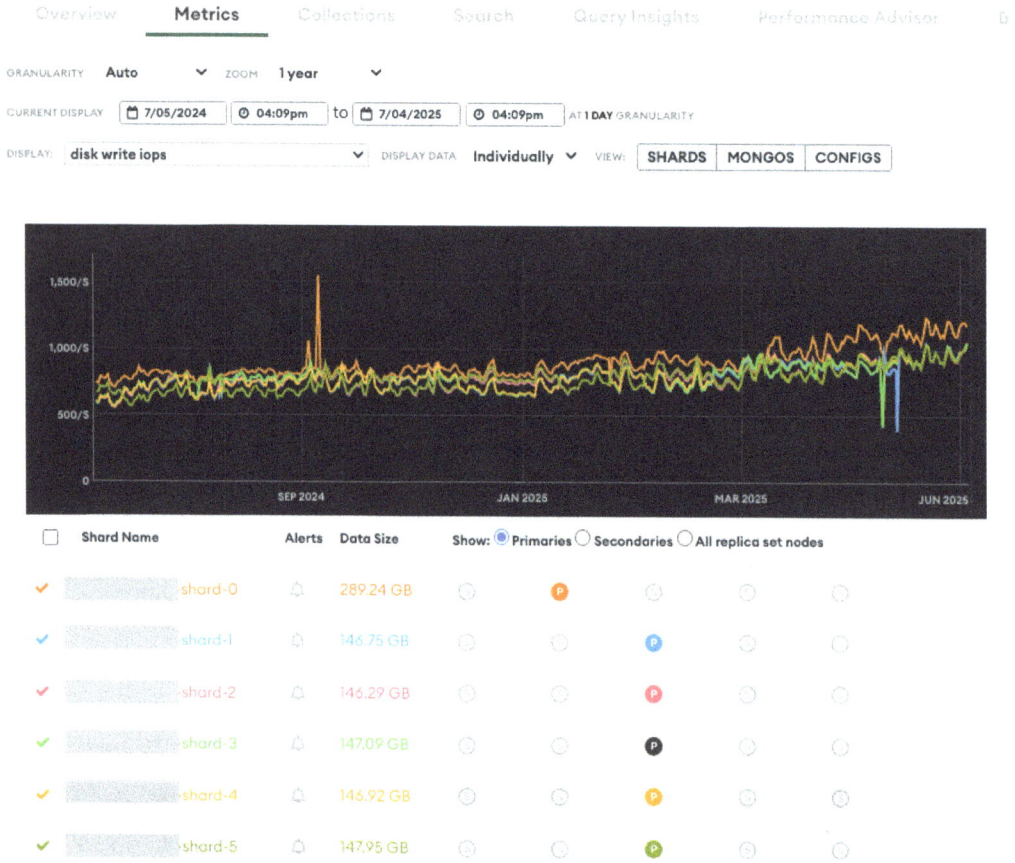

Figure 15.9: Graph showing the last year of write IOPS on shard-0

Diagnosing the cause

The root cause of the imbalance stemmed from the cluster's initial configuration. The cluster contained a single database with numerous collections, and when the database was first created, shard-0 was designated as the primary shard. As a result, all unsharded collections were placed on shard-0 by default. Over time, as the number of unsharded collections and their respective data volumes grew, shard-0 became overloaded with disproportionate workloads.

This uneven distribution led to a higher concentration of operations and data on shard-0, causing it to consistently experience elevated CPU, memory, and disk usage compared to the other shards. The heavy utilization of shard-0 also increased query latency and limited the overall throughput of the cluster, as operations on unsharded collections were bottlenecked by the resource constraints of the primary shard.

As discussed in *Chapter 1, Systems and MongoDB Architecture*, performance optimization is rarely a one-step process. Bottlenecks in database systems are dynamic. When you resolve one issue, the next constraint in the system often becomes apparent. This principle was clearly demonstrated in our case. While the indexing improvements successfully addressed the initially identified slow operations, they simply revealed another underlying bottleneck that had been partially masked by the more severe indexing problems.

Implementing the solution

The team had to determine which of the following would be the best approach to balance the workload:

- Scale up the primary shard (Atlas supports individual scaling of each shard)
- Move unsharded collections from shard-0 to other shards
- Shard more collections

The team decided to move unsharded collections from shard-0 to other shards, as this approach was simplest to implement and manage compared to alternatives. This method required no changes to the application code or data schema and could be performed without significant downtime. Additionally, it gave the team direct control over exactly which collections moved where, allowing for careful balancing based on collection size and access patterns.

But first, they double-checked which collections were unsharded and which were sharded.

1. To do this, they ran the following commands in mongosh:

    ```
    // List unsharded collections
    db.getCollectionNames().forEach(collectionName => {
        if (!db[collectionName].stats().sharded) {
            print(collectionName);
        }
    });

    // List sharded collections
    db.getCollectionNames().forEach(collectionName => {
        if (db[collectionName].stats().sharded) {
            print(collectionName);
        }
    });
    ```

They found one database with 163 collections. Of those, 20 were sharded and 143 were unsharded.

2. Next, the team analyzed the real-time panel for shard-0 to get a quick view of its workload:

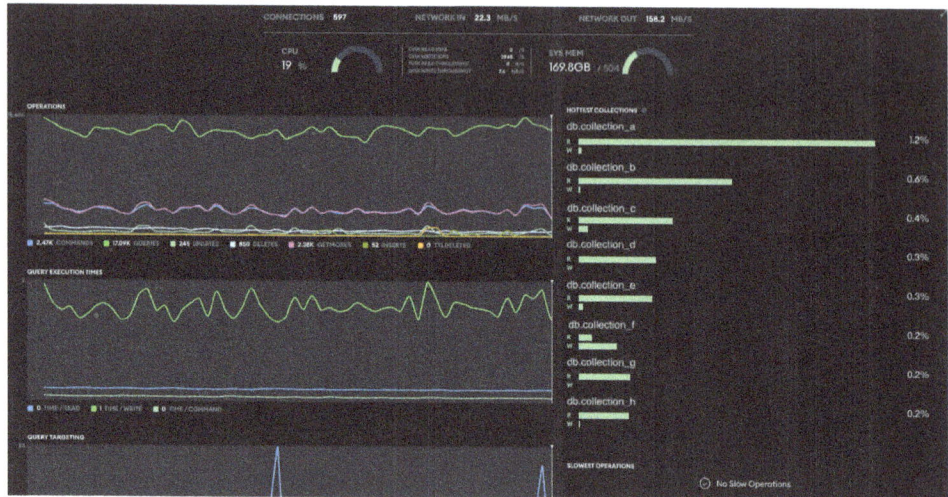

Figure 15.10: Panel displaying how hot a collection is in real time

Figure 15.10 shows the real-time view of the hottest collections in terms of operations per second. The view shows the CPU and memory utilization along with the number of connections, operations per second, and the underlying read and write IOPs going to the disks. This detailed breakdown proved invaluable for determining which collections should be moved to different shards.

By identifying the unsharded collections with the highest operation counts, largest memory footprints, and greatest CPU consumption, the team could prioritize moving the most resource-intensive collections first. This targeted approach ensured that the rebalancing effort would have the maximum impact on relieving shard-0's burden while minimizing the number of collections that needed to be relocated. Collections with lower activity levels could remain on shard-0 or be moved in later phases if necessary.

The team also analyzed the Query Insights view for a longer-term picture of the most active collections, as pictured in *Figure 15.11*.

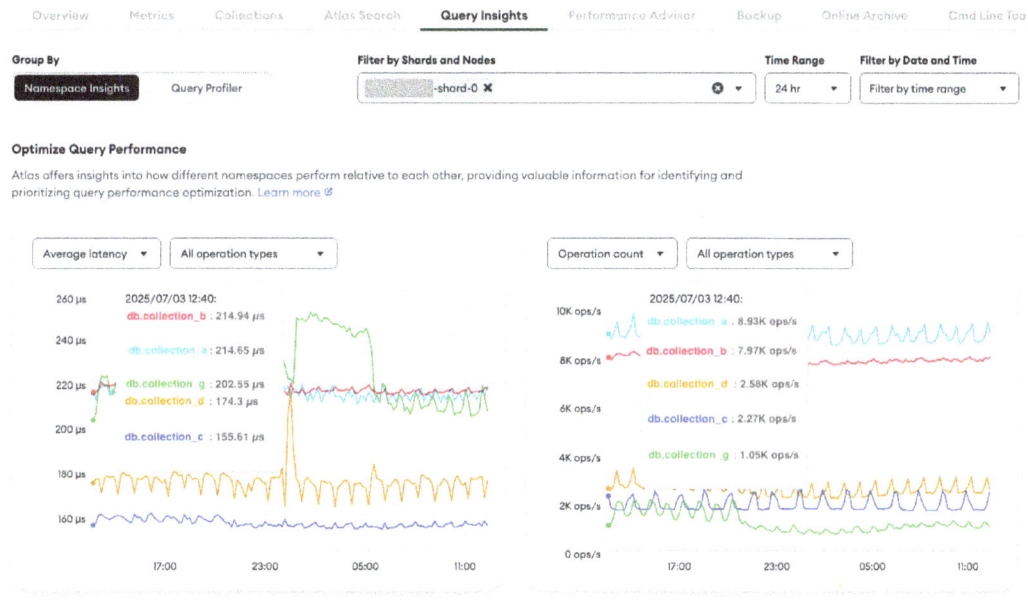

Figure 15.11: Graph showing both the count of operations per second and the average latency over the last 24 hours

The graph shows both the count of operations per second and the average latency over the last 24 hours. Using this information about shard-0's workload, the team then identified the 10 unsharded collections with the highest CPU consumption that had manageable dataset sizes to ensure quick migration.

They planned to distribute these collections from shard-0 across other shards:

- The busiest unsharded collection to shard-1
- The second busiest collection to shard-2
- Busy collections 3 and 4 to shard-3
- Busy collections 5, 6, and 7 to shard-4
- Busy collections 8, 9, and 10 to shard-5

This plan was tested in a QA environment first before running it in production. This precaution was important because moving collections between shards involves heavy operations that can significantly impact cluster performance.

They moved the smallest two collections first and checked the metrics to verify the changes were working. For each collection move, they followed this process:

1. Monitor shard-0 and the destination shard's hardware metrics and operation execution times.

2. Verify the destination shard has free disk space, IOPs, network resources, and CPU headroom.

3. Connect to mongos and move a collection:

   ```
   db.adminCommand( { moveCollection: "db.collection_b", toShard:
   "shard-1" })
   ```

4. If something goes wrong during the move, use the abortMoveCollection admin command.

5. Monitor shard-0 and the destination shard's hardware metrics and operation execution times.

> **MoveCollection causes short write block**
>
> The moveCollection command blocks writes to the collection for up to 2 seconds during its critical section. You can find more details in the documentation at https://mongodb.com/docs/manual/tutorial/move-a-collection/.

Results and learnings

The team expected that migrating most resource-intensive unsharded collections, along with earlier schema and indexing optimizations, would ease the cluster's resource demands, enabling them to downscale infrastructure, significantly reduce costs, and sustain performance levels.

This example demonstrates that addressing hardware resource constraints requires more than simply scaling up; it calls for a strategic approach that integrates monitoring, diagnostics, workload analysis, and operational planning. Tools such as Atlas monitoring and Query Insights are crucial for pinpointing resource bottlenecks and analyzing both short-term metrics and long-term workload trends. With clear visibility into these metrics, organizations can implement data-driven solutions tailored to their cluster's unique needs, ensuring corrective actions are precise and impactful.

Use case: Diagnosing insufficient IOPs in self-managed MongoDB

On self-managed systems, it's common to see a similar pattern across customer deployments: workloads naturally grow over time, often outpacing the capabilities of the underlying infrastructure. With MongoDB Atlas, this is easy to catch early using built-in monitoring tools that provide real-time visibility into key metrics such as idle CPU, disk IOPs headroom, and the number of operations being executed. However, when managing MongoDB clusters independently, teams must rely on scripts or external monitoring tools to track these metrics.

In this example, we revisit a case from a customer who was self-managing MongoDB on their cloud infrastructure. As performance issues began to surface, the MongoDB support team turned to the server's diagnostic data.

Diagnosing the cause

MongoDB servers capture system information and internal counters every second in **Full-Time Diagnostic Data Capture** (**FTDC**). This data doesn't contain any sensitive information such as queries, query predicates, results, or credentials.

Analyzing the storage read requests per second (which on Linux comes from the iostat command), they found the database server was issuing 16,600 IOPs. FTDC data from vmstat showed 39% iowait, indicating the system was spending significant time waiting for I/O operations.

The customer had provisioned the underlying storage with 15,000 IOPs. Cloud providers typically allow bursting beyond the provisioned limit for a period before throttling. This bursting, followed by throttling, was experienced as stalls by the customer's application.

Looking at the IOPS allocation, we realized we were using more IOPS than provisioned. Performance was acceptable for a time because higher burst IOPS were provided. However, after the burst allowance was exhausted, a sharp performance degradation followed. The system no longer had enough IOPS, and operations slowed, waiting for I/O.

Implementing the solution

The customer increased the provisioned IOPS from 15,000 to 18,000, which immediately resolved the performance stalls.

Results and learnings

This case highlights several important principles regarding hardware resource constraints in Atlas and self-managed MongoDB deployments. I/O limitations frequently present themselves as high iowait percentages, signaling potential bottlenecks in storage. In cloud environments, it's worth noting that temporary bursting above provisioned limits may be possible, but this is not always sustainable for growing workloads. A deep understanding of the relationship between application workload and resource provisioning is critical for maintaining optimal performance. Even without the advanced monitoring capabilities provided by Atlas, diagnostic tools such as FTDC can offer valuable insights to identify and address underlying issues. Finally, it's worth remembering that sometimes the simplest and most effective solution to performance problems is simply increasing the available resources to match the demands of the workload. This case serves as a reminder of the importance of proactive planning and monitoring to avoid resource bottlenecks.

Systematic approach to performance troubleshooting

Based on the examples we've explored, here is a structured methodology to diagnose and resolve MongoDB performance issues:

1. **Identify symptoms and gather initial data**: The first step in troubleshooting is pinpointing performance symptoms and collecting relevant data to understand the problem. Determine when the issue started, identify which database operations or collections are affected, and gather baseline metrics such as CPU usage, IOPS, and query performance for comparison. This initial information helps build a clear picture of what's happening and guides the next steps in diagnosis.

2. **Use multiple diagnostic tools**: Leverage a variety of diagnostic tools to gain deeper insights into the issue. For Atlas users, monitoring dashboards provide a visual overview of key performance metrics, while those on self-managed clusters can use system monitoring tools to achieve similar results. The database profiler is invaluable for detecting slow queries, log files help uncover errors or patterns linked to performance degradation, and the currentOp() command identifies running operations. Additionally, the Performance Advisor offers recommendations for index optimization, which can often address query efficiency concerns. Remember that the observability and monitoring ecosystem is constantly evolving, and it's important to stay current with emerging technologies.

3. **Categorize the issue**: Once the data is collected, categorize the nature of the issue to narrow down possible solutions. Is it caused by inherently slow operations, such as full collection scans or poor indexing strategies? Could it stem from blocked operations, such as locks or cursor-related problems? Or, is it the result of resource constraints involving CPU, memory, or disk I/O limitations? Understanding the root cause is critical for selecting the right approach to remediation.

4. **Determine the scope**: Next, assess the scope of the issue to ensure solutions are targeted effectively. Is the problem affecting specific queries or collections, or is it broader and system-wide? Additionally, verify whether the issue only occurs at specific times, such as during peak workloads or scheduled jobs, to determine whether timing or patterns play a role. Defining the impact and scope ensures efforts are directed where they'll be most effective.

5. **Implement targeted solutions**: Once the issue is understood, implement fixes tailored to the specific problem. For inherently slow operations, consider adding indexes or optimizing queries to improve efficiency. Blocked operations may require killing long-running or stuck processes and resolving cursor-related issues. If resource constraints are identified, scaling up CPU, memory, or disk IOPS, or redistributing workloads across shards or clusters, can alleviate performance bottlenecks.

6. **Verify the solution**: After implementing changes, monitor key metrics to ensure the problem has been successfully resolved. Verify that the issue does not recur and confirm that performance has improved to the expected level. Set up alerts or proactive monitoring to catch similar issues early in the future, minimizing downtime and user impact.

7. **Document findings and preventative measures**: Finally, document the root cause of the issue and the steps taken to resolve it. Use this opportunity to implement preventative measures, such as updated monitoring workflows or infrastructure changes, to avoid similar problems moving forward. Share these findings and best practices with other team members to ensure alignment and reinforce a culture of proactive performance management.

By following a structured approach, teams can systematically identify, address, and prevent performance issues in MongoDB deployments. Consistent monitoring and timely intervention are key to maintaining a responsive, scalable system.

Summary

In this chapter, we've explored real-world examples of MongoDB performance issues that align with William Zola's three fundamental causes: inherently slow operations, blocked operations, and insufficient hardware resources. Through case studies, we saw how to identify performance issues using MongoDB's built-in tools. We diagnosed root causes by examining query patterns, cursor behavior, and resource utilization. We then implemented targeted solutions through indexing, query optimization, and resource management. Finally, we set up preventative measures to catch issues before they become critical.

The debugging tools for MongoDB performance have improved significantly in recent years. Atlas provides comprehensive monitoring and alerting capabilities, while self-managed deployments can leverage tools such as the database profiler, log analysis, and FTDC data.

Remember that performance optimization is an ongoing process, not a one-time task. As your data grows and application patterns evolve, continually monitor performance metrics, review index usage, and adjust your configuration to maintain optimal performance.

By systematically approaching performance issues using the principles and techniques outlined in this chapter, you'll be better equipped to maintain high-performing MongoDB deployments regardless of scale or complexity.

16

Unlock Your Exclusive Benefits

Your copy of this book includes the following exclusive benefits:

- ⌨ Next-gen Packt Reader
- 📄 DRM-free PDF/ePub downloads

Follow the guide below to unlock them. The process takes only a few minutes and needs to be completed once.

Unlock this Book's Free Benefits in 3 Easy Steps

Step 1

Keep your purchase invoice ready for *Step 3*. If you have a physical copy, scan it using your phone and save it as a PDF, JPG, or PNG.

For more help on finding your invoice, visit https://www.packtpub.com/unlock-benefits/help.

> **Note:** If you bought this book directly from Packt, no invoice is required. After *Step 2*, you can access your exclusive content right away.

Step 2

Scan the QR code or go to `packtpub.com/unlock`.

On the page that opens (similar to *Figure 16.1* on desktop), search for this book by name and select the correct edition.

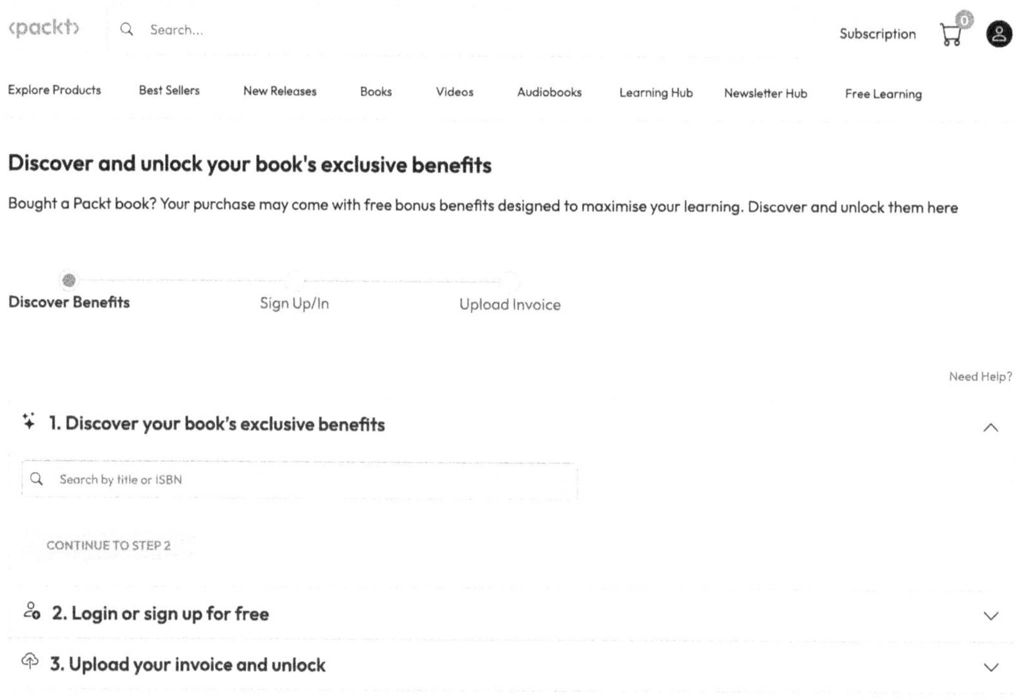

⟨packt⟩   🔍 Search...   Subscription 🛒⁰ 👤

Explore Products   Best Sellers   New Releases   Books   Videos   Audiobooks   Learning Hub   Newsletter Hub   Free Learning

Discover and unlock your book's exclusive benefits

Bought a Packt book? Your purchase may come with free bonus benefits designed to maximise your learning. Discover and unlock them here

Discover Benefits   Sign Up/In   Upload Invoice

Need Help?

✦ **1. Discover your book's exclusive benefits**   ∧

🔍 Search by title or ISBN

CONTINUE TO STEP 2

👤 **2. Login or sign up for free**   ∨

☁ **3. Upload your invoice and unlock**   ∨

Figure 16.1: Packt unlock landing page on desktop

Step 3

After selecting your book, sign in to your Packt account or create one for free. Then upload your invoice (PDF, PNG, or JPG, up to 10 MB). Follow the on-screen instructions to finish the process.

Need help?

If you get stuck and need help, visit `https://www.packtpub.com/unlock-benefits/help` for a detailed FAQ on how to find your invoices and more. This QR code will take you to the help page.

Note: If you are still facing issues, reach out to `customercare@packt.com`.

Afterword

Well, we've made it to the end of our MongoDB performance journey! But if there's one lesson that stands out from years of database optimization, it's that performance tuning never really ends. Just when it seems like everything's been nailed down, the application grows, user patterns shift, or MongoDB releases a cool new feature to try.

Remember our discussion on schema design from *Chapter 2, Schema Design for Performance*, or on indexes from *Chapter 3, Indexes*? That wasn't just for fun! Many users have struggled with performance issues that ultimately traced back to poorly designed schemas or suboptimal (or missing) indexes. You can't build a skyscraper on quicksand—no matter how much you optimize elsewhere, that shaky foundation keeps fighting back.

We've covered a lot of ground, from spotting slow queries to mastering indexing. Along the way, we've explored how complex systems interact. We looked at how to leverage features such as the aggregation framework, change streams, and transactions. We reviewed how to use replication for high availability and sharding to scale out. But performance tuning is a marathon, not a sprint. It's an ongoing process of learning and adapting as applications evolve.

Key takeaways

So, what are the biggest lessons to carry forward? Here's a quick recap of the principles that will keep your MongoDB deployment fast, stable, and ready for what's next:

- **Schema design is everything**: Seriously, the vast majority of performance headaches come from schemas that don't match how the application uses data. Think about reads and writes when designing documents. And don't be afraid to evolve the schema over time. A good schema is the foundation for great performance.

- **Indexing is your superpower**: Good indexes are the key to performant queries. A smart indexing strategy means MongoDB doesn't have to work so hard. Make a habit of reviewing indexes regularly.

- **If you don't measure, you're flying blind**: You can't fix what you can't see. Set up consistent monitoring with meaningful metrics and alerts. It helps spot trouble early and guide tuning efforts. Visibility into deployments helps you catch problems before your users do.

- **Don't forget the boring stuff**: Beyond schemas and indexes, solid day-to-day operations keep everything running. That means managing configurations, having a solid backup plan, and knowing when more capacity is needed. Automating maintenance can save a lot of future headaches.

Performance tuning might feel like chasing a moving target, but with the right habits and a solid foundation, you'll always be ready for what's coming next.

The performance mindset

Think like a performance detective. Be curious. Don't wait for things to break. Poke around in query plans, monitor baseline performance, and question assumptions. Make performance a team sport, something developers, ops, and architects all share responsibility for.

We've seen one case where a seemingly minor change to an index cut a page load time by 40%. Those kinds of wins only come when you look for them. By staying curious and building habits around improvement, optimization becomes part of the culture, not a reactive task.

Practical next steps

Knowing is great, but doing is better. Here are some hands-on steps you can take right now to turn performance theory into results:

- **Audit your schema**: Take a hard look at your schema. Does it really work for your most common queries? Check access patterns and consider whether the document structure (embedded vs. referenced) still serves its purpose.

- **Get friendly with diagnostic tools**: Become comfortable with `db.collection.explain()` and the Query Insight tab in Atlas. Use them to observe real query behavior. Hunt for slow queries and ineffective indexes—it can even be fun.

- **Set up real monitoring**: Use tools like MongoDB Cloud Monitoring or similar alternatives. Build dashboards that highlight critical metrics such as operation duration, cache hit rate, and replication lag. Let the data point to where the work is needed.

- **Test under pressure**: Incorporate load testing into your development processes. Make sure the system can handle expected and unexpected traffic. That's how you stay ahead of bottlenecks before they impact production.

- **Talk to people**: Connect with others through local user groups, events, or online discussions. The MongoDB community is large and filled with people solving similar challenges and sharing experiences that can unlock valuable insights. You can start by visiting the MongoDB Community Forums at `https://www.mongodb.com/community/forums/`.

The more you apply what you've learned, stay observant, and stay connected, the more resilient and responsive your system will become.

Future considerations

MongoDB continues to evolve. Keep up with the release notes at `https://www.mongodb.com/docs/manual/release-notes/`, test new features in safe environments, and adopt what makes sense.

Stay curious. Experiment. Measure. And always confirm that changes actually lead to improvements.

Final thoughts

Performance tuning blends art and science. With the insights shared in this book, it's possible to make a significant impact on application performance. Treat each bottleneck as a puzzle and every fix as a learning opportunity. A well-tuned database improves the experience for developers, operators, and users alike. It's a journey—but now, there's a map to guide the way.

Now go build something awesome, and make it fast!

Index

Symbols

D

E

F

W

‹packt›

packtpub.com

Subscribe to our online digital library for full access to over 7,000 books and videos, as well as industry leading tools to help you plan your personal development and advance your career. For more information, please visit our website.

Why subscribe?

- Spend less time learning and more time coding with practical eBooks and Videos from over 4,000 industry professionals
- Improve your learning with Skill Plans built especially for you
- Get a free eBook or video every month
- Fully searchable for easy access to vital information
- Copy and paste, print, and bookmark content

At www.packtpub.com, you can also read a collection of free technical articles, sign up for a range of free newsletters, and receive exclusive discounts and offers on Packt books and eBooks.

Other Books You May Enjoy

If you enjoyed this book, you may be interested in these other books by Packt:

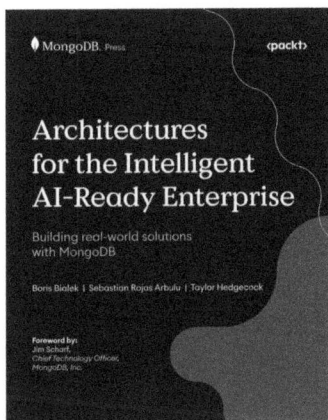

Architectures for the Intelligent AI-Ready Enterprise

Boris Bialek, Sebastian Rojas Arbulu, Taylor Hedgecock

ISBN: 978-1-80611-715-4

- Design AI-ready data architectures that scale in production
- Define systems of action and explain why they matter for enterprises
- Modernize legacy systems for AI-ready, unified architectures
- Implement governance, privacy, and compliance frameworks for AI
- Explore real-world AI implementations for over six industries
- Deploy production RAG and agentic systems with MongoDB
- Apply semantic data protection in regulated industries
- Build domain-specific AI agents and intelligent copilots
- Apply MCP, causal AI, and multi-agent systems for future-ready architectures

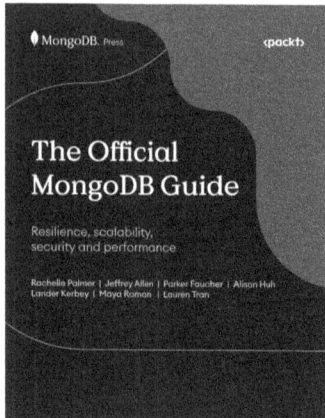

The Official MongoDB Guide

Rachelle Palmer, Jeffrey Allen, Parker Faucher, Alison Huh, Lander Kerbey, Maya Raman, Lauren Tran

ISBN: 978-1-83702-197-0

- Build secure, scalable, and high-performance applications
- Design efficient data models and indexes for real workloads
- Write powerful queries to sort, filter, and project data
- Protect applications with authentication and encryption
- Accelerate coding with AI-powered and IDE-based tools
- Launch, scale, and manage MongoDB Atlas with confidence
- Unlock advanced features like Atlas Search and Atlas Vector Search
- Apply proven techniques from MongoDB's own engineering leaders

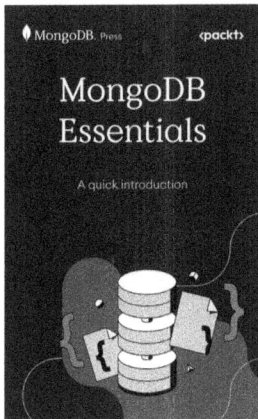

MongoDB Essentials

ISBN: 978-1-80670-609-9

- Understand MongoDB's document model and architecture
- Set up MongoDB local deployments quickly
- Design schemas tailored to application access patterns
- Perform CRUD and aggregation operations efficiently
- Use tools to optimize query performance and scalability
- Explore AI-powered features such as Atlas Search and Atlas Vector Search

Packt is searching for authors like you

If you're interested in becoming an author for Packt, please visit authors.packt.com and apply today. We have worked with thousands of developers and tech professionals, just like you, to help them share their insight with the global tech community. You can make a general application, apply for a specific hot topic that we are recruiting an author for, or submit your own idea.

Share your thoughts

Now that you've finished *High Performance with MongoDB*, we'd love to hear your thoughts! Scan the QR code below to go straight to the Amazon review page for this book and share your feedback or leave a review on the site that you purchased it from.

https://packt.link/r/1837022631

Your review is important to us and the tech community and will help us make sure we're delivering excellent quality content.

www.ingramcontent.com/pod-product-compliance
Lightning Source LLC
Chambersburg PA
CBHW081040220326
41598CB00038B/6943